SHAKESPEARE UP CLOSE

Reading Early Modern Texts

SHAKESPEARE UP CLOSE

Reading Early Modern Texts

Edited by
Russ McDonald
Nicholas D. Nace
and
Travis D. Williams

Arden Shakespeare

First published in 2012 by the Arden Shakespeare

Editorial Matter and Selection copyright © Russ McDonald, Nicholas D. Nace
and Travis D. Williams 2012
All other matter copyright © Bloomsbury Publishing Plc 2012

The Arden Shakespeare is an imprint of Bloomsbury Publishing Plc

Bloomsbury Publishing Plc
50 Bedford Square
London WC1B 3DP

A CIP catalogue record for this book is available from the British Library

ISBN 97814081158784

Typeset by Margaret Brain, Wisbech, Cambs

Printed and bound in India by Replika Press Pvt. Ltd.

To

Stephen Booth

CONTENTS

PREFACE

This collection began life as an effort to honour the work of Stephen Booth. Emeritus Professor of English at the University of California at Berkeley, editor of the indispensable Yale edition of Shakespeare's Sonnets, famous teacher, brilliant critic, occasional theatre director, legendary playgoer, shyly sly performer at the lectern, unfailing friend – Stephen Booth is also, in the opinions of the editors and of many others, perhaps the greatest living close reader, certainly one of the closest of all close readers of any time, a critical descendant of Samuel Taylor Coleridge, William Empson, and Cleanth Brooks, and an inspiration to all whose minds are excited by textual details. We concur with Michael Schoenfeldt, who calls him 'the critic laureate of close reading'. This book differs from a formal festschrift in that, while still a tribute to the accomplishments of an extraordinary teacher and critic, its connection is less personal. Some of the writers contained herein have little or no professional connection with Stephen Booth, while others have worked with him for half a century. Some refer to him glancingly in their analyses; some do not. The focus throughout is on Booth's greatest gift, in the sense of that given to him and given by him to others: the act of reading.

The editors wish to thank the contributors for their eager participation in this project, for producing such excellent work, and for doing so at an unusually accelerated pace. Robert Watson, moreover, saved us from ourselves with crucially timed comments on the Introduction. We are particularly grateful to Margaret Bartley, our publisher at Arden Shakespeare. She was invariably enthusiastic about this project from the start, and has been extremely helpful, and patient, with every stage of its progress. Finally, each editor would like to thank the other two.

LIST OF CONTRIBUTORS

Paul Alpers is Class of 1942 Professor Emeritus of English at the University of California, Berkeley, and Professor-in-Residence at Smith College.

Charles Altieri is Rachael Anderson Stageberg Professor of English at the University of California, Berkeley, where he occasionally gets to lecture on Shakespeare. His most recent book is *Wallace Stevens and the Phenomenology of Value.*

Joel B. Altman is Professor Emeritus of English at the University of California, Berkeley, and the author of *The Tudor Play of Mind* and *The Improbability of Othello.*

Harry Berger, Jr is Professor Emeritus of Literature and Art History at the University of California, Santa Cruz, and a Fellow of the American Academy of Arts and Sciences.

A. R. Braunmuller, Distinguished Professor of English and Comparative Literature at UCLA, is General Editor of both the Pelican Shakespeare and the New Cambridge Shakespeare.

David A. Brewer is Associate Professor of English at the Ohio State University and the author of *The Afterlife of Character, 1726–1825.* He is currently working on authorial names in the eighteenth-century Anglophone world.

Stephen Burt is Professor of English at Harvard. His books include *The Art of the Sonnet,* with David Mikics, and *Close Calls with Nonsense: Reading New Poetry.*

Ralph Alan Cohen co-founded the American Shakespeare Center and established the Blackfriars Playhouse and the graduate programme in Shakespeare and Performance at Mary Baldwin College, where he teaches and directs.

Drew Daniel is Assistant Professor in the Department of English at Johns Hopkins University, and the author of the forthcoming *The Melancholy Assemblage: Affect and Epistemology in the English Renaissance*.

Margreta de Grazia is the Rosenberg Professor in the Humanities and Professor of English at the University of Pennsylvania. She is the author of *Shakespeare Verbatim* and *Hamlet without Hamlet*.

Jeff Dolven teaches Renaissance literature at Princeton University. He is the author of *Scenes of Instruction*, a study of romance fictions and humanist pedagogy, and is currently at work on a book about style.

Heather Dubrow, John D. Boyd, SJ, Chair in the Poetic Imagination at Fordham University, is the author of six scholarly books and a collection of poetry.

Paul Edmondson is Head of Research and Knowledge for the Shakespeare Birthplace Trust. His publications include *Shakespeare's Sonnets* (co-authored with Stanley Wells).

Michael Ellis-Tolaydo is Professor of Theater, Film, and Media Studies at St Mary's College of Maryland and a professional actor and director.

Lukas Erne, Professor of English at the University of Geneva, is the author of *Shakespeare as Literary Dramatist* and the forthcoming *Shakespeare and the Book Trade*.

Stanley Fish is the Davidson-Kahn Distinguished University Professor of Law and Humanities at Florida International University. His most recent publication is *Versions of Antihumanism: Milton and Others*.

Donald M. Friedman is Professor of English Emeritus at the University of California, Berkeley. He has written on Marvell, Milton, Donne, Wyatt, Herbert, Carew, and occasionally on Shakespeare.

Brett Gamboa is Assistant Professor of English at Dartmouth College, where he teaches courses on dramatic literature and performance. He is currently working on a book about doubling roles in Shakespeare's plays.

Brian Gibbons, author of *Jacobean City Comedy* and *Shakespeare and Multiplicity*, is General Editor of the New Cambridge Shakespeare and the New Mermaids.

Erik Gray teaches at Columbia University. He is the author of several books about poetry and is currently working on a book about love poems.

Linda Gregerson's fifth book of poetry, *The Selvage*, will appear in autumn 2012. She teaches Renaissance literature and creative writing at the University of Michigan.

Kimberly Johnson teaches Renaissance literature and creative writing at Brigham Young University. In addition to her research focus on the lyric tradition and religious history, she is a poet and translator.

Coppélia Kahn, author of *Roman Shakespeare* and *Man's Estate: Masculine Identity in Shakespeare*, is Professor of English at Brown University.

Jeremy Lopez is Associate Professor of English at the University of Toronto. Most recently, he is the editor of *New Critical Essays: Richard II*, and he is completing a book-length study of the 'non-Shakespearean' dramatic canon.

Margaret Maurer is the William Henry Crawshaw Professor of Literature at Colgate University. She writes on Shakespeare and on John Donne's occasional poetry and his letters.

Russ McDonald is Professor of English Literature at Goldsmiths College, University of London; his most recent book is *Shakespeare's Late Style*.

Nicholas D. Nace teaches at Binghamton University (SUNY). He is at work on a book about ideation and explication in literature of the seventeenth and eighteenth centuries.

Lena Cowen Orlin is Professor of English at Georgetown University, executive director of the Shakespeare Association of America, and author of *Locating Privacy in Tudor London*.

Norman Rabkin was, until his death in June 2012, Professor Emeritus of English at the University of California, Berkeley. He was author of *Shakespeare and the Common Understanding* and *Shakespeare and the Problem of Meaning*.

Michael Schoenfeldt is the John R. Knott, Jr, Professor of English at the University of Michigan.

Daniel Shore is Assistant Professor of English at Georgetown University. He has published essays in *PMLA*, *Critical Inquiry*, *Milton Studies*, and *Milton Quarterly*.

Tiffany Stern is Professor of Early Modern Drama at Oxford University. Her most recent monograph is *Documents of Performance in Early Modern England*.

Garrett Stewart, James O. Freedman Professor of Letters at the University of Iowa, and author most recently of *Novel Violence* and *Bookwork*, was elected in 2010 to the American Academy of Arts and Sciences.

James Grantham Turner has published numerous books and articles on early modern literature, art, and culture. He is James D. Hart Professor at the University of California, Berkeley.

Robert N. Watson is the Neikirk Professor of English at UCLA, editor of Jonson's plays, and author of *Back to Nature* and several other books.

Stanley Wells, General Editor of the Oxford and Penguin editions of Shakespeare, is Honorary President of the Shakespeare Birthplace Trust.

Travis D. Williams is Assistant Professor of English at the University of Rhode Island. He is working on a book about literature, rhetoric, and mathematics in early modern Britain.

Susan J. Wolfson, Professor of English at Princeton University, is the author, most recently, of *Romantic Interactions: Social Being and the Turns of Literary Action*.

Mark Womack is a Lecturer in English at the University of Houston.

George T. Wright, University of Minnesota Professor Emeritus of English, is the author of *Shakespeare's Metrical Art*, *Hearing the Measures*, 'Hendiadys and *Hamlet*', and other books and essays. Retired, he lives in Arizona.

INTRODUCTION

Few would disagree that students of literature need to develop their skill at close reading – 'students' at all levels, from undergraduate to retired scholar, and 'literature' in any language, any genre. But what is close reading? The editors of this volume would ideally begin by defining the practice in a succinct, persuasive phrase or sentence, but since we know of no single statement by which any critic in any period has satisfactorily articulated the aims, the range, the benefits, and the process of close reading, we propose to introduce the collection without such an impossible formulation. Those who have tried to put the practice into words usually find the result either so general and bland as to be useless or so hedged with conditions and limitations as to be effectively disabled.

Given the inherent challenges, it is tempting to settle for an account that reduces the practice to something like 'pay attention'. Stephen Booth appears to take such a stance when he refers to himself and other literary critics as 'professional noticers'. However liberating it might be to suggest that all a reader needs to do is simply pay attention to how the text directs an otherwise unexamined process of reading, the simplicity of 'pay attention' may seem condescending to colleagues and scolding to students. Less rebarbative and perhaps more useful is an approach that asks readers to see (and hear and think) in as many uncoordinated ways as possible and to sustain those multiple perceptions until coordination becomes momentarily necessary or momentously rewarding, perhaps in a classroom lecture or an essay. A richer reading results when interpretive options are not prematurely discarded. Close reading can thus engage a variety of theoretical and critical approaches by starting with the literal text, itself recalled to the original meaning of 'literal': *littera*, letters and the sounds they make, and the words and patterns created from them.

In lieu of definition, this book offers illustration: forty talented people, mostly critics and scholars but also directors and actors, have agreed to read a literary text closely, to watch themselves as they do it, and to describe what they are doing. Devoting themselves to excerpts in verse or prose or in some cases to entire poems by Shakespeare and his contemporaries, they represent a wide range of approaches to the act of close reading: some attend to sounds, others to rhetorical figures, to etymology, stage directions, prosody, imagery, subtext, and a host of other textual particulars. Some of these readers are explicit about the theoretical implications of their exercise, while some mainly perform the analysis and let the performance speak for itself.

If the present collection has a polemical agenda, it is simply to assert that close reading should come out of the shadows. It is neither journeyman work, a fit task for undergraduates but not for trained scholars, nor a sanctuary into which to escape from other modes of literary scholarship. Most of us undertake the serious study of literature because we wish to read more deliberately and with greater self-awareness, to ascertain how and why texts affect us as they do. Those readers who have reflected self-consciously about what literary study entails will probably have recognised in themselves the impulse to return to a passage, to scrutinise its diction or images or sounds, to notice the presence of similar features elsewhere in the work, and to linger over the verbal hold that this bit of text exerts upon the mind. It is vital that we grasp those particulars and understand the way they function, that we come to understand how we read, in order to communicate the skills and pleasures of that experience to others.

The methods we develop for addressing various textual constructs will, of course, always need overhauling and refining, sometimes in mid-task. Language has the potential to generate new contexts even when it does not mean to: words, whether written or spoken, always exceed the instrumental need to satisfy the demands of communication. Moreover, close reading can heighten our sensitivity to extra-communicative contexts, whatever those contexts might be. Language does not lose its vitality once it has found a communicative form, and the closer we get to the words themselves – their components, origins, sounds, nuances – the clearer this fact becomes. The process helps us access the textual potentialities that our minds, prone to plucking synopses or information from what they read, habitually glide over. In this way, attention to literary particulars can extend to any use of language, which makes it a powerful tool in the classroom and beyond.

Definitional questions also appear in the long history of close reading – its rise and fall and rise in the long twentieth century. Consider the case of an earnest autodidact who has read up on reading and wishes to improve his skill at literary analysis. The student asks a professor, 'What is meant by "Close Reading"?' Typical frustration follows:

> It might be interpreted variously. My own use and construc-
> tion of the terms is in referring to diction, figures of speech,
> translation of allusion, etc. For instance, when one is directing
> the attentive soul of the pupil to the informing thought of a
> bit of real literature it is not the time to ask him the meaning
> of a particular word, especially where the meaning may be
> gathered from the context. This does not argue that exact,
> even etymological knowledge of the words is immaterial; but
> there is a time for all things, and this is not the time for
> the question, 'What does dilapidated mean?' for instance.
> At another perhaps earlier, perhaps later, lesson, interest
> may be at a white heat over the word 'dilapidated'. The little
> beginner in Latin who sees in the stem a *stone*, *stones*, and
> in the prefix *without, from*, and builds in imagination stones
> separated, thrown down or what not – feels the fitness or
> unfitness of the use of *dilapidated* wherever he sees it appear,
> and will himself ever after, use it advisedly. This is one phase
> of 'close reading' and 'there are others'. Do not, however,
> make reading the study of an 'alms-basket of words'. When
> you go to a feast of expression do more than steal the scraps.

Certainly the question, and some of the answer, could be heard in colleges and universities today. In fact, they were published in the October 1897 issue of *Popular Educator*. Over a century later there is still much of value here, and much to shrink from. The professor's inclusiveness is accompanied by a subtle prioritising founded on values that would not find much sympathy today. References to the 'attentive soul', 'informing thought', and 'real literature' now ask to be critiqued. Patronising the 'little beginner in Latin' no longer succeeds in an age when close reading has virtually no place in secondary schools and knowledge of Latin among university graduates is almost nil. The professor's lofty confidence in his command of the legible text and in his system for treating it now seems quaint. His response is characteristic of the period, with its primary attention to poetics and its figuration of text as a 'feast of expression'.[1] A century's worth of theoretical refiguring of the relationship between form and content has convinced many that the textual feast is made entirely of scraps and laid on an imaginary, ever-shifting table.

Skip forward nearly a century to consider a detailed description of how the activity of close reading affects another practitioner. We find diction more congenial to us, but observe the same concentration on the rewards of detail:

> I do it because I like the way I feel when I'm doing it. I like being brought up short by an effect I have experienced but do not yet understand analytically ... I like savoring the physical 'taste' of language at the same time that I work to lay bare its physics. I like uncovering the incredibly dense pyrotechnics of a master artificer, not least because in praising artifice I can claim a share in it. And when those pleasures have been (temporarily) exhausted, I like linking one moment in a poem to others.[2]

Stanley Fish's 1993 Clarendon Lecture registers the exhilaration and sense of possibility that can attend the activity of reading closely. His description does not go so far as to consider the experience of textual analysis an end in itself, acknowledging as it does a movement towards an analytical conclusion, but it certainly captures the dynamic mental state that most modern students of literature have felt upon inspecting the minute particulars of a passage and seeking to comprehend their operation – the 'physics' of the piece.

Close reading has a venerable history. It should probably be seen as extending at least as far back as Quintilian and Cicero, specifically in their illustration of rhetorical tactics in the art of oratory. It flourished as an identifiable critical activity among the biblical exegetes of the middle ages. One of its greatest successes occurred in the Renaissance, when the Donation of Constantine, a revered political document conferring political authority on the papacy, was exposed as fraudulent by the Italian humanist scholar Lorenzo Valla using techniques of textual analysis – close reading as political praxis. The point is that close reading is hardly a modern (or modernist) phenomenon. When the *Popular Educator* answered the inquiring student, I. A. Richards, frequently cited as the inventor of close reading, was three years old. New Criticism, which would make attentive reading a proprietary virtue and therefore a target for subsequent attack, had not yet emerged. Before the revaluation of John Donne by H. J. C. Grierson and T. S. Eliot, before John Crowe Ransom and his 'Kenyon Critics', before Empson rose with quantum mechanics, before Leavis emerged alongside behaviourism, before Fish – before all this there was close reading. Whatever its origins, close reading's history as a critical movement is one of repeated definition and redefinition, a constant struggle to undo restrictions that usually results in the imposition of new and different restrictions. It is as close to a shared methodology as literary study is ever likely to have, and it has never truly gone away, although many have cheered its return.

Some initial self-consciousness about the process of textual analysis made itself known at the University of California at Berkeley in the 1960s and 1970s, associated, at least in Renaissance studies, with the emerging school of reader-response criticism. Janet Adelman, writing in 1973, commended a new and necessary

focus on 'the reader's immediate, minute-by-minute responses
to the work of art rather than on abstract narrative or thematic
patterns'.[3] She thus gave explicit sanction to a critical style that
had been percolating throughout the 1960s, citing Paul Alpers'
The Poetry of The Faerie Queene (1968) and Fish's *Surprised by
Sin: The Reader in* Paradise Lost (1967) as foundational works
relying on this mode of reading – works still foundational in
Milton and Spenser studies. To this trend can be added Donald
M. Friedman's 'The Mind in the Poem: Wyatt's "They Fle From
Me"' which examines the techniques by which Wyatt challenges
his reader 'to find the truth of the story'.[4] Situating her own critical attention to *Antony and Cleopatra*, Adelman mentions Booth's
essay 'On the Value of *Hamlet*' as the moment such concerns
entered Shakespeare studies. Booth viewed *Hamlet* as a 'succession
of actions upon the understanding of an audience', famously
ending one passage of analytical bravura with the phrase '*Hamlet*
is the tragedy of an audience that cannot make up its mind'.[5] At the
same time Norman Rabkin extended such ideas more broadly to
any work of art that consists of 'a complex and highly determined
shaping of an audience's responses'.[6] Many of these arguments
may be traced to the pedagogical thinking of Reuben Brower, the
influential Professor of English at Harvard who taught some of
these critics and whose seminal 'Reading in Slow Motion' insists
on the sovereignty of close textual study.

As context began to dominate the critical scene after about
1975, treatment of textual detail disappeared from much literary
analysis, sometimes tacitly, sometimes vilified by its detractors as
a useless remnant of New Criticism and as a diversion from more
urgent concerns. Here is Geoffrey Hartman, an early expositor
of the limitations of one kind of close reading: 'The dominion
of Exegesis is great: she is our Whore of Babylon, sitting robed
in academic black on the great dragon of Criticism, and dis-
pensing a repetitive and soporific balm from her pedantic cup'.[7]
Following Hartman, a number of theorists, some committed to
deconstruction and some with a political orientation, sought to
displace the practice, persuaded that the 'close' in close reading

implied a dangerous intimacy with the comforts of the surface. Never mind that such criticism ignores as already political a mode of analysis upheld by its promoters as well suited to the teaching situation that prevailed when Second World War veterans returned to the classroom. Often descriptions of the process of reading noticed the spatial positioning of the critic relative to the object to be read: close to? how close? far from? inside? beneath? Steven Best and Sharon Marcus associate such suspicion with Fredric Jameson's *The Political Unconscious* (1981); they claim that 'only weak, descriptive, empirical, ideologically complicit readers attend to the surface of the text'.[8] Relying upon surface/depth models of writing drawn from critical articulations perceived as clinging to mere surface, 'symptomatic reading' became the new term for an approach by which Jameson urged readers to 'seek a latent meaning behind a manifest one'.[9]

Whereas Jameson's opposition to close reading focuses on the obscuring effects of foregrounded textual features, Franco Moretti has recently attempted to correct what he feels is nearsightedness in traditional close reading with what he calls 'distant reading'. He advocates a process built not on the surface/depth model but on the closeness/distance model that close reading asserts in its very name. Moretti's model is a spatial reconceptualisation of literary history and complex texts, one that often takes a small detail, as close reading might, but (enabled by recent database technologies) looks at its function visually across a large number of texts, a dizzyingly distant perspective that sees new kinds of large-scale forms. In an essay on *Hamlet*, however, Moretti is cheerfully aware of what he sacrifices: he claims to be 'discussing *Hamlet*, and yet saying nothing about Shakespeare's words'.[10] Speaking very broadly, we might say that doubters or opponents of close reading urge a critical penetration past or under the legible surface, whereas proponents favour a practice that looks *at* the literary object as well as beneath or beyond it.

In addition to the spatial constructions, the temporal dimension of close reading has come to the fore in recent treatments. Brower's hope that literary analysis might be called 'slow reading' has been recently revived by Marjorie Garber, who has trained our attention on time and the visual in her recent 'Shakespeare in Slow Motion'. Her overriding objective is 'to slow down the move to context, if not reverse it altogether, by redirecting attention to the language of the plays, scene by scene, act by act, moment by moment, word by word'.[11] The sequential conditions of reading prompt Garber to retard the process: successive mental activities occur too rapidly to be registered at the typical pace of reading. In a related development, critical approaches influenced by cognitive science have given a new sophistication to our understanding of what we do when we read. G. Gabrielle Starr, seeing cognition as an ally in the understanding of close reading, refers to one of the strengths of cognitive science as its 'focus on exploring the time sequence of mental activity'.[12] Not only does this return us to the process of reading the text, but it again engages the 'mental pleasures' generated by the process of reading.[13] Finally, along with space and time, the rhetoric of volume frequently asserts itself: close reading is concerned with minutiae, more ambitious analysis with 'larger' questions.

A concern for both the spatial and the temporal sometimes characterises the practice of close reading as 'hermetic': a prominent complaint is that it is inimical and opposed to historicism. It is true that the New Critics emphasised and sometimes fetishised the particulars of the verbal object, reacting as they were against a tired biographical-historical model of literary criticism; their occasional use of the critical mode as a redoubt from which to escape the vicissitudes of politics tainted the practice for many of their successors. However, concentration on the eventfulness of poetic language need not occlude the claims of history or any other pertinent context. A glance at the 'Analytic Commentary' in the Yale edition of the Sonnets discloses Booth's command of contexts aplenty – the Elizabethan rank system, for example, or early modern sexuality, or sixteenth-century philosophy.

In fact no one, not even Brower at his most heuristically polemical, seeks finally to exclude context. Rita Felski, in a recent essay in *New Literary History*, makes the point concisely: 'Context is not optional'.[14] (Interestingly, that sentence helps to introduce Felski's analysis of the perils of fetishising unexamined contexts, an essay entitled '"Context Stinks!"') An approach to analysis that privileges the textual object may feel limited because this act of reading does not make assertions about anything beyond the way language is working. If this circling back to the empirically observable phenomena of language is born of scepticism about how much we can confidently say about early texts, its hermeticism is distinct from that which has been attributed to New Critics. The putative incompatibility of formal study and the claims of history depends on misconstructions of both, as Heather Dubrow reminds us in seeking constructively to reconcile text and context: 'how can we negotiate connections and tensions among the types of close reading to which this volume is dedicated, and the historicism that, though often contrasted with close reading, in fact need not and should not be read against – in the sense of opposition to – it?'

The contributors to this volume address the problem of just what kind of activity close reading is by performing brief acts of literary analysis; mostly these performances do not frame themselves as anything more than analysis. Their approaches, though various, share a concern with the ways in which our experience is structured by linguistically dense, verbally complex texts, texts that are themselves structured by intentionally organised systems of meaning (rhyme, meter, rhythm, metaphor, syntax, and so on). But almost all these readers are likewise alert to unintentional, non-inert systems of meaning (the forces of gender ideology, social-political formations, and language itself, the ruler of them all). We here attempt to reveal the many dimensions of our experience of texts, to offer an image of the way our minds work with or against language in the process of reading. All literary criticism must finally confront the question of what is at stake in the discussion, or, putting it bluntly, 'so what?' Our hope is that an answer to this question will appear in the sparks generated when an active reader interacts with a literary text. Readings produced by such close examination need not assume – or discover, or confer – a unity or supreme interconnectedness in the texts they explore. Nor must an answer to the 'so what' question result in a grand generalisation about the text under scrutiny. Readers will answer the question in different ways.

For Booth, the question is the answer. His position may be aptly summarised in the title of one of his critical manifestos, 'Close Reading without Readings'. (It is also elaborated cogently in another such polemic, 'The Function of Criticism at the Present Time and All Others'.) Booth's mode of analysis is to inspect with minute attention and almost infinite patience the dimensions of linguistic function, taking the experience of reading as an aid to appreciating what we already and actually value in what we often unthinkingly value. It does not attempt to go further. According to this line of reasoning, close reading *can* be uncoupled from interpretation and enacted as an end in itself. Such a refusal to place the activity of close reading in the service of large interpretive claims has been controversial. Helen Vendler, for example, another of literature's greatest close readers, faults Booth's edition of the Sonnets on the grounds that he 'gives up too easily on interpretation'.[15] He apparently welcomes such a charge. Booth believes that the identification of philological, poetic, and other patterns and networks in a poem or passage or play helps us to experience the eventfulness that such verbal density confers upon a work and that causes us to delight in and to want to return to it. This is perhaps why he has tended to concentrate on those Shakespearean works that are among the most popular: *Romeo and Juliet*, *Macbeth*, *King Lear*, *Hamlet*, *Twelfth Night*, the Sonnets. Some of the contributors to this volume would stoutly defend Booth's non-utilitarian position, insisting that the activity of reading is the *telos*.

Others would argue that tiny details of text, carefully considered, open large vistas that afford a host of interpretations. Such an approach treats close reading instrumentally, making it a vehicle in the service of other critical agendas. The critic is thus permitted to 'transcend' the textual object and draw political, philosophical, or other extra-textual conclusions; indeed an approach that makes use of formal analysis in this manner is sometimes called 'transcendent criticism'.[16] Charles Altieri helps to clarify the distinction between the two poles of reading described here: 'Of course some authors do make the medium the matter. But it is much more common to consider this internal density as the means to build imaginative engagements with how characters and lyric speakers think and suffer and find satisfaction. The text's sense of the world interprets and puts to work its exploration of the powers of the medium'.[17] Finally, close reading offers a different kind of utility to those who approach the text with a deconstructive bent, a view represented by Paul de Man's claim that '[m]ere reading' can 'transform critical discourse in a manner that would appear deeply subversive to those who think of the teaching of literature as a substitute for the teaching of theology, ethics, psychology, or intellectual history'.[18] In Shakespeare studies, the use of close reading in the service of extra-textual aims is variously represented in the work of Catherine Belsey, Malcolm Evans, and Terence Hawkes.

Between these opposed positions, many practitioners have recently begun to re-evaluate the activity of textual analysis. The autumn 2009 issue of *Representations* is devoted to 'How We Read Now', and the number of *New Literary History* containing Felski's piece bears the provocative title *Context?* Sharon Marcus's 'just reading' and Caroline Levine's 'strategic formalism' both emphasise the surface intricacy of literary language as a way to configure – for any reading is also a structuring – unsounded ideological depths.[19] Recent versions of close reading, vivified and enriched by theoretical approaches elsewhere considered to be in opposition to it, have responded directly to 'symptomatic reading' and to the other proponents of distance. Whether one looks behind them or rearranges them so as to form a group picture, the words of the work – and sometimes even smaller units of language – are always the inescapable reference point. Close reading is the method for dealing with the inescapable.

Shakespeare Up Close represents a kind of practicum of possibilities. Its primary value may well be the multiplicity, indeed the inconsistencies of approach employed by its contributors. The various readings exhibited here may be said collectively to represent the range from the non-utilitarian to the practical. Some essays dwell so delightedly on selected textual particulars that close reading becomes an end in itself, whereas others move with determination from the treatment of details to their larger hermeneutic value. Students – and their teachers – are invited to consider the gradations of approach and recognise the manifold virtues of a very broad critical church.

We can all 'do' close reading, so the claim goes. Teachers who value close reading as a pedagogy usually hope to show students that they need not ignore their native instincts of literary appreciation, that they can both enjoy imaginative writing and at the same time discuss it – even those elements of it that produce enjoyment – in sophisticated ways. Close reading is not vivisection: to dissect a literary text is not to murder it. Unlike explaining why a joke is funny, which usually ruins it forever, literature does not cease to be enjoyable because we choose to pay attention to why it is enjoyable. Literary texts are remarkably resilient.[20] However, the process of modelling close reading for students, of showing them in the classroom what one can make of a text by closely examining it, is a tricky business. On whatever side of the podium, the reader with an overriding devotion to context and an impulse to leap from the text to a reading or interpretation is likely to omit or at least elide the process of reading. Under pressure to produce an analysis of the cultural or historical forces 'behind' a poem or play, such a reader may launch a Jamesonian hunt for what is obscured by the text, not what is present in it. The vigilance in looking for big pictures has become so engrained that it could now be said to be part of the way we read a text, and therefore potentially a part of close reading. However, the desire to go 'beyond' the text more often than not entails skipping over it. Close readings often seem to be the hidden work of literary scholarship because they are messy, betraying precisely too much of the clumsy indecision – the reality of reading difficult texts – that graduate education trains us not to show in finished work. A well-presented close reading requires a critic to hold in linear sequence objects and experiences that do not want to comply, while also not losing the multi-dimensional pleasure that reading should foster. It is also worth saying, especially to a potential consumer of some forty examples, that a well-presented close reading also demands patience of one who reads it (i.e., the reader of the reader).

The critical culture of the past four decades has so insistently privileged context over text that many instructors are no more familiar with the tools and *topoi* of close reading than are the students they teach. In 'cultural poetics' the adjective has for some time tyrannised the noun. One of the primary objectives of *Shakespeare Up Close* is to restore the reputation and utility of close reading as a classroom strategy, a goal that necessitates removing the opprobrium with which some proponents of contextualisation and historicism have tarred it. A related phenomenon is that teaching often generates a pressure to oversell the ends and goals and undersell the means and methods. In order to demonstrate the productivity of close reading, a teacher may offer examples that move startlingly from the specific to the general, where significance is more apparent, and thus encourage the student to perform a similar critical manoeuvre. In the process, close reading and the textual particulars it isolates may become mainly a student's retrospective support for generalisation and abstraction, the more accessible and appealing forms of critical activity. We, instructors and students alike, must recognise and articulate the particular kind of specificity close reading produces and understand the operation of the methods by which meaning can be produced from those specifics.

We must also establish a symbiotic, healthy relationship between text and context. To make legitimate claims about cultural or historical forces, to contribute to knowledge of how texts participate as large-scale agents and arbiters of meaning or as providers of intellectual pleasure, students need resources and knowledge, 'background' of a kind obtained outside the text. In short, they need extra-textual information that a limited notion of close reading does not readily provide. One way to retrain a student's focus on a text is to embrace a brand of close reading that identifies a text's various contexts and exposes the points at which meaning can be produced. Philology and rhetoric offer fruitful possibilities: to approach a passage by exploring the sixteenth-century attitudes towards the diction and syntax on which it depends, perhaps with the help of the *OED* and George Puttenham and John Hoskyns, can expand the scope of the discussion and invite connection with other relevant contexts, for example, the court, law, education, and the forces of gender. Another practical move is to shift the aim of close reading from locating and 'decoding' the hidden messages in a poem or passage to recognising that our initial responses are worth thinking about because they are textually based and rhetorically elicited. This collection hopes to help students take seriously claims that substantive and non-substantive, contextual and extra-contextual meaning *all* contribute to the nature and effect of a literary text. Doing so will perhaps lead students to kick away the heuristic division between surface and depth (a division that need get no further than a discussion of metaphor in order to collapse) and use close reading as an instrument to make visible the multiple negotiations between language and the world. As many of our contributors demonstrate, close reading can expose that which other methods of analysis leave hidden in plain sight.

The essays that follow aim to be exemplary but not, as a group, exhaustive. On this side of the theory watershed, any attempt to articulate an Empsonian 'Seven Types of Close Reading' would soon come to grief. Paul Alpers does call Empson's *Seven Types of Ambiguity* the Magna Carta of close reading, an apt comparison, since the mythologies about both texts – what they do and do not accomplish – provide useful guidance for more open consideration of the forms and goals of close reading. Nor do the essays attempt to exhaust their primary texts, or compel consensus around their readings. In keeping with their non-deterministic approach to close reading, the editors invited contributors to make their choices as they wished, without regard to any plan or organisation, except for the most general requirement that primary texts be early modern. All the contributors read convincingly. We hope that their examples will foster emulation, and we further hope that such reading will inform and nourish the relationship between stage and page. As a practical matter, the book ignores the current debate over the ontological status of Shakespeare's text: whether their author regarded the plays chiefly as theatrical documents or conceived them as eventually being made available to readers. They were first 'published' – made public – in the Elizabethan and Jacobean playhouses but soon thereafter became not only theatrical scripts but also legible objects, performed on stages (and now recorded on film) but also read and studied in libraries and dormitories and classrooms.

Even with a large helping of randomness, this selection of scholars, their choices of primary texts, and the arrangement of their work by the editors form a text that is itself available for close reading. This collection presents one cross-section of a canon (for better or worse) of early modern studies in the early twenty-first century: Shakespeare as solid as ever, Jonson (cheered on by scholars) still trying to pull out of his shadow, Milton maintaining the gains of the last century, prose still the neglected stepchild, sixteenth-century authors (Spenser, Marlowe) perhaps in decline, seventeenth-century lyric (Herbert, Marvell) striding ahead. Other readings are possible.

The groupings detailed here are admittedly artificial, and many of the essays could find placements in several of the categories, but we believe each group tends to demonstrate clearly and pointedly a particular facet of close reading. The first and last sections, 'Close Reading Beginnings' and 'Close Reading Endings', include essays that attend at least in some degree to the special poetic, formal, and rhetorical complexities of starting and stopping. In both cases, the objects of reading are diverse, and the consequences of close reading move far beyond the straitened prescriptions made for close reading in earlier decades. Reading beginnings with particular sensitivity can in fact assist in the establishment of a text to read and of a philosophy for subsequent editorial decisions, as in Lukas Erne's investigation of an ossified editorial tradition. Likewise, Charles Altieri's attention to the ending of *King Lear* finally results in an adjustment of the philosophical parameters of experiencing a text. And two pieces illustrate the utility of close reading for actors and directors.

'Close Reading Experiences' and 'Close Reading Both Ways' are also naturally related groups that could easily form a single continuum. The first includes essays that read passages closely in order to describe and inspect the ways in which literary language creates experience. Such experience often takes the form of pleasure, but it may be better to understand experience as an aesthetic encounter. Certainly, there is nothing pleasurable about the intense 'vermiculation' Kimberly Johnson investigates in John Donne's sermon *Deaths Duell*, but then there may be real delight in encountering language that comes as close as any can to making us feel what it must be like to decay in a grave. The second group includes essays that attend especially to the doubleness of complex writing. These readers emphasise the many ways in which messages conveyed by one dimension of a text are complicated, even contradicted, by messages from another dimension. Close reading provides a means momentarily to coordinate these often skewed axes of signification.

The essays in 'Close Rereading' show how close reading often has a reparative function. Interpretations that emanate from the too-comfortable grooves of literary orthodoxy can be refreshed, or swept away, by looking again, with new patience, at what is clearly staring at us from the page. The most familiar moments – Faustus's theological hubris, for example, in Drew Daniel's dazzling rereading – take on startling new lives. By contrast, Jeremy Lopez reads a text that has received little reading of any kind, and shows that John Fletcher himself was an astute close reader of his senior colleague and writing partner, William Shakespeare. 'Close Reading Techniques' is in a sense the inverse of the section on experience. Instead of taking each new detail of text as a site for the minor adjustment of a reading experience, and the major retrospective adjustment of everything that has come before, these essays select a particular technique or device as a way to open a window on an entire work or works. The topics addressed move from discrete to unbounded, from form and mechanics (monosyllables and punctuation), to rhetoric (similes and narrative culs-de-sac), to motives and modes of self-presentation. The penultimate section comprises essays about *Hamlet* – a casebook, of sorts, of the many ways close reading may be constituted in response to a single text – and attests to the enduring centrality of that play to the most fundamental intellectual concerns in early modern literary studies.

Above all, we hope that these essays will be read closely.

Russ McDonald
Nicholas D. Nace
Travis D. Williams

A NOTE ON TEXTS

Unless otherwise indicated, the works of William Shakespeare are quoted and cited from *The Arden Shakespeare Complete Works*, revised edition, edited by Richard Proudfoot, Ann Thompson, and David Scott Kastan (London, 2011). Other editions of Shakespeare's works are cited by their editors' names and listed under those names in the Bibliography.

At the first quotation of a Bible verse in each essay, the translation used throughout is indicated by 'Geneva' or 'AV' (Authorised Version).

In quotations that preserve original spelling, long-s has been modernised.

Close Reading Beginnings

ONE

Editorial Emendation and the Opening of
A Midsummer Night's Dream

Lukas Erne

THESEUS   Now faire *Hippolita*, our nuptiall hower
           Draws on apase: fower happy daies bring in
           An other Moone: but oh, me thinks, how slow
           This old Moone waues. She lingers my desires,
           Like to a Stepdame, or a dowager,   5
           Long withering out a yong mans reuenewe.
HIPPOLITA Fower daies will quickly steepe themselues in night:
           Fower nights will quickly dreame away the time:
           And then the Moone, like to a siluer bowe,
           Now bent in heauen, shall beholde the night   10
           Of our solemnities.
           William Shakespeare, *A Midsummer Night's Dream*, 1.1.1–11

Some time ago, I distributed a photocopy of the beginning of the
first quarto of *A Midsummer Night's Dream* (1600) to a group of
advanced students and asked them to think about differences to
the text in modern editions. We discussed what modern editors do
when preparing an edition such as the Arden, the Oxford, or the
New Cambridge: the modernisation of spelling and punctuation,
the expansion and regularisation of speech headings, collation,
annotation. And emendation. In the first eleven lines, editors
usually emend two words: 'waues' to 'wanes', in line 4; and 'Now
bent' to 'New bent', or 'New-bent', in line 10. My students saw
good reasons for the first emendation but – in good Genevan
iconoclast tradition – were totally unpersuaded by the second. I
remembered that all the modern editions I had consulted read

'New bent in heaven', a reading that had firmly engraved itself in my memory when I performed in a student production of the play as an undergraduate. So I tried to defend the traditional emendation (a reflex I lament in other editors but am clearly not above myself). Yet I found it hard to do so and may well have left most students unconvinced.

A few days later, I investigated the editorial history of the passage. The emendation in line 4, 'waues' to 'wanes', goes back to the second quarto of 1619 and was adopted in all later seventeenth-century editions – and by all modern editors too. 'Now bent' in line 10, however, remained the accepted reading throughout the seventeenth century. In 1709, Nicholas Rowe was the first to change the passage to 'New bent', and, with the exception of the little noted Everyman Shakespeare,[1] all modern editions agree with Rowe. The only eighteenth-century editor who did not follow Rowe's emendation is Samuel Johnson, whose text unaccountably reads 'Never bent', presumably a misprint, as H. H. Furness pointed out.[2] A nineteenth-century critic objected to what had long become a standard emendation: 'however pleasing these lines may be, they exhibit proof that Shakespeare, like Homer, may sometimes slumber; for, as the old moon had still four nights to run, it is quite clear that at the time Hippolyta speaks of there would be no moon, either full-orbed or "like to a silver bow", to beam on their solemnities'.[3] John Payne Collier agreed and thought the problem could be fixed with the original reading, 'whereof the meaning is that "then the moon, which is *now* bent in heaven like a silver bow, shall behold the night of our solemnities"'.[4] Collier's edition thus restored Q1's 'Now', but later editors returned to Rowe's emendation. So with only three exceptions, all editors from Rowe in 1709 to Jonathan Bate and Eric Rasmussen in 2007 seem to have agreed that 'Now' should be emended to 'New'.

Before discussing the emendation from 'Now' to 'New', let us look at the two speeches. They clearly form a dramatic whole, Hippolyta's speech answering Theseus's. Both are concerned with the period of time between the present and the planned wedding in four days. As it turns out, the time *A Midsummer Night's Dream* dramatises until the end of the play is only two and a half days, an inconsistency of which readers and spectators can easily remain unaware.[5] Theseus's 'our nuptiall hower' in the first and Hippolyta's 'our solemnities' in the last line frame the passage, 'nuptiall hower' and 'solemnities' referring to the event that will unite them and the first-person plural pronoun 'our', not used elsewhere in this passage, expressing that union. In between, both characters dwell on the period of time leading up to the wedding – 'fower … daies' (2), 'Fower daies' (7) – during which the 'Moone' (3, 4, 9) wanes. Both characters mention the speed with which they think the four days will go by. Theseus is remarkably inconsistent: the 'nuptiall hower / Draws on apase' (1–2), but the old moon wanes slowly: 'She lingers my desires' (4). Hippolyta, by contrast, is consistent, saying twice in two consecutive lines that the remaining time 'will quickly' (7, 8) elapse. While Theseus's tone appears to be one of impatience, that of Hippolyta is more elusive. Is she reassuring Theseus that their wedding day will come soon, or is she complaining that it will come all too soon? Does she think the quick passage of the four days leading up to their wedding is a good or a bad thing?

The 'Moone' is compared by both characters to that which 'She' is 'like to' (5, 9). Theseus' 'Moone' 'lingers [his] desires, / Like to a Stepdame, or a dowager, / Long withering out a yong mans reuenewe' (4–6), which equates postponed marriage and consummation with delayed inheritance and diminished economic potency. No less charmingly, the comparison makes Theseus cast himself in the role of the young male, in opposition to the female, who is old and withering. Hippolyta compares the 'Moone' to 'a siluer bowe … in heauen' (9-10), reminding us of the virgin warrior's reputed skill in archery. The moon and bow are associated with Diana, the goddess of chastity, who 'shall beholde the night / Of [Theseus and Hippolyta's] solemnities' (10-11).

The two opening speeches further gain in meaning if we recall other parts of the play. Theseus's 'dowager, / Long withering out a yong mans reuenewe' (5–6), who obstructs the fulfilment of love, contrasts with Lysander's 'widowe aunt, a dowager, / Of great reuenew' (1.1.157–8; I quote from Q1 but line references are to the Arden 2 edition), who enables it. Theseus's description of the old moon as a female who is 'withering' (6) looks ahead to his admonition to Hermia to agree to marry Demetrius, as her father commands: 'But earthlyer happy is the rose distild, / Then that, which, withering on the virgin thorne, / Grows, liues, and dies in single blessedness' (1.1.76–8). In both passages, it is delayed or refused marital consummation which, according to Theseus, causes the 'withering'. Theseus and Hippolyta's different perspectives on the speed with which the old moon will be replaced by the new is also revisited later in the play, when they are watching the mechanicals' performance of *Pyramus and Thisbe*, more specifically, Starveling's performance as Moonshine. To Hippolyta's 'I am aweary of this Moone. Would hee woulde change', Theseus replies: 'It appeares, by his small light of discretion, that hee is in the wane: but yet, in curtesie, in all reason, wee must stay the time' (5.1.242–5). As at the beginning of the play, the moon is said by Theseus to wane, the only two passages in all of Shakespeare in which the word refers to the moon.[6] In act 1, scene 1, Theseus is impatiently awaiting the change of the moon; in act 5, scene 1, when they are watching Moonshine, Hippolyta is. Theseus's opening lines contain in fact the first of many references to the moon in the play, the 'recurrent, incidental references to the moon' being one of the 'patterning elements' of *A Midsummer Night's Dream*, as Stephen Booth has rightly pointed out.[7]

The moment of time to which Theseus and Hippolyta are looking forward without quite naming it is that of the 'new moon'. Theseus mentions the 'old Moone' (4), but the new moon, although referred to twice in lines 3 and 9, is not actually called 'new' – or at least not until quite a bit later in the scene, when Theseus says: 'Take time to pawse; and, by the next newe moone, / ... prepare to dye, / ... Or else to wed *Demetrius*' (1.1.83–8). One reason why the emendation from 'Now' to 'New' may be appealing is that the word 'new' is otherwise conspicuously absent from the passage – unless we consider that it is hiding in 'reue*new*e' (6), just as 'old' is hiding in 'beh*old*e' (10). The passage makes explicit several temporal oppositions: between 'slow' and 'quickly', 'old' and 'yong', and 'daies' and 'nights' (even, more specifically, 'Fower daies' and 'Fower nights'). Given this pattern of oppositions, we expect 'old Moone' in line 4 to be followed by 'new Moone', but it is not, although the moon, if we accept the traditional emendation, is at least 'New bent in heaven'.

Modern editors have defended the emendation from 'Now' to 'New' in various ways. One editor claims that 'Now' is 'probably a compositor's error, due to the confusion, a common one, of "e" and "o"'.[8] Another one believes that the 'probable compositorial misreading [was] affected by "then" at l. 9'.[9] Perhaps, though 'e'/'o' confusion is less likely in secretary hand than minim misreadings, and while 'then' may invite 'now', the idea of the new moon calls for 'new', not 'now'. Even if secretary hand 'e' and 'o' can be confused and 'then' might have prompted 'now', the mere possibility of compositorial error does not, I would argue, justify an emendation. The question is whether the passage in Q1 makes sense. A third editor claims that '"Now" can only be defended as proleptic: "then the moon" will be "now bent in heaven". But an audience would hear "Now" as in contrast with "then"'.[10] A proleptic 'Now' in the given context, the editor infers, makes no sense, and so the emendation from 'Now' to 'New' is necessary.

Yet is it true that 'Now' would have to be understood as proleptic? Or can Hippolyta be understood as making one point about the moon in the future ('then the Moone ... shall beholde the night / Of our solemnities') and another point about the moon in the present (the moon is 'like to a siluer bowe, / Now bent in heauen')? In terms of the lunar cycle, 'Now' need not be proleptic: four days (or nights) before the appearance of the new moon's waxing crescent, what is left of the old moon's waning crescent is slender enough to be compared to 'a siluer bowe'. The syntax of 'like to a siluer bowe, / Now bent in heauen' is somewhat awkward, it is true, and the sentence would more naturally run: the moon is now bent in heaven like to a silver bow. The inversion of the expected order satisfies the metrical pattern, 'like to a siluer bowe' completing one pentameter and 'Now bent in heauen' starting the next, whereas the syntactically more natural order would leave the first line one foot short and the second one foot long. So did Shakespeare slightly bend the syntax (in a way of which he is also capable elsewhere) because it suited his metrics?

It is possible that he did, although I cannot be certain. So what am I to do as editor of *A Midsummer Night's Dream*? As close reader, if given the choice between the two words, 'New' or 'Now', I have a preference for 'New'. Not that 'Now' is impossible. Indeed, in some ways, it fits very well: the beginning of the first speech is echoed by the ending of the second, and the similarity is underlined by the repetition of 'now': 'Now … our nuptiall hower' (1); 'Now … our solemnities' (10). What is more, 'Now' naturally follows from 'then' in the preceding line. 'New', however, is the word which works better syntactically, and it spells out the implied opposition between the old and the new moon. Yet as editor I do not choose on the basis of aesthetic preference. Editors need to emend passages that are clearly corrupt, but the present passage, 'Now bent in heauen', is not. The Q1 reading was followed by five other editions in the seventeenth century: the second quarto (1619), and the first (1623), second (1632), third (1663–4), and fourth (1685) folios. The people responsible for Shakespeare's seventeenth-century reprints, as Sonia Massai has fully demonstrated, were not mindless copyists who let the texts deteriorate, but were often astute editors who carefully chose to alter or preserve readings in earlier editions. They believed – and I agree with them – that 'Now bent in heauen' (contrary to 'This old Moone waues') is a defensible reading. Therefore, unless we wish to practise the kind of aesthetic editing which we now associate with Alexander Pope, who liberally 'improved' the Shakespearean text based on his poetic preferences,[11] editors, I believe, have no other responsible choice than to return to 'Now'. In my text for the new *Norton Shakespeare*, I will thus eliminate the traditional emendation (and, incidentally, add waning and waxing parentheses):

And then the moon (like to a silver bow
Now bent in heaven) shall behold the night
Of our solemnities.

TWO

The Story of O: Reading Letters in the Prologue to *Henry V*

TRAVIS D. WILLIAMS

O for a muse of fire, that would ascend
The brightest heaven of invention,
A kingdom for a stage, princes to act,
And monarchs to behold the swelling scene!
Then should the warlike Harry, like himself,   5
Assume the port of Mars, and at his heels,
Leashed in like hounds, should famine, sword and fire
Crouch for employment. But pardon, gentles all,
The flat unraised spirits that hath dared
On this unworthy scaffold to bring forth   10
So great an object. Can this cockpit hold
The vasty fields of France? Or may we cram
Within this wooden O the very casques
That did affright the air at Agincourt?
O pardon, since a crooked figure may   15
Attest in little space a million,
And let us, ciphers to this great account,
On your imaginary forces work.
Suppose within the girdle of these walls
Are now confined two mighty monarchies,   20
Whose high upreared and abutting fronts
The perilous narrow ocean parts asunder.
Piece out our imperfections with your thoughts.
Into a thousand parts divide one man
And make imaginary puissance.   25
Think, when we talk of horses, that you see them

Printing their proud hoofs i'th' receiving earth.
For 'tis your thoughts that now must deck our kings,
Carry them here and there, jumping o'er times,
Turning th'accomplishment of many years   30
Into an hour-glass: for the which supply,
Admit me Chorus to this history,
Who prologue-like your humble patience pray,
Gently to hear, kindly to judge our play.

       William Shakespeare, *Henry V*, 1.0.1–34

The prologue to *Henry V* is a strange piece of verse drama. Unlike the prologues to other of Shakespeare's plays that have them – *Romeo and Juliet*, *2 Henry IV*, *Troilus and Cressida*, *Pericles*, *Henry VIII*, *The Two Noble Kinsmen*[1] – this one is not about the story, the characters, the setting or the genre, or at least not primarily so. It is not about what the play is about, but about how it is about it. The prologue to *Henry V* is very 'meta'. This contrast would not be worth much attention if it did not emphasise a deviation from the ostensible purpose of this and all prologues. A prologue is a moment of initiation. It bears responsibility for informing actor, audience, and reader of what is about to happen. In many ways the prologue to *Henry V* instead defeats the goals of explanation and seems rather to indulge in techniques of confusion. One source of confusion is the fact that the speaker does not announce his identity (on the assumption that the speaker is a man, which modern productions need not make) until the final lines of the prologue. A reader or auditor is thrown upon contextual clues, even more than usually, to answer those questions that any reader or auditor must answer: who is this, to whom is he speaking, and why? These answers are especially hard to come by because this is the first speech in the play, and it soon enough becomes apparent that the early lines are cast in a subjunctive mood (generally, if not at every verb) that further muddies the water by presenting us with a contrary-to-fact situation.

 If the prologue does two contradictory things at once – informing us about the play we are about to see and making it difficult to be informed about the play we are about to see – it is the diction that creates the dilemma. Larger structures of syntax and argument play their parts, but it is at the level of a single word that the duality of the prologue has its origin. I will approach the polysemous qualities of the prologue through special attention to the letter O, which appears as a distinct word three times in the speech. The letter-word is a reminder that even the slightest of utterances is capable of multiple, simultaneous, and contrary significations. The Chorus desires a reality of exact non-representation while admitting that only purely, inescapably hollow representation is all that will be delivered. But the Chorus also insists on the 'like'-ness of these, and other, extreme opposites: small and large, full and empty, something and nothing ('ciphers' [17]), creation and destruction ('unraised' [9]). Most prominently, the Chorus insists on the simultaneity of performed identity and essential identity, both for himself: 'Admit me Chorus to this history, / Who prologue-like' (32–3), and for the play's hero: 'warlike Harry, like himself' (5). Prompted by the flattery and encouragement of the Chorus, we (the audience / reader) are given extraordinary responsibility for putting flesh on the bones of these correspondences. Even as the Chorus formulates the task, the speech itself provides abundant opportunities for us to multiply the Chorus's words into a copious, lexically constituted world. O, in its nothingness and somethingness, provides the symbol and the limit of our task.

The first appearance of O is without context, except that which is external and prior to the moment of utterance here. Like the first word of any play, we can only approach a complete appreciation of this O's possibilities in retrospect. An actor walks onstage, and says, 'O'. There are two plausible functions for O before another word is spoken: an exclamation and an introduction to a vocative. No vocative appears, although it is syntactically possible for one to appear through the end of line 4. O as an exclamation brings with it a bewildering number of possibilities. An actor or a reader may select from among them; an audience must take what it gets. Tonal and dramatic decisions will drive semantic conclusions.

Is the speaker surprised to find an audience: 'O, I didn't expect there to be people here'; delighted: 'Oooo, there's an audience!'; uncertain, frustrated, or worried: 'O dear, what shall I do?'; disgusted, displeased, exasperated, or irritated: 'O, another bloody audience!'; reproachful and accusatory: 'O, how could you!'; filled with wonder and awe: recall Derek Jacobi at the beginning of Kenneth Branagh's 1989 film; declamatory: 'O, time for you to be quiet so I, and later my colleagues, can be heard'? The last option has much to recommend it because it does not require subsequent explanation or justification: the theatrical moment is its own justification, and acting companies have always needed to signal to the audience that talk must stop and listening must begin. Like the spluttering, ranting Herod of the cycle plays, who proclaims his self-importance while perhaps also clearing a playing space before the pageant cart,[2] the speaker of Shakespeare's prologue may supplement a musical flourish and his own rich costume with a lofty, histrionic, but otherwise empty O: it clears the space, empties it, so that it might be filled with the world created by the players and by us. The emptiness is not merely a negation, however. As the sentence unfolds, we perceive the contrary-to-fact situation I mentioned above in the form of impossible theatrical production values. With 'Then' at line 5 and the modal 'should', the first four lines suddenly take the form of a giant 'if' clause. 'O for' is then understood as 'would that there were', and 'Then' as 'in that case'. By the middle of line 8, which ends the 'then' clause, it will be obvious that the speaker depicts wild impossibilities that defeat even Mount Helicon itself. As 'But' initiates a statement of explicit concession, O acquires a tone of wistful frustration and irritation as a result of what the speaker wishes would, but knows cannot, happen on his stage.

'But' logically governs the speech through to the end of line 14. The speaker more than empties the audience's expectations of all the possibilities envisaged in the if/then clauses, now enforcing a strongly vertical comparison.[3] 'A muse of fire' (playing on the characteristic of fire to ascend higher than any other element) is now 'flat unraised spirits'. The 'kingdom for a stage', a place for valiant battle and heroic death, becomes 'this unworthy scaffold', a site for the ignoble death of criminals. ('Upreared' [21] later continues the theme of verticality.) Implied is the vast social distance between King Henry as an actor and the undistinguished actor who will appear as King Henry. 'But' also introduces an imperative, governed by the vocative 'gentles all' that could have been the vocative of the original O. 'Gentles' also carefully rescues the audience to a social position slightly closer to the monarchs that might have beheld the 'swelling scene'. 'Cockpit', in the same manner as 'unworthy scaffold', is another demotion of the playing space. It also introduces a thematically unharnessed sexual valence for O – a container for a cock – especially the O that will appear within two lines.[4] As Stephen Booth points out, the letter-word O frequently was an allusion to a vagina.[5]

A second rhetorical question introduces the second O of the prologue, and with it a large number of newly relevant senses for O. 'This wooden O' will immediately be a reference to the wood-framed round structure of the theatre that the speaker and audience now inhabit, working with the sense of O as anything shaped like the letter. *Henry V* was likely one of the first plays presented in the new Globe Theatre in 1599, so this particular theatre extends the relevance of O to a particular playing space. Both the Earth and the 'world', in the early modern sense of 'created universe', are relevant glosses for 'Globe'. Hence, O encompasses everything. '[C]ram / Within' makes the space a receptacle, recalling 'cockpit', with perhaps another bawdy reference in 'wooden' (and recasting 'swelling' [4] and '-raised' [9] above).[6] The question asks if the space could hold all the 'casques / That did affright the air at Agincourt'. The answer is no, if we understand 'casques' (helmets) – round objects and hence another example of O – to be a synecdoche for the heads of the soldiers they contain and their attached bodies. The answer might be yes if we calculate that the theatre might just be large enough to contain all the helmets – just the helmets – worn at the battle of Agincourt, but that would perhaps be to consider too curiously. More to the purpose, 'casques' sonically resembles 'casks' (the Folio spelling is in fact 'Caskes'), reminding us of yet another receptacle with an O shape,[7] and concluding a short, thematically irrelevant series of terms related to alcohol: 'port' (6), 'spirits' (9),[8] 'casques' (13).

A fourth logical partition of the speech begins with the third O. We have already had *if*, 'then', and 'but', and now we get *so*: if we had it, then we'd use it, but we don't have it, so we'll need to make do with something else. O introduces and intensifies an imperative which governs an implied vocative supplied from line 8, 'gentles all'. But O could also be the direct object of 'pardon': 'gentle audience, please pardon O'. Why should pardon be asked? It may not do to pursue this forced grammar too far, but pardon may be requested for the wooden O that is so insufficient to the tasks outlined in the if/then clauses. O as a recipient of pardon also invokes the pure letter. A more compelling explanation comes immediately after pardon is asked. O is a 'crooked figure' – 'figure' a term preferred in early modern arithmetic for 'numeral' – as is the O-shaped numeral 'zero' – more often called a cipher in early modern arithmetic. Both 'figure' and 'cipher' comment on the variable worth of the pardon-seeking person speaking and the actors he introduces. 'Zero' as nothing – something irrelevant, insignificant, or worthless[9] – neatly *and* messily balances the 'everything' invoked by O as that universe itself. Here pardon is asked for a thing that only appears to be nothing, because it can in some situations – as when one does one's 'account's (17) – be something, namely when a zero, a 'cipher', written in a low position (place-value), 'little place', 'multiplies' a quantity into something much larger: 'Attest ... a million', an arithmetical task paradoxically repeated by 'divide' (24), the inverse of multiplication. The theme of O rounds itself out with 'girdle' (19), with three available senses: an intimate garment, so another touch of the sexual image; the bands of a barrel, reaching back to 'cask', 'casque', and the deprecation of the wooden playing space; and the ecliptic or the equator,[10] returning to O as a celestial globe. 'Girdle' also reaches ahead to 'hour-glass' (31), an object shaped as if it were wearing an invisible girdle.

A series of imperatives – 'Suppose', 'Piece out', 'Think', 'Admit' – makes up the balance of the speech, which refills the space with all the impossible production values earlier evacuated by the admission of inadequacy. Only the agent has changed: now the audience or reader, rather than the actor, becomes responsible for presenting the unpresentable. The imperatives ask the audience to give life to the play, to give birth to it almost as the progeny of the otherwise irrelevant sexual senses invoked earlier and a string of words that now cohere in a theme of pregnancy and child-rearing: 'swelling' (4), '-raised' (9), 'great [with child]' (11, 17), 'vasty' (12), 'crooked' (15, perhaps implying 'round-bellied'), 'girdle' (19), and '-reared' (21).

At the end of the prologue, the speaker finally reveals that he is the Chorus: just an actor, perhaps wearing a costume, but not really inhabiting a role. (Indeed, the several utterances of O anticipate the speaker's announcement of his identity; both 'chorus' and 'prologue' include the sound of O.) This delay is of a piece with the semantic delay of the speech. The audience has had to work as hard at construing meaning as they will have to work at imagining settings, situations, and characters. Returning to the first O, we can see that the Chorus is talking to himself, to everyone, to anyone, and to no one in particular. The opening O is indeed a histrionic flourish, a initiator of pure theatricality, as empty as the representation the players will heroically fail to mount.

At the end of the play, the Chorus returns lightly to the images that thronged the prologue:

> Thus far, with rough and all-unable pen,
> Our bending author hath pursued the story,
> In little room confining mighty men,
> Mangling by starts the full course of their glory.
> Small time, but in that small most greatly lived
> This star of England.

> (5.Ep.1–6)

Now it is the 'bending author' (another 'crooked figure') who is inadequate to the task, making the best of the 'little room' of the 'wooden O'. 'Small time, but in that small most greatly lived' recalls the 'many years' crammed 'Into an hour-glass'. 'Course' starts out as a synonym of 'story', but also becomes the curved path of Henry V's star in the sky, a star proleptically – visually and sonically – present in 'starts'. Finally, the Chorus borrows for his own the glory of another group of players from another group of plays – *1–3 Henry VI* and *Richard III*:

> Which oft our stage hath shown; and for their sake
> In your fair minds let this acceptance take.
>
> (5.Ep.13–14)

Forgotten in this valediction is the role played by the audience, assigned to it by the Chorus. Praise goes everywhere – the author, other players, this Chorus, and his colleagues – but not to the gentles who had to 'make imaginary puissance' and 'deck our kings'. The Chorus is a dramatic con-artist, giving something that is nothing, pretending to take nothing but really taking everything, being all things to all people, and taking all the credit while other people do the work – rather like the hero of the play, who steals the clothes we put on his back.

THREE

The Sense of a Beginning

DONALD M. FRIEDMAN

Of man's first disobedience, and the fruit
Of that forbidden tree, whose mortal taste
Brought death into the world, and all our woe,
With loss of Eden, till one greater man
Restore us, and regain the blissful seat,   5
Sing heavenly muse, that on the secret top
Of Oreb, or of Sinai, didst inspire
That shepherd, who first taught the chosen seed,
In the beginning how the heavens and earth
Rose out of chaos: or if Sion hill   10
Delight thee more, and Siloa's brook that flowed
Fast by the oracle of God; I thence
Invoke thy aid to my adventurous song
That with no middle flight intends to soar
Above the Aonian mount, while it pursues   15
Things unattempted yet in prose or rhyme.
And chiefly thou O Spirit, that dost prefer
Before all temples the upright heart and pure,
Instruct me, for thou know'st; thou from the first
Wast Present, and with mighty wings outspread   20
Dove-like sat'st brooding on the vast abyss
And mad'st it pregnant: what in me is dark
Illumine, what is low raise and support;
That to the height of this great argument
I may assert eternal providence,   25
And justify the ways of God to men.

John Milton, *Paradise Lost*, 1.1–26[1]

We know that Milton thought about writing an epic poem for a very long time, not only because of external evidence – contemporary biographies, and his commonplace book in the library of Trinity College, Cambridge, where he recorded possible subjects for such a poem – but also because he tells us so directly, at the beginning of Book 9, the book of the fall of man, where he describes himself as 'long choosing, and beginning late' the subject of his 'heroic song' (9.6). Nevertheless, even as he begins his at-long-last attempt to fulfil his desire to 'perhaps leave something so written to aftertimes, as they should not willingly let it die',[2] his opening gesture is one of suspense: 'Of' – the first word of *Paradise Lost*. Syntactically miming the well-known epic tradition of beginning *in medias res,* he begins at a midpoint in the arc of his narrative, and in the middle of a sentence.

The awareness of time – time gone by, time going by, time to come – saturates *Paradise Lost* as it proposes to tell the story of mankind from the creation of our universe to its promised end in the fulfilment of providence and the end of time. That saturation is found not only in the specifics of its narrative, but throughout the poem in individual words and echoing phrases as well, as they suggest multiple meanings that enact different perspectives on a focal concept. A stylistic strategy thus serves to support the enormous act of memory that constitutes the epic.

As an example, consider the last word of the first line of the poem, 'fruit'. The emphasis placed on it is unmistakable: it is an accented monosyllable, and seems to refer directly to the consequences of 'man's first disobedience'. When we read 'Of that forbidden tree' in the next line the reference is specifically to the 'apple' that Eve and Adam eat, to their ill fate. But we have already been alerted to the true scope of that simple action, the unfolding history of humanity's pain and disappointment. In this way Milton enlists our recognition of the significance of the initial act of disobedience as he extends our understanding of the wider connotations of 'fruit' in the poem. We might note here that this is the same fruit that will seem 'fruitless' to Eve as she stands before the tree of knowledge, accompanied by Satan (9.648), and which will be cited by the Son as the 'fruits' of repentance (11.22) that will lead to a form of reconciliation and redemption for the fallen pair. Beyond that encompassing perspective, Milton is also pointing towards the event that will simultaneously mark the lowest point of the arc of consequences and the moment that it turns upwards towards redemption, for the 'fruit of that forbidden tree' is ultimately the Son upon the cross.[3] I would venture even further to suggest that 'forbidden' does not rest only on the absolute (and unique) ban upon 'that' tree that harbours both knowledge and the secret of immortality (or nothing at all), but that Milton has shaped a word to tell us that this particular tree was 'bidden' long before (from eternity) to bear both its foredestined 'fruits'.

Much more is going on in the first line. The unstressed syllable of the initial iamb, moreover, urges the reader forward not only to the stressed monosyllable 'man's', but the seemingly trochaic[4] emphasis on the following 'first', which in turn forces the stress pattern onward to the prefix of 'disobedience'. 'First' makes it clear that the 'original sin' was only the first of a long series of failures and mistakes, while it also suggests that it was, in some sense, the primal, archetypal, most disastrous of human actions.[5] But what we have since learned to designate as sin (as in 'original sin', with its doctrinal resonances), Milton calls 'disobedience', the prefix 'dis' marking the wrongdoing of Adam and Eve as a falling away from 'obedience',[6] which is thus placed as the normative state. Comparably, in his account of creation, the universe is made by God out of his own substance, rather than out of nothingness by an act of will; matter, traditionally the source of moral evil, is thus essentially divine in essence. The poem's language reflects its ontology.

The polysyllabic 'disobedience' comes up, abruptly, against 'fruit', the word reminding us of what follows from the failure of obedience and, at the same time, of the possibility of natural and benevolent outcomes. In this poem, choice is capable of producing both agony and joy – as the first line enacts in its seven words. The fruit of our failure to heed the imperatives of our creation is everything that has happened to all of us from the beginning and that is destined to become of us in the fullness of time.

A powerful principle of economy governs the versification of the two sentences that occupy the twenty-six lines of the opening invocation. Milton exploits enjambment to produce surprise that becomes revelation: the turn on 'fruit' is only the first instance. In an example of Milton's notorious resort to Latinisms (in the view of some of his offended critics), he plays, too, on the interinvolved connotations of tasting and knowing, derived from the Latin verb *sapio*. In this story, to experience is to acquire knowledge, with all its potential for joy, and all its dangers. The phrase 'mortal taste' defines the act that deprived our 'general ancestor[s]' (4.659) of the possibility of immortality. But it also defines the nature and origin of our mortal being – in the appropriation of knowledge. Thus, stress and apparent end-stopping combine to explain how we became human. And once again enjambment unillusions us, for that 'mortal taste / Brought death into the world'; only later (in Book 10) will that abstraction be transformed as we are shown the figure of Death (Satan's incestuous child by Sin) actually crossing to our world over a very solid bridge.

Milton has still more to teach. Death is not the worst, for along with it came 'all our woe' ('woe' echoing 'world', and acknowledging woe's scope by stressing 'all' and including us in 'our'); by comparison the 'loss of Eden' sounds almost like an afterthought, especially because we are promised, later, 'A paradise within thee, happier far' (12.587). Turning to a different mode of emphasis from the final-stressed enjambment – the caesura, or rhythmic pause within the line – 'till' sets a term for our woe; at the same moment, 'one greater man' redefines the 'man' responsible for 'all' of it. It also sets Milton's hero – the Son – apart from the 'man' who serves as the hero of many of the epics Milton has in mind as he begins his own: those 'fabled knights / in battles feigned' (9.30–31), subjects Milton rejects because he is 'Not sedulous by nature to indite / Wars' (9.27–8). The 'greater man' is promised to 'Restore us', and 'regain the blissful seat'. Both verbs speak of the correction of a previous flaw or failure; both are active, almost physical, and 'restore' suggests not only recovery of a native possession that has been lost, but also the replenishment of a natural substance. The 'blissful seat', we will learn, is not the garden of Eden, the 'happy rural seat of various view' (4.247), but a more ambiguous place, yet reminiscent of 'the seat of God' (1.383).[7]

It is at this point that the first vocative verb appears, the first call to speak – or, more properly, to 'sing' the rest of the poem. He calls upon his 'heavenly muse' to inspire him as (he, she, it?) did 'that shepherd, who first taught the chosen seed' (8), emphasising the stresses on 'that' and 'first', so as to call upon our recognition of Moses the shepherd-become-prophet and to suggest, modestly but tellingly, that he – Milton – is the latest in a long line of such truth-tellers.[8] The stress on 'that' serves a similar purpose to the way the word pointed to the tree in line 2: it reminds us of what we already know, as at the same time it suggests other, possibly unrecognised, significances. It combines with 'first' (as in line 1, meaning both important and initial) to conjure Moses' successors – those who have been visited by divine mentors – and also to revivify the ancient connections among shepherds, poets, and spiritual leaders.

But the mention of biblical sites associated with Moses' encounters with God, and Milton's declaration of his intent to 'soar above' the 'Aonian mount' (Helicon, home of the classical Muses) make clear that his 'Heav'nly' muse is someone or something other than the creative force that midwived all other epic accounts of the origins of the universe and humankind, the tradition into which he is now initiating himself. His request is not merely to be aided in his audacious endeavour (he asks, after all, for the Muse to sing the tale itself of the 'first disobedience'), but something more, and greater. With his characteristic mixture of knowledgeable respect for the tradition and a driving ambition to transcend it, he invokes Ariosto's claim in *Orlando Furioso* of writing something that has never been said in prose or rhyme ('Cosa non detta in prosa mai, ne in rima'),[9] and overgoes that boast by promising to write 'Things unattempted yet in prose or rhyme'. 'Unattempted' manages to sound both confident and diffident.

For at this point Milton turns his voice from the encapsulated narrative of lines 1–16 to his consummate challenge – to explain and do justice to the purpose of his story of creation, fall, and redemption. For this task the Muses, 'Heav'nly' or other, will not serve. He calls upon the 'Spirit' who 'from the first / Wast present', and is thus possessed of something essential to the success of the poem's 'great argument': not rhetorical skill or poetic inspiration, but knowledge – a particular kind of knowledge, not to be confused with the kind that can be acquired by 'long choosing' or by dedicated study of the poet's predecessors. Rather, it is a knowledge communicated by an action; in this case, the renovation of the hopeful hierophant's soul and mind. Milton calls upon a Spirit that prefers 'Before all temples th'upright heart and pure', choosing as the place of sanctity not a building but the human heart (nevertheless not forgetting that the body is the 'temple of the spirit'). This particular heart, however, needs to be 'built' so as to maintain itself upright, in order to wield the strength necessary to its work. The Latin for 'build' is *struere*; the denotation Milton chooses is 'instruct', by which he reminds us that the construction he asks for is inward, and that teaching is a kind of building from within, knowledge a kind of substance that provides and sustains the bricks and mortar of a moral being.[10]

That this Spirit's knowledge differs from our usual understanding is signalled by the phrase, 'for thou know'st'. 'To know' is usually a transitive verb: one knows *something*. But the Spirit's is a kind of knowing not limited by a specific object; it simply knows, a way of knowing not available to fallen humans, a way that alone can reveal the essence of his telling to the poet. More precisely, the Spirit's knowledge is not an action upon a subject, nor its possession, but rather the creation of the thing known. It has been present 'from the first', and in its 'brooding on the vast abyss', has exercised the power of 'the two great sexes' (8.151) so that 'the heav'ns and earth / Rose out of Chaos'. The knowledge that the poet seeks, then, is identified with the power that creates order out of disorder, light out of darkness. Thus he speaks of himself as a figure of the inchoate, the formless, the potential, the end-stopped enjambment once again enacting the transformation he wishes for: 'what in me is dark / Illumine', where the run-on brightens

the verse with a polysyllabic flash. 'What is low' must be raised
so as to reach 'the heighth' of the poem's 'great argument'. The
latter is double; Milton undertakes to 'assert' – that is, to advocate,
advance, show the truthfulness of – 'Eternal Providence', the
power both to foresee the future and to provide for those who will
see it. What remains is to 'justify the ways of God to men'.[11] Milton
allows us (or asks us) to consider the implicated consequences of
explaining the justice of God's ways, and the more specific task of
making apparent to men the justice of God's ways. In either case,
he is also alerting us to the multifarious, ubiquitous 'ways' he will
be describing in the verses that follow; they include God himself,
the sociable spirit Raphael, the Son, the archangel Michael, and of
course Satan and his offspring, to name only the visitors who make
their way to Eden. This is not to speak of all the other 'ways' in and
by which God creates, cares for, educates, punishes, and provides
for 'Adam the goodliest man of men since born / His sons, the
fairest of her daughters Eve' (4.323–4), phrases that manage to
include all of us.

It is perhaps Milton's peculiar talent, or perhaps his genius, to
create images, phrases, single words and entire poems whose major
mode is inclusion. (William Empson wrote four pages on 'all' in
Paradise Lost in *The Structure of Complex Words*.) In such cases as
'fruit', or 'Tree', or 'seed' (and there are many more), they range
throughout a work of over 10,000 lines, ramifying and expanding
in significance, shaping our responses and sculpturing our understanding. This in itself summons admiration; but what calls for
simple astonishment is that it is done without hand or sight.[12]
Every word, every phrase, every line, was made by the voice, was
the creation of sound, and was so imagined; and that imagination
reached to a sustained oral vision (if such there be) charged with
meaning from the beginning we have just been listening to, to the
final, oxymoronic phrase, 'their solitary way' (12.649).

At the opening of Book 3, speculating on his blindness, Milton
tell us of nightly visiting the 'Muses haunt', and then of his habit
to 'feed on thoughts, that voluntary move / Harmonious numbers'
(3.37–8). Those are the 'apt numbers' he speaks of in the note 'On

the Verse' prefaced to Book 1, which contribute to 'true musical delight', together with 'the sense drawn out from one verse into another', the device we less eloquently call 'enjambment'. Those verses came to him in the night, and he gave them voice in the light of the next day: light out of darkness, order out of obscurity, form out of chaos, poetry out of silence.

Close Reading Experiences

FOUR

Spenser Up Close: Temporality in
The Faerie Queene

Linda Gregerson

That well may seemen true: for, well I weene
    That this same day, when she on *Arlo* sat,
    Her garment was so bright and wondrous sheene,
    That my fraile wit cannot deuize to what
    It to compare, nor finde like stuffe to that,
    As those three sacred *Saints*, thought else most wise,
    Yet on mount *Thabor* quite their wits forgat,
    When they their glorious Lord in strange disguise
Transfigur'd sawe; his garments so did daze their eyes.
            Edmund Spenser, *The Faerie Queene*, 7.7.7

In Book 11 of the *Confessions*, Augustine attempts to contemplate
the mystery of time and, in particular, the temporal embeddedness
that makes human beings particularly unqualified to comprehend
eternity. Time is motion: the human mind cannot comprehend eternity directly because, says Augustine, it cannot *hold still*.[1] So the
mystery of eternity, and He who dwells in it, can only be imagined
in opposition to that which it is not: to temporality. But time,
though it is our only native element, proves almost as difficult to
comprehend as does eternity. The future cannot properly be said
to exist because it does not exist *yet*, and the past *no longer* exists.
'As for the present', writes Augustine, 'if it were always present
and never moved on to become the past, it would not be time but
eternity. If, therefore, the present is time only by reason of the
fact that it moves on to become the past, how can we say that even
the present *is*, when the reason why it *is* is that it is *not to be*?'

(11.14). The present has no duration, then, no dimensions proper to itself. It is thinner than the razor's edge. And yet it is full, is indeed the only fullness we shall ever in this life have. It can only be summoned *by feel*. 'Suppose', says Augustine,

> that I am going to recite a psalm that I know. Before I begin, my faculty of expectation is engaged by the whole of it. But once I have begun, as much of the psalm as I have removed from the province of expectation and relegated to the past now engages my memory, and the scope of the action which I am performing is divided between the two faculties of memory and expectation, the one looking back to the part which I have already recited, the other looking forward to the part which I have still to recite. But my faculty of attention is present all the while, and through it passes what was the future in the process of becoming the past ...
>
> (11.28)

In his effort to capture the dimensionless plenitude of the present, Augustine invokes the recitation, from memory, of a psalm. It is no accident that the example is drawn from verse rather than prose. When he attempts to capture something about the nature of time by means of measurement, by *telling time*, Augustine invokes the motion of the heavenly bodies and the divisions we number according to their circuits: years, months, days, and hours. He invokes the humbler rotations of the potter's wheel. He invokes, repeatedly, what he takes to be the foundational units of language: syllables long and short, the metrical foot, the poetic line. Poetry, it seems, is language acutely, perhaps uniquely, wedded to time.

And poetry is apt for memory. In Augustine's case study, the recitation of the psalm, it is necessary that the verse be already familiar, already awarded a recurrent place in consciousness. Its syllables pass through the mind and through the voice in the manner of a sacramental return, or the rotation of a potter's wheel. The future again becoming the past again through the portal of the human. It is in this way and this way only that we contrive to turn our face to the eternal. Of the past, writes Augustine, all we can say of it is that it too is an aspect of the present, the present of the past, which we call memory. And the future, or all that can be said to exist of it, which is the present of the future, we call that expectation. So, three kinds of time: the present of the past, the present of the present, and the present of the future. And all of these are qualities of attention.

Attention as a felt faculty – the future becoming the past again, by means of which we infer our own existence in the radical transience we call the present – is the particular genius of Spenserian poetics, especially the poetics that govern the epical, allegorical, post- and anti-Petrarchan, neo-antiquarian chivalric romance we call *The Faerie Queene*. The apprehension the poem is designed to induce is by its nature fugitive, the cusp between expectation and remembrance, the sense of having sensed the thing in the instant before its disappearance, or of being about to sense it again. For Spenser, the cognitive 'capture' that matters is a quality of feeling – I saw her, I was there – and is utterly at odds with fixity: try to hold the moment still and you denature it; the plenitude of radical transience resolves to 'nought but pressed gras'.[2]

If the present, as Augustine so carefully explains, is interstitial, its apprehension must be so too. And the poet who makes this apprehension the governing object of his poem must devise a method that does not, itself, belie the quest. Spenser's foundational proposition in *The Faerie Queene* – the method he devises for inciting in himself and in his readers, recurrently, the apprehension of being-in-the-present-tense – involves the cultivation of oppositional momentums. Take, for example, the oppositional timing of narrative and prosody. Were one to set about writing an expansive twelve-book historical fiction, 'clowdily enwrapped in Allegoricall deuises' ('Letter to Raleigh' [716]), one could scarcely imagine a more recalcitrant, more Procrustean vehicle than the nine-line stanza Spenser devised for *The Faerie Queene*. Its fixed dimensions, its end-stopped hexameter, and its interlocking rhymes, far more constraining in English than are the rhymes of Ariosto and Tasso in Italian, would seem to be inimical to the limber speedings-up and slowings-down that narrative momentum requires. And, indeed, although the stanza sometimes tames the narrative to a coincident cadence, as in the allegorical pageants, it most often works at odds with other forms of pacing in the poem, establishing a kind of cognitive syncopation. Rising action and deliquescence, deferral and derailment, urgency and lassitude play out against a grid of syllables and accents, metrical feet, poetic lines, stanzas and cantos and books: devices all for construing even the unknown narrative future as a species of proportioned expectation, and that which *was* the future as a measurable past. All in an effort to invoke – to summon – that dimensionless in-between, the fugitive, mortal present tense, which *is* only because it *is not to be*, but which – and this is the point – is not yet wholly lost.

When the narrator of cantos that 'appear to be parcell of some following Booke of the *Faerie Queene*' (7.6, title page) introduces the allegorical figure of Mutabilitie, he describes her as an enemy to Nature, one who has perverted Nature's 'good estate', broken Nature's laws, turned blessing to curse and life to death. And yet, in the ongoing course of narrative action, when Mutabilitie submits her claims against the Jovian dispensation, she appeals to Nature as her judge. Has she simply, disastrously, miscalculated her own interests? Or forgotten, somehow, her own origins? Admittedly, Mutabilitie has a knack for undermining herself: the very 'evidence' she marshals on her own behalf in the trial scene, the orderly procession of seasons, months, and hours, suggests a structural stability that belies her claims for perpetual change. And the fungible four elements as she describes them – earth, water, air, and fire perpetually 'chang'd ... Into themselues' (7.7.25) – uncannily anticipate, albeit by means of a grammatical ambiguity, the sentence that will be passed against her. But the slippage between Nature-as-enemy and Nature-as-arbiter is something else. It marks a fracture line, not in Mutabilitie's prideful aspirations or in Mutabilitie's forensic calculations, but in the poet/narrator's allegorical proposition.

When Spenser begins the Cantos of Mutabilitie in the form of

a lament, he conjures a model of Nature – Nature in her first estate
– before the advent of change. But this model, a false one, quickly
proves untenable. The world worth having, Nature not denatured,
has mutability running in its veins. Her very form is mutable, now
male, now female, its indeterminacy secured by variable report
and by a veil with a substantial pedigree:

> That some do say was so by skill deuized,
>   To hide the terror of her vncouth hew,
>   …
>   But others tell that it so beautious was,
>   And round about such beames of splendor threw,
>   That it the Sunne a thousand times did pass,
> Ne could be seene, but like an image in a glass.

(7.7.6)

Surface logic makes terror and beauty the touchstones of alternate
hypotheses: if one accounts for the veiling of the face, the other
must be false. But, as is so often the case with Spenserian attributes,
the qualities behind the veil evade the strictures of either/or.
Linked by their exorbitance, terror and beauty function additively,
equally mysterious, equally unbearable to human sight: both/and.
The image of an image in a glass links Nature's face to other forms
of the terrible beauty we call the transcendent, and is directly
followed by a more extended, and explicit, biblical analogy:

> That well may seemen true: for, well I weene
>   That this same day, when she on *Arlo* sat,
>   Her garment was so bright and wondrous sheene,
>   That my fraile wit cannot deuize to what
>   It to compare, nor finde like stuffe to that,
>   As those three sacred *Saints*, thought else most wise,
>   Yet on mount *Thabor* quite their wits forgat,
>   When they their glorious Lord in strange disguise
> Transfigur'd sawe; his garments so did daze their eyes.

(7.7.7)

The brightness too great to be seen is covered and conveyed by a garment too bright to be described, which is to say, too great for all comparison: the poet cannot 'finde like stuffe'. And yet, of course, in this very insufficiency, which links him to the disciples on Mount Tabor, he finds the likeness he requires. Regarding that likeness, the transfiguration of Christ, the Geneva Bible provides the following gloss: 'Christ shewed them his glorie that they might not thinke that he suffred through infirmitie but that he offered vp him self willingly to dye' (Matthew 17:2). The transfiguration, according to this reading, was itself a hermeneutic gloss, a help to the faithful in expectation of the Passion, so that when the mortal moment came they might know it for what it was: not a weakness but a strength, not an end but a beginning, not the triumph of death but the rupturing of history by eternity. Which cannot be gazed on directly.

In the Mutabilitie Cantos, the seat prepared for Nature the adjudicator, in all her beauty and her terror, is hedged about, like Nature's face, with doubleness: what was 'the best and fairest' has become 'most ill' (7.6.37). '[W]ere it not ill fitting', writes the poet, he would tell you the story of Arlo Hill (7.6.37) and, in the space thus opened up by the ever-resourceful subjunctive mood, he proceeds to do precisely that. Arlo Hill is one of those wonderful Spenserian sites where the floating world of mythic place is rudely reconfigured by the pull of the actual – actual hills, actual rivers, actual Ireland – and where unstable temporalities compete for imaginative sway. 'O Clio,' writes the poet, 'lend Calliope thy quill' (7.6.37), which is to say, apparently, that the muse of history must retire for a while in deference to the muse of epic poetry. The time-frame governed by Calliope, 'whylome', is one quite congenial to the subjunctive mood. 'At some indefinite time in the past', is how we generally construe it, though the word was also used in the sixteenth century to refer to the future: 'Therefore I purpose', writes Henry Bradshaw, 'All such ydlenes whylom to refuse'.[3] 'Whylome' is a floater, not quite commensurate with Clio's chronicles; it captures epic's double allegiance to genealogy and futurity, memory and expectation: witness the epic prophecies that read like history to epic's contemporary audience.[4] 'Whylome', writes the poet, 'when IRELAND flourished in fame / Of wealths and goodnesse' (7.6.38), Arlo was the fairest hill in the land. And then came Faunus' trespass and Diana's curse.

The Diana/Cynthia who features in the interpolated prehistory of Arlo Hill is another of the resonantly redundant but not-entirely-coincident figures who are so central to Spenser's method in *The Faerie Queene*. The goddess who curses the landscape is not, not quite, the goddess whom Mutabilitie has tried to depose in the frame narrative. And yet there is real sympathy, and a world of shared tradition, between the luminous body that lights our way by night and the maidenly body that refuses to be seen. Cynthia's gates are guarded by the allegorical figure of Tyme, and though she sits on a throne, she never 'stands', that is to say, stands still (7.6.8). Let us think of her, then, as sister to Augustine's present tense. Faunus wants to hold her in his gaze, for which the punishment is both unnatural fixity and unnatural scattering or 'spilling'. Faunus betrays his stolen gazing with a burst of laughter, an uncontrolled somatic 'breaking forth', and then is captured, or 'taken', '[l]ike darred Larke' (7.6.47). To dare: to daze, paralyse, or render helpless with the sight of something. The phrase derives from a method of capturing larks by showing them a hobby, or small falcon, 'that the larks' eyes being ever upon the hobby, should not see the net that is laid on their heads'.[5] Faunus, caught like a bird in a bush, is threatened with gelding, then subjected to a farcical version of Acteon's fate, the tearing-apart-by-hounds that in the Ovidian prototype displaces gelding and in the Spenserian reenactment comes to nothing but exhaustion. And a curse.

The curse is on the landscape, whose sweet waters and fair forests are made the haunt of wolves and thieves. That curse continues 'to this day' (7.6.55). If predatory looking was the sin, the punishment, displaced upon the place, is chronic predation. Chronic, and oddly untethered to chronological time, for the temporalities of Clio and Calliope cannot be made to align. Does the fateful encounter of Faunus and Diana take place before or after the trial of Mutabilitie? Nothing allows us to know for certain. In

the narrative sequence of the poem, the interpolated pre-history of
Arlo Hill means that we encounter the seat of Nature's judgment
as a place that has already been or, by the time of reading, will
already have been fatally changed. And yet the place is redolent
with all that is best and fairest:

> And all the earth far vnderneath her feete
>> Was dight with flowres, that voluntary grew
>> Out of the ground, and sent forth odours sweet …
>>>>>>>>>> (7.7.10)

Marking the arrival of embodied Nature, Arlo Hill itself becomes
a type, or epitome, of nature, occluding the curse that has or will
have, has *and* will have, made the place 'most ill'. The site is an
especially fertile one for non-coincident redundancy. The Nature
that sits in judgment is and is not the nature that spreads a living
carpet for her feet. The curse that targets Arlo Hill for special
desecration is and is not the more general curse with which the
cantos of Mutabilitie began:

> O pittious worke of MVTABILITIE!
> By which, we all are subiect to that curse,
> And death in stead of life haue sucked from our Nurse.
>>>>>>>>>> (7.6.6)

The sweeter vision preserves the liveliness of mutability – the
flowers grow; the mountains change their 'gray attire to green' –
and contrives for a moment to 'forget' mutability's mortal sting.

In this it anticipates the healing euphony of Nature's juridical
pronouncement:

> I well consider all that ye haue sayd,
>> And find that all things stedfastnes doe hate
>> And changed be: yet being rightly wayd
>> They are not changed from their first estate;
>> But by their change their being do dilate:

> And turning to themselues at length againe,
> Do worke their owne perfection so by fate,
> That ouer them Change doth not rule and raigne;
> But they raigne ouer change, and doe their states maintaine.

(7.7.58)

Fixity is no friend to nature. If mutability implies death, as the temporarily occluded curse portends, fixity is death itself. Nature cannot banish Mutabilitie; she can only make, has already made, Mutabilitie incorporate. In this way, her spoken judgment enacts a narrative manifestation – a working-out-in-time – of the logic that structures the very allegory that contains it. Like a host of other Spenserian antitypes, personified Mutabilitie is set in motion to illustrate – unfold to the light – an eponymous virtue, in this case, Constancy. That virtue is initially misrecognised as freedom-from-change. It is discovered to be, not fixity, but hope, the constancy of spirit required to sustain Time's subjects in the face of change. This is why Nature appears for a moment – the smallest part of a moment – without her veil.

Spenser's enthusiasm for quantitative meters in English had waned before he set to work on *The Faerie Queene*, but his understanding of verse as a living passage through temporal stays or frameworks endured. In English, the accentual-syllabic iamb is far more accessible to the ear than is the largely notional alternation of 'short' and 'long'.[6] The general accord of syntax with groupings of five iambic feet enables the ear to hear what the eye sees on the page as lineation. A pattern of rhyme – *ababbcbcc*, for example – can underscore those divisions and also the regular accruals that make for a nine-line stanza. An extra foot in the ninth line pleasantly destabilises the final couplet and marks more fully the rounding-off of stanza. Hearing and seeing conspire to form a system of simultaneous memory-and-expectation. Twelve promised books; twelve cantos apiece; four dozen stanzas, more or less, to the canto; a patterned nine lines to the stanza. All the more stunning, then, when the timepiece halts 'vnperfite'.

The narrator of the conjecturally eighth canto of the conject-urally seventh book of *The Faerie Queene* is not altogether consoled by plot resolution. He has heard Nature's judgment – those stun-ningly brief two stanzas – but is haunted by Mutabilitie's 'Large Euidence' (7.7.Arg). Evenly divided between despair and hope, he allots a single stanza to each. The former 'makes [him] loath this state of life', so utterly dependent upon the vicissitudes of time (7.8.1). The latter prompts him to turn beyond time altogether, toward 'the pillours of Eternity' (7.8.2). Or rather, it prompts him to think, like Augustine, *through* time and the ever-evanescent present tense, towards that which time, in its chronic evanescence, portends.

It is change under the aegis of despair that haunts the Cantos of Mutabilitie: not change per se, but change for the worse. When Nature, who is both the site of the insurgency and its judge, deter-mines to be at peace with Change and call her 'daughter' (7.7.59), she speaks in such a manner that all the assembled creatures on Arlo Hill, while 'looking in her face', behold a 'chearefull view' (7.7.57). The narrator appears to have 'forgotten' both her terror and her veil. Embodied Nature, who has submitted to Mutabilitie's long catalogue of elements and seasons, has assumed a human face. In this she echoes and anticipates another, transfiguring acceptation of mortality. 'Willingly to dye', as per the Genevan gloss, does not quite capture it, but willingly to live is to be the portal through which the ever-diminishing future becomes the ever-expanding past. For a moment before her vanishing, 'whither no man whist' (7.7.59), a terrible judge is imagined to be both accessible and benign.

The poem is a timepiece, an instrument for parsing time by means of measured cadences. Even in poems whose working parts are very much simpler than those of *The Faerie Queene*, the method is oppositional: phrasing now allied with, now at odds with metrical foot, duration of image now allied with, now at odds with duration of line, concordances of sound now allied with now at odds with concordances of sense. Short or long, simple or convoluted, the timepiece we call a poem is designed to heighten the feeling of being-in-the-present-tense, which does not last, the better to summon the yet-more-evanescent thought of lastingness. In Shakespeare's sonnet sequence, the paradox is configured, for a time, as procreation. In *The Faerie Queene*, it is configured, for a very brief time and in a fragment 'vnperfite', as Christian revelation. It is configured, more chronically, as the ravishment of imperfection itself: Mutabilitie's 'louely face' (7.6.31) makes Jove forget his wrath even as she challenges his rule. It is not fixity we want when we turn to the inherited figures of faith, or to children, or to poems; it is the continuing incarnation of that which we love precisely because it is fleeting. We want 'our perishing earth' in all its perishing beauty.[7] We want it whole, and we want it in all its partiality, and in our partiality for it. A poem 'vnperfite', whose untimely cutting-off is merely a final instance of its aggravated derailments and auto-interruptions, is built to parse the perishing.

FIVE

'at heaven's gate'

PAUL EDMONDSON AND STANLEY WELLS

When in disgrace with fortune and men's eyes,
I all alone beweep my outcast state,
And trouble deaf heav'n with my bootless cries,
And look upon myself and curse my fate,   4
Wishing me like to one more rich in hope,
Featured like him, like him with friends possessed,
Desiring this man's art, and that man's scope,
With what I most enjoy contented least;   8
Yet in these thoughts myself almost despising,
Haply I think on thee, and then my state,
Like to the lark at break of day arising
From sullen earth, sings hymns at heaven's gate;   12
For thy sweet love rememb'red such wealth brings,
That then I scorn to change my state with kings.

                    William Shakespeare, Sonnet 29

In what follows we offer a close reading of Shakespeare's Sonnet 29. A sonnet may be encountered in many different ways: in a volume of its author's collected works, in an anthology of love poems, in a classroom, in a practical workshop, in a song setting by Rufus Wainwright, or Hubert Parry, or Benjamin Britten. We read for a variety of reasons, perhaps most obviously a desire for the aural and therefore performative pleasure that the internal and external sounds, meanings, and associations of the words themselves may bring. We expect that our taste for poetry will be satisfied and extended by the encounter, as though each poem we read somehow expands our receptiveness and hospitality. But taste is highly subjective and is inflected by many social, cultural, and personal predilections. Perhaps there is a sense that poetry is good for us, in which case our reading will be more duty bound than a consequence of imaginative and aesthetic engagement.

What is the effect of reading a Shakespeare sonnet? An electric current energises our minds and bodies; a swimmer plunges into the ocean, is beaten back by the waves, but still forges ahead. We hear music, see landscapes and images from the natural world, and take upon ourselves imaginary feelings. We embark upon a short journey which we know will change us if we commit ourselves fully to it. As for the poet in Sonnet 27, 'then begins a journey in my head', a journey that continues long after our reading of the poem has finished, and which may haunt a sleepless night.

What does it mean 'closely' to read a sonnet? One answer – associated with the New Criticism dating back to the 1930s – is that it represents a desire to gain as full a picture as possible of how a sonnet works, to understand its constituent parts and their relationship with one another. Close reading of this kind looks as it were through a microscope and refers to nothing apart from the text itself. But the methods and aims of close reading change over time. The publication of Stephen Booth's edition and analytic commentary of the Sonnets[1] represented a major shift in close reading as a critical practice. It now no longer seems fruitful to pretend that any text exists apart from its context. Booth's commentary is alive to historical and literary contexts (critical editions have never claimed that any text exists in a vacuum), but is primarily concerned with their organic life. Here the Sonnets exist moment by moment; Booth's readings, like the waves in Sonnet 60, constantly change 'place with that which goes before'. Here the Sonnets live and breathe as word succeeds word and line follows line, and we are invited to see how they, like the living things perceived in Sonnet 15, hold 'in perfection but a little moment'.

Paradoxically, the hermeneutical emphases of Shakespeare studies of recent times, in thoroughly demonstrating the literary contingency of texts, have brought Shakespearians back to close reading with renewed vigour. There is now a heightened understanding of its purposes and rewards. It now seems possible to seek in the closeness of close reading an unashamed and intimate engagement with a text's imaginative well-spring (quite separate from authorial intention), and with how that works upon us. Consensus is not the objective; it can never be with something as vulnerable and open as the language of poetry. The hope is rather that in rigorously examining how a poem affects us, we may help other readers discover more clearly ways in which it might work – even differently – upon themselves.

Where do we start from when we turn to read Sonnet 29? We bring to it all that we have read, all our own previous readings of it, our experience of sound recordings, musical settings, films, performances at poetry recitals, seminars and conferences, and the sum total of how our personal memories of this poem interweave with our life experience.

Our previous work on the Sonnets[2] has emphasised the importance of freeing them from imaginary biographical contexts and of encouraging readers not to be deluded by lazy assumptions which have accrued around the 1609 quarto and what it represents, specifically in relation to the gender of the person addressed in each individual sonnet.

We try to read each sonnet as though for the very first time. In this critical approach our reading could be compared to the task of an actor. However many times a speech has been studied, rehearsed, and performed, any actor worth his or her salt must work to make it sound alive in the moment, freshly minted, as though it had never been spoken before. Or, as Sonnet 76 has it:

> O know, sweet love, I always write of you,
> And you and love are still my argument.
> So all my best is dressing old words new,
> Spending again what is already spent.

> (9–12)

Just as the author's metaphor here evokes the act of sex ('spending', 'spent') so the actor and the close reader turn to the sonnet to make love afresh each time. In close reading, we try to enter the very bloodstream of the poem.

The opening word of Sonnet 29, 'When', arouses expectation; a sequel is needed, we are held in suspense, on the lookout for a resolving 'then'. 'When', opening the poem against expectation with a reversed iamb, demands emphasis itself and throws even greater emphasis on the second syllable of 'disgrace', making it an important word and presence. The concept of disgrace relates to 'fortune', which can be taken as both an abstraction and a personification. As well as feeling that the poet is disgraced through difficult but unspecified circumstances, by the time we reach 'men's eyes' we sense a paradoxical evocation of the blind goddess Fortuna herself. The poet is in double disgrace, ignored by the eyes of other people who, like Fortuna, seem blind and callously indifferent to his feelings.

The next line is full of self-pity. The wide open long vowel sounds and liquid labials of 'I all alone' are both defiant and lonely in their emphases. Following naturally on from 'eyes' and the implicit pun on 'I' ('when first your eye I eyed' [Sonnet 104]) is 'beweep'. The poet has been 'outcast' by social and universal forces. These two lines alone might suggest that Shakespeare's King Richard II could be identified as a possible imagined speaker. Like Richard, the poet has lost his state. The word has multiple significances – mental and physical conditions – and in the case of Richard himself 'state' also means throne. Both poet and king find histrionic comfort in the act of weeping.

From blindness – and eyes (rhyming with 'cries') blind with tears – we move to the sense of sound evoked by the aggressive and defiant 'deaf heaven' and 'bootless cries'. The poet now feels cut off from both earth and heaven. Even language fails him, and perhaps in these 'bootless' sounds there is something of King Lear's 'When we are born, we cry that we are come / To this great stage of fools' (4.6.178–9), or the devastating non-language of his dying breath in the quarto text's 'O, o, o, o' (5.3.308).

A sense of isolation is further developed by the repetition of the first-person pronouns 'I', 'my', and 'myself'. The poet, like

Richard II again, is self-regarding, looking upon himself. The sonnet itself acts as a kind of looking-glass for self-discovery and truths ('Look in thy glass and tell the face thou viewest' [Sonnet 3]; 'that every word doth almost tell my name' [Sonnet 76]). Self-cursing now accompanies self-pity. 'Fate' harks back to 'fortune' and makes clear the importance of the now rhyming keyword 'state'. (We pause to notice that the quarto prints a full-stop after 'fate' in defiance of syntax; many modern editions replace this with a comma and present Sonnet 29 as a single, sinuous sentence.)

From the directness of 'curse' we encounter the present participle 'wishing' (impelling the sense forward with a second reversed iamb), a struggle that beats itself out in rhythmic mono-syllables for the rest of the line, the words 'rich in' half echoing the emphatic 'wishing'. The strong placing of 'hope' at the end of the line hints at possible anchorage, a moment of pause – even a breath – and in brave contradiction of the fateful, bootless, blindness that wails and sails above it.

The impetus of this hope turns the poet out from self-gazing to look, like a character in a play, at the faces and 'features' of other men. Yet even here there is multiple reflection and refraction of image and selves as in a mirror, 'like him, like him'. The longing for 'friends' (the word could also mean lover as in Sonnet 133's 'my sweet'st friend') evokes a comparison with the tragic loneliness of Richard II who 'needs friends' (3.2.176) and even with Macbeth's regret for 'troops of friends' (5.3.25).

Dramatic antithesis – perhaps indicative of a mind seeking to control – also structures the next line, 'this man's ... and that man's'. Although the word 'art' can refer to any kind of skill, its central placing in the poem draws attention to the very artistry we are experiencing. But even while the poet is expressing a desire for another's 'art', he is using his own art in order to express his desire. 'Scope' reaches forward to a renewed openness of mind, action, and possibility and deepens the sense of 'hope', underlining it with rhyme.

The self-contained lines of the octave reach their momentary summation with this directly antithetical line, expressing a state of dissatisfaction with which readers through the centuries have identified: 'with what I most enjoy contented least'. But we are still buried in an eight-line-long subordinate clause, held in suspense, awaiting the resolution and relief that a main clause will bring.

We can hear the turning point beginning to emerge with 'yet in', the third reversed iamb to open a line. So far these have occurred regularly, once every four lines. Now begins the sestet, in which reversed iambs will start each of the first three lines, shoring up a sense of dislocated rhythm as the poet's state changes. The 'state' of the poet is '*almost*' all that he has described, but 'yet' reminds us that the earlier glimmer of 'hope' is not quite lost. The 1609 quarto prints 'my self' as two words, emphasising that it is the entire sense of self-hood that is being despised. Modern editions run the risk of diminishing this loss of 'self' possession in turning two words into one, 'myself'. The extra syllable at the end of this line creates a sense of limping weakly forward; the poet is 'despising' himself, but not entirely. There may be a way out.

There is a catching of breath on 'haply', creating a sense of recovery. The 'fortune' which brought disgrace on the poet now turns. He happens happily to think of the beloved. This change of direction is not willed by the poet but seems rather to come upon him like a blessing. Heaven is not deaf after all. For the first time our self-pitying, almost despising, introverted poet is arrested by the intimacy of another person, a 'thee', rather than a 'you'. 'I think on thee' is the main clause of the sonnet and serves to reverse all that has gone before. In reading this sonnet aloud we might make a significant pause at the comma which separates 'thee' from 'and then': 'Haply I think on thee, and then my state'. The unusual repetition of a rhyme and a word – 'state' – from the poem's second line binds this new feeling together with the old.

The abstract 'state' is made real by a simile rooted in the natural, physical world. The repeated hard consonants of 'like', 'lark', and 'break' arrest our ears and bring a new and refreshing sound of dissonance as the bird flies and the sun rises. This line slows the reader down and is extended with the extra-metrical syllable of 'arising', flowing into the next line as the wintry, 'outcast state', the 'sullen earth' starts to melt with the song of that February bird, the lark ('a summer bird / Which ever in the haunch of winter sings / The lifting up of day' [*2 Henry IV*, 4.4.91–3]). Larks fly directly, vertically upwards, a sudden ascent perhaps with the suggestion of sexual arousal ('But rising at thy name doth point out thee / As his triumphant prize' [Sonnet 151]). But the sexual imagery is here only subliminally present. The emphasis is on the change of an emotional state; the lark is an image of sudden joy and morning freshness.

The lark starts to sing in line 12, and we might notice that its song has been anticipated in the rhyming words 'despi*sing*' (9) and 'ari*sing*' (11). The sibilance of '*s*ullen', '*s*ings', 'hymn*s*' and 'heaven'*s*' is itself part of the lark's music, but so too is the contrast of the dull vowels in 'sullen earth'. The lark in flight beats across the boundary of the line ending. The alliterative 'hymns' at 'heaven's gate' hark back to 'haply', evoking the actions of the bird itself heaving out the song from its heart. Larks wake up lovers with their melody (Innogen with 'Hark, hark, the lark at heaven's gate sings' [*Cymbeline*, 2.3.20]; *Romeo and Juliet*, 3.5.2–6). But here it is as if the lark 'sings hymns' incessantly, the two words conjoined by an internal rhyme in a fluent legato, reaching the gate of heaven to sing perpetually before it.

The first mention of 'love' comes as late as line 13, qualifying and concluding the nature of the relationship with the word 'for'. This love is as 'sweet' as the lark's melody. The couplet includes the second use of enjambment (the first occurs from line 11 to 12) in 'such wealth brings, / That', a flowing over of meaning in which this particular sestet excels. The couplet re-members the love and puts back together that which has been fractured, made subordinate, momentarily lost. This same re-membering brings about a final change of state which is able to countenance monarchs yet wishes for nothing more than what it already has and is. The third occurrence of the keyword 'state' acquires retrospectively the meaning of 'throne' by its association with the possessive 'kings''. But, by simultaneously rejecting royal thrones, and declaring a new 'state', the poet points most emphatically both outwardly and inwardly to a world that has changed. The closer we read, the more deeply we sense this change.

Our close reading of Sonnet 29 has attempted an emotional identification with its constituent parts and finds each line fringed with different meanings and nuances. The sound of the sonnet is important to us since we like to imagine all of the Sonnets as poetic speech acts – *sonnetti*, little sounds – which might be enacted through reading aloud. We would even go as far as to insist that a sonnet is only fully realisable as a sonnet when it is read aloud, with a mind and heart alive to its possible meanings. 'However and wherever you read them,' the actor Jeffery Dench once told us, 'whether it's to an audience of twenty or a thousand, they've got to sound as intimate as pillow talk.' We have related this sonnet incidentally to Shakespeare's plays and to other sonnets in the collection in order to understand the imaginative energies at work. We find that the sex of the real or imagined addressee is not revealed in Sonnet 29, though the poet is very definitely moving within a male-gendered, homosocial world ('men's eyes', 'featured like him, like him'). Our purpose here has been closely to read its poetry rather than its contexts. If we were to relate Sonnet 29 to its social and historical contexts, we should see links to the discourses of intimacy, friendship, melancholy, statesmanship, natural history, theology and religious devotion. There is nothing to prevent the significant state-changing 'thee' in this poem from being identified with the Christian God, bringing about God's Kingdom. The central expression of Sonnet 29 roots it very much in this world, but departs from 'sullen earth', and finds a way of expressing an ecstatic love at heaven's gate, a journey's end which coincides with lovers meeting. Readers who read closely enough might experience something of what this feels like for themselves, in earth as it is in heaven.

SIX

On Shakespeare's Sonnet 60

BRIAN GIBBONS

Like as the waues make towards the pibled shore,
So do my minuites hasten to their end,
Each changing place with that which goes before,
In sequent toil all forwards do contend.   4
Natiuity once in the maine of light,
Crawles to maturity, wherewith being crown'd,
Crooked eclipses gainst his glory fight,
And time that gaue, doth now his gift confound.   8
Time doth transfixe the florish set on youth,
And delues the paralels in beauties brow,
Feedes on the rarities of natures truth,
And nothing stands but for his sieth to mow.   12
      And yet to times in hope my verse shall stand
      Praising thy worth, dispight his cruell hand.
         William Shakespeare, Sonnet 60[1]

Seamus Heaney has remarked on the pleasure he takes in the obsolete spelling 'pibled' in this, the first edition of *Shake-speares Sonnets* (1609); 'pibled' more vividly and exactly captures the natural sound, prompting the reader to visualise the breaking waves churning pebbles; and this vivid auditory moving image of the forward surge of wave succeeding wave connects with the moment-after-moment passing of the speaker's life. It is its energy which gives the wave its momentary glassy form, triumphantly crested, but it is that very energy which causes it to topple over into dissolution. The waves, the rhythm of one's body, all press forward, 'contend', so hastening inevitable dissolution and death.

The sound is echo to the sense of the first two lines, unstressed syllables giving a quick pace ('Like as the waves make' – 'So do my minuites') while one long-vowelled word in each line ('towards', 'hasten') imposes weight on the regular iambics that follow ('the pibled shore' and 'to their end'). Then line 4 has stress on long-vowelled words weighting the beginning, middle, and end ('sequent ... forwards ... contend'), so reinforcing the pattern of line 1. The syntax in both quatrains is driven by active verbs: 'Crawles', 'crown'd', 'fight', and 'confound' – placed as they are in prominent positions at the beginning and end of lines – to sustain an underlying wavelike movement of a mass of water swelling, cresting, collapsing, and subsiding.

The sonnet rhyme scheme is designed to weave quatrains together as units and secure a conclusion by a final couplet, but in this sonnet the syntax gives to each line an independent status as a sense-unit – each is governed by a verb (the verb in line 5 being understood). Each separate line hastens forward, each adds its own successive action: 'make', 'hasten', 'changing', 'contend', 'crown'd', 'fight', 'confound', 'transfixe', 'delues', 'Feedes', 'mow', 'stand', 'Praising'. The prominent repetition of the conjunction 'And' four times in seven lines – 'And time ... confound', 'And delues', 'And nothing stands', 'And yet ... shall stand' – reinforces an accumulating impression of repetitive destruction.

There is a metapoetical aspect to this, since the poem's movement illustrates the general idea that repetition, line by line, wave by wave, can overwhelm a more complex pattern of thought. The sonnet begins by showing that a wave like a man can be said to have a nativity, swell to maturity but then be confounded in dissolution, but Shakespeare then widens the lens to show a perspective of comprehensive desolation: the final metaphor is of mowing, retrospectively adding to the ominous astrological connotation of line seven's 'crooked eclipses' the immediate physical threat, the *curved* blade of a scythe, to every ear of wheat and living thing; hence also, line 10's metaphor 'delues the paralels' reflects a more direct image of levelling as annihilation. In this wide perspective men are undifferentiated, distanced, unnumbered as drops of spray or ears of wheat or idle pebbles chafed by the murmuring surge. Defying this conclusion, the poem makes an existential stand, affirming only individual human worth as the solitary value that keeps hope alive.

Shakespeare's nearby Sonnet 64 reflects the technique of Sonnet 60, in particular its loosening of the formal scheme of thesis-antithesis-synthesis implied by the rhyme scheme. The opening words 'When I have seen' begin a sentence that cannot be completed until the twelfth line, so irresistible is the intervening succession of images of devastation after devastation, particularly of the sea's power of dissolution: an idea deep-seated in Shakespeare, as when in *The Comedy of Errors* a brother likens himself, seeking his lost twin, to a drop of water,

> That in the ocean seeks another drop,
> Who, falling there to find his fellow forth,
> (Unseen, inquisitive), confounds himself.
>
> (1.2.36–8)

Moreover Sonnet 64's final couplet, far from achieving an affirmation, can reach absolutely no conclusion, only unending, in a present tense of continuing, resistless loss: 'it cannot choose / But weepe to haue, that which it feares to loose'.

Heaney confirmed his interest in Sonnet 60 when he picked out, in *The Government of the Tongue*, the line 'Natiuity once in the maine of light'. This is what he says about it:

> Some poems ... have openings at their centre which take the reader through and beyond. Shakespeare's Sonnet 60 for example ... Something visionary happens there in the fifth line. 'Nativity', an abstract noun housed in a wavering body of sound, sets up a warning tremor just before the mind's eye gets dazzled by 'the main of light', and for a split second, we are in the world of the *Paradiso*. ... this unpredictable strike into the realm of pure being.[2]

Heaney's short sonnet-like poem in *Seeing Things* may – so it seems to me – have been influenced (probably unconsciously) by Shakespeare's Sonnet 60: the idea of repetition is a clue to a deeper affinity below the obvious surface differences, such as Heaney's use of the pronoun 'we' and his setting the speaker among his congregated classmates in the ordinary playground of a village school, in the Northern Ireland of the 1940s:

> The ice was like a bottle. We lined up
> Eager to re-enter the long slide
> We were bringing to perfection, time after time
>
> Running and readying and letting go
> Into a sheerness that was its own reward:
> A farewell to surefootedness, a pitch
>
> Beyond our usual hold upon ourselves.
> And what went on kept going, from grip to give,
> The narrow milky way in the black ice,
>
> The race-up, the free passage and return –
> It followed on itself like a ring of light
> We knew we'd come through and kept sailing towards.[3]

Scratched ice on a school playground visually recalls the white-streaked look of an emptied milk bottle (in Heaney's childhood – as in mine, although I was in another part of the United Kingdom – a free half-pint bottle of milk was a schoolchild's daily ration): and the children lining up bring to mind the traditional rhyme, 'Ten green bottles standing on a wall, / And if one green bottle should accident'ly fall, / There'd be nine green bottles standing on a wall' (next verse, 'Nine green bottles', then 'Eight', 'Seven', down to 'No green bottles').

So, one after another, the children slide down off the end of the poem's lines as two syntactic overruns enact the 'letting go / Into a sheerness', the going 'a pitch / Beyond our usual hold upon ourselves'. Repeating round and round, 'time after time' (the poem's end-stopped lines enhancing the effect) enables escape from time, transforms the earthbound slide into a mystical 'narrow milky way in the black ice'. Poetic echoes are in the air – perhaps Henry Vaughan, 'The Retreate':

> O how I long to travel back
> And tread again that ancient track!
>
> $(21-22)^4$

Or Vaughan's 'The Night':

> There is in God (some say)
> A deep, but dazling darkness
>
> $(49-50)$

– and perhaps in Heaney's final line 'We knew we'd come through and kept sailing towards' there may even be a fleeting memory of the skating passage in Wordsworth's *Prelude* (Book I, 461–77 'We hissed along the polished ice … To cut across the reflex of a star'), though the actual verbal presence in this child's intuition of paradise is Vaughan's 'The World':

> I saw Eternity the other night
> Like a great *Ring* of pure and endless light
> All calm, as it was bright
>
> $(1-3)$

The phrase 'ring of light' – when unobtrusively shorn by Heaney of 'great', and 'pure and endless' – does pass as a modern child's ordinary speech, and, when not recognised as a quotation will only increase surprise at the marvellous inspired final line that evokes the strange childhood ecstasy:

> It followed on itself like a ring of light
> We knew we'd come through and kept sailing towards.

The children follow one another, round and round they go. Distance, fifty-odd years, could have lent disenchantment to the view (so do our minutes hasten to their end). Yet in Heaney's poem the moment of transcendence is rapturous.

Shakespeare's Sonnet 60 makes its human, personal affirmation in spite of all, following what sounds like the ineluctable conclusion 'And nothing stands' with the declaration 'my verse shall stand'. The poignancy of this utterance is of crucial importance. For Heaney the word 'Nativity' cannot but allude to the Christian doctrine of incarnation, so that the metaphor 'the main of light' ('main' referring to the ocean) can be taken by Heaney as alluding to the Christian revelation. However, a more sombre interpretation is possible: 'Nativity' has no inevitably religious resonance, it may signify 'birth', or a new-born child, or its horoscope, and Gwynne Evans considers Ovid was working in Shakespeare's mind here.[5] Ovid had not the comfort of Christian doctrine. In the passage Evans cites from *Metamorphoses* XV, Ovid refers to 'Dame Nature'.[6] Evans comments that the phrase 'main of light' was suggested by the sea-imagery of the opening quatrain, since Shakespeare 'most often associates "main" with the sea or ocean'; Evans compares Sonnet 64.7 and *The Merchant of Venice* 5.1.97, 'the main of waters'. The line therefore may be read as Shakespeare deliberately avoiding (although inevitably expecting readers to be conscious of) explicit Christian resonance. That is to say, the line is poignant because unsupported by religious faith; hope is all the more fragile – and human – when unable to affirm religion; and this is no less true of Herbert in *The Temple*, for instance in his bleak depiction of hope's erosion in 'The Answer', expressed in the metaphor of evaporating morning mist:

> a young exhalation, newly waking,
>   Scorns his first bed of dirt, and means the sky;
>   But cooling by the way, grows pursy and slow,
>   And settling to a cloud, doth live and die
>   In that dark state of tears:

$$(8–12)^7$$

By contrast the assured, often rapturous poetic voice of Vaughan's 1655 collection *Silex Scintillans* expresses an unquestioning faith which sets him apart: 'The Morning-watch' celebrates 'The great *Chime* / And *Symphony* of nature':

> In what Rings,
> And *Hymning Circulations* the quick world
> Awakes, and sings;

(9–11)

'The Water-fall' sees the natural world as a reflection of the divine idea, the circular descending from and ascending to the heavens, a perfect circular harmony:

> Why, since each drop of thy quick store
> Runs thither, whence it flow'd before,
> Should poor souls fear a shade or night,
> Who came (sure) from a sea of light!

(15–18)

Marvell in 'On a Drop of Dew' presents the descent from heaven of a single drop of dew, its brief hour's stay in the world while gazing back, shining like its own tear, and its returning ascent by evaporation (lines 1–18); then follows a parallel journey by the soul, not shed from the bosom of the morn, but itself 'that drop, that ray / Of the clear fountain of eternal day'.[8] In print the letter 'o' is prominent in the poem's title and first line, offering a visual pun on the shape of a drop, and the 'o' sounds go on echoing in the diction throughout, being voiced in seventy-three words out of the poem's total of two hundred and forty-four words; here is the list: how, orient, from, bosom, of, morn, Into, blowing, roses, of mansion, For, region, born, Round, encloses, globes, How, flow'r does, touching, upon, mournful, own, so long, from, rolls, grow, to, So, soul, drop, Of, fountain of, Could, flow'r, former, blossoms, recollecting, own, Does, thoughts, how coy, wound, So, world, round, above, love, How loose, to go, How, to, Moving, on, point below, about does, though congealed, Congealed on, does dissolving, Into, glories, of.

The dates of this and other lyric poems by Marvell are uncertain; yet 'On a Drop of Dew' apparently directly echoes Vaughan, for in Marvell too the devout soul (could we but see it 'within the humane flow'r') enjoys 'pure and circling thoughts':

> Could it within the human flow'r be seen,
> Remembering still its former height,
> Shuns the sweet leaves and blossoms green,
> And, recollecting its own light,
> Does, in its pure and circling thoughts, express
> The greater Heaven in an Heaven less.
>
> (21–6)

The argument of this poem involves some typically subtle grammatical trickery: after all, even apart from the question whether or not the soul can be seen, we cannot see the mind, cannot see it remember, or think; these must remain inner, invisible activities – except when in some imaginary, absurd place such as Marvell's 'The Garden' (a poem liberally sprinkled with fantastic humour) where there is 'green' thought in a 'green' shade. Marvell begins 'On a Drop of Dew' by urging his readers to use their eyes –

> See how the orient dew,
> Shed from the bosom of the morn
> Into the blowing roses,
> Yet careless of its mansion new,
> For the clear region where 'twas born
> Round in itself incloses:
>
> (1–6)

– but this 'See' is not a quite simple present imperative, or rather, to put it another way, the object of the verb 'See' is not quite simple – we are not literally to see the 'Bosom of the morn', nor the drop of dew being shed, nor its landing on blowing roses, for the function of these words is misleadingly to bring in sensuous associations from many a Cavalier love lyric. No – we are instead to 'See', in the pure abstract sense of 'comprehend', how the drop of dew is 'careless of its mansion new', although – another cavil! – even if with 'mansion' Marvell presumably intends a biblical resonance, echoing, for example, John 14:2, 'in my Father's house are many mansions' (AV), even so, might the word 'mansion' not seem a touch durable when applied to a one-hour rest on a rose petal?

Still, the first eighteen-line part of the poem does present some perfect, delicate and precise natural description, particularly of the physical mass of the tiny crystal-clear sphere, so precariously a-quiver:

> How it the purple flow'r does slight,
> Scarce touching where it lies,
> But gazing back upon the skies,
> Shines with a mournful Light,
> Like its own tear,
> Because so long divided from the sphere.
> Restless it rolls and unsecure,
> Trembling lest it grow impure,
> Till the warm sun pity its pain,
> And to the skies exhale it back again.
>
> (9–18)

The pathetic fallacy, a conventional trope, assigns human attributes and sentiments to the non-human; here the trope serves to enhance accuracy in detailed observation and to keep in touch with the imaginary feminine character of the drop of dew: the second half of the poem, from line 19 onwards, develops an extended parallel between the heaven-sent drop of dew and the soul, which for its part (as Marvell is mystically enabled to see and convey to us) has more than a hint of some Cavalier poet's coy Julia, dancing in circles and singing by herself:

In how coy a figure wound,
Every way it turns away:
So the world excluding round,
Yet receiving in the day,
Dark beneath, but bright above,
Here disdaining, there in love.
How loose and easy hence to go,
How girt and ready to ascend,
Moving but on a point below,
It all about does upward bend.

(27–36)

Here, then, are pure and circling thoughts made metaphysically apprehensible – to echo Donne in 'The Second Anniversary', one might almost say, her body thought.

Perhaps 'grace' is the critical issue in assessing Marvell's capacity to make a 'strike into the realm of pure being': notice how even at a high point he will stop to make a slight adjustment ('that drop, that ray') of his phrasing:

So the soul, that drop, that ray
Of the clear fountain of eternal day

(19–20)

The soul *is* like a drop of dew, but crucially, it is not liquid like the drop: it is pure light, not our daylight but 'the clear fountain of eternal day'. The soul is like the drop of dew, but it is entirely pure, it is light emitted from the eternal source. Marvell's poetry is so often delicately musical, meltingly tender, fastidiously elegant, that 'curious' seems an appropriately ambiguous word (meaning both 'enquiring' and 'unusual') to describe his mind, one that gives such sharp discrimination and such precision to everything he writes, including his paradoxical conceits and jokes – as in 'The Garden':

Fair trees! Wheres'e'er your barks I wound,
No name shall but your own be found.

(23–4)

Marvell can be humorously ready to intervene (parenthetically) when one of his hyperboles gets above itself, as in 'Bermudas':

> Oh let our voice his praise exalt,
> Till it arrive at heaven's vault:
> Which thence (perhaps) rebounding, may
> Echo beyond the Mexique Bay.

> (33–6)

Yet ultimately it is right to remember T. S. Eliot's insistence on Marvell's 'tough reasonableness beneath the slight lyric grace', and to remember that this is the formidable poet of the 'Horatian Ode'.

I come back to circling thoughts: Shakespeare's Sonnet 60 confronts Time's corrosive power of annihilation with an existential, time-defying stand, for human worth, and this is what makes it a great poem. Marvell's most famous lines, too, confront nihilism squarely; they have to concede much:

> But at my back I always hear
> Time's winged chariot hurrying near:
> And yonder all before us lie
> Deserts of vast eternity.

> (21–4)

Marvell reaches the high note of 'On a Drop of Dew' in the infinitive 'dissolving': it is as if the poet of 'To His Coy Mistress' were (almost) converted by the Vaughan of 'The Water-fall':

> The common pass
> Where, clear as glass,
> All must descend
> Not to an end:

> (7–10)

SEVEN

Balthasar's Song in *Much Ado About Nothing*

MARK WOMACK

Sigh no more, ladies, sigh no more,   60
    Men were deceivers ever;
One foot in sea, and one on shore,
    To one thing constant never.
Then sigh not so, but let them go,
    And be you blithe and bonny,   65
Converting all your sounds of woe
    Into 'Hey nonny, nonny'.

Sing no more ditties, sing no more,
    Of dumps so dull and heavy;
The fraud of men was ever so,   70
    Since summer first was leavy.
Then sigh not so, but let them go,
    And be you blithe and bonny,
Converting all your sounds of woe
    Into 'Hey nonny, nonny'.   75
    William Shakespeare, *Much Ado About Nothing*, 2.3.60–75

Balthasar sings 'Sigh no more' for Don Pedro, Leonato, and Claudio, while a concealed Benedick listens on. I would like to analyse Balthasar's song in elaborate detail but not, as is the fashion in critical analyses, to reveal some heretofore undiscovered meaning or theme it might be argued into delivering. Instead my analysis will try to demonstrate how the song works its magic on the minds and ears of its audience. I am interested less in what the song says and more in what it does, how it works, and how it works on us.

Before analysing these lyrics, I want to remind you that this song is simple and easy to understand. Indeed, Kenneth Branagh begins his film version of *Much Ado About Nothing* with a recitation of these lyrics precisely because they are so easily comprehensible and thus 'allow the audience to "tune in" to the new language they are about to experience'.[1] Any analysis saying that these lyrics are really obscure and difficult would lie. I will point out many unobserved complications in these lines, but I stress from the start that they are unobserved. The complications are real, yet they never impede our graceful, easy enjoyment of the song. I describe the incidental effects in these lines not to produce an interpretation of them but because I believe that the invisible complexity of these lines is the main source of their aesthetic value. The lines enable our minds to apprehend complexities without ever having to strain. With that in mind, I will proceed with my analysis.

The song begins with a simple, straightforward imperative: 'Sigh'. The following words ('no more') both continue that imperative command and, simultaneously, completely reverse it. 'Sigh no more' is as easily comprehensible an imperative as 'Sigh', but the easy understanding we have of the imperative by the third word in the song contradicts the – equally easy – understanding we had of the song's opening word. No one ever has any trouble assimilating the latent contradiction that lurks in this opening phrase; the lines enable us to glide past such potential obstacles to our understanding.

The song continues by specifying an object for its command: 'ladies'. This also gives us no trouble, even though the onstage audience for the song is exclusively male. Then the lyrics repeat their opening command. The first word of the song's second line momentarily provides a beautifully rhetorically balanced pair of commands: 'Sigh no more, ladies; sigh no more, men'. This potential unit dissolves instantly as 'Men' shifts from being a potential object for 'sigh no more' to being the subject of a new declarative sentence. The second line does not overtly signal logical connection with the first; the lines do not read, 'Sigh no more, ladies, sigh no more. / *Because* men …'. Although we do not find any explicit logical conjunction, the substance of the lines signals their relationship. Moreover, the successive grammatical identities of 'Men' does link the lines together, silently countering their syntactic disjunction.

The newly extant declarative sentence says, 'Men were'. This suggests an emerging statement of men's past identity, and the word 'deceivers' fulfils that expectation. The phrase 'Men were deceivers', following as it does the command that women should 'sigh no more', invites us to understand that women should cease their sorrow because men have ceased their deceit. To this point, the lines say something like, 'Don't cry ladies, because although men used to be deceivers …'. That provisional understanding would be confirmed if the next word in the song were 'once', but the actual next word, 'ever', effects another revolution in our understanding. Note that 'ever' both fulfils and contradicts the expectations generated by 'were': 'ever' places the action of deceit in the past and also makes it an habitual, continually present condition.

At this point the first two lines say something like, 'Don't grieve ladies; men have *always* been deceitful'. Our minds never consciously realised that that easily comprehensible meaning emerged like a snake from a series of potential contradictions.

The song's third line provides a metaphorical description of men's deceit. It begins, 'One foot in sea'. The word 'sea' suggests fluidity and instability appropriate to the context of deceit. The phrase 'one on shore' both contradicts and complements the reference to 'sea'.[2] The shore, as solid and stable dry land, contrasts starkly with the mutability of the sea. Yet because it does contrast, the stable land reinforces the idea of mutability. Men are first associated with the fluidity of the sea then with the stability of the shore, but the very fact of the double association makes men sound all the more deceitful. This line, incidentally, provides a good description of the actions the mind performs in hearing this song. The destabilising potential of the unfolding lyrics (*one foot in sea*) coexists with the clear sense the song makes (*and one on shore*).

The intricate incidental actions of the song continue in the next line, where the word 'To' can seem momentarily to function as its homophone 'two', a function pertinent to the preceding line's implied reference to two feet. The next word, 'one', makes the sound *to* into a preposition rather than a noun, but 'one' reintroduces the concept of number in the same instant that it removes that concept from the previous word. Such a reversal unfolds in the line at large as well. The phrase 'To one thing constant' states precisely the opposite of what the completed line 'To one thing constant never' delivers to us.[3] Yet, since the line occurs in a context of male deceit and inconstancy, the word 'never' is – in that dimension – a fulfilment rather than a contradiction of implied promise.

As the song moves into its second quatrain, we experience yet another example of simultaneous conjunction and disjunction. 'Then' introduces a logical consequence of the preceding line of thought, functioning as 'therefore' typically does. Yet the action recommended does not flow logically from what came before but rather invites the ladies to abandon a reasonable reaction (sorrow) in favour of an unreasonable one (mirth). The patent illogic of the conclusion is quietly counteracted by latent links in this line with the previous lines. 'Then', for example, does not indicate time in this context, but its unharnessed potential to refer to the past links it with the song's earlier references to the past, e.g., 'Men were deceivers ever'. Similarly, 'sigh not' re-enacts the mental gymnastics demanded and facilitated by the opening phrase: 'Sigh no more'.

The phrase 'let them' momentarily says, 'stay them', 'prevent their free movement' before the word 'go' makes the completed line say just the opposite.[4] When the song urges its audience to 'let them go', we effortlessly perceive that, although it is in the previous sentence, 'men' is the antecedent of 'them'. And because a sigh is a release, a letting go, of breath the phrase also subliminally links itself to the word 'sigh'. A similarly double-jointed link exists between 'blithe' and 'bonny'. The words fit together both as complementary adjectives (happy and pretty) and as synonyms, since 'bonny' can mean happy too. Although the double meaning of 'bonny' does not exert enough pressure to push itself into consciousness and become a pun, it does establish an extra flicker of relationship analogous to the – more obvious – alliteration of the two words.

The first two lines of what turns out to be the refrain are exquisitely rich in sound patternings, including internal rhyme ('so'/'go'), alliteration ('*b*ut', '*b*e', '*b*lithe', '*b*onny'; '*Th*en', '*th*em', 'bli*th*e'; '*s*igh', '*s*o'), and other sound links ('si*gh*', 'bli*th*e'; 'no*t*', 'bo*nn*y'; 'no*t*', 'bu*t*', 'le*t*'; 'The*n*', '*n*ot', 'A*n*d', 'a*n*d bo*nn*y'). The dense interrelation of sounds gives an extra-rational coherence to the lines that enables us to accept the frivolous illogic of the statement the lines make. They give our ears a sense of easy coherence that counters the irrational message of the song.

Another manifestation of such extra-logical coherence occurs with the concluding nonsense phrase 'Hey nonny, nonny'. The phrase is meaningless and yet is also contextually glossed to mean 'sounds of joy', the opposite of 'sounds of woe'.[5] Moreover, the phrase fits perfectly into a non-rational system of coherence: the rhyme scheme (*bonny*/*nonny*). The words may not make sense, but the sounds do.

The song's second stanza opens with a line that both does and does not echo the first line of stanza one. The relationship between the two lines is encapsulated in their first words: 'Sigh' and 'Sing'. Just as their phonetic likeness and difference both push them together and pull them apart, so do their potential meanings. When we hear 'Sing', our minds apprehend both a repetition and a variation of the first line. 'Sing' presents itself as either a potential antonym of 'Sigh' or its potential synonym. The song may present singing as an alternative to the just rejected action of sighing or as a parallel activity. The imperative 'Sing no more' replicates the same positive/negative command our minds negotiated in the first line and enhances the parallel between 'Sigh' and 'Sing'. The word 'ditties' turns 'Sing' from the intransitive verb the precedent of 'Sigh' suggested it was into a transitive verb. Thus the syntax undergoes an effortless and unobtrusive metamorphosis as it progresses. Yet the words 'ladies' and 'ditties', which determine the distinct syntaxes of the two lines, rhyme and thus create continuity between these lines.

In the original quarto text, the first line of the second stanza ends on the word 'moe'. Modern editors often regularise this to 'more', but in so doing they disable yet another of the song's complexly discontinuous continuations of established patterns. Working on the model of both the song's opening line and the stanza's opening phrase, we can easily grasp 'moe' as a variant of 'more'. The word has altered in order to fit the rhyme scheme, but we do not have to wait for the sound of 'so' two lines later to justify this alteration. The word 'moe' already rhymes, both with the *go/moe* rhyme from stanza one and with the word that immediately precedes it here: 'no'. Thus, while 'moe' insists that the line it concludes is the start of a new stanza, a new stanza substantively and phonically parallel with the first as well as substantively and phonically different from it, the same word – by rhyming with 'go' and 'woe' from stanza one – *also* makes the line a continuation of the unit begun in the refrain from the first stanza.

Whereas the first two lines of stanza one provided a syntactic parallel between 'Sigh no more, ladies' and 'sigh no more / Men', this stanza's second line presents a solid parallel to 'ditties'. That parallel, however, is inexact. The lyrics do not say, 'Sing no more ditties, sing no more tunes'. The phrase 'Of dumps so dull and heavy' describes the kind of ditties we ought not to sing. Note the richness of sound patterns in these lines. The alliteration of 'ditties'-'dumps'-'dull' and the slant rhyme of 'ditties' and 'heavy' all help to reinforce the parallelism of the lines, a parallel weakened by the metrically useful, syntactically vague 'Of' at the beginning of the second line.

The next two lines continue the intricate repetitions and variations this stanza works on the one that precedes it. The lines are rich in alliterations: '*f*raud', '*f*irst'; '*s*o', '*S*ince', '*s*ummer'. And the phrase 'The fraud of men was ever so' is variously like and unlike 'Men were deceivers ever'. Both phrases, for instance, contain the sound of the conceptually pertinent verb 'sever': 'wa*s ever*' and 'deceiver*s ever*'.

The refrain, like most other elements in this song, frustrates and fulfils expectations simultaneously. The line 'Then sigh not so, but let them go' is a straightforward repetition, but its new context alters it subtly. The word 'sigh', for instance, fits perfectly into our expectation that refrains be identical. But the word 'sigh' also violates the pattern established by the refrain of stanza one. In the first stanza, 'Then sigh not so' repeats the verb of the song's opening line. The opening verb of stanza two, 'sing', does not appear in the refrain. Thus 'sigh' fits into one pattern established by the song and simultaneously violates another pattern.

The second time the refrain appears its rhymes link it to the rhymes in stanza two, whereas after stanza one the refrain established a new quatrain of alternating rhymes. The rhyme scheme of stanza one is *abab cdcd*, but the rhyme-scheme of stanza two is *cece cdcd*. And since the *e* and *d* rhymes – 'heavy'/'leavy' and 'bonny'/'nonny' – are themselves near or slant rhymes, the rhyme-scheme of the poem might more accurately be represented as: *abab cdcd cd'cd'cdcd*. The rhyme scheme is yet another pattern that makes the repetition of the refrain both a simple refrain and a complex variation of its earlier appearance in the song.

The effects I have described in Balthasar's song are, I believe, largely responsible for the song's loveliness. Those effects, however, are not available to casual observation. It requires a scrupulously close reading to make them manifest by slowing down the experience of the song and observing that experience at microscopic range. Such readings require great effort and yield little in the way of grand, interpretive conclusions. But scrupulous attention to the language is the only way to understand how Shakespeare transforms a mere vehicle for transmitting conceptual freight into an amusement park ride for the minds and ears of his audience.

EIGHT

The Persistence of the Flesh in *Deaths Duell*

Kimberly Johnson

But for us that dye now and sleepe in the state of the dead, we must al passe this *posthume* death, this *death* after *death*, nay this death after buriall, this *dissolution* after *dissolution*, this *death* of *corruption* and *putrifaction*, of *vermiculation* and *incineration*, of *dissolution* and *dispersion* in and *from* the grave. When those bodies that have beene the *children* of *royall parents*, and the *parents* of *royall children*, must say with *Iob, to corruption thou art my father,* and *to the Worme thou art my mother and my sister. Miserable riddle,* when the *same worme* must bee *my mother* and *my sister* and *my selfe. Miserable incest,* when I must be *maried* to my *mother* and my *sister, beget,* and bee both *father* and *mother* to my *owne mother* and *sister, beget,* and *beare* that *worme* which is all that *miserable penury*; when my *mouth* shall be *filled* with *dust,* and the *worme* shall *feed,* and *feed sweetely* upon me ...

John Donne, *Deaths Duell*[1]

While the fate of the body after death is the subject of recurrent rumination throughout John Donne's sermons, the topic becomes the centre of gravity in the last sermon that Donne preached, a few weeks before his death. This final performance from the pulpit, delivered at Whitehall before the king at the beginning of Lent in 1631,[2] was published after Donne's death as *Deaths Duell, or A Consolation to the Soule, against the Dying Life, and Living Death of the Body.* In *Deaths Duell,* the susceptibility of the mortal body to death is vividly and assiduously considered, from the 'winding sheet in our Mother's womb' in which 'we are dead so, as that wee doe not

know wee live' (5), to the 'final dissolution of body and soule' in the
grave (7). Against the awful mortality of the body, Donne proclaims
that Christ redeems men from both the spiritual corruptions of
sin and the physical corruptions of the decaying flesh, asserting a
consoling vision of the miracle of resurrection and its power to undo
the horrors of the grave, to restore the body to perfection. Ramie
Targoff provides a perhaps too-neat summary of the apparent
argument of *Deaths Duell*: 'However debilitating the effects
of death may seem to be, God will effortlessly overcome them'.[3]

While Donne's Christian hope may yearn towards the resurrection, his rhetorical imagination is lodged firmly in the flesh,
the text of the sermon weighted far more towards what Targoff
primly calls the 'debilitating' effects of death than towards God's
overcoming them. Like the seventeenth-century printer who
designated *Deaths Duell* a '*Consolation to the Soule*', Targoff fails
to register the dissonances that Donne's sermon sounds against
the consolations of its own argument, as repeated appeals to the
doctrine of resurrection show insipidly beside the sermon's vivid
rendering of the body as an irredeemably physical object. The
frail and fragile flesh, whose vulnerability to disease and infirmity
Donne chronicled in his *Devotions Upon Emergent Occasions*,
is for Donne ever in peril of corruption and the depredations
of mortality, and when death finally overtakes the body, as must
happen sooner or later, the repugnance of its decay exceeds the
more placid commonplaces of Christian redemption.

Nowhere is this phenomenon more apparent than in the final
sermon's extended fantasia on the decomposition of the mortal
body, that slow, unsavoury process that Donne calls '*death* after
death, nay this death after burial, this *dissolution* after *dissolution*,
this *death* of *corruption* and *putrifaction*, of *vermiculation* and
incineration, of *dissolution* and *dispersion* in and *from* the grave'
(10). His initial mention of bodily decay gives rise to a grotesque
descant on '*putrifaction*, of *vermiculation* and *incineration*', as he
imagines the breaking down of flesh and tissue, the hot dissolution
of the grave. This passage churns with the implications of its own
initial conceit – that in the grave the decomposing body undergoes

a 'posthume death' – and makes its associative leaps one point to the next with increasing intensity of horror. The commingling of substances Donne here imagines is clearly embedded in the familial lamentations of Job 17:14 ('I haue said to corruption, Thou art my father: to the worme, Thou art my mother, and my sister' [AV]), in the notion that the worm might become both mother and sister only by virtue of its having incorporated those bodies into itself. But Donne elaborates the physical mechanics underlying Job's apostrophe into such vividness that they are barely tolerable. Moreover, by identifying post-mortem decay as '*incest*', Donne reimagines this natural process, the flesh becoming fundamentally transgressive merely by virtue of its corporeality. It is a rebarbative figure, to be sure, its revulsions serving to make more powerfully present the fleshliness of the mortal body. Donne's focus on the unsublimated matter of the body prompts the explicit turn to its sensible features at the passage's conclusion. Here, the '*sweetely*' in '*feed sweetely*' provokes a specifically sensual apprehension of this worm's diet. For the word '*sweetely*' ensures that the decomposing body is registered as a material artefact, one that is fully available to the suite of perceptual senses, including taste. Inviting his audience to reflect on the flavour of a corpse, Donne overwrites any possible spiritualisation of decomposition with the vivid sense-data of vermiculation.

What's fascinating about this passage, beyond its unflinching focus on the horrors of our posthumous decay, is that in its drama and even sensuality it departs from the style of much of *Deaths Duell*. Certainly Donne constructs over the course of the sermon an orthodox argument about God's power over death, and supports his claims with a meticulous explication of both scripture and early church writings, but his method in supporting that thesis hews more towards the painstaking explications of scholasticism as he demonstrates all the ways in which '*unto God the Lord belong the issues of death*' (11). Donne's insistence upon God's power to redeem mankind from death reads as legalistic prose, its images common and even a bit vague, and certainly pale beside his imaginative rendering of decomposition. Indeed, the vivid grotesquery of the vermiculation passage is matched only by the final passage of the sermon, in which Donne lingers over the details of Christ's crucified body.

> There now hangs that *sacred Body* upon the *Crosse, rebaptized* in his owne *teares* and *sweat,* and *embalmed* in his *owne blood alive.* There are those *bowels of compassion,* which are so conspicuous, so manifested, as that you may *see them through his wounds.* There those *glorious eyes* grew faint in their light: so as the *Sun ashamed* to survive them, *departed with his light too.* ... There we leave you in that *blessed dependancy,* to *hang* upon *him* that *hangs* upon the *Crosse,* there *bath* in this *teares,* there *suck* at his *woundes,* and *lye downe in peace* in his *grave,* till he vouchsafe you a *resurrection,* and an *ascension* into that *Kingdome,* which hee *hath purchas'd for you,* with the *inestimable price* of his *incorruptible blood.* AMEN.
>
> (20)

As the sermon concludes, the body of Christ hangs in starkly corporeal contrast to the flatly exegetical treatment Donne gives the idea of redemption: the familiar biblical phrase '*bowels of compassion*' is reclaimed from trope to material as those bowels are 'conspicuous', manifested through his wounds. They are, in other words, actual bowels – intestines, rather than metaphorical sites of empathy. The physicality of Christ as Donne portrays it here ultimately resists figural identification, and Donne's last gesture leaves his congregation contemplating the body of Christ on the cross as a body, inassimilable into some symbolic scheme. And though he may reference Christ's eucharistic function at that moment in enjoining worshippers to '*suck* at his *woundes*', the specificity with which Donne has described those wounds and the bowels they reveal repels rather than invites. At the climactic moment of his sermon, then, Donne offers a Christ whose body is just too *bodily* to be sublimated into symbol.

In its jarring insistence upon the material reality of the body, Donne's depiction of the crucified Christ echoes the vermiculation passage. In each case, Donne's language becomes vibrantly corporeal, confronting the reader with a theatricality that forces our awareness of what's being described as an object in itself rather than a sign pointing to some meaning beyond itself. That is to say, in each of these passages, the physical remains merely and aggressively physical, rather than serving as an illustration of some spiritual principle or other. The grotesque body in the fires of decay, the grotesque body on the cross – each asserts itself *as itself*, as an object, steadfastly refusing to give way to what we might call a 'signified'. And it is this quality of the grotesque body that I believe animates Donne's enthusiasm for it, particularly in a sermon so concerned with the posthumous fate of the flesh: it persists, it remains interpretively present to the understanding, rather than becoming abstracted away into meaning. The body *in extremis*, in decay, sweetly in the mouths of worms, is obscenely corporeal, resisting symbolic significance, and as such it remains literal, asserting its implacable presence as it refuses symbolic absorption. The grotesque body forces our awareness of its objecthood.

It strikes me as no small coincidence that in the midst of a sermon dedicated to the doctrine of man's redemption from the grave, Donne turns to a mode of representation that registers as pure corporeality. His treatment of both mortal and christic bodies is to make them most indissolubly vivid *as bodies* at the very moment that the text confronts physical dissolution. The effect is, paradoxically, that the body becomes most present to the apprehension when its integrity is most threatened. Or, to say it another way, as the bodies Donne describes are imperilled by worms and death and swords and decay, Donne's language makes us most aware of the physical reality of bodies. By using terms that insist upon their corporeal objectivity, that refuse to dissipate into the ether of abstract symbolism, Donne assures that a sense of physical persistence permeates these texts. ''Tis less grief to be foul',[4] Donne remarks satirically in 'The Anagram', but as foulness is employed in the context of describing the body's dissolution, it has the effect of sustaining the flesh beyond the moment of its breaking down. It is indeed less grievous in these circumstances to be foul, because in the foulness in which worms feed sweetly and Christ displays his intestines there is a kind of afterlife, a vivid and persistent objecthood that doesn't dissipate into metaphor, enduring in the interpretation as a kind of embodied immortality.

NINE

The Syntax of Understanding: Herbert's 'Prayer (I)'

DANIEL SHORE

Prayer the Church's banquet, Angels' age,
    God's breath in man returning to his birth,
    The soul in paraphrase, heart in pilgrimage,
The Christian plummet sounding heav'n and earth;   4
Engine against th' Almighty, sinners' tower,
    Reversed thunder, Christ-side-piercing spear,
    The six-days world-transposing in an hour,
A kind of tune, which all things hear and fear;   8
Softness, and peace, and joy, and love, and bliss,
    Exalted Manna, gladness of the best,
    Heaven in ordinary, man well dressed,
The milky way, the bird of Paradise,   12
    Church-bells beyond the stars heard, the soul's blood,
    The land of spices; something understood.

George Herbert, 'Prayer (I)'[1]

Herbert's 'Prayer (I)' is as notable for what it omits as what it comprises. A series of twenty-eight noun phrases, it lacks both a main verb and, with the exception of the ninth line, conjunctions. It has the syntax of a catalogue or laundry list, although we might wonder whether this counts as having a syntax at all. The effect of these omissions is to compel readers to reconstruct the syntax before proceeding to interpretation. To understand the poem as a statement – as stating or asserting something – the reader must first construct it into a single, sonnet-length sentence, transforming apposition (the placement of one noun phrase after another) into copulation (the joining of subject to predicates) by the addition of a main verb, the copula 'is'. While the copula could be inserted after the first word, effectively rewriting the initial phrase, 'Prayer *is* the Church's banquet', it could be inserted equally well between any of the subsequent phrases – in the final line ('The land of spices; *is* something understood'), for example – and indeed between *all* phrases ('Prayer *is* the Church's banquet, *is* Angels' age, / *is* God's breath in man …'). Rather than adding the copula at a particular point, however, we assume it as the unwritten condition of each phrase's meaning – the ground bass, as it were, over which successive chord changes unfold.

We do the same kind of reconstructive work – work so customary that we no longer notice it – when we encounter a definition in a dictionary, joining the *definiendum* (the thing to be defined) to the *definiens* (the thing that does the defining). Herbert's poem has the surface form of a definition, but it defies the expectations that go with it. We expect a definition to explain a less familiar concept by equating it with more familiar ones, but this order is reversed; 'prayer' is in the position of the *definiendum*, but it swiftly takes on the function of the *definiens*. All subsequent phrases are understood in terms of it; the abstract 'gladness of the best' takes on definition and significance only in relation to our ordinary, pre-reflective understanding of prayer. The poem traffics in a reversed economy of familiarity. The word 'prayer' is defamiliarised by its predicates even as it renders those predicates more familiar.

Like a definition, 'Prayer (I)' does not have a tense. Yet critics have noticed that the order in which it unfolds suggests changes in tone, with the relatively conventional metaphors of the first quatrain giving way to the aggressive second, then a third that is in turn gentle and exotic, followed by a concluding couplet that, depending on the reader, is cryptic, triumphant, or quietly resolute. The poem, in other words, is a definition with a plot.[2] Like Helen Vendler, we may 'assume a single consciousness behind the metaphors of the poem',[3] reading it as the story of a mind moving through a series of moods and dispositions. The initial metaphor of a church banquet, however, suggests communal, rather than solitary prayer, and the first poem in *The*

Temple, 'The Church-Porch', recommends that 'Though private prayer be a brave design, / Yet public hath more promises, more love: / ... / Pray with the most: for where most pray, is heaven' (397–8, 402). Read communally, the twenty-eight noun phrases describe the different prayers of multiple churchgoers, arranged not, as with Vendler's 'single consciousness', as a succession in time but in space. As a country parson, the rector of Fugglestone with Bemerton, Herbert had countless opportunities to look out over those gathered in St Andrew's Church and imagine how each member of his congregation would pray. While it may be fanciful to imagine twenty-eight churchgoers gathered in a *stanza* (Italian for 'room') that is five feet wide by fourteen pews deep, it is worth remembering that the volume in which the poem was published, *The Temple*, is partly structured by the architectural space of the church; the volume's first poem, 'The Church-Porch', gives way to a subdivision, 'The Church', which includes 'The Altar', 'The Church-Floor', 'The Church-Lock and Key', and 'The Windows'. 'Prayer (I)' may describe the members of the congregation, as well as the mind of their preacher, in the act of prayer.

The poem obliquely names its own lyric form and explicitly names its chief generative trope. The word 'sounding' in line 4 refers to the measurement of depth (and, in this case, height) using a plummet, but it is also a punning translation of the Italian *sonnet*, the diminutive of *suono* ('sound'); this submerged meaning becomes manifest with the mention of music, 'a tune', and again with the sounding of '[c]hurch-bells'. Each of the noun phrases is, as the third line suggests, a 'paraphrase' (from the Greek *periphrasis*, literally 'to speak around') of the first word. Prayer, we are told, is 'the soul in paraphrase', but the entirety of the poem is prayer in paraphrase. In one of the most successful rhetorical tracts of the Renaissance, *De Copia* (1512), the humanist theologian Erasmus treats *periphrasis* as a means of generating copiousness, or eloquent abundance. As examples he notes that the word 'letter' may be paraphrased as 'what you have written to me', and 'has delighted' may be paraphrased as '[h]as brought pleasure, has been a pleasure, has been a joy, etc.'. Using incremental variations of this kind he demonstrates how a single sentence, 'Your letter has delighted me very much', can 'turn like Proteus into several forms', generating an extensive list (four pages in my edition) of nearly synonymous sentences.[4] 'Prayer (I)' is a parody of this exercise, a *copia* that has slipped its leash and is only brought to heel at the close. Where Erasmus spins out small, periphrastic variations on a single sentence, Herbert conjoins extreme paraphrases into a single sentence.

Scholars have devoted much of their energy to explicating the poem's admittedly cryptic noun phrases. For 'sinners' tower' we are directed to the tower of Babel in Genesis 11:4, for 'The six-days world-transposing' to God's creation of the world in six days in Genesis 1 and 2. More than any of these individual phrases, however, the way we read the poem depends on what the meaning of the word 'is' is. Even if we comprehend the meanings of 'sinners' tower' and 'The six-days world-transposing', we must work to understand how they could both be predicated on the same subject. The poem strains the limits of synonymy, but a few distinctions partially alleviate the strain. Two words or phrases may refer to the same thing without having the same sense; in Gottlob Frege's classic example, the names Hesperus and Phosphorus both point to the planet Venus but at different times of day. As I noted earlier, the practice of prayer may take different forms in the same person at different times or in different people at different places. And there is always the fact of polysemy: 'prayer', like any word, can have multiple meanings that we should not expect to be compatible.

Notwithstanding these reasons for differentiation, the implied copula, which underwrites the poem as a whole, presses the reader to consider not only the periphrastic equivalence of 'prayer' to the phrases that follow, but also, at a deeper level, the equivalence of the phrases to each other. What could it possibly mean to say that 'man well dressed' *is* a 'Christ-side-piercing spear', or that the 'milky way' *is* 'joy'? Such questions ask us, in the words of Thomas Greene, to 'fathom copulative depth' by looking at each successive paraphrase as an outward manifestation of an 'original unity'.[5] In addition to their implied syntactic relationships, the phrases are often bound together by non-signifying similarities in structure. Consider the third line, 'The soul in paraphrase, heart in pilgrimage', which is composed of two phrases split by a comma and a caesura. The phrases fit effortlessly together because (i) they have parallel syntax ('x in y'), (ii) they both take the definite article ('The') that begins the line (the second phrase through ellipsis), (iii) 'soul' and 'heart' are a conventional pair, and (iv) 'paraphrase' and 'pilgrimage' are both three-syllable words beginning with 'p'. Being 'in pilgrimage' is a state or action of a different order from being 'in paraphrase', but surface similarities work to diminish this discrepancy, so that paraphrase (including the paraphrase that is the poem) becomes a kind of pilgrimage and vice versa.

Other surface similarities carry out a similar, if less concerted, reduction of difference. 'Church's', 'Angels'', and 'God's' are each possessive, even though possession means something quite distinct in relation to a 'banquet', an 'age', and 'breath'. The verbal adjective, 'piercing', and the verbal noun, 'transposing', are both composed of a present active participle, hinting at the equivalence of Christ's death and the world's regeneration. On an ideational level, 'sounding', 'transposing', 'tune', and 'Church-bells' harmonise with each other, while 'milky way' and 'stars' form a minor constellation. By softening difference, such surface similarities (and there are many more) suggest that meaning, like 'God's breath in man', emanates from and returns to a single source.

The list-like structure of the poem, as I've argued, compels us to reconstruct a syntax that joins the poem's noun phrases into a unified sentence and sense, but it places only minimal constraints on what that syntax might be. Thus far I've followed previous critics in assuming that the poem's implied main verb is 'is', the third-person singular present, but other choices are possible. Taking his cue from Vendler's reading of the poem as a process of self-correction, Steven Burt suggests a more intricate syntax that allows for differentiation and qualification as well as direct equation: 'prayer is X; no, not X after all, but more like Y; not Y, or not Y alone, but also, and more important, Z'.[6] But even such an elaborate syntax does not exhaust the possibilities. One might also reconstruct the poem as, in effect, '*Let* prayer *be* the Church's banquet, Angels' age, etc.'. This syntax changes what philosophers sometimes call the 'direction of fit'. Instead of fitting the words to the world, as with a definition, it asks the world to fit the words. It stipulates or requests, rather than merely records, the nature of prayer, so that the poem traces the contours of desire rather than reality. If this syntax, like Burt's, has the disadvantage of requiring the reader to do more than the minimal work necessary for reconstruction, it has the advantage of bringing 'Prayer (I)' closer to being a prayer itself. The world-to-word direction of fit allows for an especially satisfying understanding of the final noun phrase. Instead of stopping short the sequence of extreme paraphrases with either a climactic leap of faith or an inconclusive failure,[7] the poem closes by expressing a final need, a desire, a hope, a prayer: 'Let prayer be … something understood'.

TEN

The Real Presence of Unstated Puns: Herbert's 'Love (III)'

MICHAEL SCHOENFELDT

Love bade me welcome: yet my soul drew back,
        Guilty of dust and sin.
But quick-eyed Love, observing me grow slack
        From my first entrance in,
Drew nearer to me, sweetly questioning,
        If I lacked any thing.   6

A guest, I answered, worthy to be here:
        Love said, You shall be he.
I the unkind, ungrateful? Ah my dear,
        I cannot look on thee.
Love took my hand, and smiling did reply,
        Who made the eyes but I?   12

Truth Lord, but I have marred them: let my shame
        Go where it doth deserve.
And know you not, says Love, who bore the blame?
        My dear, then I will serve.
You must sit down, says Love, and taste my meat:
        So I did sit and eat.   18

        George Herbert, 'Love [III]'[1]

One of the most beautiful and moving pieces of poetry in the English language, George Herbert's 'Love (III)' is at least as remarkable for what it does not say as for what it does. Specifically, the poem is built around a conceptual pun that Herbert chooses not to articulate, between the word 'host', which designates the bread in the Eucharistic feast, and the action of inviting and feeding another, which is the essence of the Eucharistic feast. As the former University Orator at Cambridge, Herbert would have known that the word 'host' is derived from the Latin *hostia*, which means 'sacrificial victim'. Herbert, though, is in 'Love (III)' developing a scenario which deliberately revises this notion of host. The sacrifice portrayed in 'Love (III)' is not that of humans offering their best goods to placate an angry deity, but rather a god of Love offering to serve his own flesh to his human creatures. Humans are made to sit and consume the goodness and sustenance bestowed on them by a beneficent but gently coercive divinity.

Yet it is remarkable how rarely the conceptual pun on 'host' is discussed in the many interpretations the poem has inspired. In a typically brilliant parenthetical remark, Stephen Booth observes in his edition of Shakespeare's Sonnets that 'the word "host" never appears in the poem and is the common denominator on which its uneasy analogies turn'.[2] And in a discussion of a possible pun on 'alter' in 'The Altar', Richard Strier notes that Herbert sometimes builds his poems around puns that are never fully actualised in the poem: 'Herbert does at times make spectacular use of puns not verbally actualized in the poem, as in the "host-Host" pun that underlies "Love" (3), and the puns on "choler", caller, and clerical collar that animate "The Collar"'.[3] But in general, criticism of the poem has been almost as reluctant to talk about the pun as Herbert is to exploit it in the poem.

One of the many mysteries of 'Love (III)', then, is its refusal to flesh out the conceptual pun around which it is organised. In 'Love (III)', the real presence of the unstated pun provides the linguistic equivalent of the mystery of the real presence of God in the Eucharist. By hinging on a pun the poem never speaks, the poem performs the essential mystery of faith, which is, in Paul's famous formulation, 'the evidence of things not seen' (Hebrews 11:1 [AV]). Through this unstated pun, Herbert shows us how the word was made flesh, and still dwells among us, in decidedly human gestures of love and hospitality.

Of course 'host' functions as far more than just an unrealised pun. Food and hospitality have mediated divine–human relations throughout Judeo-Christian culture, a fact that 'Love (III)' quietly exploits. If the Fall is an act of eating forbidden fruit, and Hebraic sacrifice is a surrender of one's first fruits to god, Christian redemption is a supper prepared and served by a gracious lord. In Psalm 111:5, David announces: 'He hath given meate unto them that feare him', while in Luke 22:27, Jesus declares to the Apostles at the Last Supper: 'For whether is greater, he that sitteth at meat, or he that serveth? Is not he that sitteth at meate? But I am among you as he that serveth'. 'Love (III)' is particularly interested in the hierarchical inversion whereby the Lord serves his servant.[4] In this final sublime lyric of *The Temple*, Herbert's God is a great lord who exercises gracious coercion, violating hierarchy by serving his servants: 'You must sit down, says Love, and taste my meat: / So I did sit and eat' (17–18). In 'Love (III)', though, we learn that this feast of love has a special menu: Love offers to his guest the meat of his own body.

The poem, then, offers a presence that is once decidedly real and poetically unrealised. The phrase 'real presence' is typically used in theology to describe a god that is mysteriously but materially present in what was previously just bread and wine. Throughout *The Temple*, Herbert plays with the idea of the real presence of God in the Eucharist. He is fascinated by the relationship between God's blood and the wine that is its terrestrial vehicle. But where conventional theology tends to suggest that something in the wine is transformed into blood before the communicant drinks, Herbert is far more interested in the opposite process. In 'The Agony', for example, Herbert writes that 'Love', the figure and trait at the centre of 'Love (III)', 'is that liquor sweet and most divine, / Which my God feels as blood; but I, as wine'.[5] Herbert is amazed by the perverse fact that God's bloody suffering is ritually represented by a substance – wine – that bestows gustatory and intoxicating pleasure on humans. In 'Love (III)', Herbert mentions neither blood nor wine, but he does mention 'meat', the other half of the Eucharistic menu. Rather than emphasising the liturgical transformation of bread into flesh by ecclesiastical authority, Herbert cuts out the middle man, portraying instead a consummately gracious host who offers the speaker a meal of his own substance: 'You must sit down, says Love, and taste my meat'.

The speaker enters this poem like a dusty traveller reluctant to accept the courtesy he is offered. He protests that he is 'the unkinde, ungratefull', and so undeserving of Love's solicitude; in the process, he stirs another pun that is not fully awakened. Eucharist, the name for the liturgical meal that 'Love (III)' commemorates, derives from the Greek word *eucharistia*, meaning 'thanksgiving'. The speaker's claims of ungratefulness thus become explicit statements of his unworthiness for this particular meal. But divine Love will not take no for an answer; Love is literally incarnated as the Lord of Hosts, welcoming reluctant, undeserving, ungrateful humanity with ravishing courtesy to a lavish feast of its own flesh. Although sentenced to 'repining restlessness' in 'The Pulley', humanity is here commanded to rest, to 'sit and eat'. It is as if the long-sought rest and much-hungered-for nourishment pursued throughout *The Temple* were finally to be granted. The poem also offers the discursive consummation of the volume of devotional lyrics; as Jonathan Post remarks, 'we are suddenly and finally treated to the fullest representation in language of a dialogue that has always been at the desired center of *The Temple*. In "Love (III)", the earlier "whispers" and "Methought" give way to table talk of the most profound order'.[6] 'Love (III)' is the last English lyric in the Williams manuscript, Herbert's early draft of about two-thirds of the poems that would become *The Temple*.[7] It is, then, presumably the poem with which Herbert intended to conclude his collection of sacred verse from early on. And unlike many of the poems in the Williams manuscript, this poem is not revised at all, as if Herbert the craftsman knew he had got it just right. He realised that in this moment of forced rest and welcome consumption, he had achieved a near-perfect note of closure for his collection of devotional verse, however much he fiddled with other poems.

Despite its profound sense of closure, though, the poem is filled with ambiguities that open this deeply religious poem out to a wide range of secular human experience. The figure of

'Love', for example, is addressed both as 'Lord' and 'My dear'. The former term is one of overt social distance, while the latter is one of tacit erotic intimacy; the former is one of masculine power, the latter of almost feminine endearment. As we quietly move from one to the other, the poem progressively closes the distance between the speaker and the host. Even the physical distance between the speaker and Love moves from welcome to hand-taking to entering the body as food. As Helen Vendler observes, 'The distance between God and the soul ... here shrinks, during the actual progress of the poem, to nothing'.[8] At the moment of ingestion, no greater physical intimacy is imaginable. The most quotidian of encounters is expressed in the simplest of lexicons, and yet the result is a confrontation with the deepest mysteries of incarnate love.

The poem also engages in some deliberately weird tense shifts, as if both time and hierarchy are out of sort. While opening in the past tense, 'Love bade me welcome', the poem moves in its penultimate line to a kind of eternal present – 'You must sit down, says Love, and taste my meat' – before closing in the past tense: 'So I did sit and eat'. It is as if that final commandment were narratively timeless, directed to the reader as well as the speaker. If so, the invitation, like Shakespeare's claims for the immortality of poetry in the Sonnets, is reinvigorated every time the poem is read. It is not clear, moreover, who speaks the line 'My dear, then I will serve'; it is the only line in the poem not explicitly identified with a speaker, and fascinatingly, it could be spoken by either. It could be the final utterance of the resisting speaker, offering to serve at a meal where he is destined to be the honoured guest, or the gracious invitation of an insistent host. The rhythms of conversational interchange always make me think it is spoken by the poem's speaker, but the fact that either the speaker or Love may utter it suggests the growing proximity of their positions. Like the unstated pun on 'host', the ambiguity reinforces the profound sense of immanence and mystery that emerges from the deliberately homely scenario. The occasion expresses the deepest mysteries of Christianity, but also seems available in an almost primal sense to readers of any, or no, religious persuasion. It is as if George Herbert had decided to create the poetic equivalent of his brother Edward's *De Veritate*, a book seeking the hidden truths shared by all religions (and the foundational text of English Deism).[9]

It is, moreover, telling that the last lyric in *The Temple* begins with an invitation. The entire volume has in a sense been a vigorous invitation to Christian submission. As Herbert announces in the first stanza of 'The Church-Porch', he hopes to 'Rhyme [the reader] to good, and make a bait of pleasure' (4). A poem entitled 'The Invitation' brilliantly imagines the Eucharistic feast as the culmination of various forms of sin; the poem welcomes the glutton (those whose 'taste / Is your waste' or whom 'wine / Doth define'), the fearful (those whom 'pain / Doth arraign'), the epicurean (those 'whom joy / Doth destroy'), and the lover (those whose 'love / Is your dove'). In this poem, Herbert suggests that Christianity offers a kind of universal coverage; it is difficult to imagine what sin, or what sinner, would not be welcome to this feast to which 'all' are expressly invited. 'Love (III)' attains a similarly capacious and gracious invitation through different means. 'Love (III)', moreover, is immediately preceded by a cluster of poems about the last things – 'Death', 'Doomsday', 'Judgment', and 'Heaven'. The echo-format of 'Heaven' in particular prepares us for the repartee of 'Love (III)'. It offers a studied enactment of immanence through the linguistic trick of showing that the surprising answers are embedded in the terms of the questions: 'what is the supreme delight? / *Light*. / Light to the mind: what shall the will enjoy? / *Joy*' (13–16). Some of the rhymes in 'Love (III)' function in just this way. In the last stanza, 'deserve' is rhymed with 'serve', and 'meat', most significantly, is rhymed with 'eat'. Like 'Love (III)', moreover, 'Heaven' offers a surprising emphasis on the spiritual joy and sensual delight at the core of heavenly experience.

'Love (III)' is carefully composed of alternating long and short lines. This form offers a kind of shorthand for the rhythms of impoverishment and beneficence that constitute the human experience of God in Herbert's imagination. The overt patterns of Herbert's famously shaped poem 'Easter wings' demonstrate how those rhythms make up the expansion and contraction of wings in flight. The alternating long and short lines of 'Love (III)' also provide the perfect vehicle for unleashing the musical rhythms and visual patterns in the repartee between divine invitation and human resistance. The poem is apparently simple, composed largely of monosyllables. But the more one looks at it, the more one admires the poem's quiet craft. The phrase 'guilty of dust', for example, demonstrates Herbert's remarkable ability to choose a term perfectly appropriate to both the poem's terrestrial and heavenly scenarios. Travellers, after all, are frequently covered with the dust of the road when they arrive at their destination. But 'dust' is also the material from which we were all made, according to Genesis, and the material to which we will return, according to *The Book of Common Prayer*. The tacit internal rhyme between the 'dust' of human mortality and the 'must' of divine hospitality, moreover, demonstrates how the latter finally trumps the former, how for Herbert divine grace ultimately overcomes Original Sin. That is why the speaker is, in that rich collocation of material substance and ethical transgression, 'guilty of dust and sin'.

I have elsewhere written at length about how the poem absorbs the language and rhythms of Renaissance courtesy literature, and also about how the poem exudes a tacit but powerful eroticism.[10] Twenty years later, the poem is even richer and more powerful than any context I can bring to bear upon it. There is something remarkable, even wondrous, about certain works of art that allow them to grow and deepen with long acquaintance and study. We cannot pluck out the heart of their mystery, but we can perhaps gesture towards the verbal effects that grant them the aura of greatness. The unstated pun on 'host' in 'Love (III)', suffusing the poem but never surfacing, is like the mystery of immanence the poem describes. Herbert's great power as a poet is to translate such mysteries into quotidian events comprehensible by all. And our job as critics is to use every analytical tool at hand to try to understand and appreciate some of the magic by which he does so.

Herbert in 'The Son' praises the rich ambiguity of the English language, which 'give[s] one only name / To parents' issue and the sun's bright star' (5–6). 'Love (III)' similarly exploits the verbal coincidence in English of the word for terrestrial hospitality and a term for the Eucharistic meal. A poem about material presence, 'Love (III)' hinges remarkably on linguistic absence. It is a poem that solicits, even demands, the fastidious attention to verbal effect that has been called close reading. Such reading can help us register what is there, what is not. Our critic laureate of close reading, Stephen Booth, describes beautifully the overall aesthetic presence of subtle verbal effects in great works of art:

> Non-signifying patterns and tensions also occur in great poems – as little noticed and as undeniably there as the hundreds of slightly different leaf shapes and shades of green in a middle-sized maple tree in the back yard; they contribute to a great poem's identity just as – and just what – they contribute elsewhere. A literary effect need not be special to be.[11]

A great poem, 'Love (III)' is filled with truly special effects. It rewards repeated reading and study with glimpses of the genial magic behind these quietly spectacular verbal events. Aptly termed by Simone Weil '*le plus beau poème du monde*', the poem is a testament to Herbert's remarkable ability to construct a poem around a concept, in which previously inessential poetic materials such as titles and tacit puns become a crucial part of the poetic experience.[12] The poem's richly unstated pun on 'host' is one of the many ways the poem incarnates in language the complex emotions and paradoxical ideas surrounding the imagined embrace of fallen humanity by divine Love. The courteous silence that ends the poem – one should never talk with one's mouth full, after all – is like the mute but resonant pun around which the poem is built.

Close Reading Both Ways

ELEVEN

'Hardly they heard'

JEFF DOLVEN

If thou wilt not be seene, thy face goe hide away,
Be none of us, or els maintaine our fashion:
Who frownes at others' feastes, dooth better bide away.
    But if thou hast a Love, in that Love's passion,
I challenge thee by shew of her perfection,
Which of us two deserveth most compassion.
        Sir Philip Sidney, 'Come, *Dorus*, come', 13–18[1]

In the first eclogues of Sidney's old *Arcadia*, the shepherds gather
to sing the customary mix of plaint, praise, and game that holds
their little community together. Among them on this particular
afternoon is a newcomer, a nobleman in rustic disguise: Musidorus,
prince of Thessaly, who has fallen in love with the Arcadian Duke's
daughter Pamela in her pastoral exile. (His cousin, Pyrocles, has
fallen for her sister Philoclea, and he too joins the entertainment,
disguised as an Amazon.) Dorus looks the shepherd's part, but his
lovelorn melancholy singles him out, and so one of the shepherds
– Lalus, accounted the best of their singers – challenges him to a
contest in praise of their mistresses. 'Come, *Dorus*, come', he begins,

        let songs thy sorowes signifie:
And if for want of use thy minde ashamed is,
That verie shame with Love's high title dignifie.
    No stile is held for base, where Love well named is:
Ech eare suckes up the words a true love scattereth,
And plaine speach oft then quaint phrase better framed is.
                       (1–6)

The invitation is a little condescending, allowing that Dorus may
be out of practice, and reassuring him that there is no shame in
a plain (read, beginner's) style. Still Lalus seems to be genuine
enough. He wants to make a show of his skill, but he also wants
to bring this outsider into their company. Dorus takes up the
challenge:

> Nightingales seldome sing, the Pie still chattereth:
> The wood cries most, before it throughly kindled be,
> Deadly wounds inward bleed, ech sleight sore mattereth.
> Hardly they heard, which by good hunters singled be.
> Shallow brookes murmure most, deep silent slide away;
> Nor true love loves his loves with others mingled be.
>
> (7–12)

Lalus has opened with two handsome stanzas of hexameter in terza
rima, a linked form that gives Dorus his first rhyme. The rhythms
are conservative, varied only by a possible opening trochee in
the first line, and the caesurae gravitate to the middle. If this is a
representative specimen of their eclogue verse, then the Arcadian
shepherds are well up-to-date. Next, Musidorus's answer gamely
takes up the rhyme word, but the imagery immediately takes a
dark turn, and more significantly, the rhythms are very different
– you might even say, avant garde. This is no shepherd's song. It
must fall upon the gathered shepherds' ears like a Rite of Spring.

That claim wants some justification, justification that will
have to happen at three scales: the fiction of attention that Sidney
has written between these two characters (which continues for
another hundred and sixty-two lines of close poetical combat), the
attention that he was soliciting from his contemporaries, and how
we, four hundred some years later, should tune our own attending
ears to what he has made. For you could think of Dorus's listening
to Lalus, and then responding, as a kind of fantasy of reading, and
therefore as a possible recommendation to anyone who has in his
or her hands the book that records that fantasy. If what is at stake
is reading, however, it is not interpretation – or if so, only in the

trivial sense in which everything is interpretation. Certainly there is no explicit attempt on Dorus's part to say what the preceding stanza might mean. The idiom of response is poetry, not prose; imitation, not exegesis. And while such a response requires the closest attention, its aims and its techniques are different from what we tend to practise today under the banner of close reading. This essay is a brief study in the kind of attention that this short stretch of song calls for, as a way of asking ourselves what it would mean to read closely without putting interpretation first.

I want to consider that kind of attention under two heads, skill and style, beginning within the fiction, as though Lalus and Dorus were improvising their songs in something like the real time it takes to read them once. They commit to being judged in relation to a standard that will be set on the fly, which means that they must attend closely to poetic form not as an ideal and immanent architecture, but as a set of rules for carrying on. Imagine how Dorus has to listen, hearing first the iambic movement (after that initial trochee), then the hexameter, then the three-syllable rhyme ('signifie', 'dignifie': surely an aggressive challenge to set someone you take for a beginner!). The rhyme scheme unfolds, *ababc* – so far, it seems likely to be a sixaine, with a closing couplet. (The Arcadian forest has already heard three of them, from various singers.) Then comes 'framéd is', repeating the *b*-rhyme, signalling that the form is in fact terza rima, and handing Dorus 'scattereth' at the very last moment. He has to adapt as he goes – he has the form, but again, as a way of proceeding, and it is his turn now. As he gathers all this, he must also listen for how Lalus is setting the form's tolerances. They are more or less standard for the hexameter line of the 1570s, as a poet like George Gascoigne might write it: a settled caesura, occasional inversions, mostly in the first position, decorums which were shared by the pentameter line.[2]

All of which is to say that Lalus is proposing a technical challenge and, at the same time, setting a standard by which the skill of both participants can be measured. Skill is a matter of the well-handling of agreed-upon rules.[3] It solicits praise for technical accomplishment, and does not particularly ask for a given performance to be distinctive in its manner. On the contrary, the rules can be shared entirely, the same for all. (You might say that art here comes closest to sport.) It is open to Dorus to respond in like kind, adopting Lalus's deference to love as an enabler of good verse along with his implicit account of how good verse sounds. But that is not what he does. Granted, the first line is rhythmically similar to Lalus's, with its opening inversion, and the second, though its image is arresting, is an even run of iambs. But his answer is no docile imitation, and indeed, however carefully he may be listening, it is not clear that he even addresses his opponent when his turn comes. In the new stanza, Lalus is cast as a chattering magpie, while the dayworld of pastoral plunges into darkness and the trees that shade the singing burst into flame. This revolution takes hold of the verse with the third line, 'Deadly wounds inward bleed, each slight sore mattereth'. How to hear its rhythm? There is a trochee to start, to be sure; perhaps the iambs stabilise after that, '*Dead*ly wounds *in*ward *bleed*, each *slight* sore *matt*er*eth*'. Or perhaps the second half of the line starts the same way, with another inversion, '*each* slight sore *matt*er*eth*'. Not so uncommon in the period, an inversion after the caesura. But the effect repeats itself in the middle of the next tercet, '*Shal*low brookes *mur*mure *most*, *deep* silent *slide* a*way*', scanned here to allow both inversions again. Such a double symmetry, within and between the two lines, is a bravura effect. There may moreover be a provocation to something still more radical, if we hear those openings as dactyls and allow them to coax the rest of the line to follow suit in triple rhythm: '*Dead*ly wounds *in*ward bleed, *each* slight sore *matt*ereth'; '*Shal*low brookes *mur*mure most, *deep* silent *slide* away'. Four-beat lines are intruding in a poem of sixes. Where are Lalus's rules now?

These are strong words, 'revolution' and 'radical', to use for effects that may sound subtle to unpractised ears. But not too strong. Sidney's book was written at a moment of ferment for English poetry, when metrical skill was still asserting itself precariously in relation to norms only beginning to command wide agreement. Sidney stages within his pastoral a little scene where these new norms matter greatly: the audience of shepherds is, after all, an audience of fellow makers, cultivating the same art, measuring themselves against one another even as they rely upon the standards of that measurement to hold them together. Dorus plays by the rules he is given for the first two lines, to show he can do it. But the departure that follows is sufficiently strange and defiant to carry us beyond what the rules compass, into the territory of style. If skill is expressed in relation to a standard, style will always trouble that relation: it is a word used then and now to talk both about a shared idiom and a distinctive, individual departure from it, whether wilful or not.[4] Dorus has broached the problem of style to the extent that he offers his verses not as a proposal for new norms, but as a badge of his unbridgeable difference – his virtuosic, aristocratic suffering among these shepherds, the agonised eloquence of a class of one. (Or perhaps of two, if we include his cousin Pyrocles.)

Lalus's response has something unmistakably defensive about it:

> If thou wilt not be seene, thy face goe hide away,
> Be none of us, or els maintain our fashion:
> Who frownes at others' feastes, dooth better bide away.
> But if thou hast a Love, in that Love's passion,
> I challenge thee by shew of her perfection,
> Which of us two deserveth most compassion.
>
> (13–18)

The first line returns us squarely to the conservative metrics of his overture: steady iambs, a caesura in the middle, that caesura moved a foot backwards in the second line and then to its centre of gravity again in the third. If you insist on being unseen, he says (and perhaps he means, on being unrecognisable), then you do not belong here. If you want to stay, you must maintain our fashion. 'Fashion' is an important word, one that you might say he recaptures from style – Dorus's adventurous singularity – and reassigns to skill. Play by the rules, he says, and he goes on to restate those rules as he makes a second invitation to join the game of paragons. This exchange is only the beginning of the contest. The remainder plays out this routine of thrust, counter-thrust, and retreat several times as Lalus sets new technical challenges, and Dorus meets them and then more than meets them. Needless to say, the prince could be said to win on skill alone, and William Ringler's edition of Sidney's poetry wonderfully describes Lalus's retrenchment, from triple to double to single rhymes, in the face of his opponent's inexhaustible resources.[5] But Dorus manages, at the same time, to make mere skill seem a poor part of the true poet's gift.

The scene could be said to be Sidney's fantasy of how his own gift might express itself in a field of poetic conformity. Lalus's inability to keep up, and his preference for shared norms over individual achievement, are a polemical foil for a poetic project in which Sidney may not exactly seek followers. He gives us in Dorus a voice meant both to incite and to defy imitation, that elusive charisma that makes us sometimes speak of style as a secret, even though it consists only in what we can see and hear. How then – how technically, and in what spirit – did he expect the poem to be read? It is important that his first readers, like his shepherds, were an audience of poets. Mary Sidney, *Arcadia*'s dedicatee, finished his translation of the psalms after his death; manuscripts of his poems passed through the hands of courtly makers (in Puttenham's phrase[6]) like Edward Dyer and Fulke Greville. Perhaps the Earl of Oxford, no friend of Sidney's, was looking on, and certainly Edmund Spenser and Gabriel Harvey were straining for a glimpse, from Leicester's household and Trinity Hall, Cambridge, respectively. For all of them, these subtle matters of poetic technique were tokens of membership and estrangement, of lineage and community and the desire to stand apart from both. Spenser and Harvey's arguments about the rules of quantitative meter make such manoeuvrings patent: 'I would hartily wish', writes Spenser, 'you would either send me the Rules and Precepts of Arte, which you obserue in Quantities, or else followe mine, that M. Philip Sidney gaue me ... that we might both accorde and agree in one: leaste we ouerthrowe one an other, and be ouerthrown of the rest.'[7] A version of the same half-competitive, half-collaborative adjustment is happening in Sidney's verse, implicitly, and with the same high cultural stakes.

The challenge for us as readers is to imagine having an ear tuned to such discriminations, where technical perceptions and value judgments and social proprioception are all mixed together. Such an ear is a greedy ear, as Lalus allows: 'Ech eare suckes up the words a true love scattereth'. To listen or to read for style is not a neutral disposition, such as the interpreter is often advised to adopt. It is covetous: at the least, sensitive to the self-fashioning ambitions of others, and ideally a little ambitious in its own right. It also requires experience, a wide acquaintance allowing for the recognition not only of forms, but of their origins and their tolerances and their manifold purposes. Reading with an imitative ear breaks down the differences between reading and writing upon which our modernity characteristically insists. Making a poem is a good way of knowing the poems you have read, just as making an essay can be a good way of knowing the essays you have read, when you are self-conscious about the sources, not only of your thoughts, but of your sentences. Such practices have a very long history in literary pedagogy.

Which is to say that this kind of making, in which all of the Renaissance writers we read were trained, is another form of attention, of close attention, even close reading. The contest between Lalus and Dorus is a little master class for readers of *Arcadia*. I have emphasised attention to rhythm, but the attention of the singing contest – and every poem ever written is caught up in some singing contest or other – can fall upon anything, the way the vowels grow more lax over the course of the half-line 'deep silent slide away', the dogged repetition of 'love' (a Sidneian signature), or for that matter whatever these stanzas might be said to be *about* (for example, the way such repetitions figure impasse, and the varieties of impasse).[8] What is required is an active disposition towards making and the community of makers. *I want some of that*; *I want to sound like that*; or *I can imagine what it is like to want to sound like that, I can imagine someone wanting to sound like that, I know who wants or wanted to sound like that or consort with others who do or did* and so on. Such networks of imitative desire are what hold literary history and literary communities together. There is no way of really knowing them without being part of them, without knowing how to want skill, even style; without the mutual contamination of likeness and liking. In some basic way, the New Criticism, still chief sponsor of our close reading, got its start by suspending questions of what a poem is like in favour of questions about what it means. But likeness, relations not of allusive intertext (a particularly happy hunting ground for interpretation) but of stylistic affinity, has always been a vital part of literary knowledge, of literary life, pointing as it does back into the past, around us to our sects and schisms, and forward into possible futures, poems yet to be made. 'Maintain our fashion,' says Lalus. 'Nor true love loves his loves with others mingled be,' says Dorus. Skill and style. There is a *like* inseparable from *how*, and you can only get so close to a poem without it.

TWELVE

Having It Both Ways in Juliet's 'Gallop apace' Speech

Brett Gamboa

Gallop apace, you fiery-footed steeds,
Towards Phoebus' lodging. Such a waggoner
As Phaethon would whip you to the west
And bring in cloudy night immediately.
Spread thy close curtain, love-performing night,   5
That runaway's eyes may wink, and Romeo
Leap to these arms untalk'd-of and unseen.
Lovers can see to do their amorous rites
By their own beauties; or, if love be blind,
It best agrees with night. Come, civil night,   10
Thou sober-suited matron, all in black,
And learn me how to lose a winning match
Play'd for a pair of stainless maidenhoods.
Hood my unmann'd blood, bating in my cheeks,
With thy black mantle, till strange love grow bold,   15
Think true love acted simple modesty.
Come night, come Romeo, come thou day in night;
For thou wilt lie upon the wings of night
Whiter than new snow on a raven's back.
Come gentle night, come loving black-brow'd night,   20
Give me my Romeo; and when I shall die,
Take him and cut him out in little stars,
And he will make the face of heaven so fine
That all the world will be in love with night,
And pay no worship to the garish sun.   25
O, I have bought the mansion of a love

But not possess'd it, and, though I am sold,
Not yet enjoy'd. So tedious is this day
As is the night before some festival
To an impatient child that hath new robes   30
And may not wear them.
          William Shakespeare, *Romeo and Juliet*, 3.2.1–31

Shakespeare routinely enriches our experience of language by
playing on the potential of words to signify in more than one
available context. For instance, Romeo's excuse for wanting to
hold a torch rather than dance at the Capulets' ball ('Being but
heavy, I will bear the light' [1.4.11–12]) has nothing – and much
– to do with weights and measures. Though readers effortlessly
take 'heavy' to mean 'sorrowful' and 'light' as a metonym for
'torch', the coherence of the antonymic pair keeps each word's
literal meaning alive, though the literal meanings remain isolated
from the prevailing sense of the line.[1] The force of 'bear', which
enables the complex perception that something heavy – a burden
– is also a bearer, adds to the secondary context of ponderousness,
energising the line by assigning Romeo contrary qualities while
avoiding the sense of contradiction. Here 'light' and 'heavy' are
not counterparts but companions, though readers cannot escape
their awareness that the terms exist to define a contrast.

Romeo and Juliet is filled with similar examples, from Romeo's
string of oxymoronic paradoxes ('Feather of lead, bright smoke,
cold fire') to his belief that he enjoyed the 'sweeter rest' by not
sleeping; from the play's repeated efforts at confusing night and
day to its thematic crux: the idea that, like Juliet, his 'only love' has
sprung from his 'only hate' (1.1.180, 2.3.39, 1.5.138). Attempts to
reconcile contradictions are by no means unique to Shakespeare,
but the pervasiveness and subtlety of his attempts may be. Juliet's
'Gallop apace' speech, which opens 3.2, stands out both for the
frequency with which it describes things using what should be
mutually exclusive terms, and for its elegance in keeping us from
noticing. The speech continually has it both ways, achieving unity
through contradiction and enlivening the minds of readers and

audiences by almost erasing their abilities to distinguish the literal from the metaphorical.

From its first line ('Gallop apace you fiery-footed steeds'), the speech harmonises ideas that pull in opposite directions. The ear cannot distinguish whether the syllables in 'apace' form one word or two. So 'Gallop apace' conveys the sense of 'run fast' while also posing an implicit fallacy – namely, that a horse can gallop for a single pace. The resulting tension does not impede readers who understand the idiomatic use of 'apace', but their understanding is threatened as soon as it is achieved by the word's situation in a context of literal paces, a context strengthened by the 'fiery-*footed*' steeds. The word 'footed' is urgently relevant to the root meaning of 'apace' – a meaning absent in the metaphorical context – so the line insists that readers overlook the 'pace' in 'apace' and, in the same moments, prevents them from doing so. As a result, the line enables a clear understanding of something as clearly at odds with itself. It allows readers and audiences to accomplish the casual but super-ordinary feat of accepting the pace in question as both literal and figurative, both impossible and certain.

Juliet urges the steeds to take the sun away so that night – and Romeo – may come sooner, imagining how Phaeton 'would whip you to the west, / And bring in cloudy night immediately'. The idea of entrance in the fourth line elegantly contrasts with that of departure in the first three. As described the action is impossible because the taking out and bringing in are performed by the same team at the same time. Phaeton and his team cannot return to bring anything without bringing the sun back too. The lines lean on our awareness that darkness is a natural consequence of sunset, an awareness that camouflages the fact that 'bring in' has shed its transitive force and now works in concert with a verbal phrase it should cancel. Readers and audiences typically won't realise that they arrive at their destination by two roads running in opposite directions. But their journey is richer for it.

Just when we have accepted 'cloudy night' as a consequence of the team's departure (and arrival), Juliet has it differently. Now she tells night to bring itself, 'Spread thy close curtain,

love-performing night, / That runaway's eyes may wink and
Romeo / Leap to these arms untalk'd-of and unseen'. Night alter-
nates between passive object and active agent. 'Spread thy close
curtain' extends the theme of reconciled contradictions and is
casually exciting in itself. Context suggests that 'spread' means
to close the curtain – to draw it across a formerly bright sky. But
we cannot divorce it from the idea of opening, since it combines
with 'close curtain' and 'love-performing' to carry dim but real
suggestion of a skirt being thrown open. Add the fact that the
curtain clearly is and is not the night itself and the line creates just
the kind of demonstrable confusion – in seeming clarity – as the
steeds that simultaneously came and went.

Confusion masquerading as clarity continues elsewhere in
the lines, most notably because the 'runaways' – presumably
Phaeton and his aforementioned steeds – have not run away, as
Juliet's opening imperative makes clear.[2] Readers may understand
'runaway' to mean 'headstrong' or 'uncontrolled', which suits the
primary context in light of Juliet's allusion to their absent driver.
But the root meaning of 'runaways' persists, and it is amplified when
the syllable 'roam' sounds in 'Romeo' later in the same line. The
lines gain energy, then, by harmonising 'runaways' with the steeds
presently outstaying their welcome. The rhyme-like relationship of
'runaway' and 'Romeo' – suggested not only by the ideational echo
but also by their phonic and rhythmic similarities – asserts likeness between the coming Romeo and the departing team.[3] They
had been like night and day, the arrival of one depending upon the
departure of the other, but Juliet now reverses course by proposing
that night – and Romeo – can arrive without the runaway steeds
running away. The phrase 'Runaways eyes may wink' suggests that
the team with the sun in tow can stay and sleep under the curtain
of night and thus extends the passage's effort to merge night and
day begun earlier in the passage. The 'roamers' – Romeo and the
runaway team – may now be present at once, as can night and day. In
the space of five lines, then, Juliet suggests that Romeo's approach
depends on the team's departure, its return, and its staying in
one place.

Shakespeare adds to the sequence of contradictions in the ensuing lines, when, on the heels of introducing Romeo as one 'untalk'd-of and unseen', Juliet talks of seeing Romeo – and of seeing him in the dark,

> Lovers can see to do their amorous rites
> By their own beauties; or, if love be blind,
> It best agrees with night.

> (8–10)

The core wit of the sentence is in the fact that sexual intercourse needs no ocular aid – is, indeed, customarily done in the dark. The momentary possibility that 'see to' means 'attend to' contributes to our prevailing sense that the sight in question is figurative. However, the completion of the infinitive 'to do' frees 'see' from one idiomatic usage for another: 'to see … by'. This syntactic turn renews the possibility of literal sight, at least until 'their own beauties' replaces the light source we expect with the lovers themselves. However, given the early modern notion that the eyes gave off light, 'their own beauties' confirms the possibility of literal sight in the same moment that possibility is undermined.[4] So the appointment of the lovers as the lights by which they see fulfils and frustrates expectations orchestrated by the syntax. The line plays on our awareness that lovers can't see in the dark, while arguing concurrently that they do just that. Juliet's subsequent phrase, 'or, if love be blind', complicates our perception and redefines our understanding by revealing that literal sight was at stake all along. Despite her attempts to distinguish them, for Juliet sight and blindness are two roads leading to the same city – each produces similarly positive outcomes for her and Romeo. Juliet has it both ways – love is admitted as blind even while lovers – exclusively – are endowed with supernaturally keen eyesight.

Her descriptions of night are likewise animated by paradoxes. Initially introduced as 'love-performing', night is much altered in its second appearance,

> Come civil night,
> Thou sober-suited matron, all in black,
> And learn me how to lose a winning match,
> Play'd for a pair of stainless maidenhoods.

(10–13)

It is hard to accept this 'sober-suited matron' as the aforementioned love-performer, but the descriptions sit well together in a speech that likens sight to blindness. The parallelism of the compound adjectives ('love-performing', 'sober-suited') and the references to fabrics ('close curtain', 'all in black') help to reconcile the rival portraits. A conflict that should bother readers doesn't because the speech imparts likenesses to patently unlike things. Their similarity is argued further when the matron is called to play her predecessor's part rather than her own, 'Come ... / And learn me how to lose a winning match, / Play'd for a pair of stainless maidenhoods'. The love-performer gives way to the 'sober-suited matron' and *she* is the one who teaches Juliet to have sex. In this context it is as splendid as it is apt that 'learn' must be understood inversely as 'teach' and that Juliet's sure road to victory is defeat. Likewise, 'stainless', a word that bespeaks Juliet's chastity, could hardly feel less chaste, especially when 'unmann'd blood' appears in the following line. The prefix of 'unmann'd' cannot keep the word from hinting at Juliet's imminent 'manning', just as the suffix of 'stainless' cannot remove the 'stain' present in the line – and imminent on Juliet's sheets. Juliet formerly conflated going and coming, night and day, sight and blindness, winning and losing; now she is both maid and maiden, sexualised by the very words that proclaim her innocence.

In traversing so many incidental paradoxes – incidental because they intrude upon without eclipsing the ostensible meaning of the lines – we may overlook Juliet saying 'pair of maidenhoods' when hers alone is at stake. The only prospects available to pair with Juliet are the matron, whose job description disqualifies her for maidenhood, and Romeo, who would have to take a woman's part for the purpose. But the speech works to qualify each of these obviously unqualified candidates. The general contextual pertinence of 'pair' to 'winning match' gives it the momentary sense of a marriageable pair – the aforementioned lovers that see in darkness. Meanwhile, the 'pairing' of Juliet and the matron in a student–teacher relationship, one intensified by its proposition that the teacher is also the 'learner', enables readers and audiences to experience 'pair of … maidenhoods' as more logical than it is.

As if to toy with the audience the singular noun 'hood' appears in the following line, just after we have learned to go without it, although its meaning and context are new:

> Hood my unmann'd blood, bating in my cheeks,
> With thy black mantle, till strange love grow bold,
> Think true love acted simple modesty.
> Come night, come Romeo, come thou day in night. …
>
> (14-17)

Juliet commands the night to 'hood' her as one would a hawk, extending the run of requests for night to cover things in darkness. The hawking metaphor is new, but it recalls the prior description of the steeds. Both can fly, both sleep beneath a fabric of night and both are without their riders. Coupled with Juliet's reference to being 'unmann'd' – a near-perfect double in this context for 'unmounted' – the hawking metaphor works nearly as hard to liken Juliet to the flying steeds as to a grounded hawk.

And like the night before her, Juliet is defined as both a modest woman and an eager lover. The syntax initially dictates that the conditional clause 'till strange love grow bold' depends on 'Hood my unmann'd blood'. So we must at first understand Juliet to be asking night to restrain her until she is ready to meet Romeo in bed. 'Strange' provides the sense of 'unfamiliar' and points up her modesty and inexperience. But the lines implicitly argue against this strain of modesty while delivering it. The 'unmann'd blood' extends the line of sexual imagery and desire, as does the 'mantle' with which Juliet desires to be covered. The occurrence of 'man' twice in two lines, more emphatic for occurring in the same metrical position, introduces the male lover to a context anxiously concerned with his absence, enabling readers and audiences the complex perception that he is there and not there, and that Juliet's expressions of modesty concurrently advertise her desire.

Desire intrudes upon the context of modesty further when the subsequent clause, 'Think true love acted simple modesty', repositions readers and audiences in relation to the syntax. 'Think', another of Juliet's imperatives, reassigns 'till strange love grow bold' as its own condition rather than that of the clause that preceded it. So Juliet's line tells the ultra-respectable 'civil night' to think 'love acted' is 'simple modesty', or that sexual intercourse *is* chastity, until she can boldly admit her 'strange love'. She may continue shy, but Juliet's modesty now comes in on night's behalf rather than her own. After all, she is asking night itself to wink while she goes about staining her sheets. Readers and audiences are able to credit her as the modest and shy girl she is, while everything in the alternate but available context belies her.

It is a fitting climax to the series of sexually suggestive, oxymoronic paradoxes that Juliet again calls Romeo to her in a manner that preserves her innocence and proclaims her guilt, 'Come night, come Romeo, come thou day in night' (17). Climax is the most appropriate word to describe a line filled as this one is with incidental but unsubtle references to ejaculation. Still, each word that contributes to the charged secondary context – 'stainless', 'unmann'd', 'blood', 'mantle', and 'come' – is modest, if not entirely innocent. Each line can be read – *is* read – as though Juliet is as inexperienced as she claims. And prior references to coming and going in the passage helps the phrase 'Come night, come Romeo, come …' seem innocent, though the context is so sexually suggestive that we cannot experience it innocently. That Romeo arrives to lie 'upon the wings of night' and ride atop the 'raven's back' adds to the sexual suggestiveness, the more because Juliet has just been compared to a bird (18–19). In a sense, then, Juliet is the night, and Romeo is the day *in* night. 'Day in night' is likewise climactic in asserting the co-presence of a mutually exclusive pair.

The phrase intrudes farther into our conscious experience than
other paradoxes in the passage, but its way is made smoother by
the steeds that formerly brought in both darkness and light.

Having likened the night to an eager lover, a sober matron, and
the virginal Juliet, and having asked it even to make room for the
sun, the speech takes perhaps the only leaps left to it, recasting
night as a male lover and causing Romeo and Juliet to swap their
astronomical assignments,

> Come gentle night, come loving black-brow'd night,
> Give me my Romeo; and when I shall die,
> Take him and cut him out in little stars,
> And he will make the face of heaven so fine
> That all the world will be in love with night,
> And pay no worship to the garish sun.

$$(20–25)$$

Though night is personified as female throughout the passage, the
'gentle ... black-brow'd night', introduced to a context containing
galloping steeds and the 'white' Romeo mounted on a raven's
back, allows the urgently relevant homophone 'knight' to become
active.[5] Juliet had asked night to spread its 'close curtain', though
it was that curtain; now she asks night to 'Give me my Romeo',
though he is the night/knight itself. The request that Romeo be
'cut out in little stars' creates excitement by its concerted use
of 'out' and 'in' in a phrase unrelated to entry or exit and alters
Romeo from the 'day' in night to the night itself. Meanwhile,
Juliet's reference to her death finds an ideational echo in 'garish
sun'. While reconciling yet another pair of contrarieties – the sun
not ordinarily being given to garishness – the phrase's resonance
with 'die' positions Juliet for a turn as the 'day in night' just after
Romeo has left the role.

Before the Nurse – herself a sober-suited matron full of advice
about love – enters, Juliet makes two final attempts at conflating
contradictory terms and ideas,

> O, I have bought the mansion of a love
> But not possess'd it, and, though I am sold,
> Not yet enjoy'd. So tedious is this day
> As is the night before some festival
> To an impatient child that hath new robes
> And may not wear them.
>
> (26–31)

'Bought' in line 26 echoes 'pay' in line 25 but carries a purely commercial sense that 'pay worship' does not have. In line 27, 'though I am sold' continues the idea of buying and selling but casually makes Juliet – formerly the buyer – the object sold. Moreover, Juliet buys a 'mansion', which, while repeating the syllable 'man', is a place she might enjoy by entering, but she laments not being 'enjoy'd' – the result of a man entering her. Juliet then bemoans the day's slow march, but in an attempt to contrast day and night she likens an instance of one to an instance of the other, 'So tedious is this day / As is the night'. The speech thus concludes where it began: in celebration of a night that is impossible to distinguish from day. In the opening lines night could not arrive without day returning; here Juliet cannot mention the day's tediousness without talking about a tedious night.

These examples, like 'day in night', are less subtle than many others in the speech. But the more apparent paradoxes enter a context so full of contradictions that they complement and intensify what has come before without distracting us from the primary sense of the lines. And incidental tensions, such as those triggered by harmonising 'out' and 'in' or by transforming the buyer into the object bought, continue, as do the speech's efforts to revive discarded images and reimagine them in opposite terms. Consider one final example. Juliet compares her situation to that of a child who has 'new robes / And may not wear them'. The metaphor sits comfortably in a speech charged with incidental references to fabric and clothing, but while extending one strain of coherence it undermines another. 'And may not wear them' acts as a metaphor for Juliet's impatience to see Romeo, but it also revives the pertinent idea of wearing a woman sexually.[6] Juliet, who wants to wear her 'new robes', has spent the last ten lines expressing her desire to be worn. Lines like these – and the passage as a whole – are continuously energised by contrarieties. The array of seemingly inconsequential coherences – among things like clothing, riding, and animals – makes them feel clearer, more unified and more consistent in their characterisations than they actually are. Consequently, the passage enables in readers and audiences more complex perceptions, and more pleasure, than is usual.

THIRTEEN

'To Celia': Not Too Close

ERIK GRAY

Drink to me only with thine eyes,
    And I will pledge with mine;
Or leave a kiss but in the cup,
    And I'll not look for wine.   4
The thirst that from the soul doth rise
    Doth ask a drink divine;
But might I of Jove's nectar sup,
    I would not change for thine.   8
I sent thee late a rosy wreath,
    Not so much honouring thee
As giving it a hope that there
    It could not withered be.   12
But thou thereon didst only breathe,
    And sent'st it back to me;
Since when it grows, and smells, I swear,
    Not of itself, but thee.   16
          Ben Jonson, 'To Celia'[1]

Ben Jonson's 'To Celia' falls into two distinct halves – so much so that many modern anthologies print the last eight lines as a separate stanza. But this is only appropriate. 'To Celia' is a love poem, and love requires twos, as the poem so amply demonstrates: I and thou; giving and receiving; action and response. On the other hand Jonson deliberately printed the poem as one continuous lyric without a stanza break, and this too is appropriate, since love aims at unification. Love acknowledges, even celebrates, differences and oppositions, but also seeks to join differing parts into a single dynamic whole, just as Jonson's poem does. Hence the central word of the first line is 'only', a term of unity – as reflected even more clearly in the spelling used when the poem was first published in 1616: 'onely'.

Yet the word 'only' itself, in this case, has three distinct meanings, and that too is appropriate. 'Only' can modify 'me', signifying the exclusivity of love: 'Drink to me only'. Or it can modify the succeeding phrase, to signify love's transcendence of mere conventional gestures: drink to me, but 'only with thine eyes'. Or else 'only' can be a vocative. (Again, this was clearer in 1616, where the word is set off by commas: 'Drinke to me, onely, with thine eyes'. Some manuscript versions read 'Celia' for 'onely'.) This triple meaning is appropriate, because love requires a third. It takes two to tango – that is, literally, to touch. But it takes three to tangle – to complicate the dyadic relationship, and so keep lovers sufficiently distanced from one another for desire, and for poetry, to thrive. As Anne Carson explains:

> [Since] eros is lack, its activation calls for three structural components – lover, beloved and that which comes between them. They are three points of transformation on a circuit of possible relationship, electrified by desire so that they touch not touching. Conjoined they are held apart. The third component plays a paradoxical role for it both connects and separates, marking that two are not one.[2]

Often the role of third party, the one who both marks the lovers' separation and draws them together in a common cause, is played by a rival. In Ovid's *Amores* 1.4, which was almost certainly one of Jonson's sources, that function is fulfilled by the addressee's husband, who is present throughout the scene.[3] In Jonson's poem, the role is taken over by Jove, who appears at the end of the first octave as a possible erotic rival. Jove, or Jupiter, is best known for seducing women; but by presenting him as a potential rival for the speaker's attention instead (thus casting the speaker as Ganymede), Jonson reminds us that Jove also carries off the occasional mortal male – and hence serves as a particularly effective third point in a love triangle.

Even without the introduction of Jove, however, there is already a third party mediating between the lovers, or rather a series of third parties: the glance, the cup, the wreath, and – implicitly, but most importantly – the poem itself. The first four lines present two acts of mediation, or more specifically of substitution. First the speaker asks that the lovers drink to each other (the word 'pledge' in line 2 means to toast someone in return),[4] but with glances substituting for wine; then, in lines 3–4, he suggests substituting a kiss instead. The 'Or' at the beginning of line 3 could indicate the equivalence of these two suggestions. Glances and kisses are both things that lovers exchange; both are more intimate than a mere exchange of toasts; so the speaker could be saying that a glance or a kiss is equally welcome. But 'Or' could also suggest a change of mind: 'Glance at me – or, even better, leave a kiss in the cup'. The latter possibility seems more likely, given that the speaker devotes only two lines to the glance and six to the affair of the kiss. Those six lines end, moreover, with a claim that such kisses are not fungible – the substitution of a comparable commodity ('Jove's nectar') is not acceptable.

If the speaker prefers a kiss to a glance, however, it is not because the kiss is more perfect, but the opposite. The glance is immediate: it moves at the speed of light and is perfectly reciprocal ('with thine … with mine'). The kiss by contrast is drawn out and oblique. Indeed, what the speaker desires is not a kiss but specifically, and much more awkwardly, a kiss mediated by a cup. Ovid's speaker asks for the same thing: 'When thou hast tasted, I will take the cup, / And where thou drink'st, on that part I will sup' (in Christopher Marlowe's translation).[5] But Ovid's speaker is compelled to take such indirect measures by the presence of the beloved's husband. No such impediment is implied in Jonson's poem.[6] Instead, the speaker desires a kiss-in-a-cup for its own sake; the imperfection and delay are the very source of the pleasure. This explains why the speaker refuses to exchange for a 'sup' of nectar. Jove's nectar is (presumably) more like a glance – immediate, immaculate, ethereal. The process of kissing by cup, on the other hand, is tantalisingly slow and indirect.

It is scarcely a leap to say that the pleasures described in this opening octave are recognisably poetic. Like a glance or a kiss, a poem is a communicative act, requiring cooperation between two people, writer and reader. The same could be said, of course, of any form of literature. The difference is that, more than other forms of writing, poetry moves necessarily from the eyes to the lips, since it asks to be read aloud. The alliteration that enters the poem in line 3 ('kiss … cup'), just at the moment that the speaker's desire moves from visual to oral communication, draws attention to a form of pleasure – the delight in sheer physical articulation – that is largely absent in prose.[7] Above all, the pleasures described in the poem are metapoetic in their foregrounding of the means of communication, rather than its end. 'To Celia' describes a series of messages between lovers, the pleasure of which derives in each case from the imperfection, the non-transparency, of the medium. The messages thus demand to be not just read but close read – 'close' in the sense of 'attentively', but also in the sense of 'nearly, but not quite'. The whole point of each proposed interaction is to prolong the process of communication and delay its completion; and the same obtains for the poem itself, since poetry, like erotic desire, thrives by prolongation and postponement.

Hence the poem's title. The title 'To Celia' follows a standard formula but reinvests it with meaning, since it aptly reflects the speaker's ideal. What he desires is not 'Celia', or even being 'With Celia', but rather a perpetual, asymptotic approach 'To Celia'. Hence also the confusion of lines 7–8. There has existed a long debate about these lines, which could mean (read literally, but counter-intuitively) that the speaker *would* prefer Jove's nectar to Celia's kisses, rather than the reverse.[8] The confusion is significant, not for the specific ambiguity it seems to introduce, but rather for the delay in understanding it produces. Just as the cup must pass through other hands before the speaker can achieve his kiss, so the opening octave – even as it finally achieves the kiss of a closing rhyme ('mine'/'thine') – must pass through the diversion of what

William Empson calls, in his discussion of this crux, an 'irrelevant meaning'.[9]

It is no surprise, therefore, that the second half of the poem introduces even more complication and delay: the description of the wreath and its tangled significance takes up as much space as the glance and the kiss put together. The whole of the second octave represents a step backwards, further away from immediacy. In the first place, we move back into the past tense, in contrast to the dramatic present of the opening lines (a change subliminally reinforced by the shift from 'rise' to 'ros[e]' [5, 9]). Moreover, the speaker's focus shifts away from Celia and explicitly towards the medium itself. The speaker claims that, in sending his beloved a wreath of roses, his concern was not for her but for *it*: 'it' appears five times in the final six lines, outnumbering both 'me' and 'thee'. The whole of the poem's attention and erotic energy are thus displaced onto the third party, to the extent of entirely reversing the familiar trope of the final two lines. In most love poems, the beloved smells like, or in some other way resembles, a rose; in Jonson's, the roses smell like the beloved.

Most significantly of all, the second octave focuses not only on the medium of communication but on a complex – and utterly counter-intuitive – reading of that medium. First the speaker claims (retrospectively) that his gift of roses represents not a tribute to his beloved but an act of compassion towards the flowers. Then, when the woman immediately sends his gift back, the speaker chooses to read this response not as a rejection but as a gesture of reciprocation – an amorous exchange, like the return of a glance. The deliberately tortuous logic of this reading is reflected in the self-conscious wordplay of these lines, with their reversed and repeated phonemes. All three rhymes in the second octave make use of the same few sounds. The end of 'wreath' (9) is simply turned around to form 'thee' (10), a process completed in 'there' (11). 'There' then wreathes its way through the next two lines, in 'withered' (12) and 'thereon' (13) – the end of which then expands into 'only', thus connecting back to the poem's opening line. But in place of the simple exchange of 'thine' and 'mine' with which we began, we now have the ongoing loop of 'thee' (10) rhyming with 'me' (14) rhyming again with 'thee' (16) – a tautological final rhyme that, in its very perfection, suggests something forced and awry.

But the poem by no means requires that we accept this circular conclusion as completing a true love knot. To the contrary, the repetition of 'Not … thee' (10, 16) draws attention to the insistent negative – the 'not' that recurs throughout the poem and signals its refusal of closure. Every fourth line of 'To Celia' includes a 'not'; every tentative gesture of love is almost immediately withdrawn or denied. The speaker begins by asking for a glance, only to assert that 'I'll not look' (4); he asks for a series of exchanges, but says that 'I would not change' (8). His concern in the second half is 'Not … thee' but 'it' (10–11); yet by the end, 'it' has become 'Not … itself, but thee' (16). All poetry defers closure, and love poetry perhaps most of all. But Jonson's love poem foregrounds this refusal of resolution even more than most: his speaker offers invitations to intimacy while edging steadily backwards. Each interaction or proposed interaction between the lovers, building up from the glance to the kiss-in-a-cup to the wreath, grows more distant and imperfect – and therefore more pleasurable.

This progression culminates in the poem itself. The second octave offers even more metapoetic resonances than the first: like the wreath they describe, these lines consist of flowers of rhetoric, interwoven with rhyme, and dependent upon the breath of another to provide them with continuing life. But the greatest resemblance between the wreath and the poem lies in the extended and convoluted acts of reading that both require. The poetic entanglements that Jonson provides – the puzzling syntax at the end of the first octave, the reduplicated rhyme at the end of the second, and all the other elements that divert attention to the words that mediate between me and thee – succeed by resisting total or immediate comprehension. The poem arises in the first place out of the separation of the two lovers: if they were already together, or if they already understood each other perfectly, no poem would be necessary. And the poem continues to have life and meaning only so long as lover and beloved, writer and reader, remain two and not one. Hence the combination of invitation and retreat, engagement and dissociation. The more closely we read 'To Celia', the more we realise that it deliberately avoids coming too close.

FOURTEEN

Marvell's 'Mourning'

Stanley Fish

You that decipher out the fate
Of human offsprings from the skies,
What means these infants which of late
Spring from the stars of Clora's eyes?   4

Her eyes confused and doubled o'er,
With tears suspended ere they flow,
Seem bending upwards, to restore
To heaven, whence it came, their woe.   8

When, moulding of the wat'ry spheres,
Slow drops untie themselves away;
As if she, with those precious tears,
Would strow the ground where Strephon lay.   12

Yet some affirm, pretending art,
Her eyes have so her bosom drowned,
Only to soften near her heart
A place to fix another wound.   16

And, while vain Pomp does her restrain
Within her solitary bow'r,
She courts herself in am'rous rain;
Herself both Danae and the show'r.   20

Nay others, bolder, hence esteem
Joy now so much her master grown,
That whatsoever does but seem
Like grief, is from her windows thrown.   24

Nor that she pays, while she survives,
To her dead love this tribute due,
But casts abroad these donatives,
At the installing of a new.   28

How wide they dream! The Indian slaves
That dive for pearl through seas profound,
Would find her tears yet deeper waves,
And not of one the bottom sound.   32

I yet my silent judgment keep,
Disputing not what they believe;
But sure as oft as women weep,
It is to be supposed they grieve.   36
                    Andrew Marvell, 'Mourning'[1]

Marvell's 'Mourning' might well be retitled 'Mourning?' for
it refuses to give us a stable perspective on the act it at once
overdescribes and never definitively describes. Indeed the question mark is implicitly provided by the two main meanings of
'mourning', meanings the poem hovers between, collapses, and
mocks: (1) an expression of grief from the heart, and (2) an
exhibition of grief by means of conventional signs, gestures, or
clothing; in short an affectation. The poem sets as its problem the
effort to figure out what Clora is doing. What we know (although
we don't know it until the end of the third stanza), is that Strephon
is dead and Clora is, or seems to be, weeping. The mechanics of
her weeping are carefully, even microscopically, delineated; but no
amount of detail suffices to tells us what her tears *mean*, a word
that appears in line 3 and drives the rest of the poem.

The key figure in the poem is the interpreter; Clora is just his
object. But who is he? The poem's first word 'You' indicates that
he is the reader, but lines 1 and 2 define him more narrowly as an
astrologer: 'You that decipher out the fate / Of human offsprings
from the skies'. The sense seems straightforward enough. The
astrologer looks up at the stars and extracts from them – deciphers
– the secret course of human affairs; he wrests a hitherto hidden

intelligibility from the heavens and brings it down to earth. Line 2, however, complicates the sense and threatens to turn it into nonsense. '[F]rom' can go either with 'decipher' and point to the verb's object ('the skies') or with 'offsprings' and name the location of the offsprings (they come from the skies). But that would mean (an increasingly troubling word) that 'offsprings' means both something derivative and the source or original, and these are in fact two of the meanings the word has had. A third meaning is activated in line 4 – 'Spring from the stars of Clora's eyes'. In the syntax, 'Spring' is a verb indicating emergence or origin; it thus looks back at both meanings of 'offsprings'. 'Spring' – and this is a fourth meaning – also names a body of water, and that meaning looks forward to Clora's tears, which become the focus of the second stanza, but are in the first stanza only presented metonymically as 'infants' – babies that fall from the eye – and as the offsprings (babies) of Clora's eyes, which are called 'stars'. 'What mean those infants which of late / Spring from the stars of Clora's eyes'. 'Stars', which in line 2 are the objects (not named) of the astrologer's gaze (of his eyes), have now been put inside the true object of deciphering – Clora's eyes and what falls from them, also characterised as stars.

To say these lines are vertiginous is to understate the point, and the vertigo increases when the verse focuses on those eyes and tears: 'Her eyes confused, and doubled o'er / With tears suspended ere they flow' (5–6). 'Confused', from *confundere*, to pour and mix together, to blend. The verb names what has already happened in the poem: her eyes have been mixed up with babies, stars, springs, and offsprings. '[D]oubled o'er' is a doubling of 'confused' with the additional suggestion of duplicity. Her eyes have many appearances and what they mean remains obscure. The tears that don't quite flow from them are 'suspended', that is, poised, hanging, uncertain, at once a description of an impossible physical state (tears that are arrested in slow motion) and a comment on the poem's interpretive failure: it cannot settle on the significance of the scene it presents. Contained in 'suspended' is a pun on 'pendant' (see 'Eyes and Tears' [16]: 'pendants of the eyes'), both as a noun and an adjective. Her tears adorn her by hanging there like pieces of jewellery or like stars. Are they genuine or are they ornaments? Is this mourning or is it something else?

The first word of line 7 – 'Seem' – tells us that there will be no answer; it's all seeming. The theatricality (doubleness) extends to tears that not only do not drop but appear to be ascending, 'bending upwards to restore / To heaven, whence it came their woe'. The posture is one of supplication; the suggestion is of a *pietà*: the virgin Mary mourns and looks to Heaven in the hope that her son will be restored. The ascending tears aspire to the status of stars. Once they arrive, the astrologer can try to decipher them.

In the third stanza the suspended and would-be-ascending tears finally do the 'natural' thing and drop: 'When, moulding of the wat'ry spheres / Slow drops untie themselves away' (9–10). 'When' introduces an action, but what is it? In the previous stanza gravity had been suspended but it is not reinstated here; instead the responsibility for what happens is given to the tears that 'untie themselves' as if they were defying any outside aid or influence. Self-untied, the tears are at once physically free – without supports – and free of any ties (un-tied in another sense) that would allow an observer to get a fix on them. They are 'away' from everything, unrelated, stand-alone, self-enclosed entities that repel the effort to understand them. (They are like the drop of dew in the poem of that name which 'Round in itself encloses' [6] and is said to be 'Like its own tear' [13].) All we know of them is that they form themselves in the shape of the eyes they drop from – 'moulding of the wat'ry spheres' – eyes that are their double and their mirror; 'doubled o'er', the eyes see themselves in the tears, and the tears in the eyes. Again, a relationship that is an identity and one that is entirely closed off from the prying, interpreting eyes of others.

Interpretation arrives in lines 11–12: 'As if she, with those precious tears, / Would strow the ground where Strephon lay'. Here's one way to look at it – the weeping maiden who cries rivers of tears and saturates the earth where her beloved lies dead. But the 'As if' is deadly and casts its shadow on 'precious' which can mean either immeasurably valuable or overwrought, overrefined, over the top. (How precious!) In the four stanzas that follow, interpretations proliferate, and as they do the language of the poem undergoes a change. No longer densely polysemous, it is relatively (remember, this is Marvell) straightforward, which makes perfect sense because what interpretation, the irritable reaching after meaning, does is arrest the play of language in the service of a single linear story.

Of course by presenting the interpretations serially, something of the play is recovered, as it is, in fact, in the line that introduces the catalogue of alternative readings. 'Yet some affirm, pretending art' (13). Is it the 'some' who pretend art, that is, claim a skill in the art of interpretation they do not have; or is it Clora, pretending artfully to feel grief and to mourn? In the absence of clear direction, it is both and the spectre of art – of everything that is contrived, forced, limiting, and corrupting (see 'The Mower Against Gardens') – hangs over the tableaux that succeed Clora's carefully composed *pietà*. First there is the Clora who cries only in order to soften her bosom in anticipation of another dart sent by Cupid : 'Only to soften near her heart / A place to fix another wound' (15–16). Then there is Clora 'within her solitary bow'r' (18) inseminating herself with the semen of her tears: 'She courts herself in am'rous rain; / Herself both Danae and the show'r' (19–20). (She has untied herself from all external connections and needs; she is parthenogenetic, and the perfect emblem of self-sufficiency; she is Narcissus successful, looking into the mirror of her own tears and achieving union with herself.) Then there is the Clora who cries because her devotion to joy is so complete that she must expel even the signs of grief : 'That whatever does but seem / Like grief, is from her windows thrown' (23–4). And finally there is the Clora who empties her tear ducts of grief at the death of Strephon because she has already found his replacement. She might seem to be paying tribute to her 'dead love', but she 'casts abroad these donatives, / At the installing of a new' (27–8).

In the concluding two stanzas the first-person voice enters the poem more strongly than he has before. He dismisses all the interpretations ('How wide they dream') and declares that those who dive for pearl 'through seas profound' (30), seas extremely deep and unfathomable, would find Clora's tears no less unfathomable. In fact, the divers 'Would find her tears yet deeper waves / And not of one the bottom sound' (31–2). 'Sound' is both a verb and an adjective. They will not be able to sound – determine, measure – the bottom of her tears because not one of them has a sound foundation. If you think to have sounded the bottom, push on a bit further and the bottom will drop out revealing more depths, more meanings, which will in turn fail to furnish a true, final bottom.

The speaker declines to enter the game (which he has initiated). He will not offer his own candidate for bottom, and he will not enter into debates with the interpreters he finds unpersuasive: 'I yet my silent judgment keep, / Disputing not what they believe' (33–4). He mimes the posture of his unfathomable subjects; he won't say yes, he won't say no; he remains out of reach. There is one thing, however, of which he is 'sure', a word that names everything this poem will not deliver: 'But sure as oft as women weep, / It is to be supposed they grieve' (35–6). Marvell is still playing with us. Is 'sure as oft as women weep' merely a commonplace: it is certainly the case that women weep; or is the assertion that because women weep so often, we can assume that their weeping is a device? This second reading is strengthened by 'supposed'. Supposing, not knowing, has been the repeated action of the poem, an action unchecked by any reality that is not itself a supposition. Maybe women grieve, maybe they don't. Who's to tell? Not this speaker or this poem; both remain spectacularly unreadable even as they invite reading by asking the unanswerable question – the question that animates interpretation – what does this mean?

FIFTEEN

On the Value of the *Town-Bayes*

DAVID A. BREWER

Well mightst thou scorn thy readers to allure	45
With tinkling rhyme, of thine own sense secure;	
While the *Town-Bayes* writes all the while and spells,	
And like a pack-horse tires without his bells.	
Their fancies like our bushy points appear,	
The poets tag them; we for fashion wear.	50
I too, transported by the mode, offend,	
And while I meant to *praise* thee must *commend*.	
Thy verse created like thy theme sublime,	
In number, weight, and measure, needs not rhyme.	

Andrew Marvell, 'On Mr Milton's *Paradise Lost*', 45–54[1]

Most late seventeenth-century poems about the literary world, or the experience of reading contemporary literature, conjure up a figure like 'the *Town-Bayes*' in order to make their point. Whether praising or jeering or simply surveying, writing verse about the Restoration literary scene seems to have routinely required the invocation of a few stock authorial types: the bawdy wit (or would-be wit), the scandalous woman writer, the inordinately praised courtier, and, of course, 'Bayes', the ambitious, yet hapless playwright made famous by *The Rehearsal*. In the vast majority of these poems, the type or types in question are placed almost ostentatiously beyond sympathy. No one cares, or even momentarily thinks of caring, about the inner life or felt experience of figures like the 'Charming Strephon', whose 'Monthly Flow'rs discharg'd abroad' are 'full, brim full, of Past'rall and Ode'.[2] Whether they're named generically, like Strephon or Bayes, or properly, like 'Denham, that limping old bard', authors are treated in these texts as if they were simply personifications of value (or the lack thereof).[3] They're persons only in the anthropological, largely Maussian sense of conditions in which a person in the ordinary humanist sense could be clad, but which pre-existed and often outlasted their particular occupant. Such beings neither have, nor allegedly need, any sort of depth or felt humanity.

What sets Andrew Marvell's 1674 'On Paradise Lost' apart from its contemporaries is the vicarious experience it offers readers of what it must have been like to be treated this way, and to occupy the impossible position of a figure like 'the *Town-Bayes*'.[4] The poem (quite shrewdly) goes about this project in a very unobtrusive way: after all, no one likes to think of himself as such a being, and so the prospect of temporarily inhabiting 'his' place in the literary field would be unlikely to recommend either the poet or his exaltation of Milton to potential readers. Nonetheless, if we look closely (closer than simple comprehension of the grounds on which Milton is being praised would ever require), it quickly becomes evident that almost every line somehow stumbles or otherwise begins to go off the proverbial rails. That is, 'On Paradise Lost' sounds like what one would say if one wanted to laud Milton's accomplishment: it hails 'his vast design', his inclusion of all 'that could be fit' and exclusion of 'all that was improper', the 'majesty' that runs throughout his work, the sublimity of his treatment of 'things divine' (2, 27–8, 31, 33). And yet as soon as one subjects 'On Paradise Lost' to the kind of scrutiny that it suggests ought to be paid to *Paradise Lost*, it becomes immediately apparent that the authorial persona of the poem has bitten off more than he can chew.

Consider only the first five lines: 'When I beheld the poet blind, yet bold, / In slender book his vast design unfold, / Messiah crowned, God's reconciled decree, / Rebelling Angels, the Forbidden Tree, / Heaven, Hell, Earth, Chaos, all; the argument'. This seems a clear attempt to imitate Miltonic style, what with the opening echo of Sonnet 16 ('When I consider how my light is spent'), the extensive use of enjambment, the ever-growing list of what is encompassed by 'his vast design'. But the artfulness of the ventriloquism is immediately called into question by how the list trails off, ending first with the almost desperate expansion of the epic's scope to 'all' (which is at once redundant and untrue), and then apparently adding 'the argument' as a further item in the list, which suggests – however inaccurately and momentarily – that the author of 'On Paradise Lost' was so awestruck by the comparatively pedestrian summary, added at the bookseller's behest, of what the 'first book proposes, ... in brief', that he stopped reading before he even got to Milton's verse.[5] Now the next line clarifies the situation, as does the semi-colon, if one is carefully attending to such things: 'the argument' is actually the subject of a new clause, rather than an ill-considered further extension of the opening list. But the damage is done. On its own, this sort of bungling might not seem very consequential, but, as often occurs at such moments, once one notices one infelicity, it becomes hard not to notice several others, both going forward and retroactively. Accordingly, on revisiting these lines, we might pick up on how the alliteration draws together 'beheld' and 'blind', even though their sense would push them in opposite directions; or scratch our heads at how the 'vast design' is being 'unfold[ed]' in a 'slender book' comprised of little but folded sheets of paper; or recall that, in *Paradise Lost*, 'design' is a word invariably associated with Satan, and 'vast' often hovers in his vicinity.

A similar array of inadvertently faint praise can be seen in the famous comparison of Milton to Samson offered in the closing lines of the first paragraph. The persona claims to momentarily 'misdoubt' Milton's 'intent', and so (groundlessly) fear 'that he would ruin (for I saw him strong) / The sacred truths to fable and old song, / (So Sampson groped the temple's posts in spite) / The world o'erwhelming to revenge his sight' (6–10). Milton's work is here being acclaimed through allusion: by aligning one sightless, yet all the more powerful smiter of the Philistines with another, the persona seems to imply that whatever anger one detects in *Paradise Lost* – say, the lines about being 'fallen on evil days' (7.25) – is a righteous and admirable fury. Yet the language he employs to conjure up the parallel with Samson ends up working at cross-purposes with itself. 'Blind', 'ruin', 'groped', 'spite', 'revenge': this is hardly the diction likely to rally readers to Milton's side. Indeed, at least two of these terms had been used the previous year to denounce Milton: Samuel Butler mocked 'the *blind* Author of *Paradise Lost* ... groping for a beam of *Light*'.[6] It would be pretty to think that the persona was somehow attempting to reclaim this vocabulary of Royalist reproach, but it's hard to see how that could be the case: 't[aking] hold of the ... pillars', as the biblical Samson does, has the potential to be heroic; 'grop[ing]' them ... not so much.[7]

Still another display of quiet clumsiness appears in lines 31–8 of the poem. Milton is here being praised for

> That majesty which through thy work doth reign
> Draws the devout, deterring the profane.
> And things divine thou treat'st of in such state
> As them preserves, and thee, inviolate.
> At once delight and horror on us seize,
> Thou sing'st with so much gravity and ease;
> And above human flight dost soar aloft,
> With plume so strong, so equal, and so soft.

As with the other lines I've quoted, this sounds as if it comes out of a deep and appreciative engagement with *Paradise Lost*. Milton is credited with having the true majesty of self-possession, rather than the gaudy, superficial version sported by the Stuarts, and his desire to 'soar / Above the Aonian mount' is proclaimed to have been fulfilled (1.14–15). Once again, though, if we linger, we begin to notice how the praise is not as well-wrought as the situation would seem to warrant. The line about majesty is, while certainly sonorous, a tautology: of course 'majesty' 'reign[s]'; what else would it do? Similarly, the lines about soaring inadvertently weigh themselves down by stemming from the 'gravity' of Milton's song. So too does the hair standing on end which lurks etymologically behind 'horror'. And, of course, the whole point about Milton's desire to soar was to pursue 'things unattempted yet in prose or rhyme', but the echo here extols Milton's 'plume' for being 'so equal' (1.16). No doubt the persona means 'of such consistent quality', but the uninvited sense of 'on a level with its peers' evokes a situation in which Milton's ambition simply can't achieve escape velocity.

I could continue in this vein (say, to point out how the persona's complaint about 'some less skilful hand' 'show[ing]' 'the whole Creation's day' 'in scenes' seems to indict his own rapid flurry of spectacles 'beheld' [18, 21–2, 1]), but the pattern is probably clear: again and again, the persona shows himself to be a sincere admirer of Milton's, but one who isn't quite up to the task of praising him as he apparently deserves. Grasping the consequences of this pattern, however, requires a little further work on our part. In the final paragraph (the lines quoted as my epigraph), the authorial persona wants to align himself with Milton, and against 'the *Town-Bayes*' and other dedicated followers of poetic fashion. However, he concedes that, at least in the realm of rhyme, such a distinction is unsustainable – 'I too, transported by the mode, offend' – though he tries to make a witty virtue of sonic necessity: 'And while I meant to *praise* thee must *commend*'. Alas, the very lameness of the joke (and possibly its tin ear for religious politics) calls attention to all of the other ways in which he resembles 'the *Town-Bayes*'.[8] He too composes in the slightly halting manner conjured up by the metrically ungainly (and monosyllabic) 'writes all the while and spells'. He too relies upon the 'bells' and whistles of extravagant compliment and aspirational wit. Indeed, the uncertain antecedent of 'their' (in 'their fancies'), caused by the inverted syntax of that couplet, suggests – despite the counter-evidence of the singular pronouns and conjugations of the previous lines – that 'the *Town-Bayes*' may be an entire category of authors, not just a particular figure.[9] But the persona's very desire for this sort of distinction, his wish to be something other than (at best) another '*Town-Bayes*', betrays a very un-Bayesian longing and anguish, a fantasy that if only he could get out of the system in which he works, then everything would be different. That is, the sheer eagerness with which the persona embraces Milton's 'scorn' for 'tinkling rhyme', even as he nonetheless continues to write such verse, hints that, in a literary world not governed by fashion, flattery, 'ill imitating' (20), and the like (which is to say, a world other than 'the Town'), his modest talent might have been able to flourish. A world in which an author as singular as Milton had a place is thus, for the persona, itself a lost Eden, and one whose disappearance has not even yielded the recompense of 'a paradise within …, happier far' (12.587).

Such nostalgia for a vanished literary culture isn't, of course, all that unusual in the decades following the Restoration. After all, even John Dryden, the archetypal '*Town-Bayes*' and 'tagge[r]' of Milton's 'verses', looked back longingly towards 'the Gyant Race, before the Flood'.[10] But to make room in that sweeping division of literary history for an author of such mediocre abilities as the persona of this poem, much less to make him at least wanly sympathetic, is an accomplishment indeed: one comparable, in its own quiet way, to Milton's ability to allow us to momentarily imagine life before the Fall. Nowhere else do we get such an unobtrusively poignant sense of the costs of the new literary system fostered by the growth of 'the Town', a system whose dominance would not be seriously challenged for upwards of a century. Nowhere else do we get anything like this view from within the often abject, and always less than fully human kinds of personhood accorded to authors in the brave new world of Restoration wit.

SIXTEEN

Pointless Milton: A Close Reading in Negative

NICHOLAS D. NACE

With thee conversing I forget all time,
All seasons and their change, all please alike.   640
Sweet is the breath of morn, her rising sweet,
With charm of earliest birds; pleasant the sun
When first on this delightful land he spreads
His orient beams, on herb, tree, fruit, and flower,
Glistering with dew; fragrant the fertile earth   645
After soft showers; and sweet the coming on
Of grateful evening mild, then silent night
With this her solemn bird and this fair moon,
And these the gems of heaven, her starry train:
But neither breath of morn when she ascends   650
With charm of earliest birds, nor rising sun
On this delightful land, nor herb, fruit, flower,
Glistering with dew, nor fragrance after showers,
Nor grateful evening mild, nor silent night
With this her solemn bird, nor walk by moon,   655
Or glittering starlight without thee is sweet.
But wherefore all night long shine these, for whom
This glorious sight, when sleep hath shut all eyes?
John Milton, *Paradise Lost*, 4.639–58[1]

This speech uttered by Eve in Book 4 of *Paradise Lost* constitutes
for Milton the first attempt by a human to compose what we
now call poetry. Although the blank-verse lyric contained in this
passage – the sixteen lines from 641 to 656 beginning and ending
with 'sweet' – is commonly referred to as 'Eve's love song', and

less commonly as her 'hymn' or 'aria', Milton presents no evidence that these lines were sung. Yet somehow terms of music feel appropriate to describe the *en rondeau* movements of what appears to be organised sound with little organised sense, phrases with no necessary logical relationship or graspable content – nor even any anticipation, climax, or release except what syntax alone provides. There is no urgency in the lyric's overelaborated phrases, no pressure of event. It draws us along only by giving us the feeling that Eve indeed is building towards an ever more grammatically complete utterance, however delayed and modest that utterance's predication ultimately is. The stretched forward nine-line first half picks up speed and slows down in response to the burden of cataloguing, then ponderously turns, at line 650, to repeat its elements as a kind of *da capo* during the poem's compressed and reordered second half. Even in the resounding of its echoes in that second half its language is crisp, clean, contained, with virtually none of the pop and crackle of language's potential beneath the literal meaning of its sentences. As a performance, the inset lyric proves lavishly dull and dispassionately passionate; as an act of communication, its equipoise sets it apart from the content-rich *recitativo* of the two two-line sentences immediately before and after it (and as I hope to show, those four humbly meaningful lines offer a great deal more to make our minds vibrate with intellection than the lyric itself does).

Poems and songs are both performances of sound – in Milton's 'At a Solemn Music' 'voice and verse' are 'harmonious sisters' – but if Eve's lyric constitutes a song, it proves to be one perhaps by the same logic Edmund Waller uses to characterise the dramatic songs of the 1680s: 'Soft words, with nothing in them, make a song'. Eve's mercurial, self-referential lyric sentence, set off and apart by 'sweet', shrinks at both ends and coheres only to itself. It presents to us precious little of what we talk about when we talk about poetry, yet its aesthetic success cannot be denied. After all, it appears in *The 100 Best Love Poems of All Time* (it is fifth). Poems usually have 'content', perhaps even an 'argument', as each book of *Paradise Lost* has. They generally have a point. While Eve does offer lines, I believe those lines have no real point, though they can be used to make points intertextually. The lyric is beautiful, but entirely repetitive and self-cancelling. How, then, can we read its beauty – or even explain why it seems beautiful in the first place? I believe this can be done by performing a kind of negative close reading, by showing all the expected things that are not there.

A deflated paraphrase of Eve's lone assertion would run 'life is only sweet when we are together'; but even this dewy-eyed proclamation is a product only of perception, the display of which constitutes her only proof. The presence and distribution of value in the world is dependent on the perspective of the viewer, she might be suggesting, which proves ominously similar to Satan's 'The mind is its own place, and in itself / Can make a heaven of hell, a hell of heaven' (1.254–5). Satan later finds himself 'undelighted' by all Eden's 'delights', which possibly proves the point that Eve never truly makes or supports. On its own, Eve's assertion is not falsifiable because she does not know life apart from Adam; she registers sweet perception even in its imagined absence, which renders her point nugatory. The lyric disproves whatever it might be said to prove, but in the meantime it exists, giving us experience without information, making us forget our fallen state. It may be the only poem pure enough to prove Archibald MacLeish's dictum in 'Ars Poetica' that 'A poem should not mean / But be'.

Granting Eve's speech its ontological integrity as a poem, we might still wonder what kind of poem can offer such pointless intricacy. But here lies the problem, and the perfection, of what Eve has framed as 'sweet'. It is a song, a sonnet, a loco-descriptive poem, a list, an aubade fanned by the 'breath of morn', a paean to Adam; yet it is not a song, a sonnet, a list, a loco-descriptive poem, an aubade fanned by the 'breath of morn', or a paean to Adam. Or not *precisely*. It offers parallelism, but is not parallel. It feels balanced, but proves top-heavy by two lines (and one 'tree' that has no antipodean mate). The whole feels rhyme-like in its repetitions, and indeed it rhymes at 'flower' and 'showers' and mellifluously runs together soft *w*, *s* and *m* sounds, but this is not true rhyme. Words repeat, but not exactly: 'fragrant' and 'starry' go into the turn but come out differently on the other side, as 'fragrance' and 'starlight'; the 'rising' of morn in the first half becomes paraphrased as 'ascends'. Even its modest syntactic climax is diminished by the fact that the poem's final line gives us an 'Or' that does and does not continue the pattern with 'neither ... nor ... nor', though mere sound affords that continuation by stealing a slow-moving 'n' from 'moon'. Eve ostensibly praises Adam with her poem, but in it he is effectively forgotten; the 'with thee' that hails him *precedes* the start of the lyric and only seems to balance the whole poem by the final line's 'without thee', though this return to earlier grammar is not jarring. Eve describes a world that is not sweet in language that is unrelentingly sweet. In its grammar as well as its general comportment Eve's lyric follows the logic of 'is and is not': it comes perilously close to being something recognisable, but always veers off into idiosyncrasy.

Here Eve presents herself as a different kind of poet from the author of *Paradise Lost*. Despite the cerebral toughness that Milton's verse routinely demonstrates, his definition of poetry in *Of Education* does not demand that poems have points of the kind we find throughout *Paradise Lost*, whether of argument ('shall thou dispute / With him the points of liberty' [5.822–3]), or aim ('That spot to which I point is Paradise' [3.733]), or, what comes closest to what Eve offers, indexical reference ('each place behold / In prospect as I point them' [12.142–3]). When Milton compares verse to the other 'organic arts' – the bare-knuckle stance of logic or the flowering palm of rhetoric – he asks only that poetry be 'simple, sensuous, passionate'.[2] Simple in its complex evacuation of content, sensuous in its appeal to each of the five senses, passionate in its elegiac stance on the pastness of the present: Eve's poem relentlessly satisfies this definition and does no more. It is full of nothing, finally, but the shifting densities of consciousness itself as Eve appreciates the world's sweetness. In a way it *is* sweetness.

Furthermore it is *only* sweetness. Those who wish to lick the sugar off this poem will find that they have nothing left. But we have no way of talking about sweetness beyond labelling it. Many savvy readers fall into inarticulate appreciation before Eve's poem.

It is, they say, 'pleasing', 'moving', 'exquisite', and – befitting the synaesthesia of the poem's own melodious 'sweets' – 'delicious'. The passage has been deemed simply 'beautiful' by nearly every reader who has stopped to admire it: Addison and Steele (separately) praise its 'beauty', as do Abigail Adams, Walter Scott, and John Lubbock. Gray invokes it in his 'Ode on Music'; Gay, in his *Trivia*. Cowper reduces its empty grandeurs to a mock-lyric in *The Task*. Wordsworth, Keats and Byron echo its phrases in complex post-lapsarian contexts. Yet few contemporary readers of this passage are content to appreciate Eve's beautiful pointlessness or the way we experience it; most find its meaning everywhere but in the lines themselves.

The poem has for centuries been frisked by critics in order to reveal concealed allusions that might help make extrinsic sense of it. Not surprisingly, many analogues have been found – or planted. Among them, Daphnis's songs in Theocritus's *Idylls* 8 and 9; Thyrsis's catalogue of poplar, pine, and ash in Virgil's *Eclogue* 7; the Bible's Song of Songs 2:17 and Ecclesiastes 11:7; the keenly perceived beauty of sunlight in fragment 316 of Eurpides' *Danae*; William Drummond's 'The Sun is fair'. L. L. Martz sees in it 'a complex blending of many pastoral and Ovidian devices'.[3] James Grantham Turner ingeniously hears echoes of 'St. Augustine's meditation on the love of God as a redemptive transposition of earthly love';[4] John Leonard catches a 'jarring allusion' to Hector's farewell to Andromache in Homer's *Iliad*. We might add to this list Cowley's agon between beauty and absence in 'The Spring'. Judging from this history, there was never such an allusive passage in all of literature.[5]

And there never was. Eve's deeply original poem is as unlike all those passages as it is like them. Our experience of it has nothing to do with recall. Such resourcefulness in finding allusions is our way of looking past its 'beauty' and peering into the safely echoing chasm of literary history. If this passage did not flaunt its uniqueness, one might look for echoes in Milton's own works. Perhaps it sounds a bit like the songs of *Comus*'s Lady. If it accords with anything in *Paradise Lost* itself, perhaps it suggests some affinity with what the 'Celestial Patronness' might produce had she employed an unfallen amanuensis. However, resemblances that are not obvious in the poem evidently pose a problem for the beauties that are.

When we try to bring the uniqueness of our experience reading Eve's poem into analytical consciousness, our critical vocabulary proves impoverished. If we wished to identify in it recognisable techniques, we might say it relies on the rhetorical figures of *hyperbaton*, *enumeratio* or *cancrizone*. And so on. Most significantly the whole poem constitutes an *epanalepsis*, or, more accurately, a double *epanalepsis*, since both the first line and the whole sentence share the same structure of beginning and ending with 'sweet', the evaluative label under which all the objects and phenomena of Eden are subsumed. The first line does in miniature what the rest do on a larger scale, and 'sweet' occurs, pointlessly, twice between. The resulting feeling that these lines form a self-contained unit prompts some critics to characterise these 16 lines as a 'sonnet'.[6] But classifying them, if anything, deadens us to the effects of beauty that are their sole purpose.

So how *do* we read beauty? We must account for how Eve, and through her Milton, empties language to make 'pleasant' phenomena feel coherent but weightless and easy. We must examine what is not present that, if it were, would impede our appreciation of how blissful perception itself was in pre-lapsarian Eden. We must read the poem in negative. Fortunately Eve facilitates this with the two lines before and after the lyric. We can pick at her poem's edges in order to feel the kind of poetry it is not:

> With thee conversing I forget all time,
> All seasons and their change, all please alike.

'Conversing' has more lexical potential than any word in the lyric, suggesting movement, dwelling, turning over, time and versification, as well as various kinds of verbal and physical intercourse. 'I forget all time' means 'I lose track of time', although in the emergent elliptical assertion 'I forget … all seasons and their change', 'seasons' requires some sorting out. Some editors peremptorily gloss 'seasons' as 'time of day', although most readers surely think of 'seasons and their change' as solstitial/equinoctial change, even though it is 'spring perpetual' in Eden. This word demands a mental workout, even if we do not realise it. The final 'all' prepares us for a continuation of the series established by 'all time' and 'all seasons', but it is controlled by 'please', not 'forget'. We do not know which components this final 'all' refers to, although it means something like 'everything', or, given the interactive sense of 'conversing', perhaps 'all individuals' (*OED s.v.* 'all' adj. 6). And 'pleasing alike' echoes the even reciprocity of 'conversing' while giving extra connection between the near synonyms 'please' and 'like'. Richness of this kind is everywhere in *Paradise Lost* – everywhere *but* Eve's poem.

On the other end, lines 657–8 constitute a question that, after the dilation of the preceding lyric, seems sudden and unexpected:

> But wherefore all night long shine these, for whom
> This glorious sight, when sleep hath shut all eyes?

It would change our view of Eve to see the foregoing poem as rhetorical set-up intended to soften the transgression of her first seeking of knowledge – an act that, it would transpire, forms the seed of tragedy. Not only does Eve's sense of awe return her to prosaic language in which poetic effect and childlike wonder co-exist, but line 657 reads as if it *is* prose, until one reaches the bracingly iambic 'for whom'. We do not know what entity 'these' signals, though we supplement shiny things – stars, 'moon', 'gems of heaven' – before the whole host of earlier referents is composed into a singular 'sight'. Furthermore, 'sight' and 'eyes' are an obvious ideational pair operating unexpectedly: 'sight' here means something like 'scene'. Eve's style outside her lyric offers the typical sorts of effect that the hard-working lines of Milton generally offer.

Without the support provided by communicative content or non-substantive verbal meanings, the lyric bound by these braces of lines stands full of meaningless coherence. The only non-substantive verbal meaning I can point to in the lyric is the 'delightful land' that, with the sense of subtraction in its prefix 'de-', might imply a relevantly dark or unlit place. There is also a possible but profoundly unlikely sense of 'showers' meaning 'labour-pains' (*OED s.v.* 'shower' n1 5b) that picks up some small amount of progenitive energy from 'fertile' and 'grate' of line 647's two feet 'of grateful eve-' (which also slyly describes the attitude of its speaker), then resolves with 'coming on'. My point in looking so hard for typical poetic effects is that they are few and feeble. Milton, of course, is not perfect.

So how, then, does this poem attempt to produce 'delight' that is correlative to Eve's, if not by the usual poetic means? It does this by making distinctions that do not matter, by making distinction itself not matter. Take, for instance, distinctions between the senses. There is in the poem a great deal of synaesthesia, the process whereby one sense attempts to explain a phenomenon to another. Every recounted object that composes the 'sight' of Eden proves 'sweet', though Eve does not recount any tasting, even of the esculent 'herb' and 'fruit' sandwiched between 'tree' and 'flower'. While it is hard to tell what entity in this catalogue is 'glistering with dew', and even harder to tell when the sun exerts itself on these moistened entities, we easily perceive that all the senses are engaged: 'glistering' is to sight as 'fragrant' is to smell as 'soft' is to touch as 'sweet' is to taste; 'silent' night, opposed to the 'charm'-filled morning, invokes hearing. Moreover, 'glistering' and 'glittering' are words that convey the reflection of light though their very sound. Though he rejects the viability of 'pure' poetry where phonosymbolism would reign, William Empson's description of the synaesthesia that such poetry would necessitate perfectly describes Eve's lyric: 'It throws back the reader upon the undifferentiated affective states which are all that such sensations have in common; perhaps recalls him to an infantile state before they had been distinguished from one another'.[7] Milton gives us this glimpse of an 'infantile state', though in phylogenetic terms, through Eve's pre-lapsarian perception, where all 'delight' is achingly 'sweet'.

The sense of time also does not matter as the sun 'spreads' across the catalogued 'herb, tree, fruit, and flower'. Syntax and sequence are at odds, but not in tension. The catalogue tries to slow the sentence down; the sentence tries to speed the catalogue up. It breaks rhythm with its plodding staccato monosyllables. However, unlike most other nouns in this sentence – such as 'breath', 'beams', and 'Sun' – these items are as concrete as they are concretely felt in the meter. 'After soft showers', arriving on the heels of 'fragrant' and 'fertile', asks one only to think of 'rain showers', even though the 'orient Beams' of the sun in the lines directly before are a related kind of shower ('a copious downfall of anything' [*OED s.v.* 'shower' n1 1c]). The move from dry showers to wet occurs as a casual connection between things that, though they both come to the earth from the sky, are opposed. The cycles of sunshine and rain are contracted like the cycles of time. Distinctions are made between night and day, and even between the three disordered phases of daybreak – pre-dawn ('the breath of morn'), first light ('When first … he spreads / His orient beams'), and sunrise ('rising') – but those distinctions likewise do not matter. In the final line, 'moon / Or glittering starlight' only feels as if it had given us an alternative between moonlight and starlight. Distinctions and disjunctions evanesce; all is coherent with the unity of bliss.

That feeling of coherence is the real achievement, especially considering that entire phrases could fall out without changing the meaning or meter. (Would there be a difference if the first line were to read 'Sweet is the breath of morn; pleasant the sun'?) Even the basic distinction of lineation often does not matter. Eve confers metrical coherence on these pentameter lines, but solidifies that coherence even further by overlapping pentameters, a not uncommon phenomenon in *Paradise Lost* that occurs with uncommon frequency here (eight times). The phrases cohere as pentameters within lines and as shadow pentameters across lines: 'her rising sweet, / With charm of earliest birds'; 'nor rising sun / On this delightful land'. The poem's first half offers trochaic inversions ('*Glis*tring', '*pleas*ant', '*fra*grant') that, when iambic meter resumes, give the effect of delay between the two stresses, which causes the second stress – and the pattern – to feel stronger. Weightless coherence increasingly resembles firmness. The first half feels more definite, containing as it does four instances of the definite article; the second half does not use 'the' once, repeating the first half without even the modest sense of movement and time passing in 'coming on', 'then' and 'after'.

In the long division of Eve's lines, an almost zero–sum equation is produced. Nothing carries over into it except 'with thee'; everything but 'tree' is cancelled out. Thought and afterthought are locked together into exaggerated self-dependency. Eve's poetry is language purified of meaning. It is pure aesthetic affect, like a sky full of fireworks, flashing and burning out in an ashless instant, consumed with those forms it was nourished by. It asks us only for a brief time to experience.

Close Rereading

SEVENTEEN

Marlowe's Will, Marlowe's Shall

DREW DANIEL

> *Si peccasse negamus, fallimur, et nulla est in nobis veritas*
> If we say that we have no sin,
> We deceive ourselves, and there's no truth in us.
> Why then belike we must sin,
> And so consequently die.   45
> Ay, we must die an everlasting death.
> What doctrine call you this? *Che serà, serà*:
> What will be, shall be! Divinity, adieu!
>   Christopher Marlowe, *Doctor Faustus*, 1.41–8[1]

Marlowe begins *Doctor Faustus* with an exemplary scene depicting the high stakes of close reading. Turning to theology after offering tartly pre-emptive rejections of logic, medicine, and law, Faustus picks up the Vulgate Bible of Saint Jerome, reads a passage out loud, comments upon it, and then disavows divinity with a flippant fare-well. As every schoolchild knows – because every schoolteacher and editor tells her – Faustus precipitously cuts off the text of the First Epistle of John before John can offer him forgiveness for the confession of sins, in the process committing a sophistry known as 'the devil's syllogism'.[2] But rather than flag what is missing from the text, I wish to tarry with what remains stubbornly present within it. Specifically, I want to bear down upon the final two lines of this passage, and to read as carefully, closely, and exclusively as I can a single, nagging discrepancy perched there: Faustus's translation of '*Che serà, serà*' as 'What will be, shall be'.

Sound familiar? '*Che serà, serà*' has entered the bloodstream of our culture, travelling from the Wittenberg study of Doctor

Faustus into the mouth of Doris Day, in the form of the anthem 'Que Sera, Sera', written by Jay Livingston and Ray Evans, and pounded out *ad nauseam* during Alfred Hitchcock's 1956 film *The Man Who Knew Too Much*. The clean snap of the phrase is crucial to its viral power. Proverbial tags often hinge upon a noticeably dramatic near-similarity; Cicero's alleged '*Dum Spiro, Spero*' (while I breathe, I hope), a rewrite of a phrase from his letters to Atticus, offers a case in point, and the old Italian saw '*Traduttore, traditore*' (Translator, traitor) another. But in contrast to '*Dum Spiro, Spero*' and '*Traduttore, traditore*', the parallel lines of '*Che serà, serà*' run in the opposite direction, producing not a pleasingly total difference from a slight orthographic swerve, but tattooing instead a dramatically exact and precise repetition. A foundling with an odd formulation, the phrase itself sounds suspect, as '*Che serà, serà*' is not necessarily idiomatic in Italian, in which one would render 'Whatever will be, will be' as '*quello che sarà, sarà*'. That said, given both the chaotic textual history of *Faustus*, and the uncertain orthography of the period, a printing house misprint of '*serà*' for '*sarà*' is entirely possible.

Spelled either way, what is the source and origin of this phrase? After rifling through Erasmus and other proverbial sources, and consulting with Italian speakers and colleagues, I have yet to strike paydirt with a concrete origin that precedes its appearance in this text. Did Marlowe coin it? Perhaps. Perhaps not. An honestly provisional answer is simply that, whether or not Marlowe coined this particular phrase, other proverbial, repetitive declarations of the future's identity with itself certainly do pre-date this one. In the midst of a description of the skirmish at Slioch in John Barbour's martial epic poem *The Bruce* (1375), we find the declaration that 'Thai wald defend vailye que vailye'.[3] This intrusion of Old French into the Scottish text tells us that what may come is what may come. Both Barbour's proverb and Marlowe's proverb share a noticeably doubled shape, which acoustically and typographically enforces the self-similarity of what is to come, yet also locates that eerie absolute in a virtual futurity that the speaker of the proverb cannot access in the deictic present of their delivery. Like all tautologies, the claim necessarily proves its truth at the cost of a nagging triviality: X = X. Though the phrase cannot fail to work upon its own pronouncement, the soft double gong of prophecy sounded by the phrase induces a curious mixture of certainty and ignorance: half sagacity, half childish obviousness.

But where the Italian phrase produces this effect by repeating *precisely* the same phrase twice, Faustus's English translation makes a change, inserting a certain flick of the wrist. Faced with '*Che serà, serà*', one might translate the words into English as 'whatever will be, will be' or 'whatever shall be, shall be'. Returning to the phrase several plays later into his meteoric career, Marlowe himself opted for the latter in *Edward II*, when Edward declares 'Well, that shall be shall be; part we must' (4.4.94). Marlowe might have had Faustus say something like that, but he did not. Instead, Faustus hops the rails from 'will' to 'shall': 'What will be, shall be'. What are we to make of this small but obvious difference between Italian source and English translation? What might have been at stake for Marlowe in assigning to Faustus this momentary flyspeck of deliberate deviation? What abides here on the page within the chasm between 'shall' and 'will'?

If we exit the text in search of broader intellectual backgrounds in order to determine what is really at stake at this moment in the play, we are faced with incongruous options: we can pursue the question by way of religious philosophy, and inquire into Christian theologies of predestination and divine omniscience and their complex relationship with fatalistic philosophies of determinism. When coloured by this context, 'will' becomes accordingly saturated with voluntarist associations (the scale of the human, the personal, the sinful privacy of passion, etc.). By contrast, 'shall' shifts registers towards the deontic absolutes of commandment: 'Thou shalt not'. To assert the fusion of 'will' and 'shall' is to reconcile conflicting scales and to bring rival perspectives into perfect synthetic submission: ideally, to harmonise what 'I' will with what God declares shall be so.

Alternately, one can pursue the question by way of the history of grammar, and inquire into the usage of English modal auxiliary verbs as related yet distinct operators within a changing, slippery syntax. In this case, 'will' and 'shall' are both examples of a class of modal verbs alongside 'can', 'may', and 'must' which necessarily precede other verbs because of their peculiarly defective morphology (there is no infinitive of the form 'to shall'). Semantically, both 'will' and 'shall' are sufficiently flexible to convey the obligation to do something or to simply manifest the dynamic capacity to do something.[4] Both 'you shall go to the ball' and 'you will go to the ball' sound equally imperative if delivered in the right tone of voice; both 'I shall go to the ball' and 'I will go to the ball' sound equally declarative, particularly if one stomps one's foot while saying them. Local context is key in determining how differently these words are being used. Grammar alone doesn't provide a strong means to draw out the difference, though it flags their tendencies to diverge.

Having ventured outside the text, can we honestly choose between these rival generalities: working from God downwards, or working from words upwards? To take any stand in a methodological contest between the metaphysics of freedom and the grammar of acceptable moves in English is itself to beg the question about their disjunctive relation or conceptual priority, and neither is quite as helpful to the task of a 'close' reading of Marlowe as we would like. For even if one could show that most Protestants held a particular view about 'fate' or the relationship between divine omniscience and personal freedom, one would still struggle to verify that Marlowe was one of those Protestants (or even, necessarily, a Protestant, or even a believer, at all). And even if one could show that many users of English in the period did – or did not – differentiate between 'will' and 'shall' with the clarity of which syntactical grammarians are now capable, one would still struggle to verify that Marlowe was always or only occasionally such a user of English, or that their general rules fit his specific context.

This is because dramatic speech starts at the level of the character. If 'will and shall best fitteth Tamburlaine' (Part 1, 3.3.41), that may well prove that Tamburlaine likes using both verbs and doesn't much care to distinguish between them; but it does not demonstrate that Marlowe could not and did not. In any case, where the translation of '*Che serà, serà*' is concerned, the translator here is not Marlowe, but, specifically, Faustus. And so, focusing down to this humbler level of magnitude, let us look at 'will' and 'shall' within the speech of Faustus himself to see how these words function as a pair. Looking only within the very same opening act, we can see that Faustus regularly shifts from one verb to the other, even within the same sentence:

> How am I glutted with conceit of this!
> Shall I make spirits fetch me what I please,
> Resolve me of all ambiguities,
> Perform what desperate enterprise I will?

> (1.78–81)

The first 'shall' commences a question of the form 'should I do this?', though it is not quite a sincere sounding of the moral question 'ought I to do this?' The final 'will' is an index of desire rather than possibility, and it carries over from the wilful image of spirits fetching 'what I please'; though the interrogative form persists, the sound of the phrase 'I will' seems at the sonic level to perhaps answer the initial question – shall I? – in the affirmative. Faustus knows enough of himself to know that he is 'glutted with conceit', and hints to himself of the insubstantiality of his own desires in the *quodlibet* openness of the phrase 'what I please'. Faustus's easy deployment of both in the same sentence, beginning with one and ending with the other, neatly indexes both the proximity and the faint, lingering difference between 'shall' and 'will' within Faustus's mind at this point in the play. 'Will' connotes what is voluntary and desired; 'Shall' connotes what is possible, but also shades into the moral evaluation of what one should or should not do.

With at least this minimal contextual precedent of the tethered-yet-distinct pairing of meanings in mind, let us return to the lines in question and listen to them again:

Si peccasse negamus, fallimur, et nulla est in nobis veritas
If we say that we have no sin,
We deceive ourselves, and there's no truth in us.
Why then belike we must sin,
And so consequently die.
Ay, we must die an everlasting death.
What doctrine call you this? *Che serà, serà*:
What will be, shall be! Divinity, adieu!

(1.41–8)

The forceful entry of modality as a grammatical mode into the passage starts with the two 'must's – the declaration that 'we must sin' follows from the fact of Original Sin, and the declaration that 'we must die' follows from our mortal nature. And those 'must's voice predictions about future outcomes that create an overarching sensation of compulsion, sucking the life out of the room with the related, shaming facts of death and sin, effectively creating an inclusive 'we' that links the speaker and the audience together in a perceptual community bound together by the force of Faustus's declarations. This chain of thought proceeds to colour the encounter with the proverb itself: but still, since a repetition of either verb would still enforce the same grinding sense of obligation and certainty, then, to repeat, why jump from 'what will be' to 'shall be' when translating that proverb?

The first half refers to what is going to happen – it will be the case that X – while the sound of the 'shall' – it shall be the case that X – faintly approximates a conciliatory declaration that it 'should' or 'ought' to happen. Thus the proverb, in being spoken, models a kind of performatively self-sufficient divine decree; in voicing it, Faustus appropriates the fiat reserved for creators, law-givers, and sovereigns. The feeling of an instantaneously effective power bestowed by the formal self-proof of the tautology is a kind of trial run for the equally auto-legitimating performative speech acts implicit in the ceremonial magic, invocations, and pacts to come. As Mephastophilis knows, the terrible irony here is that Faustus believes that his blasphemies literally make their theological outcomes the case; in committing 'the unpardonable sin', he thinks that he has touched the wires of possibility and certainty together, negatively fusing them by absolutely ensuring that what he wills – the selling of his soul – has the power to determine what shall be the case in the future – his damnation. The text, of course, never ceases to present the audience member or reader with counter-factual reminders of other possibilities, even up to the closing Choral announcement that: 'Cut is the branch that might have grown full straight' (13.112). The force of that modal 'might have' seems to repudiate the very tautological certainty that Faustus struggles to marshal here in the opening scene. But Faustus has already ruined the self-confirming effectiveness of the Italian tautology by rendering it into English as not-quite-tautological, thus fatally weakening its power to be self-legitimating.

The tiny hop from 'will' to 'shall' within these two final lines signals the necessarily fraught relationship between translation and interpretation, a tension with local consequences for Faustus's character, and a specific case of a general problem: one cannot translate what one cannot understand, except in a literal and piecemeal fashion that would morcellate the meaning – but all rephrasing introduces change and in doing so raises the spectre of falsification, erasure, and drift. To translate is to betray, and we can see this not only in the jump from the Italian '*Che serà, serà*' to its un-faithful English near counterpart, but in the farewell moment of literary translation within this passage, the very last two words: 'Divinity, adieu!' This phrase at once says 'Divinity, goodbye' and, more literally 'Divinity, go to God', a howler of an English/French pun that suggests that Marlowe wants us to notice Faustus's wobbly *tour de force* as a distinctly unreliable display of scholarly code-switching. The comedy of this gratuitous advice offers a neat rebuke to the person of the Divinity, and to 'Divinity' as an academic subject in one curt gesture; but its elision of the two goes deeper. It bespeaks a broader incapacity to draw distinction between the mastery of a subject on the page and the mastery of the terrains and dimensions which academic subjects purport to explain, and by explaining regulate.

This scene offers a hyperbolic example of a choice faced by every interpreter: the choice between a 'conservative' literary criticism which acts (or at least sees itself) as a steward of the best case for the meaning of the words upon the page, and a more 'liberal' habit of literary criticism which interprets, torques, and manipulates the text on behalf of some ancillary objective or interest. Of the latter party, Faustus is hardly a disinterested reader of Jerome, but his translations are not only incomplete, but disastrously arrogant. Presented with a uniquely satisfying repetition, Faustus decides to overwrite the text with a gratuitous fillip of change. In that this is a scene in which someone fools himself into thinking that he is reading carefully and closely, but does not quite read carefully and closely enough to protect himself from collapsing into folly and error, we can also take this scene to demonstrate the risks of an approach to critical problems which attempts to 'Resolve ... all ambiguities' (1.80). Does this scene model the personal limits of Faustus as a close reader, or the limits of close reading itself? If Faustus is a bad close reader, can we only see this because Marlowe believed in the possibility of a good close reading, hovering with the angels at his shoulder? Or is Faustus's failure a deliberately humbling demonstration of the insufficiency of critical reading practices as such?

I can't answer these questions within this narrow space, but I have attended to this tiny flicker of difference upon Marlowe's page as a means of declaring a certain faith in the power of the textual detail, and as a means of therapeutically confessing a certain fear of the dangers produced by hasty commentary about those details. Indeed, *Doctor Faustus* offers us a worst-case scenario for the consequences of the sloppy handling of texts. How to witness the divergences of meaning within a text while manifesting a commitment to the belief that a text can still, at least, be read? Taking up this task, Stephen Booth has described his manner of commentary as 'pluralistically-committed'.[5] While I cannot hope to live up to the precision of his example, the demands placed by both halves of that fine phrase have guided me as I have tried to read Faustus reading the Bible and translating a proverb which may or may not be the creation of Christopher Marlowe.

Forced to confess where I stand on the question of how much, ultimately, to make of the difference between 'shall' and 'will' in this line, I can only assert that Marlowe's text seems to me to want us to notice that Faustus has wilfully inserted himself into and onto the text that he translates. This minimal difference flashes momentarily across the screen of the reader's mind as a noticeable event: the manhandling of a delicately symmetrical form which is taken up, toyed with, and rendered into a lopsided trophy of its translator's narcissism and overconfidence. Faustus's gratuitously scribbled wrinkle in the shades of available futurity horribly prepares us for the bad forms of certainty he is yet to inflict upon himself, while still also reminding us, against the spirit of his intentions, of the uncanny mixture of stubborn unavailability and endless pliability characteristic of futurity itself. No less than necromancy, Faustus here demonstrates that simply reading a text can indeed be a 'desperate enterprise'.

EIGHTEEN

Reading Intensity: Sonnet 12

SUSAN J. WOLFSON

12

When I do count the clock that tells the time,
And see the brave day sunk in hideous night;
When I behold the violet past prime,
And sable curls, all silver'd o'er with white;   4
When lofty trees I see barren of leaves,
Which erst from heat did canopy the herd,
And summer's green all girded up in sheaves,
Borne on the bier with white and bristly beard;   8
Then of thy beauty do I question make,
That thou among the wastes of time must go,
Since sweets and beauties do themselves forsake,
And die as fast as they see others grow;   12
    And nothing 'gainst time's scythe can make defence
    Save breed, to brave him, when he takes thee hence.
           William Shakespeare, Sonnet 12[1]

As to my own admiration for the sonnets and grounds for attempting to redefine as a strength what Ransom calls a structural weakness, I have … a critical authority not inferior to Ransom. … Keats said, 'Poetry should be great and unobtrusive, a thing which enters into one's soul, and does not startle it or amaze it with itself, but with its subject.' … an ultimate purpose of this essay is to establish that the sonnets fit Keats' word 'unobtrusive' and his demand that a poem amaze the soul not with itself but with its subject.

        Stephen Booth, *An Essay on Shakespeare's Sonnets*[2]

Keats's vigorous insistence on 'unobtrusive' affect involves a care for poetic art trained by reading Shakespeare's Sonnets. He himself wrote dozens of sonnets, and reflected their art in a set of odes ('Ode to a Nightingale', 'Ode on a Grecian Urn', 'Ode on Melancholy') shaped with dexain stanzas mirroring Shakespeare's sonnet-art – not only in formal structuring (quatrain/sestet) but also in the intricate interplays of imagery, syntax, diction and phonetic patterning that Booth admires in Shakespeare. Both poets revel, greatly and unobtrusively, in what Booth calls 'the multiplicity of structural patterns' that insult Ransom's demand for alignment of 'metrical pattern' with 'logical pattern'.[3] By Ransom-rules, Shakespeare's Sonnets are at best 'tolerably workmanlike' or (by half) 'seriously defective'.[4] Booth means to elaborate, and celebrate, the serious-playful defections.

Keats is a mirror of Booth, and Sonnet 12 is one that arrested his attention, on greatness of effect no less than soul-amazing subject. In his own sonnet on time's urgency, 'When I have fears that I may cease to be', he caught the temporal syntax from Shakespeare, its stretch on accumulating anaphora. Sonnet 12, titled by a timely 12 (clock's hours, year's months), starts in a metrical tick-tock, pinged with alliteration: *c*oun*t* the *c*lock tha*t t*ells the *t*ime (undertoned by a soft counterpointing of *th*). Time's active agency activates this speaker's attention. He does not say 'When I count the clock' (whenever; by routine), but (disturbing the iambic pattern) 'When I *do* count' – 'when I make myself heed' or 'pay attention to'. Across the quatrain he remorselessly tells time, to himself and to us, line to line. Telling becomes quickened witnessing, from his eye to ours, of how 'brave day' sinks to 'hideous night'; of a 'violet' no sooner beheld than 'past prime' (the double stress enforcing the sentence, and rhyming to 'time', picking up the sense of a clock's 'first hour'); and then, expanding from a day, a month, to human life-span, of 'sable curls', in a beat of meter, 'silver'd o'er' (another thud), then lustreless 'white'. On the stage of time-spans packed into a phrase, Shakespeare changes words into vivid *dramatis personae* ('fast fading violets cover'd up in leaves' is Keats's expression in 'Ode to a Nightingale').

In the sonnet-text before Keats's eyes, the wording was 'all silver'd o'er', Edmond Malone's tidying of the Quarto's 'And sable curls or silver'd ore with white'. Booth supports this (now widely accepted) intervention, but I wish he had hewed to his view that impulses to 'clarity' may sacrifice 'a considerable amount of … substance and energy' (ix). Malone's eighteenth-century taste, smoothing out the semantic level, planes off some rich verbal interplay: the sheen of 'or silver'd ore' as metallic resource (not just a sign of age), in punning league with a medieval-tinged golden 'or'.[5] Lost, too, is the ghost of a conjunctive 'or', a syntax of temporal alterity that disarrays the timeline of decline with a ruffle as arresting as Sonnet 73's 'When yellow leaves, or none, or few do hang / Upon those boughs that shake against the cold'. To Booth, the homophones 'or'/'ore' bring 'no coherent surface sense' to the line 'as a whole' (151n4). Yet it is the force of Booth's general ear for phonic play that compels me to resist him here. Be 'more of an artist, and "load every rift" of your subject with ore', Keats chides Shelley, with Spenser's Cave of Mammon unembarrassedly in mind (16 August 1820 [426]). With 'or', 'ore' ('o'er') Shakespeare does it in spades.

The crux of Malone-Booth vs. Quarto-Booth leads me to a brief and not irrelevant note on that line from Sonnet 73 quoted above. Booth (83), following Malone (1:639), emends to 'cold' the Quarto's 'could'. True, 'cold' has virtue: it honours climate-sense, deflects the auxiliary verb, and tightens the visual link of the '-old' rhyme to 'That time of year thou mayst in me behold'. But 'cold' lacks the 'ou'-tempering of a metrically stressed link to 'boughs'. It is not clear, moreover, that 'could' is a printer's error and that a by-murmur of an auxiliary is to be prevented. In Sonnet 94 ('They that have pow'r to hurt') – its torturous syntax, says Booth, forcing us 'to cope with conflicting reactions, impressions, and systems of coherence'[6] – the oscillation of 'could' and 'cold' could not be more pertinent, more resonant: 'They / … / are themselues as stone, / Vnmooued,could,and to temptation slow' (so the Quarto prints it). While Booth does not comment on 'could' in his elaborate reading of this sonnet in his *Essay,* in his edition he notes the Quarto spelling (306). The crux seems to have bothered him; in 1978 he added a substantial note on W. L. Godshalk's proposal that 'could' insinuates 'something like "cold potential"'. (In a heat, they 'could' hurt you.) Although Booth thinks this 'overstates [the] case', he just about restates it: 'in this context of curbed potential', Godshalk 'is right to recognize the incidental reverberation inherent in the mere presence of a spelling that in a suitable syntax would register a form of the verb "can"' (580).

And so, too, in the reverberation of 'or'-'ore'-'o'er' ('or' itself a word of reverberation). Sonnet 12 is all in war with time, waged by an anguished reckoner. While 'I' first appears first in Sonnet 10, there it's incidental (a medial pivot in line 9). Sonnet 12 debuts 'I' as a front-line persona, a critical agent. 'I' is its second word, set to echo in the line's end-word, 'time'. Booth's protagonist is 'the reader', more particularly, the locus of a 'reading experience' of contending with 'a multitude of different coexistent and conflicting patterns – formal, logical, ideological, syntactic, rhythmic, and phonetic'.[7] In Sonnet 12 this experience is fronted by a dramatically present 'I', perceiving, considering, speaking.[8] We are so strongly startled into a cognitive identification with this reader that we may not at all identify with the rhetorical addressee, 'thou', when it emerges at the volta of line 9. This is an 'I'-witness event.

You can register this primary identification in the report of perceptual data. The violet and sheaved grass may gesture at allegorical emblems, but this is supererogatory to the dramatic presence of an 'I' who counts, sees, beholds these images in aching particularity. On the time-plate of this counting consciousness, no volta is more wrenching than the counter-chimed 'Then' at line 9. It is a rhyming conceit wrought by what Booth (admiring such syntax in Sonnet 15) calls 'phonetic and ideational interplay' (1978 rpt; 157n9), and it descends with dramatic force. 'Then' bears the syntactic thrust of 'in consequence', but by interplay allows a sense of 'at the same time'. Shakespeare's patterning of 'Then ... do I question' on 'When I do count' has the effect of making the consequence feel simultaneous with the counting. By this temporal analogy, present accounting projects a decay of present 'sweets and beauties'. To see in time is to know dying in time, the very word 'wastes' laying its claim, in anagrammatic proximity, to 'sweets'. What a devastating concentration, then, in 'Wastes of time': the wasteland of time's work; littered waste (the grim harvest); the wasting of time by improvident youth. 'Whatever syntax a reader assumes or chooses, the context will cause the meanings given by the others to impinge on his [or her] consciousness,' notes Booth about the similarly rich phrase 'time's waste' in Sonnet 30 (1978 rpt; 182n4). This is reading as active sorting, in which possibilities sorted out are not sent off, but linger in attention.

This is the charged climate in which Sonnet 12's couplet precipitates, and with its own volta, flashes into a saving clause: 'Save breed' (a suggestion latent in 'see others grow'). Some readers, noting how the sound-amped 'Save breed, to brave' answers the sinking 'brave day', wrest a lesson against lessening. Yet in the register of a percipient 'I', the final line feels less like a logic than a drama of mind, a consoling turn, with ''gainst' flaunting resistance in the moment, in anticipation of, in preparation for what is unappeasable: 'when he takes thee hence'.[9] The soundings of 'breed' and 'thee' ally against the 'he' of 'Time', now a stark personification, emerging from the twice-tolled 'time' (1, 10) that has played from the clock to fate. How odd, then, that Booth would refuse the Quarto's capital T on the last iteration – the signifier of an embodied, militant harvester of summer's green, with a scythe that Shakespeare might have spelled 'sieth' (Quarto), as if to have Time himself rue his work. It is telling that although Malone sets a lowercase in the sonnet, he wants the capital for his gloss on the personification.[10]

The couplet's tonal oscillation on the prospect of defence effects what Keats terms Shakespeare's 'negative capability': a positive aesthetic of 'uncertainties' and 'doubts' (letter, December 1817 [78]). No doubt that Shakespeare is his 'Presider' (10–11 May 1817 [52–3]). Keats's rhythms of conception move with Shakespeare's own. *Re*-reading the sonnets in November 1817, he writes to his friend Reynolds, 'I neer found so many beauties in the sonnets – they seem to be full of fine things said unintentionally – in the intensity of working out conceits' (72).[11] The syntax is canny, giving 'in the intensity of working out conceits' both to the verbal energy Shakespeare has invested 'in the sonnets' and to the activity that reading 'in the sonnets' returns on the investment. This cooperation of 'working out' the conceits makes the sonnets for ever fresh events of reading, ever renewable. Back in April Keats had suggested to Reynolds: 'Whenever you write say a Word or two on some Passage in Shakespeare that may have come rather new to you; which must be continually happening, notwithstand[g] that we read the same Play forty times –' (49).

In November he is writing to Reynolds with new admiration of Sonnet 12, and he supplies his own verbal cue for the rich wordplay:

> Is this to be borne? Hark ye!
>> When lofty trees I see barren of leaves
>> Which erst from heat did canopy the herd,
>> And Summer's green all girded   up in sheaves,
>> Borne on the bier with white and bristly beard.
> He has left nothing to say about nothing or any thing

(72)

Keats's 'borne' heralds and expands Shakespeare's rich load: endured (Keats is joking), sent over to the reader, felt with excitement. Booth strangely misjudges the playfully exasperated delight.[12] Keats has asked Reynolds to notice things said un*intention*ally, *in intensity*. Unintentionally, in the intensity of imagination, the quatrain's first line plays more than a chord of *-ty-tree-see-leaves*. There abides a palindrome embedded in 'tr*ees I see*' that sets the 'I' as the centre of the temporal change, seeing the leaving of leaves as he remembers a green world wide enough, deep enough, to canopy an entire herd – 'herd' reverberating, faintly, in 'girded'. Not for nothing did a clerk copy this letter with 'heard' for 'herd', as if hearing again the telling of the clock.[13] And then the line that kills Keats: life reduced to a harvest 'borne on' a 'bier', shimmering into a white-bearded corpse. Had Keats known the Quarto, he would have harked to see 'bier' spelled punningly 'beare'. The subversive intensity of the verse is simultaneously to evoke 'born' and 'bear' (words of life-giving) and to refuse entrance to this sense: it's all 'barren', 'borne', 'bier', 'beard'. 'Borne' is a poignant anti-pun.[14]

Keats's feel for Shakespeare's language working not just in intentions of syntax but in soul-startling intensities of sound anticipates that respect for 'phonetic and ideational interplay' in Booth's regard, and more generally Roman Jakobson's description of poetic 'function' itself: the way poetry takes words from an 'axis of selection' for an 'axis of combination' so as to exploit the forms as well as logic of arrangement, a sensuous surplus in excess of semantic function (such as the sound-patterning to which Booth gives exquisitely detailed attention in his *Essay*).[15] No slouch on 'craftsman's proficiency', Shakespeare, says Booth, still disdains to align 'formal structure, logical structure, syntactical structure, rhetorical structure, patterns of diction, and extraformal phonetic patterns' in anything so Ransomed as 'a concerted phalanx'.[16] Responsive to the intensities stored in Shakespeare's designs, Keats is the accomplished performer of Booth's story: 'The mind of the reader is kept in constant motion'; 'in making the shifts from one context to another, the reader's mind is required constantly to act'.[17]

By this dynamic, the sonnet is a voice in motion, ready for a reader's export. 'The striking peculiarity of Shakspeare's mind', said William Hazlitt, alert to a paradox, 'was its generic quality, its power of communication. ... He was like the genius of humanity, changing places with all of us ... playing with our purposes as with his own'.[18] Without knowing Keats's feel for Sonnet 12 (the letters had yet to be published), Hazlitt channelled its communication into his *roman à clef* of personal heartbreak, *Liber Amoris* (1823). Its protagonist H. has been desperately in love with S. We find out from *Liber*'s 'editor' that H. died in consequence of her refusal, but this was not before H. has taken up a place in Sonnet 12, on his last page, in a gambit of mastery: 'Her image seems fast "going into the wastes of time", like a weed that the wave bears farther and farther from me'.[19] The simile quivers with Othello's public trashing of Desdemona: 'Oh thou weed / Who art so lovely fair ...' (4.2.68–9; Johnson & Steevens, 10:582); but the real quarry is Sonnet 12's third quatrain. What Shakespeare's 'I' projects into the future, with caution and distress –

> Then of thy beauty do I question make,
> That thou among the wastes of time must go,

– H. plays with a purpose for present consolation. The sonnet gives him a voice with a vengeance. Soliciting his reader's alliance, H.'s echo is nothing if not gloating. Well on the way to mortifying the power of S.'s beauty, time has already wasted S. into a weed:

> Alas! thou poor hapless weed, when I entirely lose sight of thee, and forever, no flower will ever bloom on earth to glad my heart again!
>
> THE END[20]

The flower is past prime, claimed by Time, the force H. rhetorically impersonates. The breeding that would brave Time in Shakespeareland turns out to be the leaves, bred from heart-barren earth, of H.'s *Liber Amoris*. What the 'I' of Shakespeare's Sonnet 12 sees communicates to Hazlitt a pathos against which there is no brave defence, only this maze of the soul.

NINETEEN

'Against' Interpretations: Rereading Sonnet 49

HEATHER DUBROW

Against that time (if ever that time come)
When I shall see thee frown on my defects,
Whenas thy love hath cast his utmost sum,
Called to that audit by advised respects—   4
Against that time when thou shalt strangely pass,
And scarcely greet me with that sun thine eye,
When love converted from the thing it was
Shall reasons find of settled gravity—   8
Against that time do I ensconce me here
Within the knowledge of mine own desert,
And this my hand against myself uprear
To guard the lawful reasons on thy part—   12
    To leave poor me thou hast the strength of laws,
    Since why to love I can allege no cause.
William Shakespeare, Sonnet 49[1]

Disputing so many other issues, alert to so many other forms of doubleness, most students of Shakespeare's Sonnets nonetheless agree on the analysis of Sonnet 49 enabled by and encapsulated in their straightforward glosses on 'against', the word that begins each quatrain. Interpreting that term as 'in anticipation of' rather than as 'in defence against' at those three junctures, such critics assume that the speaker accepts the addressee's rejection, accepts it abjectly, determinedly, and, according to many of these readers, consistently throughout the poem. In other words, 'poor me' (13) is foreseeing and participating in well-deserved negative judgments on himself. One edition thus summarises the sonnet: 'As usual the poet is self abnegating'.[2]

But in fact the poem repeatedly and simultaneously implies that its speaker is both resisting and abetting the attacks on himself that he foresees. At certain junctures one or the other gloss assumes prominence; but both those potential meanings of 'against', defence and anticipation, in fact remain in play – and at war – throughout this lyric.[3] Hence Sonnet 49 stages a continuing struggle between defiance of and complicity in its addressee's condemnation of the speaker. That battle, we discover, is mirrored even in line 11, where the 'against' that appears in the middle of the line differs from the usages of the word at the beginning of each quatrain. More broadly, the uneasy coexistence of and interaction among anticipating, attempting to prevent, and attempting to prevent through anticipation, also flags the dissolution of other apparent binaries: a blurring of the line between certainty and uncertainty and an approach to both time and space that is at once centripetal and centrifugal.

Stephen Booth's reading of the poem offers a particularly subtle yet potentially synecdochal instance of how Sonnet 49 is generally approached.[4] Misleading though F. R. Leavis's work and iconic presence was in so many other ways, his well taken and often repeated insistence that the appropriate response to earlier criticism is 'Yes, but' encourages us to respond to Stephen Booth's work on the word 'against' in Sonnet 49 and elsewhere in just those terms. The 'yes': Booth rightly argues for the coexistence of both meanings in line 13 of Sonnet 12.[5] And the 'but': in contrast to his reading of Sonnet 12, like so many other critics Booth problematically glosses the word that opens lines 1, 5, and 8 in Sonnet 49 merely as 'in anticipation of, in preparation for', arguing that it acquires the meaning of 'in opposition to' only in line 11 (212). (Similarly, his interpretations of Sonnets 13 and 63 posit a movement from denoting anticipation in an earlier line of the lyric to signifying opposition in a subsequent line [153, 244–5], though an extended discussion of those two poems is outside the scope of this essay.) Sonnet 49, I maintain, exemplifies the unsettling coexistence of readings of 'against' that Booth finds in Sonnet 12, rather than the linear movement between them he posits when discussing other lyrics.

Shakespeare's delight in, and obsession with, punning and other ways of conflating divergent meanings throughout his canon may in itself further encourage us to consider the possibility that Sonnet 12 and Sonnet 49 play on 'against' in the same ways. Moreover, I will suggest that not only the diction of other sonnets in this sequence but also their rhetorical structure justifies exploring the simultaneous, not merely consecutive, presence of both meanings of 'against' in Sonnet 49.

But the proof of this pudding is in the reading. How does that putative simultaneity of meanings relate to the workings of the poem as one responds to its consecutive lines? To be sure, if like most critics we read 'against' as 'in preparation for', in the first quatrain of Sonnet 49 we do encounter the irony that Helen Vendler and many other Shakespeareans have noted. That is, on the one hand the rejection in question is positioned in the future by the opening word and by the distal deictic 'that' (1) and further bracketed and distanced by 'if ever that time come' (1) and by the future tenses; but on the other hand the poem does imply that the feared event is already present.[6] In support of that implication, observe the modal sleight of hand that presents the events in question as a *fait accompli* in the third and fourth lines ('hath cast' [3] and the past participle 'called' [4]). Notice too that when we put pressure on the word 'against', recognising meanings other than the ones on which this essay pivots, we will find in it an undertow of 'against' as 'juxtaposed to', 'pressing close to', denotations available in early modern English, suggesting that the moment is neither present nor located in a potentially distant future but rather just on the threshold.[7] The rejection is thus located both spatially and temporally.

Yet, paradoxically, that rejection is also as it were dislocated, providing what my reading would tempt us to describe as a moving target. For seconding and expanding the case for reading 'against' as 'in anticipation of' as the preceding paragraph has done certainly does not preclude also glossing the first word of the poem as 'in defence against'. In this case the phrase '(if ever that time come)' later in the same line enacts that defence by introducing the hope that rejection will not occur, conceivably because it has been successfully anticipated and thus resisted. Thus the word 'against' encapsulates, and the sonnet from its opening onwards introduces, the very question we encounter in the procreation sonnets, other lyrics about time, and many other poems in the sequence as well: under what circumstances does predicting a dreaded eventuality paralyse one and to what extent, under what circumstances, does it impel a successful resistance? This problem, of course, also haunts the history plays.

The succeeding quatrain invites the same question. Again, a distal deictic ('that sun' [6]), emphasised as it is by a rhyme – internal, slant, and rich – with 'sum' (3), implies that the rejection has already taken place, though of course the deictic in question is open to other readings as well. But again the text in no way forces us to reject the possibility that the poem refers to defence against, in addition to complicity in, the repudiation of the relationship. Indeed, one could argue that 'strangely' (5), which had connotations in the period of abnormality and even of prostitution,[8] introduces a defensive manoeuvre, a criticism of the addressee that jars with the apparently objective respect for those reasons of 'settled gravity' (8).[9] Those two words also draw attention to the text's proclivity for suggesting certainty logically and semantically within a context of whirlingly uncertain meanings, above all through the tension between the two principal meanings of 'against'.

'Against that time do I ensconce me here', the third quatrain opens. Although a volta is not as characteristic of Shakespeare's Sonnets as otherwise perceptive students of that structural practice might lead us to believe, here it does indeed signal a change from the opening quatrains, where both meanings of their initial word coexisted more or less equally, to two lines in which the defensive 'against', neglected by most readers, becomes much more promi-nent even though its anticipatory cousin remains present.[10] For 'ensconce' is associated with protection – in this case protection of and protection against – an association intensified by 'Within' (10). 'To guard against that juncture I am establishing a fortress' is arguably the predominant meaning of line 9. Admittedly, 'ensconc[ing]' may be a response to anticipation, but it is surely also a defence against and alternative to what is anticipated.[11]

If, as critics have rightly observed, 'here' (9) alludes to the text in question, it again links time and space, suggesting as it does a moment before the rejection has occurred ('I am establishing a fortress within this text and at this moment of anticipation'). That enclave is the spatial and material counterpart to – and, again, defence against – the epistemological certainty referred to in phrases like 'settled gravity' (8). Had Shakespeare written 'Against that time do I ensconce me now', he would have signalled only temporality (a reminder that at many junctures in critical writing the linkage in the phrase 'here and now' risks concealing significant differences between those two words).

To be sure, if lines 9 and 10 swerve towards reading 'against' in terms of defence, 'this my hand against myself uprear' (11) renders the issue of anticipation, the emphasis favoured by most critics, more prominent: aptly glossed by critics as involving both swearing in a court of law or striking in a battle, as well as again reflexively representing the text itself, the hand at first seems merely to suggest that the speaker is foreseeing and participating in the attacks on himself. Yet the lines may also be glossed in terms of the spatial position of the organ in question, that is, as 'And I am raising my hand close to my body'; or conceivably the statement could be read as, 'And I am raising my hand defensively to ward off your blows'.

In a critical climate where boldness is often privileged over caution and precision, one again should acknowledge that the succeeding reference to 'guard[ing] the lawful reasons on thy part' (12) does more readily suggest anticipation of and participation in an attack against oneself than protection against it. But is it not at least possible that those reasons are being resisted (i.e., 'guard myself from')? Alternatively, surely we have long known that Shakespeare read his Derrida with care; arguably lines 11 and 12 are wrought, racked, almost wrecked semantically between the meanings of 'I am raising my hand to defend myself from your reasons' and 'I am raising my hand to defend your reasons', much as the voice in them is racked and almost wrecked between the meanings of 'against' earlier.

In any event, materialising the response in question in terms of a hand draws attention not only to the inscription of words but also to the availability of the agency that that organ so often represents. In so doing, we again witness the interplay between the two principal meanings of 'against' I am tracing. That is, on the one hand, when one reads that word in terms of anticipation of an attack in which one participates, the paradox of willingly striking oneself demonstrates agency in a situation where otherwise the speaker was a passive victim of a rejection he foresees but cannot forestall. Yet on the other hand if one reads our crucial word in terms of protection from anticipated blows, the hand represents the possibility of defence even in an arena where, if one assumes the addressee is the young man, an elite member of the culture, the lion lionised elsewhere in the sequence is attacking the 'poor me' (13) thrown to him.

As is so often the case in these poems, the couplet intensifies complexities rather than resolves them. The aggression that I have attributed to 'strangely' (5) is, as Katherine Duncan-Jones has pointed out, present in the final line since it may suggest the absence of reasons to love the speaker – or to love the addressee (208). Thus, although her own comment is confined to the conclusion of the sonnet, it again supports the pull between surrender and defence that is, I have argued, present throughout.

Reading the poem in terms of that unresolved struggle between meanings of 'against' illuminates both this sequence and its genre. There is much virtue, and *pace* Touchstone much pain too, in 'if' throughout these poems: arguably their most characteristic mode is anticipation. Anticipating feared events variously encourages proposing defences against them, notably procreation, and recognising one's helplessness. And that anticipation variously involves versions of the certainty we encounter in Sonnet 49 (the young man will surely die), uncertainty (are or are not he and the Dark

Lady an item?) and slides and slippages from one to another on the dark ice of these lyrics. In short, the many meanings of our word 'against' encapsulate semantic preoccupations we encounter throughout this group of sonnets.

And those meanings encapsulate the sonnet structure itself. The volta may be *against* inasmuch as it is anticipated, though that anticipation is unsettled by the fact that, as I suggested above, a volta is not quite as normative in this group of poems as many critics have claimed; and when it does appear, that turn may on occasion also be *against* in the sense of offering an alternative viewpoint, not infrequently a defence against the positions in the preceding eight lines (thus the sestet of Sonnet 76 ['Why is my verse so barren of new pride'] rebuts the accusation that its author's poems are inappropriately repetitive). Similarly, in this sequence the couplets may position themselves *against* the rest of the poem in the sense of being an anticipated and predictable summary, as in Sonnet 2 ('When forty winters shall besiege thy brow'); alternatively, they may provide a resolution, as it were a momentary stay *against* the anxieties and confusions of the preceding twelve lines, as in Sonnet 19 ('Devouring time, blunt thou the lion's paw'); or they may insist on new perspectives that oppose, work *against*, what has preceded them, whether positively or negatively, as in Sonnet 92 ('But do thy worst to steal thyself away').

In enacting the multiple meanings of 'against' through its own semantic and formal procedures, Sonnet 49 also invites cognate questions about other texts. How does the emphasis on anticipation in not only these sonnets but many other lyrics complicate conventional generalisations about the present-ness of lyric and its distinctions from narrative? How do culturally specific forms of futurity in early modern England, notably the rise of millenarian thought, inflect types of anticipation in other spheres? And, synecdochally examining the questions in this paragraph, how can we negotiate connections and tensions among the types of close reading to which this volume is dedicated, and the historicism that, though often contrasted with close reading, in fact need not and should not be read against – in the sense of opposition to – it?

TWENTY

The Chimney-Sweepers Conceit in the Song for Fidele in *Cymbeline*

Margaret Maurer

SONG

GUIDERIUS	Fear no more the heat o' th' sun,	
	Nor the furious winter's rages,	
	Thou thy worldly task hast done,	260
	Home art gone and ta'en thy wages.	
	Golden lads and girls all must,	
	As chimney-sweepers, come to dust.	
ARVIRAGUS	Fear no more the frown o' th' great,	
	Thou art past the tyrant's stroke,	265
	Care no more to clothe and eat,	
	To thee the reed is as the oak:	
	The sceptre, learning, physic, must	
	All follow this and come to dust.	
GUIDERIUS	Fear no more the lightning-flash.	270
ARVIRAGUS	Nor th' all-dreaded thunder-stone.	
GUIDERIUS	Fear not slander, censure rash.	
ARVIRAGUS	Thou hast finish'd joy and moan.	
BOTH	All lovers young, all lovers must	
	Consign to thee and come to dust.	275
GUIDERIUS	No exorciser harm thee!	
ARVIRAGUS	Nor no witchcraft charm thee!	
GUIDERIUS	Ghost unlaid forbear thee!	
ARVIRAGUS	Nothing ill come near thee!	

BOTH   Quiet consummation have,   280
              And renowned be thy grave!
                    William Shakespeare, *Cymbeline*, 4.2.258–81

Hamlet's friend Horatio describes himself as 'more an antique Roman than a Dane' (5.2.325),[1] so it is permissible, I think, to translate him to another Shakespeare play with Romans in it. Imagine him in the army of Caius Lucius in *Cymbeline*, a play set in Britain in the reign of Octavian (27 bce–14 ce), the emperor whose agnomen (he called himself Augustus) gives us a synonym for neoclassically proper standards of taste. In *Cymbeline* Horatio could encounter two brothers (both, like Hamlet, princes) reciting what Roger Warren has called 'perhaps the most exquisite lyric in the language' over a supposedly dead body.[2] If, when he hears the elder of them say 'Golden lads and girls all must, / As chimney-sweepers, come to dust', Horatio were to respond as he does to Hamlet's 'imagination trac[ing] the noble dust of Alexander till 'a find it stopping a bung-hole' – ''Twere to consider too curiously to consider so' (5.1.193–5) – his comment that the image is far-fetched would anticipate the judgment of eighteenth-, nineteenth- and early-twentieth-century editors who disliked the song altogether, especially its couplets, most particularly the couplet closing its first stanza.[3]

Some believed the song an interpolation by a lesser writer. Others faulted Shakespeare himself and suggested excising the lines or revising them. For Samuel Johnson, who thought the whole of *Cymbeline* achieved what 'just sentiments … natural dialogues … and … pleasing scenes' it contained 'at the expense of much incongruity', the lines must have exemplified the play's shortcomings. Johnson particularly deplored 'the confusion of the names and manners of different times',[4] and a lad in first-century Wales referring to chimney sweepers is a blatant instance of such confusion. After Johnson, Richard Grant White judged the whole of the song 'pretentious' and 'unsuited to the characters'.[5] Howard Staunton found the song's couplets 'strikingly inferior both in the thoughts and expression' to the stanzas that precede them.[6]

William James Rolfe lamented especially the 'poor pun on *chimney sweepers* and *dust*', saying it 'could hardly have been tolerated by S. in his latter years; and the couplet has no natural cohesion with the preceding lines'.[7]

As the twentieth century proceeded, however, the sea-change time can work transformed the lines closing its first stanza into the most valued facet of this little gem of a lyric. These lines are admirable for their sentiment, triggered by the echo in 'come to dust' of Genesis 3:19 ('thou art dust, and to dust shalt thou return' [Geneva]), applied both to fortune's darlings ('golden lads and girls') and the begrimed poor ('chimney sweepers'). Further commentary seems impertinent. Nonetheless, I am going to risk saying some things about the chimney-sweeper conceit in the song itself and in the play overall. I know the kind of thing I am setting out to do is often deplored, especially by students, on the grounds that discussing a poem's workings can destroy its effect. In this case, however, I think I must be allowed because it was a student who started it all. Thanks to her, I ended up thinking a lot more about this song than appreciating it requires.

Her question drew my attention to the kind of footnote I now call a 'preventative gloss', a comment designed to steer a reader clear of an idea or an association that a word or phrase might otherwise suggest. The student asked why her text directed her to substitute the word 'like' for 'as' in the song's sixth line. It turned out, when I checked, that some version of that gloss is all but universal (J. M. Nosworthy's 1955 Arden 2 edition being an exception) as far back as the mid-twentieth century, when American editors began supplying same-page notes instead of end-of-text glossaries. Once called to my attention, the assertion that 'as' means 'like' had an ironically opposite effect. I mean, I saw nothing but 'like' in 'as' until I began to suspect the editor of trying to keep me from thinking something. It was only then that what (I later learned) Rolfe calls the 'poor pun' on 'chimney sweepers' and 'dust' crossed my mind. Thanks to that student's question, I began to consider what 'as' can do, by the lights of systematised English grammar, that 'like' cannot and marvel at the reverberations of its effect.

'As' permits, though it hardly invites, the reader or the listener to imagine the golden youths becoming chimney sweepers, surrendering the particularity conveyed by 'lads and girls' as they decline into a single category of ungendered living humanoids covered in reeking filth. (Jacobean chimney sweepers cleaned not only chimneys but privies.) As chimney sweepers, then, the former golden lads and girls might be said to come to dust in two senses emerging from play on the word 'dust' as verb as well as noun. 'Dust' as noun fits with 'as' as 'like' and conveys the unexceptionable idea that the decomposed bodies of dead golden lads and girls and dead chimney sweepers are similar. Because of what 'as' can do that 'like' is not supposed by punctilious grammarians to be able to do, 'dust' as a verb conveys something spookier: the golden lads and girls are transformed into creatures who are very much alive despite the extent to which their occupation makes them look and smell like bodies returned from the grave. Once that thought presents itself, other words in the stanza participate in the anamorphosis triggered by the un-'like'-ness of 'as'. 'Task' and 'wages' and going 'home' recover some of their literal significance; and the sustained figure of speech whereby the song offers the consoling thought that death is a release from the inconveniences of physicality also alludes to the harsh reality of life for people whose occupation makes them society's pariahs, the living dead.

These curious considerations might well be their own excuse for being. If we allow that the anachronisms Johnson deplored are, after all, a consistent feature of the play, the simple defence of these golden-children-turned-chimney-sweepers is that they make the reference to coming to dust a grimmer reflection on death than Genesis 3:19 is usually taken to be. The faintly registered implications of 'dust' as a verb suggest the sensory experiences of decay and putrefaction in a way that is something like imagining a king 'go[ing] a progress through the guts of a beggar' (*Hamlet*, 4.3.29–30).

But the poor pun also reverberates with the stage business that prompts the recitation of the song. At this point in the play, Guiderius and Arviragus have decided to bury the supposedly dead

Fidele (he is actually their sister Imogen) by laying flowers on him. This staple of the pastoral convention, an impractical substitute for burial (covering the body with flowers will not prevent its being ravaged by animals) is a pretext for avoiding what would be difficult to stage and would be, in terms of the play's fable, obscene (Laertes leaping into Ophelia's grave to shelter her body from the dirt that will cover it comes to mind): the living Fidele would be soiled. The pun in Guiderius's lines relates to what he and his brother are doing by seeming to imagine the consequences of what they nearly do: inter someone who is not dead, so that the couplet suggests what the undead Fidele at large again would look like had he been buried in the ordinary way and somehow managed to free himself. The image is a playful anticipation of the concern of the song's final stanza, that a dead body remain in its grave.

The two intervening stanzas make the case for staying dead, enumerating death's advantages by listing things the dead need 'fear no more' and 'care no more' about. It is just possible that the germ of the song is in a Greek text from late antiquity that imagines a scenario obliquely related to this moment in *Cymbeline*. The eighteenth-century editor William Warburton noted that the first four lines of its middle two stanzas recall Lucian's essay 'On Funerals'.[8] The lines Warburton heard echoed in the song are from the imaginary speech imputed to a dead son who rises up from his bier to mock his father for the mourning rites that custom requires. Grief, the corpse says, is inappropriate because death is a state the living should envy. Warburton, wondering if Shakespeare could have known Lucian, noted also that 'This is the topic of consolation that nature dictates to all men on these occasions'.[9]

Lucian's spin on this 'topic of consolation', having it spoken by the corpse of the deceased boy rather than by the grieving adult (as is the case with Ben Jonson's epigram 'On My First Sonne'[10]), is strangely and perhaps coincidentally (if Shakespeare did not know Lucian) varied in a way that is even further off-beat in the situation in *Cymbeline*. Shakespeare has two speakers, both young men, alternatively recite pieces of the song. Regardless of which brother says which lines, the alternating arrangement has the effect of making each part of the song register as a commentary on what precedes it. This is the technique of an eclogue or pastoral poem, conventionally recited by shepherds contesting with one another to display their poetical abilities.

In Arviragus's second stanza, the pastoral overtones stand out against the backdrop of Guiderius's preposterously wage-earning chimney sweepers. The lines promote the simple life over a civilised one as much as they might also refer to death as a way to escape 'the frown o' th' great' and 'the tyrant's stroke'. The 'reed', from which shepherds' pipes are made, is as valued as the oak, whose leaves, Pliny says, are used for the *corona civica*, 'that glorious emblem of military valour';[11] and the sophistications of human culture (metonymised as 'the sceptre, learning, physic') are dismissed as of no enduring consequence. In the last line, that these abstractions 'follow this and come to dust' almost entirely sublimates to a more generalised philosophical observation the *memento mori* that is the primary effect of the echo of Genesis 3:19 – almost, but not entirely, as 'physic' (the practices of health and healing applied to individual bodies to forestall death) joins political power ('the sceptre') and the intellectual arts ('learning') in a list of things that have no lasting effect.

The first four lines of the third stanza, shared alternatively by the two voices, similarly list threatening natural events ('the lightning-flash', 'th'all-dreaded thunder-stone') and incidents of human cruelty ('slander, censure rash'). In this stanza, the idea of personal death is emphasised: 'Thou hast finish'd joy and moan'. The alternating lines assigned to the two speakers have the effect of suggesting that there is such agreement on the peace that the oblivion of death will bring that one might even seek it. In the couplet that concludes the third stanza, spoken by both together, the word 'consign' ('submit', but with a sense of formal agreement) is an interesting qualification of the word 'must'. To be sure, not all agreements are wholly voluntary (a person can be forced to sign a contract), but the signer still picks up the pen and writes his name.

The shift from the impersonal 'All follow this' in the couplet of the second stanza to the personal 'consign to thee' of the third displeased Johnson, who suggested reversing 'this' and 'thee' in the two stanza's concluding lines.[12] Johnson was probably bothered by the way 'consign to thee' implies, as 'follow thee' does not so certainly, that whoever or whatever is addressed in the song must in some sense be alive. This returns, of course, to the issue of confining those chimney sweepers to a simile, but it also underscores the oddity of the song's prevailing mode of direct address. All the emphatic verbs are imperatives, and forms of the second-person pronoun recur: most of all 'thee', in the last line of the third stanza and as the last word of the first four lines of the fourth.

To whom or what is the song directed? However much the mind desires and may even succeed in making the object of this address at various points in the song the departed spirit of the beautiful child, in the final stanza, 'thee' must be his body. So if the first stanza flirts with the ghoulish fantasy that that body might rise again and the second retreats at least partially into abstraction, the third stanza insists that 'All lovers young, all lovers' formally accept not just death but disintegration as their end. In Christian terms, the bleakness of the idea may justify the impulse to find fault with the song, particularly with its stanza-ending couplets, which do, so to speak, the dirty work.

In the final stanza, all couplets, the word 'consummation' (also Hamlet's word, of course [3.1.62]) stands out, not just because it sprawls over two feet of the tetrameter line but because it is the Anglicised version of the word on which Jesus, in the Vulgate Bible, dies: *consummatum est* (John 19:30). Echoing a phrase translated 'it is finished', 'consummation' moves 'thou hast finish'd' of the previous stanza to the assertion of precisely what it is that the song means to effect: 'quiet consummation', an ending that is proof against the operations of exorcism, witchcraft, charms, and ghosts.

For those who desire it to be so, 'quiet consummation' might be understood as a reference to the Christian alternative to the eerie perversions these words imply; and also, of course, read in a Christian context, 'quiet consummation' can be charged with the consoling irony that, in John's gospel, there are two more chapters to the story of Jesus. (Fidele, too, will rise again in the play and not as a chimney sweeper, though somewhat fouled by the blood of a headless corpse placed next to him.) Yet, while it must be conceded that taking the word 'consummation' to look forward to Christianity is an interpretive possibility, that interpretation is challenged if not belied by the song's concluding insistence that a renowned grave is the afterlife to be desired. This emphasis makes the song a wonderfully curious ingredient of a play set in the first years of the common era, in the pre-dawn, as it were, of history's most notorious resurrection.

TWENTY ONE

Mille viae mortis

A. R. BRAUNMULLER

3. QUEEN   This funeral path brings to your household's grave:
             Joy seize on you again; peace sleep with him.
2. QUEEN   And this to yours.
1. QUEEN   Yours this way. Heavens lend
             A thousand differing ways to one sure end.
3. QUEEN   This world's a city full of straying streets,
             And death's the market-place, where each one meets.
                                                    Exeunt severally
William Shakespeare and John Fletcher, *The Two Noble Kinsmen*,
                                                    1.5.11-16[1]

Three mourning queens, having secured their respective husbands'
ceremonious interment, now depart to their respective obsequies,
each her own way, though each also has the categorically identical
journey. The stage image is also one of unity fragmented – '*Exeunt
severally*' (i.e., separately) – only to be re-established emotionally
and ritually in the dialogue. Another form of unity arises in the
rhythm and rhyme. Two couplets end the scene: the first combines
a shortened, would-be pentameter line completing the previous
one and an aggressively regular pentameter (requiring only one
elision, 'diff'ring'); the second scans regularly with the passage's
most arresting metaphor – 'straying streets' – and a vivid revision
of the previous couplet and of a proverbial image of life as a
'thurghfare' to death.[2]

    Commentators, critics, and proverb-specialists have enlisted
the first couplet – 'Heavens lend / A thousand differing ways to
one sure end' – in support of 'Death has a thousand doors to let

out life'[3] or 'There is but one way to enter this life, but the gates of death are without number'.[4] The most convincing classical origin for the widespread Tudor-Stuart dramatic repetition of the idea is Seneca's line in *Thebais/Phoenissae*, 'mille ad hanc [i.e., mortem] aditus patent' Englished by Thomas Newton in 1581 as 'Death ech where is: and wayes to death in thousand corners are'.[5] M. C. Bradbrook chose the idea as an example of the ways many dramatists employed the classical tradition in English plays ranging from Thomas Hughes *et al.*, *The Misfortunes of Arthur* (1588) through plays by Marston, Webster, Fletcher, and Massinger.[6] The verbal link among most of these supposed debts, allusions, references, or imitations is 'thousand' or 'many' or 'ten thousand'. All humans are born the same way, they die in many different ways, often unexpected or unpredicted or unpredictable. Bradbrook later described the first couplet as 'a mimetic rendering of the Virgilian "Mille viae mortis"' which implies though it does not quite state that the phrase is in Vergil's works.[7] It is not. Perhaps the closest classical analogue (along with Seneca) is Tibullus 1.3.50, '*nunc mare, nunc leti mille repente viae*'.[8]

So much for the scholarship devoted to the first of the two couplets that conclude *The Two Noble Kinsmen*, act 1, scene 5.

What of the second couplet – 'The world's a city full of straying streets, / And death's the market-place, where each one meets'? A double-couplet ending for a Shakespearean scene is unusual this late in his career. Often, the second couplet of doubled scene-ending couplets repeats its fellow in different terms. This time, the second couplet does not simply repeat or elaborate the first. Instead, it explores a new metaphorical realm, quite different from the 'thousand' deaths of the first couplet. The second couplet picks up 'ways' from the first and converts it to 'straying streets'. It proposes an equation of '[t]he world' with a 'city' and introduces 'death' as a 'market-place' in the 'city' or 'world'. One of the relatively few critics to consider this second couplet remarks that the reference to a market indicates 'the centrality of commerce to human society and the consequent futility of lofty aspirations'.[9] On the contrary, the couplet identifies death, not commerce, as the end which awaits all, loftily aspirant or otherwise. This market-place exchanges life for not-life; it stands as the sole terminus for streets, and hence the lives lived on those streets' trajectories, 'straying' or wandering or escaping 'from confinement or control' (*OED s.v.* 'stray' v.[2] 1). By 'straying' into the market-place, 'the streets' meet each other and end.

In studying a related proverb, 'Many ways meet in one town', Robert W. Dent seems to have first identified what is a remarkably strong analogue if not a source for this imagery in *The Two Noble Kinsmen*: 'As into a great Citie or into the maine Sea, so unto death there are many waies. It is at the center, wherein all the lines doe meete; a towne of Mart, wherein many waies from contrarie coasts doe end'.[10] Opposite both 'As into a great Citie ...' and 'It is as a center ...', Thomas Tuke notes helpfully in the margin, 'A Simile'. Yet, by 1599 Shakespeare already knew the essentials of the proverb and its imagery:

> ... many things having full reference
> To one consent may work contrariously,
> As many arrows loosed several ways
> Come to one mark,
> As many several ways meet in one town,
> As many fresh streams meet in one salt sea,
> As many lines close in the dial's centre.[11]

Finally, the couplets of *The Two Noble Kinsmen* may have a more solemn historical and verbal substrate than proverb lore. For a Protestant Tudor-Stuart audience, or the creating Shakespeare, the sounds of 'ways' in the first couplet and 'straying' in the second might evoke, or have been caused by, the General Confession of *The Book of Common Prayer*: 'Almighty and most merciful Father, we have erred and strayed from thy ways, like lost sheep. We have followed too much the devices and desires of our own hearts'.[12] This allusion, if it is one, or this echo – designed or not, conscious or not – introduces a moral, or ethical, valence to the passage from *The Two Noble Kinsmen*: the 'straying streets' are so in part because those who travel them err, lack rectitude, stray 'from thy ways' (see *OED s.v.* 'stray' v.² 4 *fig.*). If we detect this set of religious possibilities in the passage, then another just-possible grammatical meaning emerges from the couplet's second line: 'And death's the market-place, where each one meets'. The plainest meaning and antecedent of 'each one' is, of course, the 'straying streets', but 'each one' may be us, the travellers on the streets, the humans who have strayed and yet found the common market-place, death.

'Straying' begins to look more and more like a transferred epithet, and it starts to become cloudier just how any street *could* stray, especially any street which the couplet knows is going to end at the market-place, an outcome which means that the streets have not, at least ultimately, strayed. One further suggestion might synthesise these possibilities. We posit that any street not following a direct line between origin and destination may be said to stray; any person travelling such a street also strays topographically and, perhaps, theologically. If we accept the logic of the kinsmen's earlier conversation about the inevitable corruption they will face if they remain in Thebes (1.2.1–83), then topography can teach, preach, or inculcate immorality – 'straying'.

TWENTY TWO

Donne the Time Traveller: Reading 'The Relic'

Stephen Burt

When my grave is broke up again
Some second guest to entertain,
(For graves have learned that woman-head
To be to more than one a bed)
    And he that digs it, spies   5
A bracelet of bright hair about the bone,
       Will he not let us alone,
And think that there a loving couple lies,
Who thought that this device might be some way
To make their souls, at the last busy day,   10
Meet at this grave, and make a little stay?

If this fall in a time, or land,
Where mis-devotion doth command,
Then, he that digs us up, will bring
Us, to the Bishop, and the King,   15
       To make us relics; then
Thou shalt be a Mary Magdalen, and I
       A something else thereby;
All women shall adore us, and some men;
And since at such time, miracles are sought,   20
I would have that age by this paper taught
What miracles we harmless lovers wrought.

First, we loved well and faithfully,
Yet knew not what we loved, nor why,
Difference of sex no more we knew,   25

> Than our guardian angels do;
>   Coming and going, we
> Perchance might kiss, but not between those meals;
>   Our hands ne'er touched the seals,
> Which nature, injured by late law, sets free: 30
> These miracles we did; but now alas,
> All measure, and all language, I should pass,
> Should I tell what a miracle she was.
>
>   John Donne, 'The Relic'[1]

Celebrated for much of the twentieth century by the same readers who puzzled over its ending, 'The Relic' belongs in the group of Donne's lyric poems distinguished by their passionate devotion to a female beloved, a devotion that seems to construct, for these exalted lovers, a cosmos or else a religion of their very own. Other such poems include 'The Good Morrow', 'A Valediction: Forbidding Mourning', and 'The Canonization'. Many readers believe (although no one can prove) that Donne wrote most or all of them for his wife Anne.

In that company, 'The Relic' stands out for the haunting line 'A bracelet of bright hair about the bone', admired by T. S. Eliot and many others. It stands out, too, for its attitude towards sex. Some of Donne's other poems (e.g., 'A Valediction: Forbidding Mourning') say that these lovers do not *need* sex, because their spiritual bond extends beyond anything merely erotic or physical. 'The Relic', uniquely, says (or seems to say) that they do not *have* sex: they rarely even touch. While some readers still think the poem speaks to Anne, some scholars believe instead that Donne wrote about his friend Lady Magdalen Herbert, to whom he also addressed a letter in verse. 'The Relic' remains, in Achsah Guibbory's words, at once 'deeply spiritual, even platonic', and 'distinctly sexual', hence 'among Donne's most mysterious' poems.[2]

Even more than do the other love poems that share its exalted tone, 'The Relic' seems to speak to and about Donne's future readers, to know how it will be disputed, and read, and reread. Many poems promise to make the beloved immortal; 'The Relic' says, and almost proves, that Donne's particular powers –

his passionate tone, his intricate rhetoric, his intellectual habit
of entangling eros with religious controversy, his defiance of
received opinion, his gift for metaphor, even his attraction to such
unromantic topics as bodily decay – will give his depictions of his
lover a power that no other writer could find.

'The Relic' says, too – and it seems to have proved itself right –
that those depictions will remain hard, or even impossible, to pin
down. We can never know what the lovers know, feel what they feel;
indeed, no one else can ever feel what they feel, or do just what they
have done. True of all lovers in one sense (no two happy families
are exactly alike), that claim applies uniquely to these lovers in
another; their bond defies the expectations, and limits, that other
bonds of love or friendship meet, almost as this poem defies the
bounds of explanation that apply to other poems. That defiance
becomes its legacy to the future, in which the 'relic's' beholders,
the poem's readers, live. Donne's poem about compelling, strange,
nearly holy things sent from his present to uncertain futures – a
bracelet, a corpse or a skeleton, a 'paper' and, on it, a poem –
becomes not just a promise but a 'mystery'; we will continue to
contemplate these lovers, thanks to 'this paper' and the poem it
bears, even though – or because – we cannot understand.

'The Relic' will end by describing (or at least appearing to
describe) a non-physical, unconsummated love. The poem begins,
though, in a world of mortal bodies, a crowd at the grave: Donne's
bones will come back out of the ground not at the general resurrection, but when specific future individuals reopen this tomb. The
sign for an attachment stronger than death, the bracelet also serves
a function: it ought to 'ensure a final reunion before Judgment',
when bodies reassemble any lost parts'.[3] 'A bracelet of bright hair
about the bone' stands out not just for the gravediggers but for the
reader and listener, as well: it is the first pentameter, and the first
line that belongs to an uneven couplet (pentameter-trimeter), and
the first line that makes sense on its own. Just after that line, we
hear the core of the sentence (the independent clause), the main
verb (or first of two verbs) on which Donne's question hangs: will
he, the future exhumer, not let us alone?

He will not; the bracelet, and the grave, and the body or bodies taken out of it, will exert an illimitable fascination on every future person who encounters them, from digger to bishop to king and finally to readers: to me, to you. Donne's 'device', reuniting the lovers in this future age, is both the bracelet as object within the poem, and the conceit about the bracelet, which Donne has indeed devised: the future will ask, of the bracelet, and of the poem, not just 'what does it mean' but 'what does it do'?

Elizabethan antiquarians found an actual 'bracelet of bright hair about the bone' in what they believed was the grave of King Arthur and Guinevere. Fancy clothing could also include 'bone lace', threaded with gold, or silver, or bright human hair. And severed hair, 'bright' or otherwise, retains its original hue, while hair on heads fades: no wonder other poets have used severed hair as a symbol for immortality.[4] But we should not reduce the fascination in this 'device' to the history and biology of real hair. Not only that bracelet but the bodies it joined exert a finally inexplicable, or magical, power: imagining how that power might act on the future, Donne moves from the dead to the living, from parts of dead bodies to live bodies that act as wholes. The mystified gravediggers will 'bring' both Donne's corpse, and the corpse of his lover, 'to the Bishop, or the King', not just as curios, but as 'relics', like saints' bones, demanding attribution, veneration, interpretation. Not the token alone, but the love that it represents, give these lovers religious as well as political importance: they seem (however foolishly) to belong at the centre of some church or state.

What sort of church or state? Most readers take 'mis-devotion' as Roman Catholicism, the religion of Donne's childhood. As an adult, he repudiated Catholic belief, first for a hard-to-pin-down sceptical outlook, and then for apparent orthodoxy: in 1615 he became an Anglican priest, and in 1621 the Dean of St Paul's Cathedral in London. Sixteenth- and seventeenth-century Protestants attacked Roman Catholics for (among many other faults) their attitude towards relics, not only a cause for behaviour that looked like idolatry, but also a source of corruption, a pretext for fraud. Relics are physical things, inanimate objects; true

Christians, and perhaps true lovers, should revere things of the spirit instead.

'Mis-devotion' implies that some other time or land (now and in England, perhaps) can show true devotion: Donne's church and state would not make this mistake. Yet as the stanza goes on, it seems to imply that this bracelet, these bodies, these relics, and indeed this poem explaining them would capture any observer, command awe if not outright worship, from anyone who crossed their path. Only in a land with the wrong religion, however, would a worshipper beholden to these relics bring them before a clerical or national institution; perhaps someone with the right spirit would adore them at home.

What is that spirit? With its elevation of love, 'The Relic' 'seems straightforwardly incompatible with any orthodox religion', judges the historian David Wootton.[5] Again, the key line arrives with a pentameter that the shape of the stanza may highlight: 'Thou shalt be a Mary Magdalen, and I/A something else thereby'. Mary Magdalen, the redeemed prostitute of the Gospels, made a good choice for heterodox writers who wished to defend (against the drift of Pauline dictates) physical sex; 'something else', as many critics have noticed, has the same meter as 'Jesus Christ'. The acolytes of 'mis-devotion' think that they have found the body of Christ himself.

But Christ left no body; his body ascended to Heaven, as Mary Magdalen found out (John 20:1–17). Donne and his lover are Christ come back to Earth, their bond as powerful as the Second Coming, or else they demonstrate that there can be more than one redeemer: *a* Jesus Christ, 'logically a very different entity from the one Jesus', as the great critic William Empson, who presented a very heterodox Donne, insisted.[6] Wootton argues plausibly that 'The Relic' reflects the beliefs of the Family of Love, a persecuted Christian sect that persisted quasi-secretly during the sixteenth and seventeenth centuries. Familists, Wootton explains, 'believed that every Christian was a Mary Magdalen rescued from sin; and that every Christian was reborn through faith as Jesus Christ', though as a Christ not yet ascended in body, every Christian was also therefore 'capable of leaving a relic at his death'.[7] To state such beliefs openly would be to risk penury and jail, if not worse; to imply them in a love poem might be just the sort of thing Donne's verse would do.

Donne takes himself and his readers outside the context of his own era's Christian dogma by peopling his future with fervent misreaders, and by – very accurately – imagining that they might argue over this poem: no wonder these lines can puzzle readers still. If we do not want to find here a Christian heresy, a serious claim about a religious belief, we might instead say that this poem, like the token it contemplates, *replaces* Christian doctrine with its own interpersonal, private 'devotion'. The bracelet and the paper and the corpses' bones, taken together, not only invite but command a kind of 'mis-devotion' that Catholic doctrine cannot require: the kind of devotion, or adoration, that we might bring to a lover, or to a compelling work of art.

And here again the poem describes – in a manner at once exultant and coy – what it has in fact, and since Donne's death, accomplished, especially since Donne's twentieth-century revival. Empson first set forth his own interpretation in an essay called 'Donne the Space Man'; this poem reveals, instead, Donne the time traveller, able to visit his own future through the invention, the 'device', of his poem. 'The Relic' seems not only to anticipate its own continuing strength as a love poem, but indeed to predict the unusual history of Donne's love poems, half-buried in the frequent (though by no means universal) disapproval of eighteenth- and nineteenth-century tastes, then resurrected by such influential commentators as Edmund Gosse, Herbert Grierson, and Eliot himself: a resurrection that comes with riddles, with lasting questions about what Donne's poems can 'teach' us, what they mean.

To the riddles of its religion (unorthodox, but to what end?), we can add the riddles of sexual pleasure. Did these lovers get any? The third stanza, taken literally, says no, but the tone of the first two, and the undertones and *double entendres* that we can find in the third if we look hard, say yes. These lovers loved 'well and

faithfully', as if their love were a faith, and as if their love were a
mystery even to them, as it will be (the poem knows it will be) to
us. 'Harmless' means that their devotion hurt no one ('Alas, alas,
who's injured by my love?' Donne asked in 'The Canonization').
It may also mean that their love did no physical 'harm' – it did
not, for example, deprive any body of virginity, and it did not
make anyone pregnant, in an age when many women (among them
Anne More, in 1617) died in or shortly after childbirth. Yet the
poem does not warn us off sex; indeed, it gives a defence of sex
in general, along with a denial of sex in this case. 'Nature ... sets
free' the seals on various body parts, and only 'late law' (belated
law, or the old law repealed by Christ's coming) says we should
not break them; nonetheless these lovers did not break them.
(The line about seals is borrowed from Ovid's story of Myrrha in
Metamorphoses 10.311–518, where it becomes a defence of incest.)

   We can go on reading the poem as a show of chaste love, and
if we do so we follow it up past the body, past material objects
described (after 'meals' and 'seals' there are no more concrete
nouns), and finally beyond the reach of words, showing or telling
us (we readers of Donne's far future) that it says what no language
can say. Yet for all its apparent praise of chaste spiritual unity,
some readers (Guibbory among them) persist in believing that the
third stanza describes, not non-sexual love, but non-procreative
sex.[8] Perhaps he and she have been doing, together, the kinds of
things that men can also do with men, or women with women.
Perhaps when they kiss they are satisfied (it's like a meal) and then
move on to other action; perhaps not their hands, but other parts,
touch the 'seals', or perhaps they make love without touching
those prohibited body parts. 'All women shall adore us, and some
men', Donne says, in a potential joke about bisexuality (a term that
Donne would not have used), the first stand-alone independent
clause in the poem. As for 'coming and going', 'coming' could
denote orgasm by 1650.

   This reading seems perverse in several senses of 'perverse', but
it has been seriously advanced, and it fits well with other poems in
which Donne explores non-procreative and lesbian sex: 'Sappho

to Philaenis', for example, and Elegy XVIII. Even if we do not accept it, its persistence tells us something about the tone, and the challenge, and the mystery, presented within the poem; its passion, and its sense of indirection, and its already evident heterodoxy about a religion that sanctifies only some love, can easily and blamelessly encourage alert readers to read erotic activity into a stanza that seems concerned to keep it out. 'Were the lovers able to override the laws of society which restrain sexual encounters,' Helen Wilcox asks, 'or was it miraculous that they went against the laws of nature by controlling their sexual desires?'[9] It is hard for some of us now to believe that such an exciting intimacy could occur without sex, or at least a history of sex between these two people. It would be like belief in a miracle, the sort of miracle that has occasioned the poem, and the poem becomes a marker laid down for a future to wonder (as our own time indeed wonders) how the sexual mores, the sexual attitudes, of the Elizabethan and Jacobean years diverged from our own.

Whether or not this love became erotic, whether the lovers gave each other bodily pleasure, Donne has fashioned a remarkable stanza in which to hold whatever they did. The heterometric first section seems designed to frame those two key lines about the bracelet and the Magdalen, in the first two stanzas, with the three rhyming pentameters as a kind of emphatic coda. Donne turns that inevitably emphatic triple rhyme to another use in his last stanza, where 'alas' and 'pass' and 'was' (almost certainly full rhymes for Donne) build up to an answer that never comes. We may learn here what 'miracles we did', but no verse, no quantification, and no description can tell us 'what a miracle she *was*'; and she no longer *is*, since she has died.

This poem of devotion thus becomes, by the time we reach that last word 'was', a kind of anticipatory memorial poem, as if Donne were imagining – while his lady is still alive – how to write her obsequy, and deciding that no one can do it. Once she has died, no future can know, let alone read or 'tell', enough about her remarkable life. (In the same way, no future can reliably interpret the bracelet of hair.) Apart from the question of sex or no sex, 'The

Relic' concludes by maintaining its sense of momentum, its sense of sublime revelation, even while it says in general terms, and with a notable cluster of echoes ('alas ... all ... all ... pass'; 'miracle ... miracle'), that we cannot get to the bottom of this unique love.

'The Relic' thus seems to anticipate not only the future fame of Donne's *Songs and Sonets*, their future status atop some canons of love poetry, but also the future of debates about them, their status as objects of endless dispute or misprision. 'A hidden wish ... is oddly satisfied' in 'The Relic', writes Kenneth Gross: a wish to become 'oneself an object of study, worship or love'. The 'written 'paper' [is] itself a relic', Gross continues, 'a testimony to be read by those future persons'; and yet it concludes in a 'willful, insistent appeal to his and his lover's unreadability'.[10] That appeal, so to speak, becomes part of its appeal. Donne has, again, presented this exceptional, mutual, spiritual bond even while telling us that it cannot be presented, since its persistence amounted to a miracle – it would be another miracle if that first miracle could be put into words. Instead miracle and puzzle are propelled, by that last triple rhyme, away from Donne's time, and towards ours, all together.

'The Relic' presents a mystery all its own: ecstatic and canny, recursive and revelatory, chaste and sexy all at once. And yet the mystery in this poem can look like a special case of the general mystery presented by all lyric poems. Lyric poetry in general pretends or imagines that we can know how it feels to be somebody else, that we can participate in their presence or being; lyric poetry offers, as a sort of miracle or mystery, our sense that through these words, arranged this way, in this 'measure', we can do so. Yet we are our sole selves; we cannot truly know another person as thoroughly, through mere words from a stranger, as the best kinds of intimate friendship and marital love allow us to get to know her. Absent that first-hand experience, we have only the poem, the relic of the poet's words: they are all we can know, and it is the measure of his talents that their mystery remains alive, and enticing, long past his death, in a time so far from his own.

TWENTY THREE

Fletcher's *Mad Lover* and the Late Shakespeare

JEREMY LOPEZ

'Tis but to die, dogs doe it, ducks with dabling,
Birds sing away their soules, and babyes sleep 'em,
Why doe I talke of that is treble vantage?
For in the other world she is bound to have me,
Her Princely word is past: my great desert too   5
Will draw her to come after presently,
'Tis justice, and the gods must see it done too.
Besides no Brother, Father, kindred there
Can hinder us, all languages are a like too;
There love is everlasting, ever young,   10
Free from diseases, ages, jealousies.
Bawdes, beldames, painters, purgers die, 'tis nothing,
Men drowne themselves for joye to draw in Juleps
When they are hot with wine; In dreames we doe it;
And many a handsome wench that loves the sport well   15
Gives up her soule so in her lovers bosome;
But I must be incisde first, cut and open'd,
My heart (and handsomelie) taine from me: staie there,
Dead once, stay, let me thinke agen, who doe I know there?
For els to wander up and downe unwaited on   20
And unregarded in my place and project
Is for a sowters soule, not an old Souldiers.
My brave old Regiments: I there it goes,
That have bin killd before me ...
                    John Fletcher, *The Mad Lover*, 2.1.1–24[1]

Memnon, the mad lover of the play's title, is trying to talk himself into fulfilling a promise he has made to the scornful princess Calis, who said that she would love him if he gave her his heart – literally. This dramatic situation, quite typical of Fletcher, involves the improbable pursuit of an equivalence between metaphor and a literal idea of the image from which it is derived. Memnon's mode of self-persuasion involves insisting on the likeness of death to other experiences, and the passage is replete with formal gestures that establish a likeness between disparate things.

Alliteration helps to equate 'dogs' and 'ducks', 'dying' and 'dabling' in the first line, 'birds' and babies', 'singing' and 'sleeping' in the second. The analogies enabled by the parallel alliteration ('dogs' are to 'ducks' as 'birds' are to 'babies', etc.) soften the images over the course of the two lines. 'Ducks' follow 'dogs' sonically; the comic, diminishing image of ducks gives way to the more solemn or mythical image of the soul-singing birds through an ideational connection (birds in each line) as well as a sonic one (the second half of 'dabling' is redistributed into 'birds sing'). The dabbling ducks make dying seem easy while the soul-singing birds (very likely to be imagined as swans) make it seem mythical and perhaps heroic. Thus 'die like a dog' evolves into 'sleep like a baby' by way of the swan-song. Everything dies, and in fact you'd have to be a fool not to.

Lines 15–16 are built around the conventional pun on 'die' in its sexual sense: here Memnon, whose heart will be 'handsomelie' taken from him (18), imagines himself in terms of a 'handsome' wench dying in sport. This image is preceded, in 13–14, by the somewhat less conventional image of 'drowning for joy' in a cool drink (where 'drown' perhaps finds a sonic echo in 'draw in'). The desire for this drink is brought on not by the heat of thirst, but the heat of wine: one drink drowns out another, and the idea of 'heat' carries over, in a new form, to the sexual idea of lines 15–16. Acting as a pivot between these two images is the ambivalent half-line 'In dreames we doe it', which seems primarily to bring back the idea of death from line 1, but also contains suggestions of an erotic dream which will be elaborated in the fantasy of the handsome wench. As in the first two lines, alliteration, inversion, and substitution allow one image to blend imperceptibly with another. Drinking draws on dreams of a handsome wench who gives up her soul '*in*' her lover's bosom just as Memnon's bosom will be '*in*cisde'.

The syntax of line 12 mirrors that of line 11. Until we arrive at line 12's verb ('die'), we might hear its list as an extension of the list in line 11 which tells us what love is 'free from' in the afterlife. The temporary indistinguishability of one line from the next dramatises Memnon's fantasy of a vital continuity between life and death, and of the total freedom the latter provides. Once the distinct identity of the two lines is clear, the seedy types of line 12 perform a similar function to that of the animals in lines 1–2, but with a difference. That this sort of person dies means that an heroic general should have no difficulty. More importantly, 'Bawdes, beldames, painters, purgers' can be seen as the causes, or repositories, of 'diseases, ages, jealousies'; the mortality of the former on earth is presented as evidence of the latter's absence in the afterlife. (Memnon does not speculate whether the bawds and others might, like himself, retain their identities after death.)

A crucial difference (which is also a similarity) in this passage has to do with Shakespeare: the passage is a parody of the 'To be or not to be' soliloquy in *Hamlet*. Phrases and snatches of phrases from Shakespeare's play whisper in the background: for example, 'To die, to sleep / No more' (Shakespeare) – ''Tis but to die … and babyes sleep 'em' (Fletcher); or, 'For in that sleep of death' – 'For in that other world'; or, 'what dreams may come' – 'In dreames we doe it'; or, 'whips and scorns … That patient merit of the unworthy takes' – 'diseases, ages … purgers'; or, 'ay, there's the rub' – 'I there it goes'. (It is perhaps merely provoking to suggest that this last might be evidence of the theatrical authority, or at least a sometime theatrical performance, of the first *Hamlet* quarto.) The purgatorial image of Memnon walking 'up and downe unwaited on / And unregarded' may recall old Hamlet who, 'unhouseled' and 'unaneled' is doomed to 'walk the night'.

An anti-Hamlet of sorts (or, perhaps, an early modern Cole Porter), Memnon sees sex rather than death as the great leveller, and is unafraid of suicide. He is also not plagued with uncertainty about the afterlife: it is a paradise of eternal youth and love, where the general will be honoured as he has been on earth. Death, therefore, is not a final solitude. Indeed, Memnon will require a retinue when he arrives in paradise – so that he does not have to 'wander up and downe unwaited on'. He arrives at this realisation at the very moment the passage seems closest to registering the terror and physical reality of the death he faces: 'I must be incisde first, cut and open'd' (17). With 'staie there' (18), he seems to be on the verge of contemplating the abyss. Then, with exquisite patience, Fletcher draws out the pauses over half of the next line, springing on us the laugh-line that also embodies the passage's search for equivalence: 'who doe I know there?' The world to which Memnon goes will be the world he left.

Of course he can expect to find there, waiting for him, his 'brave old Regiments', who fought and fell alongside him, as well as 'those I have conquer'd'. These will make his 'traine full' (25–6). What he will most want, however, are some captains. The next part of the scene involves him explaining, comically deadpan, to the increasingly alarmed Chilax that he and the other captains must accompany him into the afterlife. Memnon is no solitary traveller to the undiscovered country. Suicide is a collective enterprise.

Definite and deliberate (I believe) as the echoes of and responses to *Hamlet* are, it's hard to imagine an actor playing them, or an audience being alert to them. Richard Burbage almost certainly played the role of Memnon, and there is some evidence that Hamlet would have been seen by early modern audiences as a kind of mad lover, but Fletcher's play can hardly be seen as a reworking of Shakespeare's. *The Mad Lover* is thoroughly Fletcherian, and indeed it was printed at the head of the first Beaumont and Fletcher folio (1647). It was also performed at court on 5 January 1617, which means that it was probably the first play Fletcher wrote after the deaths of Beaumont (6 March 1616) and Shakespeare (23 April 1616). There is no extant memorial written by Fletcher for either of his great collaborators, but I suggest that this might be one way to think about the *Hamlet* parody in *The Mad Lover*. That the passage's fantasy is (also) that of a literary man rather than (solely) that of a military man is suggested by its most incongruous element: while the high level of coherence in the apposition/repetition of 'Brother, Father, kindred' (8) as well as the sonic echo between 'kindred' and 'Can hinder' (8–9) perhaps anticipates and helps to situate it so that we don't really notice, there's no reason why Memnon should imagine that, in the world after death, 'all languages are a like' (9). Noodling around rather impressionistically, even superficially, in a soliloquy whose recollection is occasioned simply by the circumstances of his plot, Fletcher, suddenly on his own at the top of the King's Men's play-writing lineup, finds a way of keeping Shakespeare's voice alive and expressing a wish for his own death. In the merging of voices is an answer to Hamlet's soliloquy and a hopeful dramatisation of the afterlife as a poets' paradise: even now, Fletcher and Shakespeare continue to speak together.

Of course, this is only a dream. *The Mad Lover*, like so many Fletcher plays, is full of improbable resurrections, but they all depend on death never having actually happened in the first place. As much as the character of Memnon becomes a site where the playwright represents his mourning to himself, he is also a figure of theatrical fun – a satirical limit-case in the dangers of taking metaphor literally. At the end of the play he will be as solitary as at the beginning – his brother wins the love of Calis – and will believe, falsely, that there are new wars in which he can return to his role as a general: these wars were invented by Memnon's brother as part of an elaborate plot to win Calis. This is not to say, however, that Memnon, here or elsewhere, is wholly ridiculous. To perform the character in the theatre would demand an eerie and even optimistic sense of conviction. This conviction lies in the ghostly presence of the playwright behind the fantasy of the afterlife's universal language – the way Memnon's, Fletcher's, and Shakespeare's words come to be alike; and in the refusal to acknowledge the permanence of physical death which governs the minutest elements of Memnon's speech. The passage is full of the sound, and the idea, of 'in': the general imagines Calis's obligations to him '*in* the other world', he imagines death in terms of drawing '*in* juleps', and he thinks about dying '*In* dreames'; he worries that when he arrives in the other world he will be unrespected '*in* my place and project'. These 'in's jingle quietly with those in 'Pr*in*cely', 'k*in*dred', 'h*in*der', '*in*cisde', and 'b*in*'. They imply but cannot quite call forth their antithesis, 'out', which Memnon just manages to avoid speaking when he thinks of his heart being 'taine from' him – as though, after death, even if it has been broken during life, it will be returned to him.

Close Reading Techniques

TWENTY FOUR

'And Ten Low Words Oft Creep in One Dull Line': Sidney's Perfection of a Sonnet Device

†Norman Rabkin

'Foole', said my Muse to me, 'looke in thy heart, and write'.
Sir Philip Sidney, *Astrophil and Stella*, Sonnet 1

With how sad steps, ô Moone, thou climb'st the skies
Sir Philip Sidney, *Astrophil and Stella*, Sonnet 31[1]

The two most familiar lines in Sidney's *Astrophil and Stella* share the use of a striking device: each one consists entirely of monosyllabic words. Moreover, they occur in prominent places: the first is the last line of the opening sonnet of the cycle, and the second is the first line of its sonnet. I am going to argue that this device, though not Sidney's invention, scarcely existed before he wrote *Astrophil and Stella*, that he used it frequently and often powerfully throughout the cycle, that the influence of his use of the device on subsequent early modern sonneteers is palpable, and that by the seventeenth century it produced some of the most memorable lines in English verse.

In the 108 sonnets of *Astrophil and Stella* Sidney uses the device in all but fifteen. Seventeen last lines consist of ten monosyllabic words. In Sonnet 74 six such lines comprise virtually the entire sestet. In Sonnet 93 the opening and closing pairs of lines follow the pattern. In Sonnet 44 monosyllabic lines open octave and sestet. Such numbers suggest that Sidney is employing the device consciously and deliberately. The two famous lines with which I began reveal how powerful it can be. Other examples show the wit and force of Sidney's technique:

1. *Love* gave the wound, which while I breathe will bleed (2)
2. For me in sooth, no Muse but one I know (3)
3. I can speak what I feele, and feele as much as they (6)
4. But she, most faire, most cold, made him thence take his flight (8)
5. Of touch they are, and poor I am their straw (9)
6. If that be sinne which in fixed hearts doth breed (14)
7. But she in chafe him from her lap did shove (17)
8. Lookes to the skies, and in a ditch doth fall (19)
9. Flie, fly, my friends, I have my death wound; fly (20)
10. With me those paines for God's sake do not take (28)
11. Come let me write, 'And to what end?' To ease (34)
12. What may words say, or what may words not say (35)
13. As good to write as for to love and grone (40)
14. I may, I must, I can, I will, I do (47)

Such lines belie Pope's contention in his *Essay on Criticism* that ten monosyllabic words make a 'dull line'.

Note the many poetical devices Sidney uses in these typical lines. Most of the lines have strong caesuras, with both halves carefully set against each other: thus examples 3, 5, 8, and 12. In some lines opposing phrases are linked by alliteration and assonance: thus examples 1, 2, 3, 9, 11, and 12. Two of the lines accentuate the monosyllabic structure by cramming several clauses into ten syllables: three clauses in example 11 and, most dramatically, five in example 14.

We might look for a moment at Sonnet 74 of Sidney's cycle. In this virtuosic piece all but the final line of the sestet is built of monosyllables:

> How falles it then, that with so smooth an ease
> My thoughts I speake, and what I speake doth flow
> In verse, and that my verse best wits doth please?
> Guess we the cause: 'What, is it thus?' Fie, no:
>   'Or so?' Much less. 'How then?' Sure, thus it is:
>   My lips are sweet, inspired with *Stella's* kisse.

The opening lines of this passage flow with the smooth ease of verse that is described, the monosyllables tumbling along like pebbles in a stream until the motion is stopped by the rhyme word 'ease'. In the terse fourth and fifth lines of the passage Sidney conducts a vigorous dialogue, repeating the word 'thus' in the first and last lines for dramatic closure and rhyming 'no' and 'so'. The monosyllabic structure of the entire passage calls attention to itself and creates a palpable tension. This is a typical example of the wit that underlies Sidney's use of the monosyllabic line.

Before *Astrophil and Stella* the phenomenon I am exploring occurs rather haphazardly. Of the twenty-nine sonnets by Wyatt in Egerton MS 2711 only ten employ monosyllabic lines, and only two have as many as two such lines; of his twenty-four sonnets in Tottel's *Miscellany* twelve have monosyllabic lines; one has seven and one five, and in one the last line is monosyllabic. Wyatt may indeed be the innovator who added this device to the sonneteer's equipment, but he seems often to employ it as if he doesn't know that he is doing so. Here, for example, are the first two lines of the sonnet that Hyder Rollins lists as 49: 'I find no peace, and all my warre is done: / I feare, and hope: I burne, and frese like yse'; again, line 12 of Tottel 50: 'The starres be hidde, that leade me to this payne'.[2] Sometimes the half-lines are slightly antithetical, but not at all as strongly as Sidney's practice.

Surrey has only two sonnets in that volume and only one line in monosyllables. Nicholas Grimald's contribution to Tottel includes eight sonnets, of which six have monosyllabic lines, one has three, three have two, and one has opening and closing lines that fit the model. None of the lines is memorable, and there is no discernible pattern in their placement. There is no evidence to suggest that these poets thought of the monosyllabic line as part of their poetic armamentarium, but the not infrequent appearance of such lines in the work of Sidney's predecessors, particularly Grimald, may well have inspired Sidney's transformation of an occasional phenomenon into an important convention. The penultimate line of Grimald's Tottel 156 shows similar artistry, with assonant long *e* sounding in both halves and opposed nationalities across the caesura: 'From thee that held both Scots, and frekes of Fraunce'.[3]

After *Astrophil and Stella* the next major English sonnet sequence, Spenser's *Amoretti*, shows Sidney's influence in many ways, including the dominant trope of the thwarted lover and the use of both Petrarchan and English structural models. Spenser deploys the Sidneyan device fifty-six times in his eighty-nine sonnets. But he does it less emphatically: only two sonnets have four such lines, and only two have three. And while eighteen of Sidney's sonnets close with monosyllabic lines, only three of Spenser's do. The implication is that Spenser, although he is aware of Sidney's practice, does not consider it an important convention. It does not serve him, as it did for his predecessor, as an instrument for wit or drama, and one would be hard pressed to find quotable lines. The major sonneteers who come after Spenser, however, adopt Sidney's trope often and forcefully.

Not surprisingly, Shakespeare adopts Sidney's device and runs with it. Of his 154 sonnets, 114 have monosyllabic lines, beginning with the ultimate line of the first. Thirty-three conclude with such lines, and forty-two have ten monosyllables in their penultimate lines (to be compared with Sidney's thirteen penultimates). Seven sonnets have four monosyllabic lines each, and three more have three. Most notably, many of the most memorable lines in the Sonnets are of this sort:

1. And all in war with time for love of you (15)
2. Nor Mars his sword nor war's quick fire shall burn (55)
3. Shall you pace forth; your praise shall still find room (ibid.)
4. But weep to have that which it fears to lose (64)
5. That in black ink my love may still shine bright (65)
6. To love that well which thou must leave ere long (73)
7. They that have pow'r to hurt, and will do none (94)
8. That do not do the thing they most do show (ibid.)
9. Of hand, of foot, of lip, of eye, of brow (106)
10. All this the world well knows, yet none knows well (129)

11. To shun the heav'n that leads men to this hell (ibid.)
12. If snow be white, why then her breasts are dun— (130)
13. If hairs be wires, black wires grow on her head (ibid.)
14. I love to hear her speak, yet well I know (ibid.)
15. Make but my name thy love, and love that still (136)
16. And then thou lov'st me, for my name is Will (ibid.)
17. When my love swears that she is made of truth (138)
18. In faith I do not love thee with mine eyes (141)[4]

From our discussion of Sidney's lines it will be easy to see how Shakespeare imitates and improves on him. Example 3 uses both alliteration and assonance to link its halves, and the whole line marches with the pace it describes. Example 2 rhymes 'Mars' and 'war's' across the caesura. Strong antithesis marks examples 4, 5, 10, 11, and 12. Like Sidney, Shakespeare packs five symmetrical phrases into example 9. In all these instances, the plethora of words established by restricting each to one syllable allows the exercise of wit and dramatic force.

After Shakespeare, the device Sidney exploited becomes an established sonnet convention. Donne's poems are a major example. *Songs and Sonnets*, oddly, contains no fourteen-line sonnets, though it has innumerable lines consisting of monosyllables. The one poem in the book designated as a sonnet (actually it has eighteen lines), 'The Token', ends with the Shakespearean 'But swear thou think'st thou lov'st me, and no more'. Later in his poetic career Donne does produce conventional sonnets, and almost every one he writes uses the device prominently. The first cycle of 'Holy Sonnets' has monosyllabic lines in both the 'dedicatory' sonnets and in each of the poems within the cycle. 'Resurrection' has five, 'Ascension' has four (including the ultimate), 'La Corona' and 'Nativity' each have three. Of the nineteen mature and better known sonnets of the 'Holy Sonnets', only three do not employ the convention. One has four such lines, two have three; four have monosyllabic opening lines, and five have similar closing lines.

Many of the monosyllabic lines are among Donne's most characteristic and powerful:

1. Die not, poor death, nor yet canst thou kill me (6)
2. And death shall be no more; death, thou shalt die (ibid.)
3. Your force, to break, blow, burn and make me new (10)
4. I run to death, and death meets me as fast (13)
5. Show me dear Christ, thy spouse, so bright and clear (18)

And finally the last line of the sequence:

6. Those are my best days, when I shake with fear (19)[5]

Not surprisingly, Donne's use of intralinear antithesis leads sometimes to paradox (examples 1 and 2). In example 3 he presents five strong phrases, a floating caesura, and alliterated *b*s and *m*s to create a dynamic line. In example 4 the antithetical halves run smoothly towards and away from the caesura, and the repeated word 'death' in each half intensifies the opposition. In example 5 assonance ('Christ', 'bright') and internal rhyme ('dear', 'clear') make the line virtually glitter. And example 6 is another case of Donne's turning antithesis to paradox.

Herbert is another major Renaissance poet who employs this convention. His poems are idiosyncratic, often formally inventive, and he does not often use the sonnet form. When he does, however, he frequently writes effective monosyllabic lines. In 'Love (I)' there are two, in 'Love (II)' there are four, in 'Avarice' there are four. I shall cite a few strong examples.

1. And though my hard heart scarce to thee can groan ('The Sinner')
2. A kind of tune, which all things hear and fear ('Prayer (I)')
3. All knees shall bow to thee; all wits shall rise ('Love (II)')
4. And praise him who did make and mend our eyes (ibid.)
5. And while he digs out thee, falls in the ditch ('Avarice')
6. Which they that know the rest, know more than I ('The Answer')
7. Or, since thy ways are deep, and still the same (Sonnet I)
8. Will not a verse run smooth that bears thy name! (ibid.)[6]

The last of the early modern sonneteers I shall consider is Milton. Nine of his seventeen English sonnets contain monosyllabic lines; one has four, two have three. And as with Donne, a number of these lines are powerful:

1. Yet be it less or more, or soon or slow (7)
2. All is, if I have grace to use it so (ibid.)
3. Ev'n them who kept thy truth so pure of old (15)
4. Ere half my days in this dark world and wide (16)
5. Bear his mild yoke, they serve him best, his state (ibid.)

And, most dramatically of all, the final line of his last sonnet, describing his dream vision of his late wife:

6. I waked, she fled, and day brought back my night (23)[7]

All of these lines are characteristically Miltonic – the slow pace, the shifting caesura – and all of them use the monosyllabic structure effectively. Example 5 is preceded by two more monosyllables ('who best') that tie all twelve syllables together while embracing a powerful paradox. The most extraordinary line, example 6, consists of three simple bald statements. 'Waked' and 'day' are assonant, and 'waked' at the beginning of a line that ends with night underlines the paradox of the whole unit; the opposing pronouns 'she' and 'my' in the two halves of the unit intensify the unity of the statement; and the assonance of the first and last words of the line – 'I' and 'night' – is a final element in making one feel that this single line is an entire, coherent drama.

What is the value of the device that Sidney refined? There is no single answer. At times, as in the last line of Milton I cited, a palpable slowing down of the verse occurs. But in many instances, like Donne's 'I run to death, and death meets me as fast', the effect is an increase in speed. Occasionally, as in Shakespeare's Sonnet 55 – 'Shall you pace forth; your praise shall still find room' – the march of monosyllables is onomatopoetic, in this instance dramatising the 'pace' described. Frequently, as we have seen, the trope enables witty, apothegmatic statements, but this is not always the case. One universal trait, however, marks the monosyllabic line: it forces the poet to use language derived rather from the Anglo-Saxon than from the Latinate stratum of the English language. This is particularly notable in Milton, who is normally attracted to the Latinate. Whatever its effects, however, it is clear that the device Sidney developed is an important convention of the Renaissance English sonnet.

TWENTY FIVE

The Fox and His Pause: Punctuating Consciousness in Jonson's *Volpone*

ROBERT N. WATSON

Celia's husband proves himself even more greedy than jealous, by insisting that she climb into bed with old Volpone to win his inheritance. Locked in the bedchamber, she soliloquises:

> O God and his good angels, whither, whither
> Is shame fled human breasts that with such ease
> Men dare put off your honours and their own?
>
> $(3.7.133–5)^1$

That's what she would say if the play's editor obeyed the preference of modern publishers for minimal punctuation and no serial commas. Yet the First Folio (1616) text of the play, carefully supervised by Jonson himself, reads:

> O God, and his good angels! whither, whither,
> Is shame fled human breasts? that, with such ease,
> Men dare put off your honours, and their own?

At first she is simply exclaiming in helpless horror, which leads her to think about the angels as God's emissaries to protect the virtuous, and to wonder where they have gone, since they have not intervened, then (we may suspect) thinking about how to escape that room and her marriage; the 'whither' works both ways before becoming a third thought, which asks why people seem to have become so shameless, so shamelessly shameless in fact; then adding that her husband's wittol pimping is surely an insult to God's honour, before remembering that it is an insult to her husband's personal honour too.

This original, heavily punctuated version is not only more interesting than the fully preconceived conventional speech that current usage offers us. It also fits Jonson's own definition of a comma as 'a mean breathing, when the word serveth indifferently, both to the parts of the Sentence going before, and following after'.[2] And it refutes the familiar slander that Jonson draws static 'humours' figures who lack the implicit developing interior consciousness of Shakespeare's characters.[3] In pure kindness, editors have buttered Jonson's hay. No wonder he complained, in a characteristically pugnacious epigram addressed 'To Groom Idiot', that careless recitation 'disjoints ... my sense, loosing my points' – 'points' being the old word for small punctuation marks. The first-do-no-harm ethos of current editors is certainly admirable, but much too casually equated with minimising punctuation. The theory goes that, the fewer marks, the more opportunities opened up for the actors. It ain't necessarily so. What Stephen Booth observed about Shakespeare's Sonnets applies equally to Jonson's plays: 'modern directive spelling and punctuation ... often pays for its clarity by sacrificing a considerable amount of a poem's substance and energy'.[4]

Granted, the handwritten parts from which Elizabethan actors learned their lines evidently lacked much of what we would now consider normal guiding punctuation. But published texts might be marked to capture the rhythms of performance. The prologue to the *Pyramus and Thisbe* playlet in Shakespeare's *A Midsummer Night's Dream* shows how badly a speech could misfire if the speaker paused in the wrong places, leading to Theseus's quip that Quince 'doth not stand upon points' (5.1.108–18); in *Love's Labour's Lost*, Berowne's sonnet to Rosaline may be misdelivered in this second sense also, when Nathaniel 'find[s] not the apostrophus' (4.2.119). Nor is it only Shakespeare's joke: in what may be the earliest surviving comedy in English, Merrygreek similarly butchers Ralph Roister Doister's love letter.

In our historicising period of scholarship, editors face a

dilemma: how should they punctuate texts printed in an era when commas were primarily understood as marking a breathing space in speech,[5] for readers who assume they are syntactical dividers in grammar? Over time, the grammatical theory has overcome the vocal or physiological theory – perhaps another facet of the way mental events have become increasingly divorced from and exalted above the physical in the wake of Cartesian dualism. Descartes' *Discourse on Method* – published in 1637, the year Jonson died – made logical thought the immortal essence of humanity and the breathing body a lowly dubious accident.

Jonson's unfinished *English Grammar* handbook shows him trying to have it both ways – a tension that evokes the persistent struggle of aspiring Renaissance minds to reconcile themselves to the limitations imposed by the body. The commas my New Mermaids edition of *Volpone* tries to resurrect are a mixture of the two kinds: neither exactly the syntactical commas modern editors are sometimes willing to preserve, nor the breathing-pause commas to which some actors attribute a kind of mystical revelatory power. Instead, they mark a slight hesitation as the speaker discovers a new direction for an incomplete sentence to take. That makes them conversationally verisimilar, and evocative of psychological depth: a breathing-rhythm, but the breathing of the mind on its errant jogs. Jonson identified the comma and the semi-colon as 'distinctions of an *imperfect* Sentence'.[6] Character is imperfection. Long before Molly Bloom, Jonson's speakers flow from one idea to another, from one phrase to another that arises from hearing their own previous phrase. Properly respected, the punctuation allocates segments for different vocal tone, and allows us to hear afterthoughts as such, rather than letting them devolve into mere subordination.

A. C. Bradley and Sigmund Freud taught people to look for a certain kind of depth-psychology in drama that favoured Shakespeare's great comedy of individuals over Jonson's great comedy of types (it resembles the assumption that linear per-spective somehow paints more truth than iconic representations). Perhaps it is dramatic justice that Jonson, after complaining that

Shakespeare's late plays were unrealistic, nowadays gets devalued for producing satiric caricatures rather than Shakespeare's psychologically realistic creatures.

It is an easy mistake to make, if one fails to read, not just between the lines, but the little pauses between the words. That, however, is exactly where a renowned master of the poetic caesura might be expected to do some work. Jonson's handbook described commas as a handy invention 'whereby Men pausing a pretty while, the whole Speech might never the worse be understood'.[7] All the better understood, I would say, and their speakers better understood as well. The standard critique of Jonson's characterisation – in both senses of this phrase – misses the point.

There is no clearer vindication of Freud's theory of the narcissism of minor differences than disputes among editors of canonical literature. But both editions of *Volpone* from Jonson's own time – the 1607 Quarto and the more readerly 1616 Folio – do contain useful punctuation that modern editions choose to erase. And otherwise punctilious textual notes often neglect to list these deletions.

The main plot shows childless old Volpone (like the fox in the fables) playing almost dead to attract greedy birds of prey whom he can then devour: 'This draws new clients, daily, to my house, / Women, and men, of every sex, and age' (1.1.76–7). These commas pry open opportunities for the actor, repeatedly adding things in a way that makes the effect much greater than an efficient little unbroken statement about how many clients his scheme draws. The 'daily' takes on the weight of astonishment, 'women' can be played with a smirk, then 'and men' with a raised finger (like Hamlet's 'Nor woman neither'), 'every sex' with a snicker (this same author wrote *Epicoene*), and 'age' standing at the end to emphasise the irony of men older than himself seeking a place in his will. Only one other modern edition saves the comma after 'women' that opens up a moment – valuable in the open-stage daylit Jacobean theatre – for interplay between actor and audience.

When Volpone longs for a next gift, his wily servant Mosca responds, 'That, and thousands more, / I hope, to see you lord of'

(1.2.117–18). Unpunctuated, it's a banal piece of courtesy. Because Mosca sometimes seems to recognise the destructiveness of Volpone's greed, however, and secretly hopes to seize the legacy for himself, the commas make the first part – 'that, and thousands more' – momentarily a warning about the unquenchable nature of Volpone's thirst for gold. Mosca then nearly reveals his own greed with 'I hope' before hastily smoothing it over (after a revealing pause that modern editors consistently erase) into obsequious praise.

Supposing he is shrewdly investing what may be a twenty-four-carat jewel to buy Volpone's favour, Corvino urges Mosca to 'Tell him, it doubles the twelfth carat'. That oft-dropped comma suggests a man deciding what Volpone should be told, rather than necessarily what the truth is. Mosca replies. 'Sir, / He cannot understand, his hearing's gone; / And yet it comforts him, to see you – ' (1.5.14–16). Is 'it' the diamond or – by a polite revision – the companion? The comma – scarce in modern editions – sets the materialistic view against the sentimental pretence. Jonson often helps us enjoy Mosca enjoying flirting with the truth that the legacy-hunters are wilfully blind to, letting that truth hover exposed for just an instant before slipping it back into concealment; here is another such moment, bravura brinkmanship at the micro-level Stephen Booth has mined so richly, with the misprision now at the level of dramatic irony on stage rather than evanescent false scents in the verbal cognition of the audience.

Later in this exchange, Corvino's feigned solicitousness is exposed again by a (rarely retained) comma:

CORVINO   I will not trouble him now, to take my pearl?
MOSCA   Puh, nor your diamond. [*Taking the jewels*] What
      a needless care
      Is this afflicts you? Is not all, here, yours?
      Am not I here? whom you have made? your
        creature?
      That owe my being to you?

(1.5.75–9)

Thus Mosca's reassurance that Corvino need not worry about his investment is broken up by non-terminative question marks in the First Folio. That heavy punctuation makes for much richer lines than what some editors now give: 'Am not I here, whom you have made your creature?' The Folio's Mosca says, first, don't worry, I am on the job; then (perhaps recognising that Corvino suspects him of mixed loyalties) adds that he owes Corvino so much, then finishes by suggesting at once that he has been made into Corvino's dependant, and that Corvino essentially *is* Mosca's creator. The phrases are each separate expressive units, as well as finally blending into a single sentence that, normally punctuated, would be far less than the sum of its parts.

A few lines later Mosca tries to attract Volpone to Celia by describing her as 'a beauty, ripe, as harvest' (1.5.109). Removing one or both of those commas, as versions now in print generally do, throws away the provocative pauses that make Mosca's description a developing series of associated erotic ideas: 'ripe' works by itself (and possibly with a hint of 'rape'), before becoming subsumed into the conventional comparison (with a residue of 'reap'). Mosca then attributes to Celia 'A soft lip, / Would tempt you to eternity of kissing! / And flesh, that melteth, in the touch, to blood!' (1.5.111–13). Those lines makes perfect sense without commas – but lose their sensuality. The busy Folio text offers time to think (if that's the right verb): delicious hesitations between the object of desire and the kissing of it, between the first kiss and the timeless feeling it offers and the infinite desires it opens towards, and thence to the rest of the flesh, so soft and warm it seems to be melting – melting, that is, when it responds yieldingly to your touch – into a blush and an intimate wet heat.

Volpone's attempted seduction of Celia adopts the same additive rhythm: demanding sensual attention, offering a beautiful object to gaze upon, then a thought about the object, then a thought about that thought:

> See, a carbuncle,
> May put out both the eyes of our St Mark;
> A diamond, would have bought Lollia Paulina,

When she came in, like starlight, hid with jewels,
That were the spoils of provinces. Take these,
And wear, and lose 'em ...

(3.7.192–7)

Volpone keeps raising the ante; and the commas – however grammatically dispensable editors now find them – are the steps he raises it on. The jewels keep getting bigger and brighter, but also shrinking in importance compared to the fortune Volpone is offering her.

Jonson generates the same heavy-breathing effect when Mosca impresses Voltore with the wealth supposedly awaiting him upon Volpone's death: 'When you do come to swim, in golden lard, / Up to the arms, in honey' (1.3.70–71). For so many twentieth-century editors to decide, merely for the sake of cleaning up the page, that the swimming should be associated only with the lard, and the immersion separately with the honey, is a waste of Mosca's mesmerising artistry, and Jonson's behind it.

When Volpone says he might be able to endure another legacy-hunter (the talkative Lady Wouldbe) 'When I am high with mirth, and wine' (1.5.99), we can hear him deciding to add an ingredient to the palliative prescription – but in only one modern edition I could find when editing my own. Volpone keeps hinting that Lady Wouldbe should depart, but each reason he offers only launches her into another verbose exposition on that topic, leading him to exclaim, 'Is everything a cause, to my destruction?' (3.4.82). Even very conservative modern editors pull out the tooth of that line by extracting the comma – forgetting that a 'cause' to Jacobeans would have suggested a lawsuit, *causa*; so Volpone is remarking with exasperation that Lady Wouldbe can make a disputatious forensic oration out of anything, before punningly blending the rhetorical term into the idea of a cause of the destruction of his eardrums. When Volpone begs Mosca to get rid of her instantly, Mosca warns that she hasn't yet given her present, but Volpone says, 'I'll take her absence, upon any price' (3.5.13). Yanking out the comma, most editions have him merely saying that forfeiting her gift would be a small price to pay to be rid of her, but really he is first quipping that her absence will itself be a present, then escalating to suggest that he'd even be willing to pay her for that present.

Eventually one legacy-hunter overhears Mosca conspiring with another, and challenges Mosca: 'You are his, only? and mine, also? are you not?' (3.9.19). The pauses sarcastically evoke the contradictions in Mosca's conduct, mounting the rhetorical challenge so much more dramatically and effectively than, 'You are his only, and mine also, are you not?'

Such readings may offer only a faint flicker, compared to Stephen Booth's strobe-like illuminations of the way great literature (such as Jonson's epitaphs on his children) engages the human mind's appetite for seizing meanings and then rapidly revising them as new phonemic and syntactic information arrives.[8] But – to venture into contextual territory Booth abjures – this 'aggregative urge' and 'indefinitely additive speech'[9] seems profoundly characteristic of Jonson. A man who, by the time he wrote *Volpone*, claimed to weigh about 280 pounds might habitually feature ever bigger things perpetually gobbling up the next smaller ones; and Jonson's comedies are (I have argued) built on this kind of cumulative system, with parodies of various rival plays finally triumphantly subsumed into his own.[10] So the pattern that Jonson's original punctuation reveals, whereby a clause originally intended to speak for and as itself opens the way to another clause that incorporates the previous ones, is congruent on a micro level to construction of the plots on a macro level. Both the sentences and the playwright pause for breath and then consume their progenitors. Commentators generally dismiss the familiar plot-elements as mere comic formulas, whereas I believe that Jonson was realistically evoking the way people fantasise themselves the heroes of formulaic stories. So both those failed melodramas and those interrupted sentences are ways of implying a complex inner process in his dramatic characters.

In the final act of *Volpone*, the additive effect that we kept hearing in the first act – characterisation by *parataxis* – comes roaring back. The out-scammed lawyer Voltore could simply repent that he'd been 'Out-stripped thus by a parasite, a slave / [who] Would run on errands and make legs for crumbs'; but instead Jonson the punctilious punctuator lets us see Voltore's exasperation with himself and his nemesis rising step by beseeching step: 'Out-stripped thus, by a parasite? a slave? / Would run on errands? and make legs, for crumbs?' (5.7.1–2).

The same self-pummelling pattern appears when Volpone finds that he, too, has been out-foxed by Mosca:

> To make a snare for mine own neck! and run
> My head into it, wilfully! with laughter!
> When I had newly 'scaped, was free, and clear!
> Out of mere wantonness!
>
> (5.11.1–4)

It is a fate editors should fear, as they needlessly sweep up Jonson's scattered commas and other archaic punctuation, officiously assuming they are helping Jonson reach the modern reader. What recent textual practices have done is bury Jonson's living intricacies under a pavement of good intentions. Ironically, they have made Jonson seem old-fashioned precisely by over-eagerly modernising the oddities of his syntax and punctuation which, in their original form, reveal exactly the process of a human subjectivity spontaneously and realistically developing from moment to moment that Jonson is commonly accused of lacking.

Editors must listen for everything a play-text could have meant, all the jokes and the shadings of human presence – in other words, they must remain literary critics. Jonson said (although he himself makes a dubious example) that it was impossible to be a good poet without being first a good man. I am saying it is possible to be a good literary editor only by being first a good close-reader. In this case, that means giving the fox back his pause.

TWENTY SIX

Some Similes in *Paradise Lost*, Book 9

PAUL ALPERS

> Much he the place admired, the person more.
> As one who long in populous city pent,   445
> Where houses thick and sewers annoy the air,
> Forth issuing on a summer's morn to breathe
> Among the pleasant villages and farms
> Adjoined, from each thing met conceives delight,
> The smell of grain, or tedded grass, or kine,   450
> Or dairy, each rural sight, each rural sound;
> If chance with nymph-like step fair virgin pass,
> What pleasing seemed, for her now pleases more;
> She most, and in her look sums all delight.
>
> John Milton, *Paradise Lost*, 9.444–54[1]

Like other literary epics, *Paradise Lost* imitates the so-called epic similes which are a prominent feature of the Homeric poems. These similes begin with an initial point of comparison and then continue for several lines; they characteristically represent scenes from a world other than that of the poem. Critics have paid a good deal of attention to some of Milton's similes, as well as to the similes as a general feature of *Paradise Lost*. Less attention has been paid to their uneven distribution in the poem, and even less to the fact that, in each of the books in which they appear, their use is distinct.

Most of the similes in Book 9 occur between Eve's separating from Adam (9.385) and the arrival of Satan and Eve at the Tree of Knowledge (9.679ff.) These three hundred lines are a particularly challenging part of the narrative. On the one hand, the Fall now seems inevitable. As soon as Eve leaves Adam, the poet exclaims,

'O much deceived, much failing, hapless Eve, / Of thy presumed return!' (404–5). At the same time Eve remains 'yet sinless' (659). It is natural to read the epic action with a sense of impending doom, and as in the lines just quoted, the poet helps us along. The ravishing description of Eve tending her flowers (425–31) – one of the peaks of representing her in a state of innocence – concludes, 'Herself, though fairest unsupported flower, / From her best prop so far, and storm so nigh' (432–3). But the similes work quite differently. Instead of carrying us along with the action, they place us firmly on its far side – after the Fall, after the expulsion from Eden, very much in the world we know. Their effect is often the reverse of foreboding, even when they indicate what will happen to Eve.

The first question to ask of an epic simile is whether and how its details are aligned with the action of which it purports to present a likeness. In our example, the correspondence is close. Both Satan and the protagonist in the simile have left a noisome place to discover a benign natural scene, whose delights are enhanced by the chance appearance of a lovely maiden. A second, equally important question is how an epic simile positions the reader, and here is where this simile becomes most interesting. It is almost unique in *Paradise Lost*, in that it is an unproblematic representation of something like ordinary life. As an eighteenth-century commentator remarked, 'The beautiful assemblage of proper circumstances in this charmingly natural and familiar simile lead[s] one to think, that Milton took the hint of it from some real scene of this sort'.[2] Its appeal can be widely documented, for example in Romantic poetry. But if we put our two questions to it, the answers take us in opposite directions. If the simile presents so clear a likeness between its human protagonist and Satan, how do we explain its equally clear loveliness and air of innocence? Alastair Fowler, the editor most alert to such difficulties in *Paradise Lost*, meets this one head-on by aligning the simile with medieval *pastourelles*, in which a knight seduces a shepherdess: 'Any sympathy with the city-dweller's need for a holiday, or appreciation of beauty, fades before his taking advantage of the countrywoman's innocence'.[3] But this last detail is 'wide remote' from anything stated or implied in the simile. Rightly objecting to Fowler's moralism, Neil Forsyth says that 'the effect of the whole passage is to draw the reader very close to Satan's perspective'.[4]

It will be seen that assessing these ten lines raises the central question of *Paradise Lost*: what do we make of human nature? What do we make of ourselves? Are we called upon to interrogate a walk in the country (and hence ourselves) with Fowler's severity – matched, of course, by many, many Miltonists – or do the delights of the represented excursion bear witness to some present capacity, some remnant of our original condition, even after the Fall? And if these are the questions, how do we go about answering them?

Defending his procedures in *Seven Types of Ambiguity*, the Magna Carta of close reading, William Empson argued against certain 'appreciative critics':

> [They] have been perhaps too willing to insist that the operation of poetry is something magical, to which only their own method of incantation can be applied, or like the growth of a flower, which it would be folly to let analysis destroy by digging the roots up and crushing out the juices into the light of day. Critics, as 'barking dogs' on this view, are of two sorts: those who merely relieve themselves against the flower of beauty, and those, less continent, who afterwards scratch it up. I myself, I must confess, aspire to the second of these classes; unexplained beauty arouses an irritation in me, a sense that this would be a good place to scratch; the reasons that make a line of verse likely to give pleasure, I believe, are like the reasons for anything else; one can reason about them; and while it may be true that the roots of beauty ought not to be violated, it seems to me very arrogant of the appreciative critic to think that he could do this, if he chose, by a little scratching.[5]

This is at once hilarious and profound, and it offers an invaluable tip: to understand the force and interest of a poem that engages us, we should find 'a good place to scratch'. In our passage, the detail that 'irritates' me is the line, 'Or dairy, each rural sight, each rural sound', in particular its striking rhythm. It begins with an unusual elision (dair[y ea]ch), strong because of its sound and its bridging grammatical units. The last four feet are two matching phrases, each with three accented syllables, and divided by a strong caesura. (Compare the preceding line, more fluent with its easy iambs and light caesuras.) In a way, the use of this rhythm is obvious: it supports the summary effect of these parallel phrases. (Though it adds, as well as summarises: rural sounds are new in the passage.) This effect of summation and closure is important for the whole simile. It prevents a steady building up to the 'fair virgin' and a sense of climax in 'her look sums all delight'. Instead, 'If chance ... fair virgin pass' seems just one more detail, and its conditional is firmly registered. We note that the next line, framed by 'pleasing' and 'pleases more', could end the simile, and this too mitigates the force of the final line. Because of this reducing of emphasis, the fair virgin's 'look', which 'sums all delight', is not only the way she appears, making her the ultimate object of a (male) gaze, but also (and, I think, primarily) her own act of looking and thus her own delight.

This overall movement, line to line, shows that though readers may be drawn 'very close to Satan's perspective', they are not identified with it. Here is Satan, as he first moves through the Garden:

> In bower and field he sought, where any tuft
> Of grove or garden-plot more *pleasant* lay,
> Their tendance or plantation for *delight*,
> By fountain or by shady rivulet
> He sought them both, but wished his *hap* might find
> Eve separate, he wished, but not with hope
> Of what so seldom *chanced*, when to his wish,
> Beyond his hope, Eve separate he spies,
> Veiled in a cloud of fragrance. ...
>
> (9.417–25, my italics)

The italicised words are picked up in the simile, as if to bring out the country sojourner's likeness to Satan. But Satan is seeking a 'purposed prey' (416), and so the verse representing him has a different movement. For the first few lines, 'he sought' might be absorbed into all that gives delight, as the simile allows us to dwell in and on its pleasant details. But 'he sought them both', repeating the verb, turns 'by fountain and by shady rivulet', from spots of repose to what is passed through on a 'quest' (414): purpose and pleasure are now contradictory. (In his moment of wonder at Eve, right after our simile, Satan can only be 'stupidly good' [465].) From this point, the verse, moving from 'hap' to 'hope' and then 'beyond his hope', builds to a climax (as the simile did not) at the vision of Eve among her flowers.

At a time when most Miltonists espoused a God-centred, 'top down' view of the poem, Frank Kermode said, '*Paradise Lost* deals most directly with this basic theme, the recognition of lost possibilities of joy, order, health, the contrast between what we can imagine as human and what is so here and now; the sensuous import of the myth of the lost Eden'.[6] What is striking about 'As one who long …' is that its sensuous pleasures are so firmly in our world – smells of grain, cattle, grass 'tedded' (spread to dry) – and yet remain connected to the pleasures of Eden. Distinguishing the representations of Satan and of the country sojourner is one of many ways in which the verse of *Paradise Lost* enables readers to accept our humanity without Satanic bitterness or triumph. I would say that this is a main purpose of the whole poem, for example in its questioning and seeking to replace traditional modes of heroism. But to remain within the scope of this essay, we move on to a group of similes fifty lines later. Here too the verse brings us close to Satan and yet distinguishes us from him.

> Pleasing was his shape,
> And lovely, never since of serpent kind
> Lovelier, *not those that in Illyria changed*
> *Hermione and Cadmus, or the god*
> *In Epidaurus; nor to which transformed*
> *Ammonian Jove, or Capitoline was seen,*
> *He with Olympias, this with her who bore*

Scipio the height of Rome. With tract oblique
At first, as one who sought access, but feared
To interrupt, sidelong he works his way.
As when a ship by skilful steersman wrought
Nigh river's mouth or foreland, where the wind
Veers oft, as oft so steers, and shifts her sail;
So varied he, and of his tortuous train
Curled many a wanton wreath in sight of Eve,
To lure her eye; she busied heard the sound
Of rustling leaves, but minded nought, as used
To such disport before her through the field,
From every beast, *more duteous at her call,*
Than at Circean call the herd disguised.

(9.494–522, my italics)

These similes are very different in character. The first, as one
editor says, is 'a passage of virtuosic classical allusion'.[7] The
second seems so transparent as to need no commentary. The third
is of unusual brevity. We begin with the second, about which,
indeed, editors and critics have had almost nothing to say. But
surely it is striking in the same way as 'As one who long …': it
is an even less problematic representation of human activity in
the world we know. There is enough likeness to Satan's serpentine
approach to establish a 'narrative link', but not enough for even
the strictest moralist to undermine its admiring account of the
'skilful steersman' – a wholly different figure from the 'pilot of
some small night-foundered skiff' who naïvely and ominously
moors by Leviathan's side in the first epic simile in the poem
(1.203–8). For the moment the reader can recognise an analogy
with Satan without the danger of a deeper likeness to him.

   The problematic aspect of this simile emerges indirectly, in
the way it follows and reflects on the one preceding. That simile
is as oblique and difficult as any in *Paradise Lost*. The grammar
of 'changed' is obscure: is it transitive, as it seems to be, or
intransitive, as it needs to be to be consistent with Ovid's story of
Harmonia and Cadmus?[8] The symmetry between Alexander the

Great and Scipio Africanus, the two offspring of Jove and human mothers, is rhetorically unsettled by the fact that Alexander is not named. And the content is thoroughly ambiguous. The human figures seem admirable, as indeed do the gods (especially the Epidauran Aesculapius, the god of healing); but they appear in the form of serpents, like Satan of course, but also suggestive of the obliquities and guises of the language that represents them. When we go on to the next simile, we can recognise, in the tacking and veering of the 'skilful steersman', a likeness not only to Satan's movements, but also to our own skills in picking our way in and around the first simile. And if we are really skilful steersmen, we will have noticed that the first letters of the lines that link the two similes are an acrostic, S-A-T-A-N.[9]

Like the steersman's, our skill as readers is not Satanic, but it quite separates us from Eve, 'our credulous mother' (9.644). It makes us capable of understanding Satan's devious rhetoric and ambiguous usages, and we may well ask whether this skill makes us simply resistant to them or somehow complicit in their spell-binding skill. (A later simile compares Satan, gathering himself to speak, to 'some orator renowned / In Athens or free Rome' [9.670–71].) Our ambiguous (self-) identifications are at the heart of the third, and most remarkable, of the similes in this passage. The comparison is certainly surprising. Empson called it a piece of Eve-baiting, one that 'goes so far as to suggest that it was she who tempted Satan and turned him into a serpent'.[10] If we do not apply it to the immediate situation, it at least seems to anticipate the Fall, when Eve has a Circe-like effect on Adam. Hence one critic calls it an 'ominous allusion'.[11] But its effect seems to me more complex, because of the way it emerges from the unfolding narrative and situates us in relation to it. (If it is merely ominous, we stand outside as knowing observers.)

After the simile of the steersman, we can immediately apply the skills it implies in reading 'tortuous train' and 'curled many a wanton wreath'. Both these phrases can bear innocuous readings, but they invite more sinister interpretations. But the lines that follow turn to what may be called naïve narrative. It is initiated by the move from 'lure her eye' to 'heard the sound', and is established by the mimetic effect of 'rustling'. This change encourages an uncritical engagement with Eve in the next lines. 'Disport' is not a loaded word, and it may prompt us to recall the earlier description of beasts 'frisking' and 'sporting' in Eden, including innocent wreathings by 'the unwieldy elephant', who 'wreathed his lithe proboscis' (4.340–47). The naïve mode of these lines relaxes our post-Fall knowingness; when it re-emerges in the simile, the effect is no longer that of the transparently ambiguous 'wanton wreath'. The simile is surprising not only because of 'Circean call' but because 'the herd disguised' transforms Eve's innocently sporting beasts. Surely we cannot explain the phrase solely by referring it to Satan: he may be disguised but he is certainly not a 'herd'. What happens, I think, is that our momentarily Edenic responsiveness to Eve and the scene becomes an awareness of a more problematic vulnerability, the recognition that according to the Circe myth, we potentially belong to 'the herd disguised'. We can become beasts through sensuousness (the standard Renaissance interpretation of the Circe story, as in Spenser's Bower of Bliss), and like Satan, we are capable of disguise. This suddenly ambiguous sense of our susceptibility to Eve extends the pathos that often attends her *before* the Fall to the situation of all her descendants *after* the Fall.

Who is the sorcerer who so transforms us? It can scarcely be Eve. She is actually quite unlike Circe here: as when she was among her flowers, she is 'mindless the while' (9.431), hardly conscious of any control she might be exerting. Satan is more like Circe: physically here and verbally later he weaves spells that will transform humankind. But the real magic is the poet's. When he springs this simile on us, he once more places us in the world we know. But this time it is neither the ordinary world of the sojourner in the country and the 'skilful steersman' nor the historical world of Greek and Roman gods and heroes. As he positions us between Eve and Satan, recalling in yet another guise his sense of what it means to be human, Milton turns to the world of pagan myth and Homeric epic – all that he meant his epic to supersede, but whose captivating powers he emulates and here makes his own.

TWENTY SEVEN

Telling Stories

Russ McDonald

POMPEY	... I beseech you, look into Master Froth here, sir; a man of fourscore pound a year; whose father died at Hallowmas – was't not at Hallowmas, Master Froth?
FROTH	All-hallond Eve.
POMPEY	Why, very well: I hope here be truths. He, sir, sitting, as I say, in a lower chair, sir – 'twas in the Bunch of Grapes, where indeed you have a delight to sit, have you not?
FROTH	I have so, because it is an open room, and good for winter.
POMPEY	Why, very well then: I hope here be truths.
ANGELO	This will last out a night in Russia When nights are longest there. I'll take my leave ...

William Shakespeare, *Measure for Measure*, 2.1.121–34

Pity the poor actor cast as Master Froth in *Measure for Measure*: this extract contains most of his part. He speaks briefly earlier in the scene (when asked his whereabouts as Mrs Elbow entered the tavern) and later (when questioned about his background and warned to stay out of taverns), but it is on this central exchange that I will concentrate. The introduction of Master Froth represents a staple of Shakespeare's narrative strategy, a device employed, often with minor variations, in virtually every play; it is a creative manoeuvre that contributes much to the richness of texture that we think of as distinctively Shakespearean. The key to this passage is its irrelevance. By 'irrelevance', of course, I mean comparative irrelevance, since it's hard to think of a word that Shakespeare wrote that is absolutely irrelevant to the words around it. But the value of Master Froth's moment lies in its vividness and its evanescence. Close reading of these ten lines of prose dialogue helps to illuminate Shakespeare's commitment to the pleasures of fiction, his exploitation of the gratuitous, and his encouragement of imaginative exercise in the audience.

The character and history of Master Froth can, of course, be related to the larger concerns of *Measure for Measure.* That relation is marginal but undeniable. Froth's brief contribution appears in the midst of the arraignment of Pompey Bum, Froth being one of the 'two notorious benefactors', as Constable Elbow malapropistically puts it. As with so many of Shakespeare's clowns, Elbow's fuzziness and verbal inadequacies make it difficult to determine what Pompey is being charged with; it is even less clear how Master Froth is involved; and no one ever explains thoroughly and exactly what happened to Elbow's wife in Mistress Overdone's establishment.

M. M. Mahood, in her excellent *Playing Bit Parts in Shakespeare*, summarises with admirable concision and reticence the problem about what happened between poor Master Froth and Mrs Elbow, as related in an exchange preceding this one. We are invited to look carefully at Master Froth, and

> [a]s we gaze, Jonsonian scenarios race through our minds. Froth, the archetypal gull, believes the Bunch of Grapes to be a room in an inn, and is as startled as Elbow's wife when he finds himself alone with her. Or else Froth knows perfectly well where he is and, reassured by Pompey ... that there are no health hazards in this house, has just asked for a girl, when Mistress Elbow innocently enters in quest of refreshments. ... But here the scenario becomes confused: ought Mistress Elbow to be 'respected' or 'suspected' for her part in the encounter? Stewed prunes have other meanings, and her dull and poverty-stricken life with Elbow may have

generated other longings. Pompey's innuendos imply that she knew very well what she was about when she entered Mistress Overdone's house. None the less, he persists in maintaining Froth's innocence to Escalus.[1]

Mahood imaginatively sifts the conflicting, inconclusive evidence. Master Froth had apparently eaten the stewed prunes that Elbow's wife longed for, prunes that had been in a china dish and for which he paid threepence. 'Stewed prunes', with the pun on 'stews' or brothels, does substantial work, yoking together longings of different kinds. Froth enters from the play's underworld, the morbific sphere of pimps and johns and hookers of which Lucio and Mistress Overdone and Pompey are the principals, which the Duke's laxity has allowed to flourish, and which Angelo seeks to suppress. Froth is, apparently, a regular customer of Mistress Overdone; whether his custom involves whoring or merely drinking is not made explicit. Indeed the dubious status of the Overdone trade is vital to the effect of this scene, particularly this segment: does she run a brothel or tavern? Is Pompey a tapster or pimp? Is Froth an innocent or a felon?

It is worth lingering over the nuances of the name. To modern ears, 'Froth' suggests something trivial, a bit of fluff, the head but not the beer (i.e., a minor player). In the early seventeenth century, however, it could also have ugly connotations: it was 'used contemptuously of persons' (*OED s.v.* 'froth' n. 3), a synonym being 'scum', as in Dekker's *Patient Grissill*, 'Out you froth, you scum',[2] and *The Merry Wives of Windsor*, 'Froth and scum, thou liest!' (1.1.152). But there are further connotations still: 'froth' is also an adjective 'Applied to what is tender or immature' (*OED s.v.* 'froth' adj. 2b), as in Thomas Tusser's *Points of Husbandry* (1557): 'Eat up thy pig, veal and lamb being froth'.[3] Escalus apparently thinks of Froth as a naïf, vulnerable to gulling, as we see when he lectures Froth on the danger of taverns, warning that the tapsters will 'draw' or drain him (2.1.201). The 'Names of all the Actors' printed in the Folio lists Froth as 'a foolish gentleman', and 'Master' as a title normally points to youth. But these conclusions are speculative. Much depends on the close reading by the actor playing the part and by the director conceiving the scene.

What matters, at least for my purposes in reading Froth's story, is Pompey's demand that Escalus – and we – scrutinise Master Froth. He is described first as 'a man of four score pound a year'. Scholars differ on the value of this sum, but the Oxford editor believes that 'With an unearned income of eighty pounds a year Froth was moderately wealthy by the standards of the time'.[4] According to Brian Gibbons in his New Cambridge edition, 'James I required all Englishmen in 1603 who had land worth forty pounds a year to accept a knighthood, or be fined, which shows that they were considered well-to-do, and Froth had twice that income.'[5] Froth seems to have inherited his money from his father, recently deceased: Pompey misses by a day ('Hallowmas', 1 November) and is corrected by Froth ('All-holland eve', or Halloween). At the time of the alleged offence against Elbow's wife, Froth was present in one of the rooms of the tavern, the Bunch of Grapes – here, as in other Shakespeare plays, such as the Pomgarnet in *1 Henry IV*, rooms in pubs are named – sitting in a 'lower chair'. (The precise nature of this piece of furniture has stumped editors, who have never been able to explain the phrase persuasively.) He enjoys sitting here 'because it is an open room and good for winter'. Some nineteenth-century commentators take this as evidence that Froth is an idiot, since no one would want an 'open' room in winter. But 'open' can mean 'well-ventilated' (i.e., warm from the fire but not smoky). More likely, 'open room' in this instance means 'public', a common room in the tavern where a fire would have burned all day and for which the individual customer would not have been required to pay, as he would in a private room.

'I hope here be truths', Pompey's capstone remark (and his second use of the sentence), signals his parodic attitude towards the legal proceedings, a contemptuous edge evident also in his mockery of Elbow. More importantly, of course, it foregrounds the complexity of discerning exactly what occurred at Mistress Overdone's, and anywhere else, for that matter. Truth is elusive throughout *Measure for Measure*. Moreover, Angelo's sudden departure at this moment subverts his commitment to justice: he impatiently dismisses the laborious process of determining the facts, hoping instead that Escalus will 'find good cause to whip them all'. Whereas Angelo thinks of the law grandly and abstractly, the play implies that real justice requires diligence, patience, and meticulous care.

But what about Master Froth and his father and his money and his chair before the fire in his favourite room? Renaissance theory of story-telling, the guidelines for which were often taken from the classical masters of oratory, particularly Cicero, Quintilian, and the pseudo-Ciceronian *Rhetorica ad Herennium*, can help to illuminate these images. In the *Institutio Oratorio* Quintilian advises the would-be orator that one way to polish his argument is to exchange the general for the specific (or to establish the general by means of the specific). He takes as his term for this attempt at 'vividness' the Greek word '*enargeia*, which [he] mentioned in giving instructions for Narrative, because vividness, or, as some say, "representation", is more than mere perspicuity, since instead of being merely transparent it somehow shows itself off. It is a great virtue to express our subject clearly and in such a way that it seems to be actually seen'.[6] The key to the classical trope, and thus to Shakespeare's creation of visual specificity, is its power to appeal to the imagination. Quintilian reverts again and again to the virtues of that faculty and its sensitivity to detail: 'Could anyone be so unimaginative as not to feel that he is seeing the persons and the place and the dress and to add some unspoken details for himself into the bargain'; 'I certainly imagine that I can see the face ...'; 'the mind finds it easiest to accept what it can recognise'.[7]

The picture of Master Froth before the fire in the Bunch of Grapes illustrates Shakespeare's use of one or two vivid details to stimulate the spectator's imagination and thus to enrich the dramatic action. By means of the slightest visual cues, we are treated to a story within a story, invited to enter momentarily another world. It is not too much to say that this packing of fictions within fictions is one of the primary features of Shakespearean drama. For all the unreality of the early modern stage

– the artifices of character (males playing female parts, for example), the absence of scenic decoration, the formality of poetic speech – it is nonetheless true that the Elizabethan and Jacobean playwrights, Shakespeare above all, lure the spectator into an imaginative realm, creating a mimetic world in which we willingly lose ourselves, a fictional space to which we are eager to return again and again. The Viennese palace in which the interrogation of Pompey Bum takes place is one corner of the fictional dominion of *Measure for Measure*, a congeries of legal figures and criminals. The various forms of authority displayed herein are especially compelling. Political: Angelo, the Olympian, self-satisfied moralist who would prefer to elide the process and skip to the whipping. Constabulary: Elbow, the half-witted officer who habitually 'misplaces' linguistically (and otherwise as well). Judicial: Escalus, the long-suffering executive who tries patiently to assemble and evaluate reliable data. Finally, Theatrical: Pompey, whose ironic attitude to his predicament and mocking interaction with his interlocutors make him arguably the most powerful figure on the stage. We find ourselves immersed in this fiction, caught up in its narratives, attentive to its details.

The recent history of Master Froth represents another fiction within this fiction, a movement, to use a spatial metaphor, deeper into the imaginative locus and further from ourselves and the familiar realm we normally inhabit. We concentrate only briefly on the death of Froth's father and the young man's custom of sitting in the Bunch of Grapes. Perhaps we wonder for an instant about the relationship between father and son: did Froth experience fierce grief at his father's death? Or was it the occasion of joy, thanks to the inheritance? What about his attachment to the fire at Mistress Overdone's? Is he a hanger-on, manipulated by Pompey as some of Jonson's figures are by a strong figure such as Bobadill? Is he kept around for his money? Or is he himself a criminal? For all of Froth's apparently callow mien, it is just possible that he is Pompey's stooge, that the story of the dead father and the open room good for winter are quotidian lies – Pompey's fictions – concocted to furnish authority to Froth's exoneration of the tapster-pimp. For the briefest of moments we are allowed to dally in this vivid, persuasive illusion. And with Angelo's exit lines the world of Master Froth evaporates, whisked away as Angelo departs and Escalus regains control, returning us to the seriousness of the investigation.

The effect of these compounded illusions is mimetic: they create the semblance of reality and depth in the fictional realm. If we think spatially, regarding *Measure for Measure* as a painting, with the Duke, Angelo, Claudio, and Isabella as the central group, then the arraignment of Pompey becomes a secondary grouping, a minor episode clearly subordinate to the narrative center. To extend this analogy, the trivial, irrelevant details of Master Froth's history and habits are doubly subordinate, so far in the background as to be almost invisible, especially when the picture is seen *in toto*. But it is such details that furnish texture to the object of art: they generate a sense of perspective and thus manufacture the illusion of layered reality. To shift to another kind of made object, we might think of a tapestry, reminding ourselves of the origin of the word 'text' in weaving; such stories as that of Froth create texture, giving body and hence reality to the surface of the play.

For an audience, the experience of embedded fictions represents a case of Shakespeare's doing what he does best, which is to set the mind in motion. The value of such pictures is that they take us on a brief imaginative holiday, contriving an instantaneous transit to another realm and then an immediate return. We glimpse into the backstory of Master Froth, and then the view disappears as we snap back to Escalus and Pompey. The compounding of multiple minor fictions impels us back and forth between two levels of 'reality'. The tactic works, then, in the same way that a pun functions, or an allusion, moving the mind rapidly between two points, both of which are absorbing. Moreover, the quick flight into the world of Master Froth is a holiday from the fictional world of *Measure for Measure*, but then *Measure for Measure* is itself a holiday from the actual world. The creation of Master Froth offers one small instance of Shakespeare's unfailing capacity to manipulate levels of reality, just as he does in those meta-theatrical festivals, *A Midsummer Night's Dream*, *Hamlet*, and *The Tempest*.

This narrative tactic reminds us of the fecundity of the Shakespearean imagination, which – surprisingly – may need some defence. It is a commonplace that Shakespeare is not known for making up stories, that he invented almost none of his own plots. Starting (usually) with Ovid and Holinshed and Plutarch and sometimes borrowing from Plautus and Painter and other popular fiction writers, he developed his gifts as adaptor, not deviser. But this bald axiom needs modification. The artistic imagination is hardly to be gauged only by what it makes up out of whole cloth. As the ancients knew, and it was in their school that Shakespeare learned, *inventio* meant finding something usable in the *inventory* of narrative materials. And Shakespeare not only invented, in that sense, but also invented hosts of minor stories to buttress and accompany the central narratives.

Many such narrative intrusions pop up in the plays, one of the simplest occurring in the hectic race to the church near the end of *The Taming of the Shrew*. As Biondello urges Lucentio to take Bianca to the priest and marry her while her father is occupied, Lucentio is doubtful, flummoxed by the haste and confusion; but Biondello reassures him: 'I cannot tarry. I knew a wench married in an afternoon as she went to the garden for parsley to stuff a rabbit, and so may you sir' (4.4.97–9). This is a textbook example of the Shakespearean turn I have identified. The tiny tale has no bearing on the plot and little to do with the action or the meaning of the text before us. Rather, it presents a self-contained story, a miniature narrative or indeed a playlet which opens a window onto another world, invites the audience to linger over the wonders of this story within the story, and then bangs that window shut, shifting from the extraneous character or narrative episode back to the main plot. A preliminary list of such stories would have to include, among many others, Iago's toothache; Othello's memory of Aleppo and 'a malignant and a turbaned Turk'; Falstaff's recalling the youthful Shallow at Clement's Inn, his body so thin that he looked 'like a man made after supper of a cheese-paring: when a' was naked, he was, for all the world, like a forked radish, with a head fantastically carved upon it with a knife'; the injured and outraged Dogberry's defence of himself as 'a rich fellow enough, go to; and a fellow that hath had losses, and one that hath two gowns and every thing handsome about him'; the masturbating Spaniard in *Pericles* who, when he heard about Marina, his 'mouth so watered, that he went to bed to her very description'; in the Pageant of the Nine Worthies in *Love's Labour's Lost*, Costard's standing up for poor Sir Nathaniel, despite his inadequacies as an actor: 'He is a marvellous good neighbour, faith, and a very good bowler; but, for Alisander, alas, you see how 'tis, – a little o'erparted'; or, perhaps the greatest of all such moments, Sir Andrew Aguecheek's 'I was adored once too'. Readers are invited to compile their own favourite examples.

TWENTY EIGHT

Richard's Soliloquy: *Richard II*, 5.5.1–49

Harry Berger, Jr

Enter RICHARD *alone.*

RICHARD   I have been studying how I may compare
This prison where I live unto the world;
And, for because the world is populous
And here is not a creature but myself,
I cannot do it. Yet I'll hammer it out.   5
My brain I'll prove the female to my soul,
My soul the father, and these two beget
A generation of still-breeding thoughts,
And these same thoughts people this little world,
In humours like the people of this world   10
For no thought is contented. The better sort,
As thoughts of things divine, are intermixd
With scruples, and do set the word itself
Against the word,
As thus: 'Come, little ones'; and then again,   15
'It is as hard to come as for camel
To thread the postern of a small needle's eye'.
Thoughts tending to ambition, they do plot
Unlikely wonders: how these vain weak nails
May tear a passage through the flinty ribs   20
Of this hard world, my ragged prison walls
And for they cannot, die in their own pride.
Thoughts tending to content flatter themselves
That they are not the first of fortune's slaves,
Nor shall not be the last – like silly beggars   25
Who, sitting in the stocks, refuge their shame,

That many have and others must sit there;
And in this thought they find a kind of ease,
Bearing their own misfortunes on the back
Of such as have before indur'd the like.   30
Thus play I in one person many people,
And none contented. Sometimes am I king;
Then treasons make me wish myself a beggar,
And so I am. Then crushing penury
Persuades me I was better when a king;   35
Then am I king'd again, and by and by
Think that I am unking'd by Bolingbroke,
And straight am nothing. But whate'er I be,
Nor I, nor any man that but man is,
With nothing shall be pleas'd, till he be eas'd   40
With being nothing.   *The music plays.*
                    Music do I hear?
Ha, ha! keep time – how sour sweet music is
When time is broke and no proportion kept!
So is it in the music of men's lives.
And here have I the daintiness of ear   45
To check time broke in a disordered string;
But for the concord of my state and time,
Had not an ear to hear my true time broke:
I wasted time, and now doth time waste me;
          William Shakespeare, *Richard II*, 5.5.1–49

'Enter Richard alone'. He tells us first what he has been trying to do, 'studying how I may compare / This prison where I live unto the world', and then why he 'cannot do it': 'because the world is populous / And here is not a creature but myself' (1–5). Nevertheless, he continues bravely,

                    I'll hammer it out.
My brain I'll prove the female to my soul,
My soul the father, and these two beget
A generation of still-breeding thoughts,

> And these same thoughts people this little world,
> In humours like the people of this world;
> For no thought is contented.

> (5–11)

These thoughts/people compose into a social hierarchy of three classes, each with its own form of discontent: 'The better sort, / As thoughts of things divine' are troubled by moral 'scruples' – self-doubt – as they sophistically take advantage of contradictions in scripture ('set the word itself / Against the word' [11–14]). Perhaps this leads to the desperation of 'Thoughts tending to ambition' that 'do plot / Unlikely wonders' and, when they fail, 'die in their own pride', which in turn leads 'Thoughts tending to content' to rationalise their acceptance of their miserable lot as 'fortune's slaves'. In this third and longest of the three descriptions, the speaker's impatience comes through most sharply. His contempt flares up at those who 'find a kind of ease' by comparing themselves to 'silly beggars', thus 'Bearing their own misfortunes on the back / Of such as have before indur'd the like' (29–30).

With one exception (the personal reference to 'my ragged prison walls' at line 21) these increasingly bitter reflections have the ring of general cynical wisdom. Yet the speaker summarily incorporates them in a self-portrait, 'Thus play I in one person many people, / And none contented', and goes on to describe his vacillation between the thoughts of kingship and of beggary as if his actual changes of fortune were the consequences of his wishes and thoughts (30–38).

In 4.1 Richard disingenuously used the two-buckets figure to highlight his dominance in the perverse game of 'Here, cousin, seize the crown'. He implied that he, the tear-laden-down bucket, controls the upward motion of the empty bucket he describes in an image more applicable to himself than to Bolingbroke ('The emptier ever dancing in the air' [4.1.182–7]). Now, as the soliloquist reviews actual changes of status he recently suffered, he resituates them in the floating present tense of fantasy, and depicts his thought and desire as controlling the seesaw between kingship and beggary. It is both a superficial evasion and a profound truth for the already deposed king to imagine himself operating both ends of the see-saw, as he does when he says 'by and by [I] / Think that I am unking'd by Bolingbroke, / And straight am nothing' (5.5.36–8).

From this glimpse of the truth of self-deposition, he turns and wings away on the redundant whir of a generalising jingle:

> But whate'er I be,
> Nor I, nor any man that but man is,
> With nothing shall be pleas'd till he be eas'd
> With being nothing.

(40–41)

This not only recalls the desire to 'find a kind of ease' he had just implicitly disparaged in his reference to the self-demeaning flattery of 'Thoughts tending to content'. It *illustrates* and *enacts* that desire. It bears the marks of a biting recoil from the flattery of the victim's discourse, and so the conclusion of this exercise in 'the generation of still-breeding thoughts' circles back like a boomerang from human nature – any man that but man is – to the speaker.

'Enter Richard alone'. Until now he has always directed his eloquence – whether sardonic or self-pitying – towards others. This is the play's first and only soliloquy. Do we infer from this that he suddenly becomes aware of the audience offstage and moves forward to address them? He begins his speech with a verb phrase in the present perfect tense: not, 'I am studying' but 'I have been studying'. Does this mean that he assumes his fans in the theatre audience have been wondering what he's been up to since they last saw him, and that he considerately brings them up to date? Perhaps he thinks they think he spends his time offstage working out the poetic comparisons he is famous for, and are eagerly waiting for the progress report he now shares with them (or at them).

Maybe, then, this is an example of the convention of extra-dramatic address frequently used in Tudor drama before Shakespeare, especially by such figures as the Vice in the morality plays. Yet Anne Righter argues that by Shakespeare's time soliloquies were distinguished from addresses to the audience and tended to be contained within the dramatic fiction: 'it was understood that almost all speeches of this kind were overheard by the spectators as the result of stage conventions, not through conscious intent on the part of the speaker'.[1] In other words, it was understood that although the actor knows he is playing to the audience in the theatre, the character doesn't know he is a fictional character being performed by an actor on stage.

If the presence of the theatre audience to the actor reminds us of its absence to the character, we become aware that the soliloquising character-as-actor is deprived of the very conditions he needs in order to resemble the performer or role-player he desires to be. He may be his own audience by default. The contrast may then establish the missing audience as the object of the speaker's anxiety or desire.

Of course an actor may play a character who performs as if he is an actor playing roles before his onstage audience, and Richard is famous for this. The soliloquy is a special case of performative behaviour, and it poses a problem: since, in contrast to the actor, the character is by convention unaware of the theatre audience he appears to address, whom does Richard address here? Is he imagining or constructing the audience he wants to be heard by, the audience he wants to persuade or be judged by, an audience that may include (or consist entirely of) himself?

Righter quotes a wonderful example of a moment of hesitation between extra-dramatic and dramatic address performed by the Vice in an earlier play, *Kyng Daryus* (*c.* 1565). After he 'opens the performance by hailing the audience in what seems to be the old manner ... he deliberately and rather slyly withdraws this initial recognition of the spectators' in the following lines:

> But softe, is there no body here?
> Truly, I do not lyke thys gere;
> I thought I should haue found sum bodie.[2]

'Enter Richard alone' and teasingly runs up the question of the audience like a flag in his statement that 'here is not a creature

but myself'. Although he attributes his failure to the difference
between the populous world and the empty prison, the emphasis
on enforced isolation suggests an additional obstacle. Accustomed
as he is to public speaking, he finds it hard even to elaborate a figure
of thought when there is no audience of flatterers or adversaries
for him to dominate with his superior rhetorical firepower.

Perhaps, Lois Potter speculates, if Richard has been 'playing a
power game where he loses in order to win', the soliloquy shows
'his realization that you can't play these games by yourself'.[3] But he
tries anyway. 'The people of this world' may have shut him out but
they can't shut him up. He will now replace the missing audience
with himself, will divide himself into the auditor or receiver or
mother and the speaker or sender or father of his comparison ('My
brain I'll prove the female to my soul'), will posture for his own
approval or disapproval as if checking his performance in a mirror.

But hasn't he always done that? 'Enter Richard alone' is the
phantom stage direction that I am tempted to slip behind the one
that heads the play's opening scene ('Enter King Richard, John of
Gaunt, with other Nobles and Attendants'), for even in Richard's
acts of dialogue he seems always to be talking and listening to
himself. What he has been saying to himself throughout the play
is a variation or illustration of what he says in this soliloquy. He
has 'been studying' since 1.1. The problem he poses for himself
is stated portentously enough to justify the amount of study
he suggests he has given it, since 'This prison where I live' can
be – and has been – taken as a reference not only to his literal
incarceration but also to his self-imprisoning state of mind.

If he succeeds in persuading himself that he has overcome
either or both of these prisons, he will have risen above his
isolation and victimisation. On the one hand he will have proved
his self-sufficiency to himself and on the other hand he will have
asserted his resemblance, his connection, to the world. Yet both
that project and its failure are mocked by the desperate and vio-
lent futility, the melodramatic pathos, of the image he uses to
illustrate the 'Unlikely wonders' plotted by 'Thoughts tending
to ambition':

how these vain weak nails
May tear a passage through the flinty ribs
Of this hard world, my ragged prison walls;
And for they cannot, die in their own pride.

(19–22)

Thus, now and always, whether alone or in public, for him to listen to himself thinking or speaking is to divide 'one person' into 'many people', none of them ever 'contented'.

'Enter Richard alone' and marks his awareness of his dilemma by representing the act of soliloquy as a monstrous act that is at once self-dividing, self-confining, and self-coupling. Shifting apparitions of escape, suicide, and caesarean trauma converge to register the confusion and impotence of the 'still-breeding thoughts' produced by what he depicts as the intercourse between his soul and brain. The conflicted senses of 'still-breeding' dramatise the causal relation between frenetic activity and futility: 'always breeding' and 'still-born' (breeding 'still', or dead, thoughts).

However strained or strange this figure of self-coupling and generation is, it is charged with meaning by its inclusion in, its allusion to, a network of apprehensions that pervade the play and manifest what may be called paedophobia (fear of children). The precariousness of generational continuity is suggested by the glimmers of several troubled father–son relationships. Gaunt quietly betrays his son in 1.3, York loudly disparages his in 5.2–3, and Bolingbroke worriedly mentions his 'unthrifty' son in 5.3.

In the deposition scene York announces that Richard has adopted Bolingbroke as his heir (4.1.108–13). This makes it possible for Richard legally to resign the crown by designating his cousin as his 'son', a strategy that comically exemplifies one of the troublesome properties of sonship that produce paedophobia: fathers are expected to raise their sons not only to perpetuate the paternal image but also to replace the mortal father, and replacement may sometimes take the form of displacement or deposition.

'Time broke in a disordered string' (5.5.46): Richard's phrase provides an apt figure of the tensions and surrogations that untune the genealogical string of patriarchal succession. The plays of the *Henriad* are bound together by their exploration of the impact of the failure of paternal authority on social and political behaviour and on the fears and desires that motivate it. Like so many phrases in the play, Richard's 'disordered string' chimes with an earlier expression used by another speaker: 'He that hath suffered this disordered spring / Hath now himself met with the fall of leaf' (3.4.48–9). This is the gardener, describing Richard's folly in the terms provided by his analogy between care of the state and care of gardens.

Even before his assistant proposes the analogy of garden to kingdom, the gardener rakes politiculture into horticulture by translating the anxiety of fathers into an arboreal figure of self-endangering virility:

> Go, bind thou up young dangling apricocks,
> Which like unruly children make their sire
> Stoop with oppression of their prodigal weight,
>
> (3.4.29–31)

The bizarre pun on 'dangling apricocks' together with that key word of the *Henry IV* plays, 'prodigal', turns apricots / sons into limp penile figures. It produces a caricature of anxiety that rubs off on the gardener as a pompous representative of youth-hating oldsters: if Richard had 'cut off the heads of too fast growing sprays, / That look too lofty' (3.4.34–5) he could have kept the crown. The gardener subordinates his critique to the unruly spray of examples that happen to be available in his horticultural analogue. His discourse thus illustrates the unruliness he critiques.

Richard II's soliloquy not only demonstrates but intensifies his sense that since, as Wolfgang Iser puts it, 'he cannot reconcile himself with any of these roles, and therefore has to act them all, he enhances the dissatisfaction with his own nothing – a nothing from which only death can liberate him'.[4] In the best commentary on representations of the nothing that is despair, not even death can liberate the ambitious sinner who tries vainly to get rid of himself and dies in his own pride. Kierkegaard describes 'the sickness unto death', the self-loathing of the sinner despondent over his sin, in terms that assimilate it to the dark side of what might be described as the Christian version of narcissism: 'A person in despair … despairingly wants to be … a self that he is not. … He would be in seventh heaven were he the self he wants to be …, but to be forced to be the self he does not want to be, that is his torment – that he cannot get rid of himself'.[5]

To the extent that Richard finds himself in a prison and world he recognises as partly – perhaps largely – the effects of self-incarceration in despair, he stands before himself as his own jailer. Among the indications in the soliloquy that he bitterly acknowledges this bitter truth about himself is the awkward redundancy of lines 9–10, in which he says he will 'people this little world' with thoughts that are 'In humours like the people of this world' because both – thoughts and people – are discontented. Apart from the fact that the assertion displays the bad humour of the speaker ('no thought [of mine] is [ever] contented'), it seems at first glance to be an arbitrary criterion of resemblance. But when we take into account the effect of the redundancy Richard's focus on discontent becomes plausible, for it amounts to an acknowledgement that the discontented subjects he creates as soliloquist are doubles of those he created as king.

TWENTY NINE

Virtual Presence and Vicarious Identity
in the First Tetralogy

Joel B. Altman

In act 5, scene 3 of *King Henry VI, Part 1*, William de la Pole, Earl of Suffolk, bids a reluctant farewell to the woman he has just arranged to marry his king, then turns aside:

> O, wert thou for myself! But, Suffolk, stay;
> Thou may'st not wander in that labyrinth:
> There Minotaurs and ugly treasons lurk.
> Solicit Henry with her wondrous praise.
> Bethink thee on her virtues that surmount,
> And natural graces that extinguish art;
> Repeat their semblance often on the seas,
> That when thou com'st to kneel at Henry's feet,
> Thou may'st bereave him of his wits with wonder.
>
> (*1H6*, 5.3.187–95)

And sure enough, just two scenes later a bedazzled Henry declares to the newly arrived Suffolk:

> Your wondrous rare description, noble Earl,
> Of beauteous Margaret hath astonish'd me:
> Her virtues graced with external gifts
> Do breed love's settled passions in my heart:
> And like as rigour of tempestuous gusts
> Provokes the mightiest hulk against the tide,
> So am I driven by breath of her renown
> Either to suffer shipwreck, or arrive
> Where I may have fruition of her love.
>
> (*1H6*, 5.5.1–9)

Such are the effects of love at first sight, a focused imagination, and some serious rehearsal.

But what has happened to enable this *translatio libidinis* between subject and king? How does the passion that one man feels for a woman become infused into another so that the second man experiences not only the love of the first but also the conditions he endured during rehearsal – crossing the tempestuous Narrow Seas while envisioning the virtues and graces of Margaret – and converts them into an extended simile of his own boisterous passion, likening himself to 'the mightiest hulk ... driven ... against the tide ... by breath of her renown'?[1]

The answer is to be found by examining the 'breath' in question – namely Suffolk's. The first thing to notice is that Henry praises Suffolk for having performed a 'rare description' of the beauty and virtues of Margaret of Anjou. What is a 'rare description'? For someone trained in the Tudor grammar school curriculum (anachronistically, Suffolk seems to be an alumnus), it is the anglicised form of *descriptio*, the Latin translation of *ekphrasis* – which is the Greek term for a kind of speech that renders in vivid, concrete detail the qualities of persons, times, actions, places, animals, plants, or works of art. It is often referred to as word-painting because its aim is to bring the object described before the eyes of the listener – that is, to transform something *heard* into something *seen*. To do this effectively, the rhetoricians claim, the speaker must feel the emotions he wants to arouse in the listener, and he achieves this by summoning a *visio* or, in Suffolk's words, a 'semblance' of the object before his own imagining power.

Now Margaret exists for Henry only in the words that convey Suffolk's imagination of her, yet those words have induced a substantial psychosomatic change in him. He participates vicariously in Suffolk's passion for a woman who is merely a virtual presence, although Suffolk has encountered the thing itself. The writer or writers of *1 Henry VI*, 5.3 and 5.5 were alert to a phenomenon that Shakespeare had already explored in *The First Part of the Contention betwixt the Two Famous Houses of York and Lancaster* (*2 Henry VI*) and its successor, *The True Tragedy of Richard Duke of York* (*3 Henry VI*), and would develop further in *The Tragedy of Richard III*.[2] It is the phenomenon of vicarious identity and its complement, virtual presence. By the first term I mean assuming in one's imagination another's person; by the second, existing for oneself or for another in a hypothetical, 'as if' mode, which sometimes shades into a subjunctive or optative mode (to use grammatical terms) – a 'would that it were' state of mind – even as one conducts oneself in the indicative mode of actuality that recognises what 'is'. Many of the *dramatis personae* in these plays participate in such parallel mental modes and this becomes a source of psychological tension for the individual and of dramatic tension among those who struggle against one another for dominance. At the epicentre stands Margaret of Anjou.

As Suffolk opens *The First Part of the Contention*, we discover that Henry's capacity to vicariously experience Suffolk's passion for Margaret in the last scene of *Part 1* has retroactively anticipated Suffolk's ritual assumption of Henry's person at the royal wedding in France. He has married Margaret in the person of his king at Tours, he says, and now sets aside that identity:

> I have perform'd my task and was espous'd:
> And humbly now upon my bended knee,
> In sight of England and her lordly peers,
> Deliver up my title in the Queen
> To your most gracious hands, that are the substance
> Of that great shadow I did represent.
>
> (*2H6*, 1.1.9–14)

A shadow – what is less, the mere *representation* of a shadow – is all that Suffolk was during the diplomatic espousal. Now the shadow vanishes as Suffolk hands over the title he had assumed to the substance to which he stood at two removes, and resumes being the man he is.

The new Queen herself is not unaccustomed to such vicarious experience. She greets her real-life husband with free, unpremeditated speech, she says, because

The mutual conference that my mind hath had
By day, by night, waking, and in my dreams,
In courtly company, or at my beads,
With you mine alderliefest sovereign,
Makes me the bolder to salute my king
With ruder terms, such as my wit affords,
And over joy of heart doth minister.

                                                         (*2H6*, 1.1.25–31)

As Suffolk had vicariously married Margaret for Henry, so
Margaret has already summoned the virtual presence of Henry
and conversed with him. Indeed, she tells him later in the play
how it was possible: Suffolk had infused his person into her
imagination, 'as Ascanius did / When he to madding Dido would
unfold / His father's acts, commenc'd in burning Troy!' (3.2.115–
17). Her hint of their imagined pre-nuptial intimacy thrills the
King, who promptly elevates procurator Suffolk to the rank of
Duke and sweeps his new wife off to be crowned.

By the third scene of *The Contention*, however, Margaret is
restive under Gloucester's Protectorship. 'Am I a queen in title and
in style', she asks Suffolk, 'And must be made a subject to a duke?'
Not only is there a gap between her social identity, which she feels
to be coterminous with her self, and her experience of power; she
has also discovered that Suffolk's assumed personhood, when he
ran at tilt in Tours for her honour, was false: 'I thought King Henry
had resembled thee / In courage, courtship, and proportion'. She
has since found that 'His study is his tilt-yard, and his loves / Are
brazen images of canoniz'd saints' (*2H6*, 1.3.48–9, 53–4, 59–60).
This disappointing disparity between Henry's virtual presence
and his actual behaviour drives her to undermine not just the Lord
Protector but the King himself.

The interplay of actual and vicarious experience – of real
presence and virtual presence – is a familiar Shakespearean theme,
but in these early plays about royal power and who has the right
(and might) to exercise it there is a persistent anxiety that what
appears to be real and may even feel real is only an imitation or,

in Elizabethan parlance, a 'shadow', and that one can easily find oneself in a situation that is inauthentic. An early instance of this preoccupation is the slippage between apparent and real identities that occurs when the Countess of Auvergne invites Lord Talbot to her castle, with the intention of entrapping him. On his arrival she mocks his stature, which, she claims, doesn't live up to his reputation. Finding himself abused, he prepares to leave, but the Countess tells him he's her prisoner:

> Long time thy shadow hath been thrall to me,
> For in my gallery thy picture hangs;
> But now the substance shall endure the like.
>
> *(1H6*, 2.3.35–7)

Talbot laughs at her folly in thinking she has Talbot's substance in her power, for

> I am but shadow of myself:
> You are deceiv'd, my substance is not here;
> For what you see is but the smallest part
> And least proportion of humanity
>
> *(1H6*, 2.3.50–53)

and he sounds his trump, whereupon English soldiers enter, and Talbot asks, 'How say you, madam? Are you now persuaded / That Talbot is but shadow of himself? / These are his substance, sinews, arms, and strength.' (*1H6*, 2.3.61–3). No more than his portrait is the body of Talbot his substance, which lies in the military power he commands in support of England's legitimate claim to France.

The exemplary Talbot has no problem with his liminal identity – composed of both substance and shadow. More problematic and dramatically compelling is Richard Plantagenet's plight. It is the ur-instance of the fact of life registered by a historiography concerned about legitimacy in a culture where public identities deeply inform selfhood and can be easily conferred and taken away: those at the top must live simultaneously in actual and hypothetical mental modes. When the dying Mortimer informs him of his royal lineage Richard murmurs, 'Well, I will lock his counsel in my breast; / And what I do imagine, let that rest' (*1H6*, 2.5.118–19). Thenceforth everything he does *actually* is in the service of 'what I do imagine' – his legitimate but (as yet) hypothetical kingship.

The Contention reprises his existential duplicity several times before Richard, now Duke of York, declares himself publicly to Henry in 5.1.[3] Meanwhile, his condition grows contagious. He persuades Jack Cade to test the commons' reaction to York's claim while he's in Ireland: 'This devil here shall be my substitute' (3.1.371). As was Suffolk to Henry in France, so Cade will be to Richard in England, albeit in the register of black comedy. For Cade predictably slips from the indicative mode of hireling actor to the subjunctive mode of true aspirant. By the time he arrives in London, he is killing even his own followers for calling him anything but 'Lord Mortimer', and one scene later he declares, 'my mouth shall be the Parliament of England' (4.7.13–14). Cade acknowledges his flight from actuality when he leaps the wall into Iden's garden, having escaped Buckingham's troops – and his role reverts to its rightful owner, for whom he was but a stand-in, when York arrives to challenge the crown himself.

An illuminating way to study the grasping at and wresting of power in Shakespeare's first history cycle is to consider it as, literally, a struggle for self-substantiation. Since nothing seems more substantial than flesh and blood, it takes the cutting of flesh and spilling of blood to be assured that one possesses and does not merely represent power. Yet it inevitably turns out that substance is shadow after all. For actual presence easily shades into virtual presence, in a grim parody of the Elizabethan controversy over the real and virtual presence of Christ in the sacrament of the Eucharist.[4] So the struggle is renewed, more blood spilt and flesh carved, to prove who is really endowed with royalty, who only vicariously so.

Blood seriously begins to flow and flesh to part at the Battle of St Albans toward the end of *The Contention*, after York kills

Clifford and the younger Clifford rages, 'Meet I an infant of the house of York, / Into as many gobbets will I cut it / As wild Medea young Absyrtus did' (5.2.57–9). His words anticipate his pitiless slaughter of Rutland in *The True Tragedy*, whose relic becomes the symbol of Lancastrian power:

> Plantagenet, I come, Plantagenet!
> And this thy son's blood cleaving to my blade
> Shall rust upon my weapon, till thy blood,
> Congeal'd with this do make me wipe off both.
>
> (1.3.48–51)

Thus shedding blood becomes a means of self-substantiation, in a perverse mockery of Eucharistic participation and empowerment. In the next scene at Wakefield, a weary York notes proudly, 'Three times did Richard make a lane to me', and 'full as oft came Edward to my side / With purple falchion painted to the hilt / In blood of those that had encounter'd him' (1.4.9, 11–13). Then, in swift reversal, Margaret and her followers capture him and mock his doctrine of real presence, setting him on a molehill to exhibit the vanity of his claim to royalty:

> Come make him stand upon this molehill here,
> That raught at mountains with outstretched arms,
> Yet parted but the shadow with his hand.
>
> (1.4.67–9)

To taunt him further, she presents *her* eucharistic relic – a napkin stained with Rutland's blood wiped from Clifford's rapier – and when he refuses to weep, she corroborates her blood token by turning him into a player king and placing a paper crown on his head so he may act out his grief and fully stage his shadow kingship.

But York turns the tables once more. Player King accuses his tormenter of being a Player Queen:

> But that thy face is vizard-like, unchanging,
> Made impudent with use of evil deeds,
> I would essay, proud queen, to make thee blush.
> …
> O tiger's heart wrapp'd in a woman's hide!
> How could'st thou drain the life-blood of the child,
> To bid the father wipe his eyes withal,
> And yet be seen to bear a woman's face?
>
> (1.4.116–18, 137–40)

From woman in player's mask to beast in woman's costume, it is *Margaret*'s inauthenticity that York proclaims before pouring forth his passion. But is that passion real or assumed? His very posture, paper-crowned upon the molehill, blurs the line between performance and actuality, as he draws tears from Lancastrian Northumberland before tossing back the crown and yielding himself to be sacrificed in the real world of his audience.

Actual and vicarious identities remain continuously in play in *The True Tragedy*. First Henry, withdrawn from battle and sitting upon – a molehill! – envisions himself as homely swain in an imaginary pastoral landscape of orderly temporal succession (2.5); then Edward of York, deposed by Warwick, claims he will continue to bear himself as king, for his mind exceeds the compass of Fortune's wheel. The pragmatic Warwick responds:

> Then, for his mind, be Edward England's king;
> *Takes off his crown*
> But Henry now shall wear the English crown
> And be true king indeed; thou but the shadow.
>
> (4.3.48–50)

Yet Warwick himself becomes a shadow, along with Clarence, when Henry declares his intent to lead a private life and proclaims them Protectors of his land. Says the kingmaker to Clarence: 'We'll yoke together, like a double shadow / To Henry's body, and supply his place —' (4.6.49–50).

Shadow, however, yields to substance as blood violence increases. First Warwick is dragged onstage, 'my glory smear'd in dust and blood' (5.2.23), as Edward (newly crowned) exults over him and runs off to kill Warwick's brother Montague. Then, in 5.5, King Edward and Prince Edward square off, demanding that each confess himself a traitor. Invective turns to ritual slaughter as the Yorks then further quantify civil sacrifice. It took one Clifford to kill Rutland; one Clifford and one Margaret to kill the Duke of York; now the Yorks go the Lancastrians one better, as Edward, Gloucester, and Clarence each takes a turn cutting into the young Prince. When Gloucester stabs King Henry in the following scene and observes, 'See how my sword weeps for the poor King's death. / O, may such purple tears be always shed / From those that wish the downfall of our house!' (5.6.63–5), it would appear that the Yorks have partaken enough blood from their Lancastrian communion to ensure their royal salvation. But they haven't counted on Queen Margaret.

'Why should she live to fill the world with words?' asks Richard of Gloucester, when Edward prevents him from killing Margaret at Tewkesbury (5.5.43). A question to be asked. For this is precisely what she does when she returns to the English court from France at the beginning of *Richard III*. She appears only twice – in 1.3 and 4.4 – but enjoys a virtual presence in much of the play through the words she utters in the earlier scene. Her words serve two important functions: to desubstantiate the actuality inhabited by the quarrelling York factions, and to linger with sacramental efficacy in the memories of her addressees, who receive them with scoffs but recall them with recognition as the circumstances of their lives begin to match Margaret's predictions and her word turns flesh.

The eeriness of Margaret, who began as a virtual presence in the imagination of Suffolk, was thence transmitted to Henry, and afterward became all too real, consists in this: she enters as a revenant from the Yorks' past who claims that *their* present actuality is merely *virtual*, for it belongs to her. Addressing first Richard, then Elizabeth, then the full assembly, she declares:

> A husband and a son thou ow'st to me;
> And thou a kingdom; all of you allegiance.
> This sorrow that I have by right is yours;
> And all the pleasures you usurp are mine.

$$(1.3.170–3)$$

In these words the struggle for legitimacy, which informed the two previous plays, is resumed in a new elegiac vein: who is the true inheritor of grief, who of power, privilege, and pleasure? Margaret is attempting nothing less than to wrest the Yorks' reality from them. When they retort that she justly suffers the curse laid on her by the Duke of York for Rutland's death, she is unrepentant and returns the curse, multiplied. These words hang remorselessly over the remainder of the play.

In her second appearance, after Richard's murders are done, she joins the Duchess of York and the late Queen in mutual lamentation, and repeats the terms she had used to address Queen Elizabeth in her prosperity:

> I call'd thee then vain flourish of my fortune;
> I call'd thee, then, poor shadow, painted queen,
> The presentation of but what I was
>
> …
>
> A dream of what thou wast; a garish flag
>
> …
>
> A sign of dignity; a breath, a bubble;
> A queen in jest, only to fill the scene.

$$(4.4.82–91)$$

Elizabeth was Margaret's surrogate; Margaret, Elizabeth's vicarious identity. As she rehearses the words spoken in 1.3, the substance of Elizabeth's royal presence grows thinner and thinner, and to prove its unreality Margaret asks, 'Where is thy husband now? Where be thy brothers? / Where are thy two sons? Wherein dost thou joy?' (92–3). She concludes that having usurped her place, it is only fair that Elizabeth usurp the sorrow that is her reality. With that she makes her final move:

Now thy proud neck bears half my burden'd yoke,
From which even here I slip my weary head,
And leave the burden of it all on thee.

(111–13)

The transfer of identities is complete. Margaret disappears from the first tetralogy as a real presence, to linger virtually in her words as one for whom 'These English woes shall make me smile in France' (115) – but not before consigning the last York king, 'hell's black intelligencer', to the ultimate vicarious existence (71–8).

THIRTY

Unmuffling Isabella

George T. Wright

ANGELO   O my dread lord,
I should be guiltier than my guiltiness,
To think I can be undiscernible,
When I perceive your Grace, like power divine,
Hath looked upon my passes.

(5.1.364–8)

DUKE   Come hither, Isabel

   ...
Not changing heart with habit, I am still
Attorney'd at your service.

ISABELLA   O, give me pardon,
That I, your vassal, have employ'd and pain'd
Your unknown sovereignty.

(5.1.379, 382–5)

DUKE   For this new-married man approaching here,
Whose salt imagination yet hath wrong'd
Your well defended honour, you must pardon
For Mariana's sake: but as he adjudg'd your brother,
   ...
The very mercy of the law cries out,
Most audible, even from his proper tongue:
'An Angelo for Claudio; death for death.
Haste still pays haste, and leisure answers leisure;
Like doth quit like, and Measure still for Measure'.

(5.1.398–401, 405–9)

MARIANA   O my good lord – sweet Isabel, take my part;
             …
DUKE   Against all sense you do importune her.
           Should she kneel down in mercy of this fact,
           Her brother's ghost his paved bed would break,
           And take her hence in horror.

                                        (5.1.428, 431–4)

DUKE   He dies for Claudio's death.
ISABELLA   [*kneeling*]   Most bounteous sir:
           Look, if it please you, on this man condemn'd
           As if my brother liv'd. I partly think
           A due sincerity govern'd his deeds
           Till he did look on me. Since it is so,
           Let him not die. My brother had but justice,
           In that he did the thing for which he died …

                                        (5.1.441–7)
                  William Shakespeare, *Measure for Measure*

Encouraged by ostensibly bold and innovative productions of the play, and in harmony with several kinds of fashionable political rhetoric, viewers and readers of *Measure for Measure* have in recent years taken pleasure in mocking the Duke, finding Lucio amusing and relatively blameless, and sympathising with Isabella in the final scene as she endures, first, badgering and threats by the Duke and others, and, later, a marriage proposal many regard as entirely inappropriate, even insulting. I have argued before in favour of a different reading of the final scene (and, indeed, of the whole play),[1] one that sees the Duke's behaviour as, if sometimes stumbling, in character entirely benign, and the present essay supports this reading by looking more closely at some passages in the final scene and noting how shrewdly and trenchantly Shakespeare has contrived the logic of the Duke's triumph.

   The question of Isabella's character is central to this inquiry. Earlier in the play, we have been impressed by her youth and innocence, and her fervour for purity, which leads her, on entering the convent, to wish for even sterner rules of conduct than it requires. What surprises us is that on her first encounter with authority, and with a little encouragement from Lucio, she should turn out to be such an effective arguer on behalf of her brother's claim for a lighter sentence, for clemency. When Claudio later suggests that to save a brother's life she might accede to Angelo's demand, we may be surprised as well at the intensity of her anger, and at her subsequent willingness to take part in the bed trick. But once it appears that Claudio has been executed, she enters the final scene as, with Brother Lodowick's support, a strident advocate for 'justice! Justice! Justice! Justice!' (5.1.26).

This appeal is strangely turned against her, as the court, in the person of the Duke (a person she has never met) pretends to regard Isabella as a troublemaker, bringing substanceless charges against his virtuous deputy, Angelo. Witnesses call her testimony and integrity into question, and it appears that she herself will be subjected to all the abuses that human courts are capable of. Not that we, the audience, don't know better. We know, as most of the principals do not, that the Duke and Brother Lodowick are the same, and we understand or should understand that the Duke, in accepting and furthering the accusations against Isabella, is doing so for a reason – not to torment her but as a means of bringing out the truth of what has happened, and, equally important, *to test her*, as, in other measures of the final act, he also tests Angelo, Mariana, and Lucio, among others. This, after all, is nothing more than what a just magistrate ought to be doing, indeed is obliged to do: by one means or another to test persons brought before the law, to subject them to trial, and to judge them (as God presumably will be doing at the end of time).

But what of the biblical injunction, 'Judge not, that ye be not judged', a text of which Shakespeare was acutely conscious as he composed this scene and this play? For it appears (in Matthew 7:1– 2 [Geneva]) along with the words that clearly undergird this scene: 'For with what judgement ye judge, ye shall be judged, and with what measure ye mete, it shall be measured to you again' – words especially applicable to Angelo and, we should note, to Isabella herself.

The biblical point is pursued in the verses that follow. It is not, it cannot be, that earthly judges never pass judgment. But they must see to it that they are not guilty of the same moral flaw for which they are condemning an accused, that they do not ignore the 'beam that is in thine own eye' (Matthew 7:3–4) while casting the mote out of their brother's. This is the fault of Angelo, and it renders him unfit to judge Claudio. The Duke, on the other hand, is not guilty of Claudio's sin, nor of Angelo's, and is therefore not only competent but, because of his position, duty-bound to judge them.

For a just judge, Angelo's case is relatively simple, but it is entangled with Claudio's, for Claudio has presumably been executed for an offence of which Angelo also is guilty. 'He dies for Claudio's death', the Duke insists (5.1.441), not simply for the crime of putting Claudio to death but for having committed virtually the same crime that he condemned Claudio for committing with Julietta. If Claudio died for that, should not Angelo die for it as well?

This is the matter the Duke must now explore, as he begins to review the various guilts of the persons before him. This trial, this inquisition, is not easy, but it is necessary in order that justice be done. In this court, to be sure, the Duke already knows pretty well beforehand how other accused persons are going to be judged, and that their punishments will depend in part on their behaviour when they are put in the position of having to acknowledge their misdeeds. In this respect, Angelo's conduct is exemplary: full confession and repentance, and deep respect for the Duke. Mariana's appeal, though passionate, is always phrased courteously.

So, too, is Isabella's, but hers is a tougher, and subtler, case than the others. Her treatment in the final scene is at first painfully harsh; it amounts, ironically, to the 'more strict restraint' she had sought in entering the convent (1.4.4). But for her, as for all the chief persons in the scene, everything changes at the moment when Lucio unmuffles Brother Lodowick and shows him to be actually the Duke. Angelo sees immediately that the game is up and that he has no alternative but full confession; Lucio sees he is in for it; Mariana sees that the husband she hoped to have may very well be going to be executed; and Isabella – what does she feel? She knows now that the Duke, for all his earlier apparent hostility, is on her side, that his earlier apparent impatience with appeals for justice was only a pretence. She even begs his pardon: 'That I, your vassal, have employ'd and pain'd / Your unknown sovereignty' (5.1.384–5). Now Mariana begs her to plead for Angelo's life – that is, in place of her earlier cries for *justice* against Angelo, to recommend *mercy* for him.

What should she do?

The Duke doesn't make it easy for her, and now we begin to see why. As many critics ask, why doesn't he tell her – and everybody – that Claudio is still alive? But his purpose in concealing this fact is not to torment her, but to make sure she sees what is at stake in such an appeal for mercy as Mariana makes to her and the Duke warns her against acceding to lightly. In deciding whether to appeal for justice or mercy for Angelo, she is really also deciding on – judging – her own case.

It's clear now that with the Duke's support she herself will not suffer further persecution. But what about Angelo? She is not, of course, an official juror or judge. She has no power to render a decision on whether or how Angelo should be punished. But like every human being she can judge whether people who have injured her should be treated with charity or vengeance. As the Duke makes clear, there is every reason for Isabella to be unforgiving and to favour a harsh penalty for Angelo. He puts it forcibly in words that must be wrestled with if we are to understand this crucial moment in the play:

> The very mercy of the law cries out
> Most audible, even from his proper tongue:
> 'An Angelo for Claudio; death for death.
> Haste still pays haste, and leisure answers leisure;
> Like doth quit like, and Measure still for Measure'.

This is forcefully put and sounds irrefutable. That is, if Claudio has been executed for what he did, Angelo, whose crime was similar ('like'), should be executed, too.

If we understand the system of justice and mercy, then not only our sense of justice but our sense of mercy as well should insist, 'An Angelo for Claudio, death for death'; 'And with what measure ye mete, it shall be measured to you again'. Angelo himself understands that he has committed the same offence for which he condemned Claudio. That he believes this is shown by the celerity with which, once exposed, he embraces death as his punishment. The Duke, apparently seconding this view, tells Isabella, who has come to court crying for justice, that not to insist on these equivalences would be deeply unjust:

> Should she kneel down in mercy of this fact,
> Her brother's ghost his paved bed would break
> And take her hence in horror.

Even as she still seems uncertain, he reminds her again:

> He dies for Claudio's death.

But Isabella is not so sure. The Duke's argument, she senses, is flawed. It's the Old Testament view – an eye for an eye. If one wrong is done, it must be answered by another. If Claudio was put to death unjustly, the just response is to put Angelo to death for the same offence: 'death for death'.

But the New Testament's authority is different, not death for death, but measure for measure, and though the Duke appears to say that the two phrases are equivalent, Isabella evidently knows the difference. For this is a play unusually rich in counterparts, and Isabella is, as the Duke wants her to be, intent on sorting them out. The equivalence she sees now is not between Angelo and Claudio but between herself and Angelo. They have almost traded positions. In 2.2 he was judging Claudio; now Isabella is judging him. There she pleaded, 'Yet show some pity', to which Angelo replied, 'I show it most of all when I show justice' (2.2.100–101). That is the Duke's ostensible position now: 'The very mercy of the law cries out / ... / "An Angelo for Claudio; death for death"'.

But Isabella's argument against Angelo earlier, and against the strict condemnation that the Duke appears to be urging now, turns on the fallibility of the judge. A morally perfect God may devise an exemplary system involving justice and mercy, but the presence of weakness and corruption in human judges requires that they and we adjust our understanding of justice and mercy as we recognise the part played by human fallibility in their decisions and the possibility that, as in Angelo's case, the judge is guilty of the crime for which he condemns the prisoner. In effect, to move from 'death for death' to 'measure for measure' is to evaluate not only the judgment but the judge: 'and with what measure ye mete, it shall be measured to you again'.

For Isabella to realise this requires that she recognise also how fallible her own earlier judgment on Claudio was, not in 2.2 and 2.4, when she is debating with Angelo, but in 3.1, when Claudio pleads with her to save his life by polluting her own. 'Die', she tells him, and Shakespeare is careful to show her using judicial terms, italicised here, to condemn him:

> *Die*, perish! Might but my bending down
> *Reprieve* thee from thy fate, it should *proceed*.
>
> (3.1.143–4)

In effect, Isabella in act 5 is forced to judge herself as well as Angelo, to recognise that her own condemnation of Claudio confirmed Angelo's death sentence and was also, like his, tainted by personal fallibility. She has come to court to plead for 'justice', but now that she sees how her position and Angelo's have been reversed, should she really behave as he did then and call for his own execution? No wonder she is flustered. To do that would be to betray all the fine arguments she made then for mercy. If those arguments on Claudio's behalf were valid then, they are valid now, *whether Claudio is dead or alive*.

And while she hesitates, the Duke continues to make the case for the 'justice! Justice! Justice! Justice!' (5.1.26) she herself was appealing for earlier. He is testing Isabella, offering her the chance to recognise that, by the very arguments for mercy that she has made earlier to Angelo on Claudio's behalf, the beam in her own eye (her absolute condemnation of Claudio) hardly qualifies her now to condemn the beam in Angelo's. The Duke has overheard the earlier harsh words with which she scolded her brother. Now when this sister of charity, recognising the common element in Angelo's case and her own, appeals for mercy for Angelo, as she had earlier done for a similarly charged Claudio, the Duke can move on. In a moment, to scramble the proceedings again by another unmuffling, he produces Claudio himself. If he had done so earlier, the crucial test of Isabella's charity – and justice – could not have occurred; it would have been too easy for her to say, in effect, 'Well, no harm's done; let's have amnesty for everyone'. The Duke's purpose, throughout this denouement, has been to unmuffle all the chief characters – Angelo, Lucio, Claudio, Isabella – and to determine especially whether Isabella's consistent goodness and mercy, even towards Angelo, can survive her belief that he has had Claudio executed. That is the test.

And once she has passed it, not with the eloquent arguments she has produced earlier, but with a convincing and hard-earned generosity of spirit, which offers only a feeble set of mitigating factors to extenuate Angelo's crime (5.1.443–7), the Duke, secretly pleased but pretending to be annoyed, can turn to other matters, to Barnardine first, and then to Claudio. Unmuffled now as the Duke was earlier, Claudio does not need to say a word when the Duke pardons him, any more than Angelo does when the Duke declares he's 'safe' (5.1.492), any more than Isabella needs to when the Duke asks for her hand. Only Lucio cannot keep still when the moment calls for stillness. It is true that no one is punished much, except Lucio, the slanderer, but that is because somehow, by accident or by the disguised Duke's benign manipulation of events, no crime of magnitude resulting in death has occurred (always excepting Barnardine's) in what is after all a comedy but a comedy concerned from beginning to end with dangerous matters. If a formula like 'An Angelo for Claudio; death for death' has any validity, then the amendment, 'life for life', must also be followed – or even, before Claudio's resurrection, 'life for death', a far more Christian principle. That is where *Measure for Measure* leaves us. Claudio, unmuffled at last, is surely grateful for life; Isabella, too, having gained immeasurably in understanding (of herself and of justice) must surely be grateful that everything has turned out so well. Why should they speak at the end? What more is there to say? Hasn't her future husband managed it beautifully? Far from treating Isabella as an inferior, the Duke pays her the high compliment of judging her capable of understanding, as no one else in the play quite does, what is at stake in the moral choices he puts before her.

Close Reading Hamlet

THIRTY ONE

Hamlet's 'Serious Hearing': 'Sound' vs. 'Use' of 'Voice'

GARRETT STEWART

> ... the whole ear of Denmark
> Is by a forged process of my death
> Rankly abus'd
>
> Upon my secure hour thy uncle ...
> ...
> ... in the porches of my ears did pour
> The leperous distilment
>
> Thus was I, sleeping, by a brother's hand
> Of life, of crown, of queen at once dispatch'd
>> William Shakespeare, *Hamlet*, 1.5.36–8, 61–4, 74–5

These extracts recover a backstory whose logical overtones – and phonic undertow – are of the sort no critic has better prepared us to appreciate than Stephen Booth, and not least because in an essay on *Hamlet*, Booth notes an earlier instance of the abused ear. His emphasis is on the way the play keeps us disoriented in each of its early speeches, including the one in which a sentinel guarding the fortress uses the very metaphor of siege to describe the assaulted credulity of Horatio in reports of the ghost: '[L]et us once again assail your ears, / That are so fortified against our story' (1.1.34–5).[1] Booth does not extrapolate from this trope, this metaphor of attack, but the reverberations are there. Stormed, rankly abused, invaded, and poisoned ears: these are the figures among which Shakespeare's own appeals to the ear in this play must negotiate their claims.

After waiting four scenes for an answer to the play's opening words ('Who's there?'), we are finally enjoined along with Hamlet ('List, list, O, list!') to a very 'serious hearing': so serious already (phonology has its own logistics) that, while massing in exhortation to a virtual 'enlistment' of response – and beyond putting the echoic *ear* back in 's*ear*ious' – the further ghostly sibilance requires a judicious listening to keep the second *s* from confounding the very name of attention with its eventually *searing* result. Such 'double phonetics' – like Empson's 'double grammar' one level up in the food chain of semantic digestibility – is everywhere in Shakespeare.

In an early allusion to contested territory between Norway and Denmark, I have noted elsewhere the syllabic 'play' when territory confiscated from old Fortinbras by Hamlet's father is referred to in Horatio's second mention of 'lands' – in 'foresaid lands' (1.1.91, 106) – with a clear overtone of 'forcéd lands'.[2] This only helps set up the syntactic 'give' I now hear in mention of the dead king's role in this tug of war. Still flummoxed by the apparition, Bernardo recognises the ghost as 'so like the King / That was'. Grammatically if not ontologically, so far so good: the king that was and is no longer; but also, posthumously, with the line completing itself by double grammar: 'that was and is the question of these wars'. Such recursive syntax, as well as the dramaturgic shifting of gears that interests Booth in the play, surfaces again when Horatio, confronting the ghost, stammers his deferential way across his choppy (too *to*-ed) grammar, wondering if there's anything, so it would sound at first, 'to be done / That may to thee do ease and grace' – until 'grace' is pulled forward across another prepositional phrase into the symmetrical balance, and deferential officiousness, of 'grace to me'.

The answer would require speech from the Ghost, of course, but only 'If th*ou* hast any s*ound*', where Horatio's own aural rhythm isolates a stratum of sound divorced from its strict recruitment to meaning until completed with the strained disjunction of '[any sound] or use of voice' (1.1.131). This rounding out in apparent wordiness offers a further complication of the (noun) and (noun) of (noun) structure so powerfully audited in its recurrent oddity (its technical name ungiven) by Empson and then later codified as 'hendiadys' by George T. Wright.[3] The 'two-for-one' figure of hendiadys, inserting coordination where there should be subordination, appears in even a more baroque form when the ghost is said by Horatio to have been spotted 'in the dead waste and middle of the night' (1.2.198) instead of in the somewhat more logical 'the dead waste of night's middle' – but in either case a seemingly unnerved circumlocution for 'midnight'. This is the same slightly unhinged grammar by which Horatio has earlier allowed that 'in the gross and scope of my opinion' (1.1.67) – meaning something like 'in my general view' – there is a sense of omen in this supernatural sighting. His grammar seems not only partly derailed under distress, in the way Empson would suggest about such phrasing; it also marks a certain bureaucratic wordiness, which lends support to Franco Moretti's sense that in the go-between function of Horatio's bland, 'flat' language we overhear, in effect, the early modern birth of State discourse out of Court rhetoric.[4] Horatio's eventual appeal to the ghost – again, 'If thou hast any sound or use of voice' – may bespeak a similar discursive fussiness as much as a grammatical splutter triggered by doubts about the ghost's own somatic materiality, including its ability to verbalise desire in shaped breath.

It is of course Hamlet who springs disclosure at the start of 1.5 by his ultimatum: 'Whither will thou lead me? Speak, I'll go no farther' (1.5.1). And when immediately enjoined with the obligation to 'serious hearing' (5), Hamlet answers with 'Speak; I am bound to hear' (6). He doesn't mean, as we might today, 'can't help but hear' (a usage not evolved until the mid 1800s), but instead deploys 'bound' in the obsolete sense of 'ready' or 'ready bound', closer to modern English's 'I am bound and determined to hear': committed to it on his own, as well as explicitly obliged by the ghostly voice. But that 'to' is about to give pause by iteration in the ghost's mouth, anticipating a later speech by Claudius about a painful indecision that mirrors and travesties Hamlet's own. Defeated by competing purposes, the guilty usurper feels 'like a

man to double business bound' (3.3.41). *To*, not *for*, which may
be why the *OED* avoids giving the widely understood usage as
'bound *for*' (in the sense of 'toward') and opts instead for 'bound'
as 'readied' ('ready *to*'?).

In any case, Claudius's 'to' would carry as well the sense of
'compelled', as it does for Hamlet, twice over, when his 'bound to
hear' is shot back to him in slant echo across the ghost's elliptical
parallelism: 'So art thou to revenge, once you shalt hear' (1.5.7).
Immediately again Hamlet, as if he were querying the grammar
as much as the cliff-hanger: 'What?' Rather than a freestanding
if inverted syntax of injunction (a variant of 'Once you hear, you
are to revenge'), two false parallelisms instead vie for dominance
over the inferred second 'bound', an unsteady dominance at that.
Either the expected infinitive 'to revenge' is intended (taking no
object as yet, direct or indirect), or, if 'revenge' seems nudged
over into a noun rather than a verb, then 'bound to' as 'ready
to' doesn't quite fit the reiterated bill. This is because 'art thou'
would grammatically anticipate something more like 'directed
inexorably towards', which of course does in fact lurk there in the
commanded 'hearing' of the paternal admonition.

Divided between the separate semantic overtones in this
ghostly interchange, we encounter a less common syntactic
figure in Shakespeare than hendiadys, but one related no less to
a double-voicing beneath meaning. At play in these ricocheting
lines is an alternate mode of syntactic twofer: namely, the twinning, bundling, or 'taking together' of syllepsis. This is a rhetorical
turn of grammar, sometimes known as zeugma (with its etymo-
logical sense of 'yoking') that highlights a non-congruity in the
logical relations between, most often, a verb and its two different
objects. This is a divided sense of relation frequently manifested
as metaphoric versus literal. In Shakespeare, the textbook example
of zeugma is the illogically phrased rage against the French
king in *Henry V* for having ordered the destruction not only of
British provisions but of the boys who guarded them. As the
scene of carnage is discovered, the nefarious French command
is ventriloquised after the fact by a Welsh voice: 'Kill the poys

[for 'boys'] and the luggage! 'tis expressly / Against the law of arms' (4.7.1–2), where the crime of mass murder is too stark to be subsumed to a generalised verb of violence like 'destroy'. In *Hamlet*, divergent claims are similarly pried open across a spreading sense of the predicate in the counterpoint of 'I am bound to hear ... and then to revenge' – as if the infinitive echo, shifted to preposition ('towards') and dragging the verb with it into new territory as noun object, returns us to Hamlet's opening of the scene with a second and more portentous sense of direction in 'Whither wilt thou lead me? Speak'.

There's almost a rhetorical parable behind all this. Die by syllepsis, revenge by it. For a three-pronged forking grammar soon emerges from other lexical densities in the ghost's account of his own murder by Claudius. Seeking out the King in his afternoon nap, the poisonous villain 'in the porches of my ears did pour / The leperous distilment', a toxin that is absorbed through 'the natural gates and alleys of the body' until it 'doth posset and curd' the 'thin and wholesome blood'. The listener's ear can perhaps resist the faint aura of hendiadys, or redundant double duty – to say nothing of a mixed metaphor with 'porches' – in that architectonic conceit of the body's 'gates and alleys' (alternatively 'gated alleys'?), since the ear's orifice (like Horatio's 'fortified' hearing 'assailed' in the first scene by rumours of the ghost) does offer a portal or gateway to its own canals before connecting to the whole vulnerable bloodstream within. But there is no explaining, except in the overkill of repulsion, the splitting open of cause and effect in the emphatic redundancy of 'posset and curd' (when 'posset' already means 'make curdle'). No explanation – except of course the clotting of grammar itself in imitative thickness.

Then, too, if in a different way, effect is put before cause in the double inversion beginning 'Thus was I', the past-tense grammar already implying the 'not to be' of ghostly retrospection. This is followed, at the apogee of disclosure, by a subordinate inversion that springs into sylleptic mode by a strange use of the past participle 'dispatched'. With a potential shadow even of 'speed' in the noun form 'dispatch', this is a word nevertheless conjured by Shakespeare, in this first recorded *OED* usage, for the rare and now obsolete sense of 'deprived' or 'bereaved' – more like 'taken away' than the usual 'sent away'. There are, it would seem, barely any normal words for the horror of this violation. In descending order, that is, the ghost remembers having been bereft, and by a literalised 'hand', first of mortal being and then of its metonymic objects of desire: 'Thus was I, sleeping, by a brother's hand / Of life, of crown, of queen, at once dispatched'. When the usurper later unconsciously echoes in his guilt the dead brother's charge, the ghost's inversion at 'of ... dispatched' is straightened out by his treasonous successor to a less semantically wrenching 'possess'd of' to itemise the fruits of his crime: 'my crown, mine own ambition and my queen' (3.3.55), where 'queen' (rather than 'wife') joins with 'crown' as not just emblematic spoils but virtual synonyms for his 'ambition'. The harsher torque of the ghost's own original phrasing has installed a more marked syllepsis. Life is inherent, crown is adjacent or metonymic, royal wife is further separated yet. One can't be robbed of each in the same breath or sense – except, that is to say (and to say in vocal rhythm as much as in so many words), by a perverse and unnatural violence registered *in* as well as *by* the paced speech of accusation.

Now, one can see why Stanley Cavell, in a tendentious reading of this scene in light of the later play-within-the-play, is inclined to distrust the ghost's claim about poison in the ear, noting the way the dumb show of this accusation doesn't perturb Claudius at first with any tremors of recognition.[5] Cavell wants it otherwise so that the poisoned blade that ultimately kills Hamlet will be a truer revelation, in repetition, of the father's death – with which, given the son's elided lifeline, consumed as it is in revenge, Hamlet's doom is virtually consubstantial. Explicit forensics aside, in the father's murder lurks the son's consigned fate. But another structural symmetry, rooted earlier yet, seems more clearly to bind the two deaths. For the ghost must first dispel the rumour that he was 'stung' by a non-metaphoric 'serpent' (1.5.34), and in doing so he predicts the way the son, too, will die of speech's own lethal effect in the ear: the poison of compelled revenge – 'to' which the son is instantaneously 'bound' in a verbally contracted double bind.

And for this ironic symmetry, the listening or reading ear is primed by an eventual phonetic overload, once the cover story has been exposed. Personified as a global audial entity, the 'whole ear of Denmark' has been 'by a forged process of my death / Rankly abus'd'. That collective ear must be cleansed by the truth, even as we recognise that in the incarnational personification of the King *as* Denmark, the 'ear of Denmark' would more normally stand in for the King's own openness to remark, to 'audience'. It turns out to be exactly such a private aperture that is in question, as we know, for the symbolic evil of the murderer has been (once again, since the verse deserves its full echoic resonance) 'in the porches of my ears' to 'pour / The leperous distilment'. What streams at one remove through our own present ears across the enjambment from 'por' to 'pour' to '(le)perous' works to insinuate in its unimpeded lexical flux the vulnerable condition of the ear's own *porous* state. Such is the unspoken (but still half sounded, half intoned) phonetic matrix of this particular drama. For *Hamlet* is a play in which overlapping syllabic increments as well as variable syntactic ligatures keep the pace of meaning's heard duration in the syncopated 'sound' and 'use' of voice. Even in silent reading, the perked ears of Shakespearean audition pick up – and pick up on – the latent semantic noise that literature employs rather than voids, floats on rather than drowns out, retaining all the while its risky porosity to a residual voicing never wholly regimented by script. So it is that, even though discouraged by Booth as a programmatic critical agenda, readings close enough to the text can gather towards *a* reading after all.

THIRTY TWO

Hamlet's Couplets

JAMES GRANTHAM TURNER

> Let us go in together;
> And still your fingers on your lips, I pray.
> The time is out of joint; O cursed spite,
> That ever I was born to set it right!
> Nay, come, let's go together.
>> William Shakespeare, *Hamlet*, 1.5.184–8

So Hamlet closes the powerful scene in which he confronts the Ghost and swears his entourage to silence. This oddly satisfying expression of dissatisfaction owes much of its finality and memorability to its prosodic form, a single pentameter couplet emerging from blank verse. Horatio has just rebuked him for 'wild and whirling words', and Guildenstern will later tell him to 'put your discourse into some frame' and not speak 'so wildly' (1.5.132, 3.2.300–301). This couplet provides the 'frame' and assures Horatio and Marcellus that he is not essentially wild. Or does it? Throughout *Hamlet*, I suggest, sudden irruptions of rhymed verse pose exactly the question of which 'frame' fits his 'discourse' and which cramps and tortures it into a false shape.

This shapely couplet ironically performs what it declares impossible, the first line with its strong central pause offset by the fluent second line, bound by rhyme and meter into a measured resolution or 'setting right' of a caesura in history. Yet its placing in the final five-line sequence seems irresolute, even awkward. The ringing *forte* declaration sounds jarring after the *pianissimo* injunction to silence, and might foreshadow the notorious Folio rendering of his last words, 'The rest is silence. O, o, o, o'. The couplet appears between two separate invitations to 'go in together' – that is, within a social interaction attentive to etiquette, precedence, and companionship – yet it seems directed to nobody in particular and interrupts, rather than furthers, the gesture of togetherness between the prince and the two commoners bound by his secret.

As couplets go, however, this is highly competent. One danger of the polished distich, as Pope warned, is that the relation of the rhyme words becomes too predictable, too pat:

> If *Chrystal Streams with pleasing Murmurs creep*,
> The Reader's threaten'd (not in vain) with *Sleep*.[1]

The opening line should promise, or 'threaten', something that stimulates thought as well as satisfying the ear; the perfect consonance of sound should deliver an intriguing cognitive dissonance. (Shakespeare had ample opportunity to practise this skill in the closing couplets he invented for the sonnet.) Here 'spite' threatens 'right', and in Hamlet's very first couplet, snapping shut his haughty 'Seems, madam?' address to Gertrude, 'that within which passes show' rhymes with 'the trappings and the suits of woe' (1.2.85–6; the garbled version in Q1 still manages to preserve the rhyme).[2] More than a merely acoustic effect, the pairing-with-difference of 'spite'/'right' and 'show'/'woe' encapsulates virtually the whole of *Hamlet*. Not every couplet promotes speculation about the relation between its end-words, however: the rhymes on 'is'/'amiss' (4.5.17–18) and 'this'/'amiss' (5.2.385–6) are altogether slacker, even though one is delivered by Gertrude at a moment of high distress and the other by Fortinbras at the solemn close of the tragedy.

Though the lexical structure of Hamlet's 'out of joint' couplet is clear and forceful, in performance certain ambiguities appear. The actor can deliver it with normal stress, making the first half-line a generic, chorus-like proclamation of these evil days. But Hamlet may well be responding to a speech he was forced to hear in 1.2, where Claudius represents Fortinbras foolishly 'thinking by our late dear brother's death / Our state to be disjoint and out of frame' (1.2.19–20). If Hamlet paid keen critical attention to his hated uncle (as he later wants the uncle to pay keen attention to his play), then the stress of the present couplet should be 'The time *is* out of joint! Fortinbras was right and Claudius has been misrepresenting him!' An actor so tuned to the first line might also place an extra stress in the second, so that a generic lament for the oppressive task ahead becomes instead a sharp realisation of the grotesque mismatch that makes *Hamlet* special: 'that ever *I* was born to set it right' – that ever the grand duty of revenge and purgation should fall to *me*, John-a-dreams, and not to a hotspur like Laertes. In one respect, Hamlet's couplet does alter the report on Fortinbras: the Norwegian is said to believe that the *state* is out of joint, whereas the Dane refers to *time*. But this difference may be less than first appears. Fortinbras infers the dislocation of Denmark precisely from the particular moment in time, the old king's sudden death. And Hamlet's prosody, 'setting right' the fracture by resolving it into a perfect couplet, implies that he sees time *as* a state, a metrical or musical keeping-time.

The sudden couplet is, of course, a conventional device to close a scene or act, still used in the prosiest Restoration comedies. It seems unwise to infer anything about a dramatic character from a moment when the actor's voice is as it were expropriated by the Stage Manager, subordinated to the practicalities of staging. Other characters in *Hamlet* formalise the end of a speech or a scene by breaking into rhyme, most notably the stagey and managerial Claudius. Laertes concludes his moralising 'good lesson' to Ophelia, immediately undermined when she admonishes him to practise what he preaches, with a couplet that practically forces the actor to wag his finger rhythmically: 'Be wary then: best safety lies in fear. / Youth to itself rebels, though none else near' (1.3.43–4). I would still argue, however, that these lines express character as well as structure, that their internal poetics are carefully matched to the speaker, and that their placing is far from automatic. Scenes 'wrapped up' with a shaping rhyme contrast with others that end on blank verse or even an extrametrical phrase, suggesting hurry or panic. Laertes' moralising couplet is in fact his only one, and (in pointed contrast to Hamlet himself) his exits never place him in metrical control.

Even Hamlet must struggle to establish mastery over rhyme in the many soliloquies he is dealt by Shakespeare. The first has no rhyme at all, while the second, anticipating an encounter with the Ghost later that evening, ends quite badly: 'Till then sit still my soul – foul deeds will rise / Though all the earth o'erwhelm them to men's eyes' (1.2.255–6). The couplet seems forced by the arbitrary rhyme 'rise/eyes', which adds little to the meaning – the opposite problem to the Popean 'creep'/'sleep', lulled by excessive conformity of the rhyme words. The more decisive ending of the 'rogue and peasant slave' soliloquy, 'the play's the thing / Wherein I'll catch the conscience of the King' (2.2.539–40), still leaves a lingering suspicion of weak rhyming, 'thing' being rather flat. The 'witching hour' and 'all occasions' soliloquies end more soundly (3.2.38–9, 4.4.64–5). But the most intense prosodic effect comes in the scene where Hamlet declines to kill Claudius at prayer, when both protagonists, separately and serially, in their very different styles, close on a couplet:

HAMLET   My mother stays;
           This physic but prolongs thy sickly days. *Exit*
KING   My words fly up, my thoughts remain below.
           Words without thoughts never to heaven go.

                                (3.3.95–8)

In addition to the psychological and theological reasons he gives for his deferral, Hamlet the artist may also recoil from 'doing it pat' as he says in the Folio text, rejecting facile closures and neat symmetrical endings.

For the Elizabethan dramatist a sudden break into rhyme can mark a lyrical heightening of the love scene, as in *Romeo and Juliet* 1.5, or an added ritual solemnity, as when Helena promises to heal the King in *All's Well That Ends Well* (2.1.164–9) – a moment comparable to the opening lines of *The Murder of Gonzago* (which is of course entirely in couplets). But the distich itself seems associated with *sententiae* or moralising (hence Romeo and Friar Lawrence converse almost entirely in couplets). Ophelia certainly uses the paired rhyme, when giving back Hamlet's love-tokens, to convey sententious wisdom and detached generalisation: 'Take these again, for to the noble mind / Rich gifts wax poor when givers prove unkind' (3.1.99–100). This makes Hamlet's 'mad' prose response ('are you honest?') quite intelligible, since 'honesty' carried the modern sense as well as the meaning 'sexually chaste', and the couplet strikes him as contrived and insincere. One of Gertrude's short soliloquies, composed of two distichs, is actually printed with '*sententia*' marks in Q2 (4.5.17–20).

Hamlet's suspicion of formalised *sententiae*, especially when uttered by a female character, begins in his opening scene. As his mother publicly comforts him she slips into rhyme –

> Thou know'st 'tis common all that lives must die,
> Passing through nature to eternity.

– and he immediately responds 'Ay, madam, it is common' (1.2. 72–4), scornfully associating commonplace platitudes, rhyming distich, and 'common' female sexuality. And yet he shapes his own ends in the same style, adopting a theatrical way of proclaiming his own authenticity and freedom from theatricality. External signs and gestures of mourning

> are actions that a man might play,
> But I have that within which passes show,
> These but the trappings and the suits of woe.
>
> (84–6)

He 'plays' contempt for play, fashions an exterior frame to declare his absolute independence from the exterior. The couplet, with its reconciliation of antitheses, captures his contradictory attitude. But it also threatens to envelop him in convention: Gertrude incorporates his 'common' interjection into a second distich rhyming 'be'/'thee' (74–5).

Shakespeare created many poet-characters (Richard II, Pistol), but none is as attuned as Hamlet to the techniques of prosody and the process of composition. His speeches seem to contain invisible quotation marks. We see him coming up with phrases, jotting them down in his tables so as not to forget them, emending them at high speed, even failing to complete rhymes and tossing them aside. He enters into every detail of the Players' art, recites whole speeches and composes new ones for insertion into his *Mousetrap*, and even makes telling remarks about prosody on stage: 'the Lady shall say her mind freely or the blank verse shall halt for't' (2.2.289–90). Hamlet associates blank verse with two crucial attributes that he seems to link causally: fluid easy movement – 'halting' (limping, or grinding to a halt) being its chief defect – and speaking one's mind freely. Conversely rhyme must be associated with artifice and constriction.

One of Hamlet's central paradoxes is that, like many critics and professors of literature, he is constantly pondering rhyme and attempting to perform it, yet knows he has little gift for it. He is a bad poet as well as a bad revenger, which makes him doubly fascinating for Shakespeare – and doubles the length of the play. The awkward, self-conscious letter to Ophelia admits 'I am ill at these numbers. I have not art to reckon my groans' (2.2.118–19). But this seems to spur him all the more to collect, recite, relish, and make up 'numbers'. His citation of ballad snatches, for example, seems motivated by curiosity about their misshapen form, even more than by the aptness of their content to the present situation. The Jephtha ballad in 2.2 of course alludes to Polonius as the old father whose daughter bewails her virginity before dying, but Hamlet seems to select his quotes for the lumpish double rhyme rather than pursuing the father–daughter motif: 'As by lot, / God wot ... It came to pass, / As most like it was' (2.2.352–6). These jogtrot internal rhymes, which recur in the bawdy ballad that Ophelia sings when mad, can be understood as telescoped or syncopated couplets. Hamlet plays with them again when he simulates mania for Rosencrantz and Guildenstern: 'the King is a thing ... of nothing' (4.2.26–8) sounds as if he is still hammering out that earlier, tinnier couplet in his mind, 'the play's the thing'.

Shakespeare gives free rein to Hamlet's parodic rhyming in *The Mousetrap* scene, not in his public faux-mad mode before the play but in the excited babbling he shares in private with Horatio after Claudius seems to have revealed his guilt. Rhyme *per se* had been thematised already in this scene, in the archaic, stylised heroic couplets of the play-within-the-play itself, which enacts the fidelity of the royal couple at an agonisingly slow pace, heavy with multiple *sententiae* and Polonius-like explications of its own rhetorical patterning ('But orderly to end as I begun ...' [3.2.204]). It is difficult to imagine the Player King and Queen's parts delivered 'trippingly' (3.2.2), unless by dramatic irony this means tripping over each ponderous and marble rhyme. (*The Murder of Gonzago* is even more end-stopped than the Ghost's speech or the Pyrrhus monologue, the opposite of Hamlet's own fleet and impetuously enjambed blank verse.) In contrast the prologue goes *too* trippingly, its simple triplet form accentuated by the folksy rhyme on 'tragedy'/'clemency'/'patiently' – an effect that Hamlet mocks as 'the posy of a ring' (3.2.142–5). He may be an expert witness, since the speech of Lucianus, the most plausible candidate for the lines that Hamlet himself wrote and inserted, ends at the bloodcurdling rhyme 'dire property'/'immediately' (252–3). In the exhilarated gloating that follows, maggots of rhyme keep jumping into Hamlet's mind just when he should be showing the steely rationality of the detective-avenger. Giddy with the triumph of an insecure author on opening night, he improvises no fewer than three fragments in quick succession. First, the 'stricken deer' quatrain (263–6) seems to be a fresh composition and not an authentic ballad quotation, and next the 'Damon dear' quatrain, in the same measure and directly alluding to the Jove-like father and his worthless successor, actually breaks off before completing the *b*-rhyme with 'ass'. As Horatio pointedly remarks, Hamlet 'might have rhymed' but instead breaks the frame with a jarring 'paiock' – emended by editors to existing words but perhaps an onomatopoetic representation of contemptuous spitting (273–6). Yet a third time the challenge of rhyming is met and mocked in an inane improvisation,

but this time it is a full-blown (and flyblown) couplet: 'For if
the King like not the comedy / Why then belike he likes it not,
perdie' (285–6).

Couplet-as-closure and couplet-as-antic-improvisation battle
it out, appropriately, in the confrontation scene with Gertrude
(3.4). Hamlet begins with a word-doubling worse than rhyme –
the flat, insolent repetition of his mother's end-words:

QUEEN   Hamlet, thou hast thy father much offended.
HAMLET   Mother, you have my father much offended.
QUEEN   Come, come, you answer with an idle tongue.
HAMLET   Go, go, you question with a wicked tongue.

                                                              (8–11)

Killing Polonius sets off a bout of grimly humorous couplet-
making – 'almost as bad, good mother / As kill a king, and marry
with his brother' (26–7) – which recurs as he begins to lug the
corpse away: punning on 'drawing to an end', he jeers that
Polonius 'Is now most still, most secret and most grave, / Who was
in life a foolish prating knave' (212–13).[3] Within the confrontation
itself, of course, he adopts a less puerile tone, indeed overacts the
thunderous moral authority. At one point he tries to bring the
scene to a dignified close with a sententious distich ('I must be
cruel only to be kind. / This bad begins and worse remains behind'
[176–7]), only to boil over again with frothing imprecations against
the bloat king and his reechy kisses. Again he reasserts control
over the rhyme and the circumstances, but now in the exultant
mode of the murderous prankster who will hoist Rosencrantz and
Guildenstern with their own petard

And blow them at the moon: O, 'tis most sweet
When in one line two crafts directly meet.

                                                              (207–8)

George Puttenham could hardly define better the rhetorical and
emotional effect of a good couplet.

In his last incarnation, the blithe existentialist who returns to Denmark on the pirate ship, Hamlet continues to spout his trademark improvised couplets. In the graveyard he rattles off two in a row on 'Imperious Caesar, dead and turn'd to clay' (5.1.202–5) – to the evident concern of Horatio, who now comments not on the rhyme (which is highly competent, even Augustan) but on the obsessive, 'too curious' thinking behind it (195). How ironic that Hamlet will soon be denouncing Laertes for rhetorical excess, for histrionic verbal virtuosity detached from true expression or 'speaking the mind' – in short, for show not woe.

Though couplets do not feature in this particular verbal duel, Gertrude does use the phrase 'golden couplets' in her attempt to assuage it (5.1.276). Her usage is strange, apparently unique in English, since she refers not to twinned verse but to baby birds.[4] She associates the word with her son because, she explains, he can be violently mad one minute and the next minute as calm as the dove hatching her chicks; she actually calls them 'cuplets' in Q2, perhaps combining the root 'couple' with the little cup of the eggshell. In F Claudius delivers these lines, but Gertrude is the apter speaker for two reasons: she had initiated the mothering couplet back in 1.2, and now she describes herself by dramatic irony, the dove hatching then mourning her plan to marry Hamlet and Ophelia. Hamlet himself surely senses these multiple meanings when he throws over his shoulder his final satiric burst of rhyme, equally contemptuous of Laertes, Claudius, *and* the mewing Gertrude:

> Let Hercules himself do what he may,
> The cat will mew and dog will have his day.
>
> (5.1.280–81)

He hatches a brazen couplet to answer her golden. Whether the association is with adorable fluffy creatures in matching pairs, or wholesome nuggets of commonplace wisdom in tidy verses, he wants none of it. Hamlet, ill at these numbers, embraces then disjoints the rhymed distich to resist becoming a couplette.

THIRTY THREE

The Dumb Show in *Hamlet*

TIFFANY STERN

Dumbe show followes.
Enter a King and a Queene, the Queene embracing him, and he
her, he takes her up, and declines his head upon her necke, he lyes
him downe uppon a bancke of flowers, she seeing him asleepe,
leaves him: anon come in another man, takes off his crowne,
kisses it, pours poyson in the sleepers eares, and leaves him: the
Queene returnes, finds the King dead, makes passionate action,
the poysner with some three or foure come in againe, seeme to
condole with her, the dead body is carried away, the poysner
wooes the Queene with gifts, shee seemes harsh awhile, but in the
end accepts love.

William Shakespeare, *Hamlet* (1604, 'Quarto 2', H1ᵛ)

The dumbe shew enters.
Enter a King and Queene, very lovingly; the Queene embracing
him. She kneeles, and makes shew of Protestation unto him. He
takes her up, and declines his head upon her neck. Layes him
downe upon a Banke of Flowers. She seeing him asleepe, leaves
him. Anon comes in a Fellow, takes off his Crowne, kisses it,
and powres poyson in the Kings eares, and Exits. The Queene
returnes, findes the King dead, and makes passionate Action.
The Poysoner, with some two or three Mutes comes in againe,
seeming to lament with her. The dead body is carried away: The
Poysoner Wooes the Queene with Gifts, she seemes loath and
unwilling awhile, but in the end, accepts his love.

William Shakespeare, *Hamlet*, in *Comedies,*
Histories, & Tragedies (1623, 'Folio', 267)

The same story – of the murder of a king by poison – is presented three times in *Hamlet*: as the Ghost's single-person blank verse narrative in 1.5.59–79; as the players' dumb show between 3.2.137 and 3.2.138; and as the players' rhymed playlet in 3.2.157–262. Of these, the dumb show is seemingly the most unnecessary, as it presents in pantomime what will immediately be narrated in dialogue as *The Murder of Gonzago*, and enacts a wordless version of the tale already told by the Ghost in act 1. The first half of this essay will analyse, in performance terms, what the dumb show contributes to *Hamlet*, and why it is there.

The second half will turn to the dumb show in literary terms. It will look at the words of the dumb show as found in two printed texts of *Hamlet*, Quarto 2 (Q2, 1604) and Folio (F, 1623) (the earliest *Hamlet* text, Quarto 1 [1603], seems to recall performance rather than dictate it, so its stage directions are unlikely to be authorial). Since the text for the dumb show has been altered and, this essay will argue, authorially revised between Q2 and F, consideration will be given to what the dumb show adds, textually, to a reading of *Hamlet*.

The travelling players who are about to put on *The Murder of Gonzago* at the Danish court do what actors sometimes did before 'real' plays: they mime part of the story in advance as a dumb show. The play that follows will then be able to focus on verbal complexity and literary features without alienating its audience. Indeed, dumb shows were used, on occasion, to gloss over or conceal the sketchiness of the written scenes they flanked, as the *Hamlet* dumb show has been said to do. Because dumb shows encapsulated the narrative of the play to come, they were sometimes called, like their paper counterparts, 'arguments':[1] comparing life to a play, Francis Quarles writes 'That fainting gaspe of Breath which first we vent / Is a Dumb-Shew, presents the Argument';[2] and Ophelia, when she sees the dumb show entering in *Hamlet*, speculates 'belike this show imports the argument of the play' (3.2.142–3).

What follows the dumb show in *Hamlet* is somewhat different from its real play equivalents, however. Usually a dumb show's additional symbolic import was 'explained' by an 'interpreter'. In the Shakespeare and George Wilkins play *Pericles*, for instance, the narrator Gower introduces a scene that is 'dumb in show' offering to 'plain' (explain) it 'with speech' (3.0.14) afterwards, which he does. Ophelia, after the dumb show, awaits an interpreter, first asking Hamlet to take on the role – 'What means this, my lord?' (3.2.138) – and then wondering, when an actor enters the stage, 'Will a tell us what this show meant?' (3.2.145). Hamlet, too, suspects that the actors are about to explain the dumb show. Fearing that his attempt to stir the king's conscience will take place too early, he protests when a player (in fact the Prologue) enters, 'we shall know by this fellow. The players cannot keep counsel: they'll tell all' (3.2.142–3).

Dumb shows required interpreters because they were nuanced, and were more than simply narrative. Resembling 'emblems' in books, or 'impresa' on shields, they provided enigmatic visual images that were not to be wholly understood until glossed. Readers/watchers knew to accrue their understanding sequentially, starting with the visual image, moving on to the words, and finally providing their own analysis of the amalgam. In *Pericles*, for instance, the 'devices' the knights bear are flanked by written mottos. The onlookers first look at the image, then at the explanatory words, and finally interpret the combination:

THAISA   … his present is
                    A wither'd branch, that's only green at top;
                    The motto, *In hac spe vivo.*
SIMONIDES   A pretty moral;
                    From the dejected state wherein he is,
                    He hopes by you his fortunes yet may flourish.
                                                            (2.2.41–6)

Yet for Ophelia, Hamlet, the courtiers, and Claudius, the expected explanation for the dumb show is not supplied, and the playlet *The Murder of Gonzago* immediately follows. This has led critics to accuse the dumb show in *Hamlet* of being merely 'anticipatory' rather than, like a proper dumb show, emblematic.[3] Yet the absence of an interpreter does not mean that the show lacks symbolic import. Rather, the show's significance is never drawn out, so that the fictional and factual audience's interpretation – indeed, the very amalgam of information they draw on – remains undirected. This enables the dumb show to convey one set of symbolic messages to the fictional courtier audience, another to Claudius, another to Hamlet, and a further set to us, the actual audience.

The courtiers are to be imagined viewing the dumb show, with its king and poisoner, as a depiction of the corruption of power. For Claudius, who is a king and poisoner, however, the dumb show is a revelation: it tells him what Hamlet knows, and warns him about the play to come. Yet directors, unable to explain why Claudius should sit calmly through the dumb show but call off the subsequent play so vigorously, tend to have Claudius distracted or absent for the show itself. Critics, too, have struggled to come up with explanations for Claudius's varying reactions. Greg suggested that Claudius does not react to the show because he is not in fact guilty of the murder; Pollard, more circumspectly, advanced the 'second tooth' theory: just as one might stand a single tooth being pulled, but not two, so perhaps Claudius was able to see his crimes presented once, but couldn't stand their repetition.[4] Yet all these explanations misunderstand what effect the dumb show has on Claudius and Hamlet.

Encouraged, perhaps, by Ophelia's demand to have the dumb show explained, Hamlet takes on the role of interpreter. He 'explains', during the playlet that follows, that Gonzago was murdered, and that Lucianus is the poisoner. Unfortunately, he goes on to 'interpret' Lucianus as nephew to the king (as Hamlet is to Claudius) rather than as brother to the king (as Claudius was to Hamlet's father). To all intents and purposes, then, he tells the court that he would like to kill Claudius. As a result, Claudius is able to halt the troubling play 'legitimately': his disquiet can now be traced to the behaviour of his nephew. Thus the uninterpreted dumb show ruins Hamlet's plans in two ways. On the one hand, it forewarns Claudius, who does not respond to the play as intended; on the other, it forces an overwrought Hamlet, disastrously, to become interpreter himself.

The dumb show is probably responsible for Hamlet's over-excitability in the first place. It is a retelling of what has haunted Hamlet from the moment he met the Ghost – the method of his father's murder. Shorn of explanatory words, the dumb show starkly encapsulates the events that altered Denmark's politics: the poisoning and death of the old king, and the sexual relationship that developed between the king's widow and his killer. So the dumb show gives physical form to Hamlet's darkest imaginings, while suggesting that the past is not just shaping the present – it is, here in the most literal fashion, entering into it.

Like Hamlet, we, the actual audience, see this show not as a foretaste of *The Murder of Gonzago* but as a reiteration of a murder already passed. Watching a story we already know, bereft of its words, makes us alert to the show's 'additional' symbolic meaning. It becomes clear that the gestures and props in the show are taking themes from the rest of the drama: an ear being infected; a crown being kissed; a woman exchanging her passions – verbal notions that are suddenly, shockingly visualised. Even the bank of flowers, an extravagant piece of property, is proleptic. It foreshadows the flowers that Ophelia imagines growing through her father's body, the flowers she distributes, and the 'weedy trophies' that slip with her into the stream as she drowns.

Placed midway through *Hamlet*, the dumb show also raises questions asked by Hamlet about the relationship between past and present, and performance and reality. Indeed, through the dumb show, our identification with the inner workings of Hamlet's mind is intensified and given visual form, not least because the content is slanted towards Hamlet's point of view; in the show, the queen's exchange of lovers is as central to the tragedy as the murder itself. The dumb show, then, gives shape to the story behind *Hamlet*, while emphasising and literalising some of the major themes of the play – and creating havoc with Hamlet's plans.

In the written text of *Hamlet*, the lengthy description of the dumb show has to substitute for a telling performative moment. A look at its vocabulary will show how it does this – for its phrases do not simply instruct the actors: they also inform the readers.

Firstly, the dumb show seems to express Hamlet's point of view. Its stress on the queen, on her behaviour, and on the ease with which she moves from man to man, conveys Hamlet's notion that Gertrude is behind the tragedy. The events are even framed in 'Hamlet' words. The queen's 'passionate action' when she discovers that the king is dead, picks up Hamlet's obsession with untrustworthy passions as against real emotion – it is 'a dream of passion' (2.2.552) that made the player cry, not real passion; the performers Hamlet values are those who do not 'tear a passion to tatters' (3.2.10), or become 'passion's slave' (3.2.73) as this 'queen' (and, by implication, Gertrude herself) does. The hypocritical nature of both the poisoner and queen is shown by use of another important Hamlet word, 'seems'. The poisoner 'seems' to condole with the queen, while she 'seems' harsh, but then accepts his 'love', mirroring Hamlet's earlier distrust of seeming (pretending) against being: 'Seems ... Nay, it is. I know not "seems"' (1.2.76). Even the fact that the first king expresses his love through declining his head on the queen's 'neck' is a Hamlet obsession; Hamlet is nauseated when he imagines his mother's new husband 'paddling in your neck with his damn'd fingers' (3.4.187). These references, available only to the reader, are part of the verbal patterning of *Hamlet* on the page; they are a substitute for the parallels in the action, for they draw us closer to Hamlet's way of thinking, while highlighting themes from elsewhere in the play.

Importantly, the text of the dumb show, between Q2 in 1604 and F in 1623, is sharpened, and made more verbally complex. Yet its changes seem not to be overtly playhouse ones, as the action will be virtually the same whichever version is followed. As with the rethinkings to be found elsewhere in the play, these revisions seem to show Shakespearean second thoughts.[5] Some of the alterations, of course, do simply add clarification for the people backstage: 'the sleepers eares' becomes 'the kings eares'; 'follows', a narrative term, becomes 'enters', a stage term, and 'leaves him' likewise becomes 'exits'. But even the one actual addition made to the action, when the queen, having displayed her love to her first husband, 'kneeles, and makes shew of Protestation unto him', emphasises and adds to the Hamlet terminology. Visually the queen humbles herself, but verbally the queen 'makes shew' of her subjection, suggesting again that her emotions are performed rather than real.

Some words in the dumb show are changed between the earlier Q2 and the later F text for what appear to be literary reasons. In the F text, the king and queen enter 'very lovingly', so that 'love' is inserted into the first sentence, where it stands in apposition to the final line, where the queen 'accepts ... love' from the poisoner: good love has given way to bad love in a single paragraph, prompting us to ask what 'love' in this play actually is. In F likewise the poisoner's 'three or foure' followers have become 'two or three Mutes': 'mute', though a theatrical word, also reflects another theme – *Hamlet* is filled with people who are reduced to silence by the events. Even we, the onlookers of Hamlet's death, are forced to join the courtiers as 'mutes or audience to this act' (5.2.342). In another alteration, the people who had once seemed to 'condole' with the queen, now seem to 'lament' with her, words that are practically interchangeable in terms of meaning, but that pick up other textual moments of *Hamlet*: 'lament', explains the Player King, is often untrustworthy – 'Where joy most revels, grief doth most lament; / Grief joys, joy grieves, on slender accident' (3.2.192–3). Perhaps, at least in the world of the dumb show, no one is really mourning the death of the king. Finally there is the fact that the queen, who had seemed 'harsh awhile' in Q2, in F seems 'loath and unwilling awhile'. Her earlier anger has yielded to sexual repulsion, rendering her emotions closer to those Hamlet feels, and making the *volte face* of her conversion even more outrageous.

Shakespeare himself is likely to have written both versions of the dumb show, since only he will have known the precise sequence of actions needed to herald *The Murder of Gonzago*; he is likely to be responsible for the revision too, as the alterations are of a piece with other 'literary' modifications he makes. As shown, the language of the dumb show both in Q and, more so, in F appears to join the network of words and images that make up *Hamlet*. And, depending on Shakespeare's literary intentions, a further textual possibility emerges. As Q2 and F alike present the words of the dumb show in italics, separating them from the roman lettering of the rest of the play, just as letters, songs, and other 'documents' in plays were sometimes isolated, the dumb show looks on the page like an 'inserted' piece of text. To the reader, this may even appear to be the 'dozen or sixteen lines' (2.2.541), originally conceived of as a speech, placed into the entertainment by Hamlet himself. After all, the addition of dumb shows to a play otherwise written by someone else was quite normal. One copy of *Locrine*, for instance, has a manuscript note attached to it by George Buc, briefly Master of the Revels, who recalled retaining copies of dumb shows he had written for it, though he had lost track of the rest of the play: 'Charles Tilney wrote a Tragedy of this matter which hee named Estrild: & which I think is this. it was lost[?] by his death. & now[?] some fellow hath published it. I made dumbe shewes for it which I yet have. G. B.'[6] Just possibly, then, the reason the language is so redolent of Hamlet's preoccupations and words is that, on one level, it is 'his' text. That would add poignancy to the fact that the show so disastrously ruins his plans. And, if this is 'Hamlet's' dumb show, no wonder he worries when he thinks the players are about to interpret it.

Whether or not the words are literally 'Hamlet's', this essay has suggested that the dumb show makes visual, performative connections with other moments of the enacted play, and verbal, textual connections with other moments of the read play. Sometimes, indeed, it does both: the words that make up the very term 'dumb show' are repeatedly and disparagingly spoken on stage. The ghost of Hamlet's father was inexplicably 'dumb' (1.1.176) to the watchmen, who hoped he might speak to Horatio, yet they 'Stand dumb' (1.2.206) when they see him. Throughout the play characters are repeatedly rendered dumb, just as they are regularly 'mute'; there are no trustworthy interpreters. In a drama where the word 'show' is also always open to criticism – 'I have that within', says Hamlet, 'which passes show' (1.2.85) – a 'dumb show' is bound to be untrustworthy. Yet though the dumb show does not aid the playlet it supposedly glosses, *The Murder of Gonzago*, it does magnificently gloss and complicate *Hamlet*, both on stage and page.

THIRTY FOUR

Claudius on His Knees

COPPÉLIA KAHN

O, my offence is rank, it smells to heaven;
It hath the primal eldest curse upon't—
A brother's murder. Pray can I not,
Though inclination be as sharp as will,
My stronger guilt defeats my strong intent,   40
And, like a man to double business bound,
I stand in pause where I shall first begin,
And both neglect. What if this cursed hand
Were thicker than itself with brother's blood,
Is there not rain in the sweet heavens   45
To wash it white as snow? Whereto serves mercy
But to confront the visage of offence?
And what's in prayer but this two-fold force,
To be forestalled ere we come to fall
Or pardon'd being down? Then I'll look up.   50
My fault is past – but O, what form of prayer
Can serve my turn? 'Forgive me my foul murder?'
That cannot be, since I am still possess'd
Of those effects for which I did the murder—
My crown, mine own ambition, and my queen.   55
May one be pardon'd and retain th'offence?
In the corrupted currents of this world
Offence's gilded hand may shove by justice,
And oft 'tis seen the wicked prize itself
Buys out the law. But 'tis not so above: 60
There is no shuffling, there the action lies
In his true nature, and we ourselves compell'd

Even to the teeth and forehead of our faults
To give in evidence. What then? What rests?
Try what repentance can. What can it not?   65
Yet what can it, when one cannot repent?
O wretched state! O bosom black as death!
O limed soul, that struggling to be free
Art more engag'd! Help, angels! Make assay.
Bow, stubborn knees; and heart with strings of steel,   70
Be soft as sinews of the new-born babe.
All may be well.   *He kneels.*
William Shakespeare, *Hamlet*, 3.3.36–72

As act 3, scene 3 opens, Claudius dispatches Rosencrantz and
Guildenstern to accompany Hamlet to England, seemingly on a
diplomatic mission 'for the demand of our neglected tribute', but
actually, we later learn, to meet instant death (3.2.172). Polonius
then exits to overhear the prince's conversation with his mother,
and Claudius is left alone onstage to confront his conscience in
a thirty-seven-line soliloquy. If we remember an earlier moment,
when he and Polonius were preparing to spy on Hamlet's encounter
with Ophelia, this soul-searching soliloquy is not as surprising as it
might seem. As Polonius handed his daughter a book to read, so as
to create the impression of piety, he made this moralising comment:
''Tis too oft proved, that with devotion's visage / And pious action
we do sugar o'er / The devil himself' (3.1.47–9). In an aside the
king responded, 'O 'tis too true. / How smart a lash that speech
doth give my conscience' (3.1.49–50). He uses the same word that
the prince will use later when he jubilantly proclaims, 'The play's
the thing / Wherein I'll catch the conscience of the king' (2.2.600–
601). This soliloquy, delivered in the aftermath of that play, offers
a more extended look into Claudius's conscience and at the same
time, through verbal parallels to and echoes of Hamlet's language,
forms part of a chilling chiasmus. The virtuous prince, convinced
of Claudius's guilt, has now become a ruthless revenger who would
'drink hot blood' (3.2.381) while the man he called 'Bloody, bawdy
villain!' (2.2.576) now struggles to pray, hoping for divine mercy.

In the first three lines, Claudius abruptly indicts himself: 'O, my offence is rank, it smells to heaven; / It hath the primal eldest curse upon't – / A brother's murder' (36–8). In calling his offence 'rank', he echoes Hamlet's depiction of the world in his first soliloquy as a fallen paradise possessed 'by things rank and gross in nature' (1.2.136). Claudius sees himself as Hamlet sees the world Claudius created by marrying Hamlet's mother. The word 'rank' carries a cluster of meanings pertaining to sex: 'Grossly rich, heavy or fertile', 'Having an offensively strong smell', 'Lustful, licentious, in heat', and 'Grossly coarse or indecent'.[1] By characterising his 'offence' as 'rank', Claudius associates it with his marriage – somewhat as Hamlet has associated the rankness of the world with his mother's desire for Claudius. Claudius's allusion to 'the primal eldest curse ... A brother's murder' (37–8), also links him to Hamlet. Cain, first son of Adam and Eve, earned God's curse for murdering his brother, the first murder ever committed.[2] Earlier, persuading his stepson to stop mourning King Hamlet, Claudius mentioned 'the first corse', an allusion that will resonate later with Hamlet's musing upon a skull the gravedigger throws up 'as if 'twere Cain's jawbone, that did the first murder' (5.1.75–6). Brother-murderer Claudius and his enemy-nephew Hamlet are obsessed with the same deed.

The soliloquy focuses on the spiritual impasse between guilt and repentance that the king experiences: he cannot pray, he says, because 'My stronger *guilt* defeats my strong intent' (40, emphasis mine). The king is so conscious of his guilt that he is prevented from believing that God's mercy is sufficient to absolve it. Thus, '... like a man to double business bound' he 'stand[s] in pause' between guilt and repentance, presumably his 'intent' (41–3). More ambiguously, though, Claudius parallels two oppositions, which in the chiastic structure of these lines, change positions: the opposition between 'inclination' (to pray) and 'will' (the desire for crown and queen which led him to murder) in line 39, and that between 'stronger guilt' (of murder) and 'strong intent' (to pray) in line 40. As Harold Jenkins notes, 'Though inclination be as sharp as will' can modify either the preceding line, 'Pray can

I not' (38) or the following one, 'My stronger guilt defeats my strong intent' (40).[3] If it modifies the preceding line, Claudius's inclination to pray is as strong as the will that led him to murder in the first place, or, if it modifies the following line, despite his inclination to pray, his guilt defeats his intention to do so.

Much hinges on how one defines 'will'. The meanings invited in this context are 'what one wishes to have or do' and 'lust, carnal desire'.[4] That Claudius is inclined to pray as much as he wishes to do so seems tautological; that he is inclined to pray as much as he carnally desires Gertrude, in the light of his later reference to her as one of the reasons he murdered his brother (55), makes more sense as expressing the tension between wanting to repent and wanting to continue enjoying the fruits of his crime. Taking 'will' to mean 'what one wishes to do or have', however, makes more sense if 'Though inclination be as strong as will' (39) modifies the following line. In that case, if Claudius's inclination is as strong as his desire to repent, nonetheless, his 'stronger guilt' and concomitant lack of belief in mercy, prevails over that desire. Either way, Shakespeare's diction creates ambiguity as to which is stronger among three forces: Claudius's guilt, his desire to repent, or his desire to continue wearing the crown and possessing Gertrude. This ambiguity is the subject of the soliloquy, and these three lines (38–40) carry something of the image Claudius invokes near the end, of a bird struggling to free itself from the sticky substance smeared on twigs to ensnare it: 'O limed soul, that struggling to be free / Art more engaged' (68–9). The more he tries to decide which is stronger, the more ambivalent he becomes.

A further ambiguity inheres in the resonant phrasing of lines 41–3, 'And, like a man to double business bound, / I stand in pause where I shall first begin, / And both neglect'. Jenkins notes that 'Bound' is both an adjective 'as in "bound" for a destination', and the past participle of the verb 'to bind', as in being obligated to do something. He comments, 'The meanings of these etymologically different words cannot be kept distinct. There is a "double" objective, but also a dual obligation'.[5] One might say that Claudius seeks to move towards heaven (repentance) but in his inability to

repent is inevitably drawn towards hell, or, that he feels obligated
to repent but cannot repudiate his 'obligation' to continue being
king. In the following twenty lines (43–63), Claudius struggles to
elucidate these dualities.

First, in a series of three rhetorical questions in lines 43–50,
he tries to convince himself that God's mercy is real, abundant,
and fully efficacious to forgive his rank offence. Like the simple
but vivid image of a man standing 'in pause', torn between two
alternatives, his forward motion arrested by his ambivalence (42),
each question evokes body language in trying to make divine mercy
present and believable. The hesitation evoked in all three questions
recalls the First Player's image of Pyrrhus who, upon hearing the
crash of the citadel's wall, '... stood, / And like a neutral to his will
and matter, / Did nothing' (2.2.476–8). In this moment, as Jenkins
comments, Pyrrhus 'temporarily images Hamlet'.[6] Similarly,
Claudius 'to double business bound ... in pause', also images him.

The first question is cast as hyperbole: Claudius, who killed
his brother bloodlessly by pouring poison in his ear, pictures his
'cursed hand ... thicker than itself with brother's blood' (43–4),
but washed 'white as snow' by 'rain ... in the sweet heavens'
(45–6). The echo of Ecclesiasticus 35:19, 'Oh, how faire a thing
is mercie in the time of anguish and trouble! It is like a cloude
of raine, that cometh in the time of a drought' (Geneva), lends
a note of fervent conviction. The second question evokes a face
to face encounter between God and the sinner: 'Whereto serves
mercy / But to confront the visage of offence?' (46–7), the Latin
word for forehead (*frons*) in 'confront' serving as synecdoche for
God's face and the sinner's. The third and last equates prayer with
mercy, and attributes to it the 'two-fold force' of preventing the
sinner before he 'come[s] to fall' and pardoning him 'being down'
(48–50), in the traditional spatial and physical metaphor for sin.

The syntax of these three rhetorical questions is fairly
elaborate. In stark contrast, two four-beat declarative sentences
seemingly bring doubt to a halt: 'Then I'll look up. / My fault is
past—' (50–51). Claudius would 'look up' to God, confident that
divine mercy would in turn 'confront' him. 'My fault is past',

then, could be read as prolepsis – the king imagining that he has repented, and that God has forgiven him. The two sentences, alike in syntax and length, travel over a line break, mimicking a kind of suture, smoothing over a rupture. This healing moment, however, is brief, for the dash following 'past' announces another break, as does 'but O' (51). Claudius now pivots back to the reality of the present moment, initiating a new train of thought in lines 51–64. Having convinced himself that if he prays for mercy, he will find forgiveness, he now addresses the interim step between prayer and forgiveness – repentance – and here he stumbles.

Ironically mimicking the 'form of prayer' he might use, he nullifies its efficacy in the brutal self-indictment of 'Forgive me my foul murder' (51, 52). The alliteration of 'Forgive' and 'foul' suggests that the latter negates the former, a conclusion then stated with crisp certainty: 'That [forgiveness] cannot be' (53), because he is not willing to repent. Repentance requires that he repudiate his sin, and surrender 'those effects for which I did the murder— / My crown, mine own ambition, and my queen' (54–5). The resounding triad of crown, ambition, and queen, each preceded by the possessive pronoun ('My ... mine own ... my') rings with as much stubbornness as honesty, and conspicuously lacks remorse or regret. Yet Claudius presses on, to pose another ironic rhetorical question: 'May one be pardon'd and retain th'offence?' (56). For the third time, he uses the word 'offence' (see previous instances in lines 36 and 47), and he will use it once more in answering the question he just posed (58). His speech is haunted by these repetitions: he can't get over the fact of his offence, no matter how he tries.

The answer to his question takes the form of an opposition between 'this world' (57) and 'above' (60). Again, body imagery elegantly captures the *habitus* of the sinner. 'Offence's gilded hand may shove by justice' counters the earlier 'cursed hand' that mercy's rain could wash clean (43–4), and in the play of words on 'gilded' – gold-bearing (whether from illicit gain or for bribe-making) and guilty – compresses a history of crime and consequence. 'Shove by' suggests the criminal's arrogance and the complicity of 'justice'. In contrast, 'above', in heaven, 'There is no shuffling' (61) – no evasion or concealment – but rather a harsh courtroom in which the earlier mild, forgiving confrontation between 'mercy' and 'offence' (46–7) yields to the rigorous demands of justice: 'we ourselves compell'd / Even to the teeth and forehead of our faults / To give in evidence' (62–4). Stymied yet insistent, Claudius ends this comparison between his present state of successfully concealed sin and the inevitable judgment he expects to face, with peppery, impatient, fragmented questions: 'What then? What rests?' (65).

'What rests' is the same 'double business' that stalled Claudius at the beginning of the soliloquy. His stubborn reluctance to repent is exquisitely balanced against his wish to believe in God's mercy, as the chiastic construction of these two lines demonstrates: 'Try what repentance can. What can it not? / Yet what can it, when one cannot repent?' (65–6). Claudius can, and cannot, repent. Is not the king experiencing an ambivalence similar to Hamlet's in the prince's 'To be, or not to be' soliloquy? In that all-too-famous speech, the prince considers two divergent options and in doing so, manages to confuse the distinctions between them so that he is consigned, as it were, to life as the default position. 'Thus conscience doth make cowards of us all', he concludes (3.1.83). In this soliloquy, Hamlet has in effect 'caught' the king's conscience as he wished to, although he doesn't know it.

Three lines of paralleled exclamations begin the concluding movement of the soliloquy: 'O wretched state! O bosom black as death! / O limed soul, that struggling to be free / Art more engag'd! Help, angels! Make assay' (67–9). In his successive Os, the king moves from the self-indictment with which he began to what serves in the third exclamation as a description of the process the soliloquy dramatises. The more Claudius examines his alternatives, and tries to move from his present state of sin to a state of repentance, the more he is mired between them. After calling for divine aid ('Help, angels!'), he 'makes assay' in his own fashion as he commands himself, 'Bow, stubborn knees; and heart with strings of steel, / Be soft as sinews of the new-born babe'

(70–71). Here the body language that has run through the soliloquy culminates. The posture of kneeling, he hopes, will soften his obdurate sinner's heart. Somewhat like the First Player who forced his soul to his own conceit so that he felt in his body the emotions he faked, Claudius hopes that the posture of repentance will induce the feeling itself. Ramie Targoff remarks that in staging Claudius's prayer, 'The play interrogates ... the belief that external practices might not only reflect but also partly transform the internal self'.[7] She argues that the institution of standardised devotional practice through *The Book of Common Prayer* in 1549 rested on the belief that external behaviour, such as kneeling and repeating a scripted prayer, could indeed work upon the heart and change it.

With regard to the praying king, then, his kneeling body might make his soul 'kneel' too, and repent – or it might not. As Claudius falls silent and bows his head, Shakespeare withholds from us the knowledge of whether, as the king prays, he succeeds in humbling his soul as well; whether he actually reaches, through repentance, a state of grace. Shakespeare constructs the sequence of events with unparalleled dramatic canniness. Hamlet arrives only after Claudius kneels and falls silent, to misread the king, in the words of R. A. Foakes, 'as if he were the silent embodiment of contrition'.[8] What might be, from the prince's perspective, the perfect moment for revenge, he interprets as the wrong moment that would in effect reward the king with heaven, rather than punish him with hell as Hamlet wishes. The audience, privy to Claudius's inmost thoughts, watches Hamlet, standing behind Claudius with his sword lifted, misinterpret the kneeling man. Like Pyrrhus in the First Player's speech as mentioned above, the prince stands 'like a neutral to his will and matter' (2.2.476), and also like his enemy Claudius, 'a man to double business bound' (3.3.41). At this point, we might recall Thomas Wright's warning: 'hearts ... be inscrutable, onely open to God' while 'externall physiognomy and operations' offer but 'an Image of that affection that doth raigne in the minde', not 'a perfect and resolute knowledge'.[9] We, and Hamlet, see Claudius kneeling in prayer, but we do not know, until after Hamlet puts up his sword and exits, whether he has in fact succeeded in wresting his soul to repentance.

Claudius's soliloquy, I think, has never received its critical due, in general because our cultural obsession with Hamlet's 'delay', as Margreta de Grazia demonstrates, has blocked out Shakespeare's dramatisation of Claudius as – in this moment at least – a sinner struggling with his conscience. More specifically, for centuries, the horror of critics at Hamlet's determination not merely to kill the king but to damn him to hell for ever, and their attempts to excuse him for it, have eclipsed attention to the interpretive dilemma – Hamlet's and ours – of reading Claudius's inscrutable heart in his words.[10]

THIRTY FIVE

Gertrude's Gallery

LENA COWEN ORLIN

You may chance to nose him as you go up the lobby.
                        Q1 *Hamlet*, 11.143

But if indeed you find him not within this month you
shall nose him as you go up the stairs into the lobby.
                        Q2 *Hamlet*, 4.3.34–6

But indeed if you find him not this month you shall
nose him as you go up the stairs into the lobby.
                        F *Hamlet*, 3.6.32–3

In the First Quarto of *Hamlet*, the 'closet scene' does not take place in a closet. The Second Quarto and the Folio are uncharacteristically insistent about the location of act 3, scene 4: Rosencrantz advises Hamlet that his mother 'desires to speak with you in her closet'; Polonius reports to Claudius that Hamlet is 'going to his mother's closet'; and Claudius tells Rosencrantz and Guildenstern that Hamlet has 'dragged' the body of Polonius 'from his mother's closet' (Q2 3.2.322–3 and F 3.2.321–2; 3.3.27 in both; Q2 4.1.35 and F 3.4.225). Where these versions perform three acts of specification, however, the First Quarto has none. Instead it relies on a series of locational signifiers that are generally unintelligible to modern ears. Gertred receives Hamlet in a room that has an arras (11.2) and pictures (11.24–5), the Ghost appears there wearing a nightgown (11.57sd), the Ghost exits through a portal (11.81), and Hamlet eventually allows that the body of Corambis is to be found by going 'up the lobby' (11.143). The title of this essay betrays its proposition, that the First Quarto imagines Hamlet to confront his mother in a gallery (Figure 1). In the Second Quarto and Folio, furthermore, the place-name that goes unspoken may be as implicitly present as the name said thrice.

Figure 1 *The long gallery at Albyns House in Essex, with a period fire surround (c. 1620) but an eighteenth-century doorframe. From Jourdain, courtesy of B. T. Batsford.*

Corambis establishes the domestic setting of the First Quarto's eleventh scene by announcing that he will 'shroud' himself 'behind the arras' (11.2). Alan Dessen has shown that the catalogue of Elizabethan spatial signifiers includes costumes and props; hunting weapons carried by an actor, for example, can serve to set a scene in a forest.[1] This helps us understand the First Quarto's unique and otherwise mysterious stage direction that the Ghost, who earlier appeared in 'complete steel' (4.28), now wears a nightgown. Had he entered in armour, he might have dislocated the sense of an interior that the scene works to maintain. Both the arras and the portal indicate, moreover, that it is a space of status. Were we to envisage a room of no distinction, then any plain or painted cloth would have sufficed to conceal Corambis. William Harrison, writing in 1577, associated 'arras' with noblemen specifically.[2] And 'portal' is a twenty-five-cent word when the five-cent 'door' would in fact have been less unruly metrically.

A portal, in its first *OED* definition described as an entrance 'of stately or elaborate construction', featured columns, pilasters, cornices, pediments, and various other mouldings and architectural embellishments. It was understood to announce a room of size and significance. The second meaning of the 'portal', equally associated with large and ostentatious spaces, was the so-called 'interior' porch (Figure 2). This was a human-height wainscot box with two doors that functioned to stage entries and eliminate draughts (the outer door would be shut before the inner one was opened). As an occasion for the display of skills in woodworking, painting, and sometimes gilding, it was as striking a feature as a monumental fire surround. Small or private rooms – that is, closets – would not have been dressed or addressed so dramatically. But the Great Gallery at William Cecil's palatial country house, Theobalds, is recorded to have had a 'carved wood "portal"'.[3]

Figure 2 *The drawing room of Bradfield House in Devon, with an early seventeenth-century portal, or interior porch. From Gotch, courtesy of B. T. Batsford.*

With three galleries, each ornamented by a themed series of wall paintings, Theobalds was sufficiently splendid that James VI and I acquired it in 1607. In galleries elsewhere, the decorative scheme often involved easel paintings. Mark Girouard characterises portrait collecting as a sixteenth-century fad and galleries as the places to display them; thus, Robert Cecil received a request for his portrait from Viscount Howard of Bindon, who described 'The gallery I lately made for the pictures of sundry of my honored friends'. Howard anticipated that it would 'greatly delight' him 'to walk often in that place where I may see so comfortable a sight'.[4] As early as 1546 the Duke of Norfolk could boast twenty-eight 'physiognomies of divers noble persons' embellishing his long gallery. In travel diaries, building accounts, and inventories, we learn of painting collections in the galleries of Whitehall (1592), Hardwick Hall (1601), Hampton Court (1610), St James's Palace (1611), Beddington (1611), Northampton House (1614), Somerset House (1616), and others. Thomas Heywood's *If You Know Not Me, You Know Nobody, Part Two* (1606) features an urban, middle-class 'Gallery, wherein I keep the pictures / Of many charitable citizens'.[5] Judging by *1 Henry VI* – 'in my gallery thy picture hangs' (2.3.36) – Shakespeare was well aware of the association. Thus, when Hamlet enjoins his mother 'See here, behold this picture. / It is the portraiture of your deceased husband' (11.24–5), and especially when the portrait then becomes one of a short royal series of two, the First Quarto might be understood to locate its eleventh scene in an imagined gallery.

The Second Quarto and Folio versions of *Hamlet* include references to the brisk market for 'picture[s] in little' of the new king of Denmark (2.2.300–303 and 2.2.361–4; at Q1 7.274–7, the size of Claudius's 'picture' goes unspecified). The portraits of the 'closet' scene are sometimes also represented, in glosses and in performance, as miniatures. But *Hamlet* would not have been unique for incorporating at least one gallery-sized, wall-hanging painting. The second dumb show in the 1599 *Warning for Fair Women* offers a precedent in terms of stage action as well as stage properties: a woman who has murdered her husband is forced by the personification of 'Chastity' to confront what a stage direction describes as 'her husband's picture hanging on the wall'.[6] In a *White Devil* dumb show, the portrait of Bracciano is large enough to have a curtain, and Isabella dies from kissing limned lips overpainted with poison.[7] A curtained portrait in *The Traitor* is specified to have 'a poniard sticking in it'.[8]

The gallery's role as a picture hall is an important condition of the spatial implications of *Hamlet*. But galleries had other meanings, as well. They were the signature spaces of audacious builders in the sixteenth and early seventeenth centuries, appearing first in royal palaces but soon included in houses of any pretension. They were long and narrow because, as suggested by Viscount Howard, their pretext was to provide room for walking in inclement weather. They attracted extravagant ornamentation both as visual entertainment for walkers and also to celebrate their own spatial profligacy. Always at least one staircase away from the ground floor, sometimes set independently in wings of their own, they were inimical to eavesdroppers. Early moderns who were desirous of confidential conversation knew to take themselves up to the great room in which others could not approach unheard.[9] This understanding of the space may have informed not only Corambis's need to pre-position himself but also one other aspect of the design of Hamlet's meeting with Gertred. What looks like a textual garble in the First Quarto, with Corambis 'hear[ing] young Hamlet coming' even before Hamlet calls out to his mother (11.1–4), would in a gallery have had a material basis.

The spatial associations are disambiguated in *Der bestrafte Brudermord oder Prinz Hamlet aus Dännemark*, the German dramatic manuscript of 1710 that probably documents performances by a company of English actors who toured Europe in the early 1600s. They are known to have staged the *Tragoedia von Hamlet einen Printzen in Dennemarck* in Dresden in 1626. In *Der bestrafte Brudermord*, Horatio informs Queen Sigrie that 'Prince Hamlet is in the antechamber, and desires a private audience'. She orders Corambus to 'Hide yourself behind the arras'. Having been admitted, Hamlet then gestures out: 'look, there in that gallery [*jener Gallerie*] hangs the counterfeit resemblance of your first husband, and there hangs the counterfeit of your present one'.[10] For travelling players, as perhaps even for those in residence at the Globe, the portraits would presumably have been word-paintings rather than stage properties, given imaginative substance by their association with a word-painted gallery.

The 'antechamber' of *Der bestrafte Brudermord* intersects with Q1 *Hamlet*, too, where the series of spatial signifiers – 'arras' at line 2, 'portrait' at line 24, 'portal' at line 81 – climaxes in the 'lobby' at line 143. A 'lobby' was 'a passage or corridor' that was 'often used as a waiting-place or ante-room' (*OED s.v.* 'lobby' n. 2). The long and narrow form of the lobby may account for the fact that the term 'gallery' came to share its conventional functions. This is the way the word was used by Donne in the elegy 'On His Mistress' ('a worthy gallery, / To walk in expectation'), by Jonson in *Volpone* ('let him entertain himself awhile / Without i'th'gallery', as also 'if you please to walk the while / Into that gallery'), and by Beaumont and Fletcher in *The Maid's Tragedy* ('Go wait me in the gallery').[11]

Gallery is a word that Shakespeare uses rarely, mostly early (as in *1 Henry VI*) or late (as in *Pericles*, *The Winter's Tale*, and *Henry VIII*). It appears in *Pericles* in a scene generally credited to George Wilkins, and in *Henry VIII* it is a direct carryover from the sources. Without a text or a confident attribution for the *Ur-Hamlet*, we cannot know whether this use of the term was original to Shakespeare in mid-career, but it occurs twice in the First Quarto. Ofelia's encounter with a distracted Hamlet takes place when 'He found me walking in the gallery all alone' (6.42; compare Q2's 'as I was sewing in my closet' [2.1.74] and F's 'as I was sewing in my chamber' [2.1.75]). Later, Corambis directs: 'The Prince's walk is here in the gallery: / There let Ofelia walk until he comes' (7.104–5). In the Second Quarto and Folio, the gallery becomes a lobby: 'You know sometimes he walks four hours together / Here in the lobby' (2.2.157–8). It might seem that the textual variants have differing spatial conceptualisations, except that, through their common use for leisure walking, 'gallery' and 'lobby' could be employed almost interchangeably. Thus, in

Jonson's *Epicene* comes the question: 'Do you observe this gallery, or rather lobby, indeed? ... You two shall be the chorus behind the arras, and whip out between the acts and speak'.[12] The use of 'lobby', in other words, confirms the implication of the earlier nexus of associations. All versions of *Hamlet* furnish the meeting between Hamlet and his mother with an arras, portraits, and a portal, and all have Hamlet drag a murdered body to or across a lobby that is associated with going 'up'.

The important difference between the three is that the Second Quarto and Folio add references to the 'closet' in the lead-up to the scene and after its completion. Although this again seems like a reimagination of the spatial definition of *Hamlet*, the fact is that by this term or as its sometime-synonym, 'study',[13] the smaller space was closely implicated in the history and design of the gallery. It is often a companion space: in *Epicene*, where the gallery is imagined with 'a couple of studies at each end one';[14] in the First Quarto of *Hamlet*, where Corambis suggests that while Ofelia walks in the gallery, he and the King should 'stand close in the study' (7.106); and in the architectural scheme identified by Simon Thurley as 'the gallery-and-closet plan'.[15]

The arrangement was common in royal building. During the reign of Henry VIII, the king and his queen shared a gallery and each had a closet off it. Generally, the gallery connected independent, his-and-her suites of domestic chambers with the palace chapel, and closets looked down into the chapel so that the monarchs could hear the celebration of the mass or could worship in solitude. As appropriate to its function, the closet was generally furnished with a prie-dieu or prayer desk. Thurley recognises the gallery-and-closet arrangement at Whitehall, Havering, Hull Manor, Dunstable Priory, Waltham-in-the-Forest, and 'at every other house belonging to the King'.[16] A 1530s survey of Hampton Court described 'the cross gallery' running 'from the king's lodgings unto the holy-day closet'.[17] Hamlet, coming across the kneeling king while en route to meeting with his mother, is probably to be imagined looking into his uncle's prayer closet. This would suggest that hers was a prayer closet, too.

The two-closet scheme was not needed for Edward VI or Elizabeth I, but it was employed by Mary and Philip and, having maintained its functional viability through all the Tudor years, was revived for James and Anne. Meanwhile, Sir William Petre re-created the royal plan in his Essex seat, Ingatestone. He constructed an upper-level gallery ninety-four feet long and eighteen feet wide with, according to a 1566 survey, 'a door, which door leadeth into the chapel chamber over the chapel, where the priest in his ministration from beneath may very well be heard'; in the plan of the house, the 'chapel chamber' is labelled the 'closet over the chapel'. There were also two other closets off the gallery, one, as became more common in gentry construction, 'at the gallery end'. Petre had an additional 'study at the end of the gallery' in his London house.[18] In 1556, Sir John Sackville bequeathed to his widow 'free going in to the chapel closet through the gallery' at Old Buckhurst.[19] The 1558 will of Sir Thomas Hilton indicated that he, too, had a closet 'within' his gallery in Northumbria.[20] The twinning of gallery with closet was well known even among those with limited access to great buildings. In his diary, the merchant Henry Machyn recorded that 'The 21 day of March [1557] the King and the Queen [went] through the gallery unto their closet' to hear mass.[21]

There are ample reasons why none of this has previously seemed relevant to *Hamlet*. The drumbeat of before-and-after references to the closet in the Second Quarto and the Folio has deafened us to other locational signifiers. We have not appreciated that arras, portal, stairs, and especially pictures might imply a gallery. We have not understood the gallery and lobby to be sister spaces. We are not as familiar with the closet-and-gallery plan as was Henry Machyn. And we do not recognise that in this convergence of material contexts, the posture of a king in prayer was a locational signifier for the scene that followed.

In 1709 Shakespeare's first editor, Nicholas Rowe, began the process of naming his play-places. Edward Capell and Edmond Malone were more aggressive scene locators, but subsequent editors have sometimes had to admit that the spatial indefinitions of Shakespeare defeat them. He often seems a scenic minimalist by comparison with his contemporaries. Bernard Beckerman distinguishes Shakespeare's resistantly 'unlocalized' scenes from such 'localized' ones as 'Brutus' orchard, Gertrude's closet, Timon's cave'.[22] Beckerman is not alone in having taken for granted that *Hamlet*'s 'closet' scene is a closed case locationally, and from this assumption have flowed others about its 'utter seclusion' and 'erotic possibility'.[23] It may be, however, that the internal logic of the play is culturally denser, if less sensational, and that we can better understand the 'closet' scene by undefining it.

Der bestrafte Brudermord preserves a vision of how a single scene could evoke both closet and gallery, with Hamlet pointing out towards a gallery as if from a room adjoining it. Whether this is another trace from *Hamlet* is an open question. There is no knowing if the Hamlet of any English performance understood himself to be walking the length of a gallery as he approached his kneeling uncle, to be moving then from the king's closet to that of the queen, or to be acting on the plausible assumption that the eavesdropper behind the arras was the man he knew to have been in the companion closet just before. The most likely of the possible effects of this chain of associations is that the scene would have been thought to take place in rooms of state, not domestic and private ones, and that it may have opened with the queen genuflecting as if in prayer, matching her husband's pose in a matching space. Finally, if a credible reading emerges from this reading of *Hamlet*, it would go also to suggest an undiscovered coherence in Shakespeare's spatial imagination. His invention is at once less indefinite for evoking the two idiocratic spaces of closet and gallery in near simultaneity, and more.

Close Reading Endings

THIRTY SIX

The Fool's Promised Exit

MARGRETA DE GRAZIA

At dead centre of the Folio's *The Tragedy of King Lear* is a prophecy of endtime.[1] It ends a scene that has trouble ending. This is the Fool's doing. There is every reason for him to follow his master to shelter. It is dark and stormy, and he is shivering from the wind and rain: 'Art cold?' asks Lear (3.2.68). Lear prepares to leave, solicitous that the Fool should join him, 'Come on, my boy' (3.2.67). Instead the Fool sings a song. Lear then bids Kent to take them both out from the storm, 'Come, bring us to this hovel' (78–9), and in the quarto *The History of King Lear* this is where the scene ends: all three men exit.[2] But in the Folio, the Fool slips back and tells a bawdy joke. Still he does not leave: 'I'll speak a prophecy ere I go' (80).

> When priests are more in word than matter;
> When brewers mar their malt with water;
> When nobles are their tailors' tutors,
> No heretics burn'd, but wenches' suitors;
> When every case in law is right
> No squire in debt, nor no poor knight;
> When slanders do not live in tongues,
> Nor cutpurses come not to throngs,
> When usurers tell their gold i' the field,
> And bawds and whores do churches build,
> Then shall the realm of Albion
> Come to great confusion:
> Then comes the time, who lives to see't,
> That going shall be used with feet.

(3.2.81–94)

After song, joke, and prophecy, the Fool still has a one-liner to go: 'This prophecy Merlin shall make; for I live before his time' (95–6). And then, at last: *Exit*.

In William Warburton's 1747 edition of *King Lear*, the Fool's prophecy is printed as two prophecies, and his introductory line is emended accordingly, 'I'll speak a prophecy *or two* ere I go'.[3] A footnote explains the change, 'The judicious reader will observe through this heap of nonsense and confusion, that this is not *one*, but *two* prophecies'. The Folio editors, 'by an unaccountable stupidity', had jumbled together two distinct predictions, the first of '*present manners*' and the second of '*future manners*'. What Warburton saw as two independent 'When'/'Then' prophecies, they had collapsed into a single inchoate one. As a result, the first prophecy had no culminating 'Then' clause, while the second prophecy closed with two. Warburton solved the problem by lifting the extra 'Then' clause from the second prophecy and tacking it to the last line of the first. In addition to setting the emended version in the text proper, he reproduced it as footer to highlight the partition. A space divides the two units; they are numbered 1 and 2, with 'Now' appended to 1 and 'Never' to 2.

> 1. *I'll speak a prophecy or* two *ere I go.*
>   *When priests are more in words than matter,*
>   *When brewers marr their malt with water;*
>   *When nobles are their tailors' tutors;*
>   *No hereticks burnt but wenches' suitors;*
>   *Then comes the time, who lives to see't,*
>   *That Going shall be us'd with feet.   i. e.* **Now.**
>
> 2. *When every case in law is right*
>   *No squire in debt, and no poor knight;*
>   *When slanders do not live in tongues;*
>   *And cut-purses come not to throngs;*
>   *When usurers tell their gold i' th' field;*
>   *And bawds and whores do churches build:*
>   *Then shall the realm of* Albion
>   *Come to great confusion.   i. e.* **Never.**

Most twentieth-century editors have followed Warburton's bold transposition, sometimes even reproducing his typographical break.[4] They, too, have assumed that the prophecy has been corrupted, though by printers or players rather than the Folio editors.[5] While stopping short of emending 'a prophecy' to 'a prophecy or two', they produce two autonomous syntactic units by introducing a full stop after the transposed first 'When'/'Then' unit. Commentators have also followed Warburton's logic in defending the separation. The first unit pertains to Shakespeare's 'Now', listing social abuses already prevalent in early seventeenth-century London: hypocritical priests (81), dishonest brewers (82), foppish nobility (83) and syphilitic lovers (84). The second unit refers to, if not Warburton's 'Never', then some millenarian future made up of social ideals: just court proceedings (85), fiscal solvency (86), and the end of slander (87), theft (88), usury (89), and prostitution (90).

Even when the prophecy is printed in its 1623 form, editors agree that the text is scrambled. It is the result, however, not of the printers' or players' ignorance, but of Shakespeare's intent.[6] Shakespeare, they assume, purposely mixed up the two prophecies in order to parody the practice of predicting the future on the basis of the fulfilment of signs.[7] Thus whether they divide the Folio prophecy in two or retain it as one, editors share the assumption that two 'When'/'Then' prophetic units have been shuffled, whether accidentally or purposely. The split between the two is marked or imagined at line 85 when after a series of social ills comes a utopian ideal: 'When every case in law is right'.

But is this projection unequivocally utopian? A close analogue to the Fool's prophecy suggests otherwise. Scholars have assumed that Shakespeare based his prophecy on one of George Puttenham's examples for the figure *merismus*, in *The Arte of English Poesie* (1589):

When faith failes in Priestes sawes,
And Lords hestes are holden for laws,
And robberie is tane for purchase,

And lechery for solace
Then shall the Realme of Albion
Be brought to great confusion.[8]

In Puttenham, the condition correspondent to Shakespeare's 'When every case in law is right' (85) is 'When lords' hests are holden for laws'. The anticipated future is not one of uniform justice but of justice determined by power: might makes right. The Fool's rendering implies the same: 'When every case in law is right' *by the judgment of those who wield it*.

The prophecy's other utopic conditions also can be flipped to their dystopic opposites. In an ideal realm, knights and squires would be solvent (86), but if the rest of the commonwealth remains in the red, social inequity would be not eliminated but widened. So, too, if detraction were stopped 'in tongues' (87), it might *in print* still spread, and more rampantly. The double negative of the next line allows for what it appears to foreclose, 'Nor cutpurses come not to throngs' (88). A world in which usury were conducted openly 'in the fields' (89) rather than behind closed doors suggests its acceptance or even legalisation. If the final utopic condition were to be realised literally, prostitution would have had to become so profitable that it could fund the erection of steeples (90).

Conversely, and just as readily, the prophecy's dystopic conditions reverse to utopic. In a reformed mass, priests are meant to pay more attention to words (signifiers of Christ's flesh and blood) than matter (Christ's flesh and blood) (81). So, too, from a magistrate's point of view, watered-down malt would be a boon (82). In a perfect society, nobles would feel obliged to set examples for their social inferiors (83). And while one would prefer that citizens burn with divine passion rather than syphilitic lust, what Protestant would to want bring back the days of the Marian bonfires?

The Fool's prophecy then is not two different prophecies but rather one perfectly equivocal one – one that, to borrow phrasing from another play of prophecies, does 'palter with us in a double sense'.[9] Flouting the law of non-contradiction, each condition is both one thing and its opposite: vice and virtue, dystopic and utopic, real and ideal. Conditions which should be mutually exclusive are instead in a relation of handy-dandy interchangeability. Like the raging storm and Lear's madness, the Fool's parting prophecy confounds distinction. The prophecy's climactic outcome, the consequence of the build-up of all its 'When's, is thus self-fulfilling: 'Then shall the realm of Albion / Come to great confusion'. It instantiates what it predicts.

But this is still not the end of the Fool's doomsday prophecy. An additional prediction follows, culminating not in revelation but truism, 'Then comes the time, who lives to see't / That going shall be used with feet' (93–4). The prophecy foresees a time that has never been otherwise, at least for bipeds (and quadrupeds): a time when feet are used to get places. The prophecy ends in business-as-usual, pedestrian at that. Rather than ending in revelational *eschaton*, it ends in humdrum tautology. And like its antecedent prediction, it is self-fulfilling. The Fool in the end does what Lear enjoined him to do twenty-six lines earlier (66), what he himself promised (78), and what the play requires: 'go'. If while speaking the final two lines, he were emphatically to put one foot before the other, he would be performing what he predicts: *going done with feet.*

Indeed the prophecy allows throughout for this kind of coordination of footing with saying. The Fool doesn't want to finish his prophecy; he doesn't want to go. So each of the prophecy's conditions, rather than resolving, circles back *da capo*, to another condition. At nine points when the audience might expect a climax, he winds up all over again, before reaching the expected (and redoubled) conclusion. Each of those verbal false starts might be accompanied by a motion to leave that backtracks as the prophecy rewinds. This is just the kind of programmatic stalling for which clowns were notorious, if Hamlet's critique is to be credited: they hold up the action with their antics.[10] Because they are unbound by the script, licensed to improvise, there is no telling how long they might go on. The audience and plot are both at their mercy.

But it is not just clowns who bide their time before endings. So, too, does Everyman. Confronted with the prospect of doomsday, he procrastinates. When summoned by Death to make his final reckoning, he begs for 'longer leisure' and tries literally to buy time by offering Death a bribe. Death loses patience, 'Come hence and do not tarry!'[11] George Puttenham identifies a figure that serves a similar function in rhetoric: '*Merismus* or the Distributer'.[12] It occurs when a proposition is given 'peecemeale and by distribution of every part for amplification sake'. This happens to be the very figure Puttenham illustrates with the analogue to the Fool's prophecy. The prophecy could have been said in one line – 'when vice abounds, and vertue decayeth' – but is instead amplified to eight. The Fool amplifies Puttenham's amplification in order to draw out the already drawn-out prophecy of doomsday.

Still there is more to come: a prophecy of a prophecy, the very one the Fool has just delivered – 'This prophecy Merlin shall make, for I live before his time'. The prophecy is postponed until the time of Merlin, Britain's first prophet – in the rule of King Arthur, a long way off from the rule of Lear who, as Shakespeare's sources specify, was contemporary with the Judaean prophets Isaiah and Elijah. So the prophecy is retracted until a time some fourteen centuries in the future; for its apocalyptic fulfilment, even longer than that. A long time to wait indeed.

The Fool's prophecy is no jumble, no parody. It is a sublimely self-conscious protraction of an exit routine designed to delay the close of the scene, calculated to push the audience's amusement to the limit, or beyond. In this respect, it resembles the ending of *The Tragedy of King Lear* itself: it, too, draws out its final moments, but with the King's suffering rather than the Fool's antics.[13]

THIRTY SEVEN

How Can Act 5 Forget Lear and Cordelia?

CHARLES ALTIERI

KENT   I am come
      To bid my King and master aye good night.
      Is he not here?

ALBANY   Great thing of us forgot!   235
      Speak, Edmund, where's the King? And where's
            Cordelia?
      Seest thou this object, Kent?
                  [*The bodies of Goneril and Regan are brought in.*]
KENT   Alack, why thus?
EDMUND Yet Edmund was beloved:
      The one the other poisoned for my sake,
      And after slew herself.   240
            William Shakespeare, *King Lear*, 5.3.233–40

Every time I read *King Lear* I am startled by the moment when
the characters recognise they have forgotten Lear and Cordelia.
Kenneth Muir's Arden 2 edition suggests that this forgetting
should not be surprising because 'there is no reason why Albany
should suspect that Lear and Cordelia were in danger; and he has
plenty to occupy his mind'.[1] But this seems almost as serious a
myopic statement as the play's forgetting King Lear and Cordelia.
If we are concerned only with the action of the play this footnote
might be right. But why then would the play call attention to the
forgetting?[2]

Shakespeare could have been lazy and just decided to get back
to Lear in the easiest available way. But he also could have been the
typical Shakespeare of the tragedies and had something surprising

and powerful in mind in insisting on the distance between the practical world of struggle for the other characters and the kind of space that Lear and Cordelia create for one another. Once we attend to that possibility, we are likely also to notice that the forgetting does not end with Albany's recognition. The play insists on the contrasts involved by immediately switching attention again. Albany asks Kent to see 'this object', the bodies of Goneril and Regan. It is only when the play turns to the dying Edmund's intention to do 'some good' (241) that it gets around to recognising something must be done for the imprisoned pair. And Edmund by this point in the play is in many ways no longer part of the action. He shares more with Lear and Cordelia than with Edgar and Albany.

The basic critical challenge posed by the end of *King Lear* is probably the need to characterise the kind of world Lear and Cordelia come to inhabit. We know that this space is composed by the power of their love for one another. But how are we to judge the relevance of that love for those who must obey 'the weight of this sad time' (5.3.322)? Is it a figure of transcendental grace, or does it force Lear to self-delusion in order to maintain that sense of difference after Cordelia is dead? I want to propose a third possibility that may occur only to a modernist, and that requires a mode of abstraction that does not entirely satisfy me. Yet it does explain the possible philosophical energies at work in this conclusion, primarily through the negatives and the contrasting imperatives.

If we ask what links all the villains in the play, clearly the answer is that they all commit themselves to various versions of Edmund's faith in something like raw nature. And the storm plays its role in reinforcing this texture of correspondences. The crucial step here is to recognise that Edmund's naturalist metaphysics is of a piece with the Machiavellian ethics that he brings out as the yet unrealised potential of Goneril and Regan. Naturalism deals with desires and ambitions as also pure facts that are caught up in wills to power and resist any moral constraints, which in nature seem mere weakness and cowardice.

So far nothing I have said is news for Renaissance scholars. And it is not at all incompatible with a Christian reading of the play. But the case gets more complicated when we have to assess the good but ineffectual characters like Kent, and Gloucester, and even Edgar. They have no power in a world that encourages and rewards Machiavellian behaviour. And they have no alternative world on which to look for power: Gloucester's despair and Edgar's sheer dogged coping are logical responses to their situation. Christian explanations can handle this, but with some strain since the characters seem condemned to the order of nature rather than choosing it. There seems no redemption for them.

Not so for Lear and Cordelia who have learned to occupy a different world, where Edmund's death is plausibly just a 'trifle' (5.3.294). That world is defined largely by the great speech when they must go off to prison. The focus there is not on eternal salvation but on the particular state of two persons who now have suffered enough for Lear simply to offer a repeated series of negations of Cordelia's depressed acceptance of the need to see Goneril and Regan again:

> No, no, no, no. Come, let's away to prison;
> We two alone will sing like birds i'the cage;
> When thou doth ask me blessing I'll kneel down,
> And ask of thee forgiveness. So we'll live,
> And pray, and sing, and tell old tales, and laugh
> At gilded butterflies, and hear poor rogues
> Talk of court news …

(5.3.8–14)

The repeated negatives are motivated primarily by the space Lear's reunion with Cordelia opens for his imagination. That space is not devotional. Rather it is experienced as the permission to explore a logic of parataxis radically opposed to the logic of imposed contradiction facing the other characters. Lear sees himself and Cordelia entering a world where possibility flows into adjacent possibility for pleasure and fulfilment. Something about the world they share warrants an attitude very different from the versions of scarcity economics that his daughters impose on Lear and that society imposes on the daughters to compete to be the one wife of Edmund. This new world of freedoms is a place where one can, as Cordelia does, utter without paradox the claim that finally she is completely recognised by her father, 'And so I am, I am' (4.7.70).

But what can this assertion of identity entail since she has so little time to live? This is one basic question that demands the audience make a judgment of Lear's final speech. What can he see that he demands we also observe:

> And my poor fool is hanged. No, no, no life!
> Why should a dog, a horse, a rat, have life
> And thou no breath at all? O thou'lt come no more,
> Never, never, never, never, never.
> Pray you undo this button. Thank you, sir. O, o, o, o.
> Do you see this? Look on her: look, her lips,
> Look there, look there!
>
> (5.3.304–10)

Christian salvation provides one such story. But I think that model would have been too easy for Shakespeare. It is not an accident that *King Lear* is set in a world where the gods have no bonds to humans; in that world the secular would be the best the characters could get. Everything else might be demonic. So we need to be more abstract, and possibly thereby more concrete. What kind of life can Cordelia still have after all these 'never's? I propose that she has the kind of life that can live at least in memory as something simply different from the order of nature that defines life and death for the other characters. The relation between father and daughter exemplifies something not subject to nature, even if it also may not secure transcendental life.

So rather than turn to Christian thinking, I want to invoke almost its opposite – the tradition of Positivist thinking that tried to stabilise what we could know about nature when we completely expunge it of all transcendental elements. But I want to view these Positivist demands under the distinct project of Wittgenstein's *Tractatus Logico-Philosophicus* that paid careful attention to what becomes of our values when we see they have no place in nature. Wittgenstein's is by far the most compelling version of the Positivist spirit for me because his is by far the most appreciative of what cannot be thought or found in the world where empiricist values prevail. Machiavellian principles are not quite the same as Positivist ones, but given Edmund's grounding of them in a theory of nature, they are more consistent with empiricism than one might think. And by using Wittgenstein we can recast the Manichaean absolute divide of good from evil into the picture of a domain of fact ineluctably divided from a domain of value. This enables us to take Lear's sense of a space in which Cordelia still lives as not just an escapist failure of character showing that he has learned nothing from his adventures except perhaps better manners to his servants.

I need draw from the *Tractatus* only two statements. Then I can return to one more feature of the play that these quotations establish as central to its power. First there is Wittgenstein's most general statement about the incompatibility of fact with values in the same way that a language capable of picturing the world is incompatible with one that expresses a personal stance:

> The sense of the world must lie outside the world. In the world everything is as it is, and everything happens as it does happen: in it no value exists – and if it did it would have no value.
>
> If there is any value that does have value, it must lie outside the whole sphere of what happens and is the case. For all that happens and is the case is accidental.
>
> What makes it non-accidental cannot lie within the world, since if it did it would itself be accidental.
>
> It would lie outside the world.[3]

I am not arguing that Edmund believes anything like this formulation. The case is more interesting than that. Positivism offers a strange reversal of Christianity with much the same force. In the Christian world, value is stable, fixed by the incarnate Word, while the truth of the senses is unstable and unreliable. In basing his life on the senses Edmund denies the stability of value. For Wittgenstein the stable world is oddly the world of accidents because that is the world of natural law. Logic deals with accidents because there is no reason why facts are as they are: logic displays what is given, not what is justified by purposes. But even though there are opposed pictures of what is stable, these traditions share an absolute divide between naturalism and the domain of values. From the perspective I am developing Edmund causes such trouble because he wants to treat values as if they were merely facts, as if they were accidents subject to human will rather than goals which promise meaning for that will. Because Edmund comes to dominate the world of facts, and because the human economy in the play is shaped by the horrors of valueless existence, there is considerable pressure on the audience to treat as sentimentality any claim like Lear's about distinctive values established by or for the play – gorgeous and noble sentimentality but sentimentality nonetheless. Hence the history of criticising Cordelia for her unwavering goodness and the corresponding sense of Lear as figure of ultimate pathos. There is no escaping history and the perspectives it establishes.

But that does not mean the historic-empirical perspective is always the only one we can take. If we stand only within history we can only ironise Shakespeare's obvious heroising of Lear at the end – from his caring behaviour to others to his heroic killing of the man who killed Cordelia, to the sentiments that flow from his identifying Cordelia as his daughter despite his madness (4.7.68–9). But if we are driven to ask how his heroism can be taken seriously as something other than sentimentality, we can also focus on how they in part shift the drama on to a plane where sheer value seems to work out its own imperatives. One can see the relationship between Lear and Cordelia as their learning through extreme suffering that 'the sense of the world must lie outside the world'. The man who could imagine 'We two alone will sing like birds i'the cage' is capable of seeing something at the margin of the world, especially when he repeats his imperatives to 'Look' at the end of the play.

We cannot be sure he sees anything real or even sees anything beyond his need to have something to see. But 'Look' is an interesting imperative in part because it does not necessarily connect to a proposition that will bind itself to the world of fact. Looking can be content with appearance, or content with a world in which something might be discovered or pursued even though it yields no clear objective manifestation. 'Look' asks us to observe Cordelia not just as this dead body but as this being given matter and spirit by the play. So while we cannot be sure Lear sees anything at all, we can wonder what the cost is of our determining that we must reproduce the object in order to believe in the importance of the seeing.

The play seems to demand a choice between ironising and idealising readings. But I think it is wise to maintain both poles of the choice. The choice is whether to accept the empirical stance in which we only respond to 'Look' if the observer provides proof, or to accept the possibility that there is a scene of seeing subject to other conditions of response. We have to acknowledge the logic arguing for the first option. But we risk impoverishing ourselves if we do not also sympathise with Lear's call at the end of the play for keeping some principle of value alive because Cordelia still responds to it, or responds to what love makes it possible to see. Lear's repeated imperatives suggest that there is something significant just in the spectacle that Cordelia becomes in the end, framed by her love and fidelity and honoured by his capacity to enter into the space that his love and fidelity have the strength to compose.

This is where my second borrowing from Wittgenstein becomes appropriate: 'There are, indeed, things that cannot be put into words. They *make themselves manifest*'.[4] This inaugurates an extended meditation throughout Wittgenstein's career on what has to be displayed rather than described. Ultimately the fullest appeal a person can make is not to ethical principle but to what confession displays that cannot be grasped by reason's universals:

> The criteria for the truth of the *confession* that I thought such and such are not the criteria for a true *description* of a process. And the importance of the true confession does not reside in its being a correct and certain report of a process.

It resides rather in the special consequences which can be drawn from a confession whose truth is guaranteed by the special criteria of *truthfulness*.[5]

The domain of human value here cannot be encompassed within 'a true description of a process' because the language of value is not something we find or argue for. It is something we display, and we hope that an audience will see into the display what reason cannot establish.

Lear offers no confession. But he does make a total unguarded commitment to his speaking at the end that serves very much the same purposes. Suppose then that Lear's repeated imperative to 'Look' leads beyond the dramatic situation to Shakespeare's reflection on the possibility of spectacle recuperating for this play something fundamental to drama that was at risk of being lost as playwrights tried to make its home in Edmund's world. There have been countless studies of the motif of seeing and blindness within this play. But how many of these worry about the play itself as something to be seen as different from what realism dictates as our mode of viewing? Minimally the spectacles of Lear denying Cordelia in public and then being humiliated by his begging and raging on the heath in a kind of recompense have to confuse the audience because they make remote any possibility that the play will produce heroic action that can provide imaginative alternatives to the play's unrelenting cruelty. We even have to admit that practically speaking Goneril and Regan are largely right about their father in his dotage. And by this kind of understanding Gloucester almost deserves his punishment for how he treats Edmund. It is spectacle that dignifies suffering and makes sympathy overrule what judgment might be tempted to conclude. And it is ultimately spectacle that makes Lear's display of seeing something in Cordelia sufficiently believable that we look for a world in which that might be possible. That world 'must lie outside the whole sphere of what happens and is the case', but it may be no less central for our sense of being human. We can only look and not act, but one major accomplishment of the play is defining what we might see by that looking.

THIRTY EIGHT

Exits without Exiting

RALPH ALAN COHEN

Hover through the fog and filthy air.
William Shakespeare, *Macbeth*, 1.1.11[1]

On the stage of the American Shakespeare Center's Blackfriars Playhouse in Staunton, Virginia, we try to attend to stage directions sanctioned either explicitly by the quarto or Folio texts (*'exit pursued by a bear'*) or by indisputable embedded stage directions ('kneel not, gentle Portia'). One merit of this approach is that the visual patterns that emerge in our productions have a claim to some authority as a representation of Shakespeare's stagecraft. Some of these patterns amount to visual rhymes, rhymes we may not consciously register any more than we register the networks of auditory connections in Shakespeare's verse that Stephen Booth describes as 'overlapping networks of casual, substantively inconsequential relationships'.[2] As he suggests with regard to those auditory rhymes, that may be just as well; but on an unconscious level these visual rhymes become a part of our experience of the play. I would like to suggest that these visual moments create a network of mirrored movements – however fragmentary – and that Shakespeare's plays are as extraordinary for this multitude of mirrored patterns of motion as they are for their aural echoes. In *Macbeth* one of those patterns is a person hesitating to exit.

Many of the visual rhymes in the plays are obvious: people reading documents aloud in *Love's Labour's Lost*; announced messengers appearing repeatedly in *Antony and Cleopatra*; and young men taking out their naked weapons in *Romeo and Juliet*. Sometimes the patterns are less obvious. In *Hamlet*, for example, two eavesdropping scenes involve the arras, but the play persistently stages other kinds of eavesdropping: Hamlet observing Claudius from the margins of the court scene in 1.2, Ophelia observing Polonius's advice to Laertes, the offstage Ghost listening to Hamlet require an oath of Horatio and Marcellus, Horatio – by Hamlet's order – observing Claudius during *The Mousetrap*, Hamlet listening to Claudius at prayer, and Hamlet and Horatio observing the beginning of Ophelia's burial. All of these moments are scenic refractions of eavesdropping.

During rehearsals for the 2006 ASC production of *Macbeth*[3] we discovered one remarkable visual rhyme (linked, as it happens, to aural rhyme): an insistent pattern of false exits. The aural rhymes connected to these false exits are the couplets that Shakespeare frequently used to end a scene. This essay assumes that the implied stage direction for an early modern actor using a couplet near the end of a scene in which there is otherwise no rhyme is that he should exit. It equally assumes that the early modern audience attending to an otherwise unrhymed scene whose business was concluding heard a couplet as a signal that the actor speaking the lines would exit on his second rhyme word.[4] If these overlapping assumptions have merit, then over half the scenes in *Macbeth* present the audience with an unnoticed but noticeable visual rhyme – a character hesitating to leave the stage.

Of the 30 scenes in *Macbeth*, 25 end with couplets; of those 25 scenes, 8 end with a single couplet, 4 end with one character speaking several couplets, and 13 end with two characters alternating couplets. None of that is remarkable; what is remarkable is that in 13 of the scenes in which a couplet appears to signal an exit and the end of the scene, a line or lines come after the couplet but before the final exit.

Consider the ending of 1.5, the first scene between the Macbeths. Lady Macbeth tells Macbeth that he must put into her hands 'the night's great business',

> Which shall to all our nights and days to come
> Give solely sovereign sway and masterdom.

                                                         (67–8)

For the audience, the expectation created both by the way the words function as a conclusion to the discussion and by the couplet in a scene otherwise without rhyme is that the two characters will exit. For the actor playing the Lady, the couplet would normally also signal exit. Of course in this case, the actor playing the Lady would know that other lines will follow, but the convention would, I am arguing, suggest to the actor that Lady Macbeth starts to leave, and Macbeth's line – 'We will speak further' – interrupts and impedes that exit. The Lady then, sharing that line, has another couplet:

> Only look up clear
> To alter favour ever is to fear.
>
> (69–70)

Like the first couplet, these aphoristic lines are a fitting conclusion to the scene, and the convention of the couplet as exit line would tell the audience to expect an exit and would suggest to the actor playing the Lady to begin exiting again. However, the half line that follows – 'Leave all the rest to me' – makes clear that she must do more to persuade Macbeth to that exit and repeats the pattern we have just seen of the Lady attempting to exit on a couplet and Macbeth resisting.[5]

At the end of this first scene between the couple, the pattern the audience sees is (1) Lady Macbeth intends to leave, (2) Macbeth hesitates, (3) Lady Macbeth intends again to leave, (4) Macbeth still hesitates, and (5) Lady Macbeth must urge him off the stage; but in 3.2 Shakespeare reverses this pattern. Macbeth has just told his 'dearest chuck' that he is going to do a 'deed of dreadful note' but will not answer her question, 'What's to be done?' Adding to her puzzlement, he launches into an apostrophe to the night and then begins an incantatory description of the time of day in which 'the crow / Makes flight to the rooky wood'. Macbeth seems 'rapt', as he has been before in 1.3 and in 1.4 and as he will be again at the banquet (another repeating visual image). Here he begins his first couplet:

Good things of day begin to droop and drowse,
Whiles night's black agents to their preys do rouse.

(3.3.53–4)

This couplet, like Lady Macbeth's first couplet in 1.5, sums up
what the character has just been saying and, as does her first
couplet, indicates that the actor will exit. But, as in her case, he
does not. Instead, he speaks a second couplet:

Thou marvell'st at my words, but hold thee still.
Things bad begun make strong themselves by ill.

(55–6)

The first words of this second couplet give us a glimpse of the
staging. 'Thou marvell'st at my words' tells the audience and
the actor playing her not only that Lady Macbeth is 'struck with
surprise' (*OED s.v.* 'marvell' v.1 2a) but that Macbeth thinks his
words are the cause of her amazement. Thus, the line works as
an embedded stage direction requiring Macbeth to look at Lady
Macbeth and the Lady to be 'marvelling' at what she has heard.
I would argue that the line suggests that Macbeth, who has been
rapt, has not been looking at Lady Macbeth, that he gives his first
couplet and begins the exit that couplet would normally prompt
before he notices that she is 'marvelling'.[6] If I am right, then he
must stop his first attempt to exit, and his second couplet is a
repeated attempt to end the scene and exit. But, in a mirror image
of 1.5, this time she is the hesitator, so much so that even after
his second couplet signalling an exit, he must add a half line and
another attempt: 'So prithee go with me'. They exit on this third
attempt as they had before, this time with their roles reversed.

The end of the banquet scene (3.4), the last scene the two
characters share, has exactly the same pattern. Here are lines 138
to 143 with my editorial stage directions in brackets:

MACBETH   Strange things I have in head that will to hand,
            Which must be acted ere they may be scanned.

[*He starts to exit.*]

LADY MACBETH   You lack the season of all natures, sleep.

[*She interrupts his exit.*]

MACBETH   Come, we'll to sleep.

[*He stops his exit and invites her out.*]

My strange and self-abuse

Is the initiate fear that wants hard use.

[*Starts to exit again, but her hesitation
or his requires the added half line.*]

We are yet but young in deed.   *Exeunt*

Of course my stage directions are conjectural, but the aural evidence that in *Macbeth* Shakespeare is repeatedly playing variations on the convention of the couplet as an exit line is unmistakable.[7]

A similar pattern appears even when Macbeth is alone on stage, most remarkably in the scene (2.1) prior to his murdering Duncan, a scene in which 'a dagger of the mind / ... / marshall'st [him] the way that [he] was going' (38–42). The last third of his 33-line monologue is a description of his exit, and that description ends with the couplet that would normally signal his exit and end the scene:

The very stones prate of my wherebout,
And take the present horror from the time,
Which now suits with it. Whiles I threat, he lives.
Words to the heat of deeds too cold breath gives.

(58–61)

The last line of that couplet is a self-remonstrance to stop talking and start doing, another perfect place to exit. But this time Shakespeare stops the exit with a sound effect – '*A bell rings*'. Macbeth's next line – 'I go, and it is done. The bell invites me' – are two sentences: the first seems to be urging action and therefore suggests it follows either a brief inaction or a slowness in moving; the second seems to be a kind of justification. In either case the actor would need to stop in order to speak the next two lines of the couplet on which he finally exits:

> Hear it not, Duncan; for it is a knell
> That summons thee to heaven or to hell.   *Exit*
> (63–4)

Productions of *Macbeth* in which the actors are aware of the disruption of this aural pattern and respond to its prompt will present audiences with a visual pattern of hesitation that, however incidental or accidental, appears in more than half its scenes – scenes with exits that start and stop.[8] This pattern of hesitation is deeply inscribed in the hesitation at the heart of the narrative: Macbeth's decision about whether or not to act on his ambition. We see this hesitation as early as 1.3 when the Witches first predict he will be king. Banquo's 'Good sir, why do you start[9] and seem to fear / Things that do sound so fair' gives us the first occasion of Macbeth's being 'rapt' – suspended, hovering – and whether to stop or to go is the subject of Macbeth's monologue at the beginning of 1.7 – 'If it were done when 'tis done, then 'twere well / It were done quickly'. That hesitation is the occasion of Lady Macbeth's dismay later in the scene and the subject of the exhortation that resolves him to the deed, and with that resolve, for the only time in the play, the Macbeths exit on the couplet in accordance with the convention and without hesitation:

> Away, and mock the time with fairest show.
> False face must hide what the false heart doth know.
> *Exeunt*
> (1.7.81–2)

THIRTY NINE

Playing Prospero Against the Grain

Michael Ellis-Tolaydo

You do look, my son, in a moved sort,
As if you were dismayed. Be cheerful, sir.
Our revels now are ended. These our actors,
As I foretold you, were all spirits and
Are melted into air, into thin air;   150
And – like the baseless fabric of this vision –
The cloud-capped towers, the gorgeous palaces,
The solemn temples, the great globe itself,
Yea, all which it inherit, shall dissolve,
And like this insubstantial pageant faded,   155
Leave not a rack behind. We are such stuff
As dreams are made on, and our little life
Is rounded with a sleep. Sir, I am vexed;
Bear with my weakness; my old brain is troubled.
Be not disturbed with my infirmity.   160
If you be pleased, retire into my cell
And there repose. A turn or two I'll walk
To still my beating mind.

William Shakespeare, *The Tempest*, 4.1.146–63

I am an actor, and therefore my joy in tackling Shakespeare, apart
from the depth and complexity of his linguistic and poetic art,
is his fundamental understanding of human behaviour, and his
ability to set forth – without judgment – complex and believable
characters for people like me to portray on a stage. Shakespeare's
main characters provide opportunities for actors to create and
reveal psychologically motivated, three-dimensional human beings

whose actions are entirely playable and understandable within the context of the play.

Generally, Prospero's 'revels' speech is seen as beautiful, sentimental, and sad. To me, however, Prospero is a man who is utterly unsentimental. I see this speech not only as the turning point of the play but as one of the most self-revealing passages in all of Shakespeare's plays. To my thinking, it ranks with Gloucester's 'As flies to wanton boys, are we to the gods, / They kill us for their sport' (*King Lear*, 4.1.38–9). It is an existentialist and frightening recognition that one's life and powers are incapable of changing the world and human behaviour. Prospero – the artist-magician-man – cannot control everything.

In my reading, Prospero is above all an angry man. Betrayed by his kin, he is sent off by boat with his daughter to die and then, arriving on an island, spends his time making sure that he has absolute control of all that happens on it as he prepares to take revenge on his enemies. He is driven chiefly by revenge against those who have betrayed him. When the opportunity to punish his enemies arrives, he begins by torturing them. Traditionally, Prospero, moved by the genuine love between Miranda and Ferdinand, recognises that he has lost the ability to feel remorse and forgives his enemies. I find it difficult to reconcile this interpretation with the role in its entirety; rather, I see the character coming to terms with his powerlessness, grudgingly accepting that life will go on and that it is time to let the next generation begin muddling through.

In 1999, I was offered my first chance to play Prospero, at the Pennsylvania Shakespeare Festival. At our first rehearsal, director Patrick Mulcahy stated that he wanted to concentrate on the clarity of language and the story of the play. He was not interested in exploring issues of imperialism and colonialism that resonate in current critical discourse. He was intent on following traditional character interpretations. Prospero, through his magic arts and his supernatural servant Ariel, controls the events that happen on the island. Mulcahy saw Prospero's journey as one of redemption.

In support of his view, he shared with the cast and crew a contemporary translation of Montaigne's essay 'Of Cruelty':

> He that through ... genuine mildnesse, should ... contemne injuries received, should no doubt performe a rare action, ... But he who, being toucht and stung to the quicke, with any wrong or offence received, should arme himselfe with reason against this furiously-blind desire of revenge, and in the end after a great conflict, yeeld himselfe master over-it, should doubtlesse doe much more. ... the one action might be termed goodnesse, the other vertue.[1]

As I listened, I began to worry that Prospero would be reduced to an egomaniac suddenly converted to sainthood, or that I would be directed to play a mainly static character.

I wanted the opportunity to explore the emotional rage and vulnerability which I believed constrain Prospero. During the period before rehearsals began (and for many other summers as well), I served with Stephen Booth on the faculty of the Folger Shakespeare Library's Teaching Shakespeare Institute. Between classes and sessions there, I mentioned to him my concern about whether Prospero's journey is truly one from revenge to forgiveness. Stephen immediately replied, 'It isn't. That's a sentimental answer that won't let go'. I headed off to Pennsylvania and to rehearsals mulling over that remark as well as two other Booth-isms from earlier, more general conversations, both relevant to Prospero's and to my own journey: 'Art does not traffic with the imposition of morality', and 'Art gives us experience, not information'. The director agreed that many of my ideas about the character of Prospero were worth working on in rehearsal, but he worried that not playing him as a forgiving, converted man at the end seemed not in service of the play. He was willing, however, to consider my belief that in Prospero's 'The rarer action is / In virtue than in vengeance' (5.1.27–8) 'virtue' suggests a noble or moral excellence rather than the Christian idea of forgiveness. If I could justify Prospero's actions in the final act, he was willing to give it a go.

In and out of rehearsal, I asked myself a series of questions and tested possible answers to see if they were playable. How did Prospero's alienation from family and state begin? How did it lead to isolation and his imprisonment on the island? How does Prospero love Miranda? Does he change and/or does his love for her change because he recognises that the love between her and Ferdinand is pure? Does he forgive his enemies? And most importantly, why did he withdraw from his duties in Milan? Years ago, before he was deposed and exiled, Prospero retreated from society to a self-created prison. Prospero cut himself off from the world – 'to my state grew stranger' (1.2.76) – and by withdrawing to devote his energies to his secret studies, he provided Antonio with the opportunity to depose and banish him. He has withdrawn from his official duties, his subjects, and society, trusting that his subjects will forgive his absence because they love him. But in fact Prospero is the architect of his own downfall and deserves to lose his dukedom.

The Tempest takes place on the island tamed by Prospero. He has spent years there, obsessing on those who have betrayed him. This has turned him into a bitter, rigid man focused exclusively on revenge. This is the Prospero we meet at the beginning of the play. This is a father who loves his daughter, I think, in the same way that one loves a pet. He needs to make sure that she clearly understands why and what he is going to do.

> O, a cherubin
> Thou wast that did preserve me. Thou didst smile,
> Infused with a fortitude from heaven,
> When I have decked the sea with drops full salt,
> Under my burden groaned, which raised in me
> An undergoing stomach to bear up
> Against what should ensue.
>
> (1.2.152–8)

In order to prepare Miranda for what he is about to do, Prospero goes to great lengths to clarify the history of their presence on the island. He constantly questions her attention and is insistent that she understand the enormity of the personal injustices committed against him, and, by association, against her as well. He wants her to appreciate fully that the actions of Alonzo and Antonio, a family member, were lethal in their intent. During this exposition, Prospero bitterly relives the experiences of the past. When he is satisfied that Miranda understands the details of his tale, he puts her to sleep.

He becomes agitated as he calls for Ariel: 'But are they, Ariel, safe?' (1.2.217). He needs to know that his enemies have survived the storm and are sequestered so that he can carry out his plans. Thus Prospero instructs Ariel to spy on his enemies 'invisible / To every eyeball else' (1.2.303–4). And though he expects Ariel to immediately do his bidding, the sprite at this moment reminds Prospero of his promise of freedom. Prospero's agitation about the arrival of the royal party and the opportunity to carry out his revenge is extreme and makes him impatient to begin, but Ariel is not moving fast enough. This pace upsets Prospero, who finally berates Ariel with every detail of the servant's rescue, ending with an explosive threat:

> If thou more murmur'st, I will rend an oak
> And peg thee in his knotty entrails till
> Thou hast howled away twelve winters.
>
> (1.2.294–6)

Diverted by a variety of events, primarily the developing relationship between Miranda and Ferdinand, Prospero promises after their marriage 'Some vanity of mine art. It is my promise, / And they expect it from me' (4.1.41–2). He will do what artists and magicians do. He will create a wondrous spectacle. He will show off.

He instructs Ariel to make the preparations for the spectacle, and Ariel responds with

> Before you can say 'come' and 'go',
> And breathe twice, and cry 'so, so',

> Each one tripping on his toe,
> Will be here with mop and mow.
> Do you love me, master? No?

(4.1.44–8)

For me, the question 'Do you love me master?' brings Prospero
up short. He says nothing. Ariel asks the question again: 'No?'
Prospero, flustered and not knowing what to say, replies off-
handedly, 'Dearly, my delicate Ariel. Do not approach / Till thou
dost hear me call' (49–50). Ariel's question shocks Prospero. He
realises that in his isolation he has lost his way. The only feelings
he has are those of hate and anger.

Several factors now compound to cause Prospero to question
what he has become: the vanity of the Masque, the purity of love
he sees in Miranda and Ferdinand, his treatment of his enemies,
and Caliban's plot to murder him. Prospero reconsiders the value
of his power. He abruptly stops the show. He realises that he is
losing control.

> PROSPERO   I had forgot that foul conspiracy
> Of the beast Caliban and his confederates
> Against my life. The minute of their plot
> Is almost come. Well done. Avoid, no more!
> FERDINAND   This is strange. Your father's in some passion
> That works him strongly.
> MIRANDA   Never till this day
> Saw I him touched with anger so distempered!

(4.1.139–45)

Aware that he is disoriented and has upset the young couple,
Prospero makes light of curtailing the masque and of his apparent
confusion. However, he feels only hopelessness regarding his value
as a scholar and as a man, and this despair pours out of him in the
revels speech. Try as he might to carry on otherwise, he recognises that nothing is permanent, that whatever we create 'shall
dissolve, / And like this insubstantial pageant faded, / Leave not a

rack behind'. Aware that he is alarming Miranda and Ferdinand, he asks them for forgiveness:

> Sir, I am vexed;
> Bear with my weakness; my old brain is troubled.
> Be not disturbed with my infirmity.
> If you be pleased, retire into my cell
> And there repose. A turn or two I'll walk
> To still my beating mind.

Prospero changes gears now, trying to calm his own confusion. He is grasping for clarity and frustrated – 'Come with a thought' (4.1.64). He cannot think clearly. Therefore, Prospero resorts to acting on what has been a driving force since his usurpation – revenge: 'I will plague them all, / Even to roaring. /... / Now does my project gather to a head. /... /... At this hour / Lies at my mercy all mine enemies' (4.1.192–3, 5.1.1, 4.1.263–4). He deals with Caliban's plot, and after chasing off Caliban, Trinculo, and Stephano, he is shocked again by Ariel's description of the state of the king's party:

> ARIEL   ... Your charm so strongly works 'em
>   That, if you now beheld them, your affections
>   Would become tender.
> PROSPERO   Dost thou think so, spirit?
> ARIEL   Mine would, sir, were I human.
>
>   (5.1.17–20)

It is at *this* moment, and not earlier, that Prospero realises and feels the enormity of what he has become as a man – arrogant, incapable of compassion, with powers that contribute nothing to humanity. He renounces his powers, frees the royal party, and absolves his enemies. Yet I find it difficult to accept that Prospero's forgiveness of Antonio is heartfelt or genuine. Antonio will remain true to his nature, a villain. He offers no repentance at all. Prospero offers a noble/virtuous 'forgiveness' that is grudging and rooted in pragmatic reason. Milan and Naples are to be jointly ruled, a concession that provides the next generation with a clean slate. Accepting that in order for him to '... retire me to my Milan, where / Every third thought shall be my grave' (5.1.312–13) is not a depressing thought but Prospero's truth, an old man's truth.

In this production, Prospero's journey was a story about the consequences of arrogance. The ruler-scholar-artist-magician learns that through his powers, he does not have the ability to effect any meaningful change in the world. By excusing his enemies' actions and giving up his powers, he will remain vulnerable, and like everyone else will have to muddle messily through life. Prospero learns that he must do this in order to give the new generation an opportunity to succeed.

Many audience members and critics were supportive of the interpretation, but some hated it because it did not have the clear, happy ending they expected. Cary Mazer's review in the *Philadelphia City Paper* surprised, upset, and eventually pleased me:

> Being exiled on a deserted island for 12 years must do some strange things to you. This certainly seems to be the case with Prospero, as played by Michael Tolaydo in the Pennsylvania Shakespeare production of *The Tempest*. Years of sitting and brooding, waiting for the opportunity to take revenge on his brother Antonio (who usurped the dukedom of Milan from Prospero and cast him adrift with his infant daughter Miranda), has turned Tolaydo's Prospero into a genuinely peculiar person, who storms and rages and lurches about the stage, consumed with unspeakable rage and unspoken hangups. I've never seen a Prospero on such a power trip, demanding total, groveling subservience from his magical servant Ariel, for no apparent reason. Nor have I seen a Prospero so fretful and preoccupied during the magical masque that he conjures to celebrate the engagement of Miranda with the shipwrecked prince Ferdinand, slapping his shaven head with both palms as though trying to knock his obsessions out of his own skull.[2]

I was surprised at the vehemence in the review and upset that I may not have succeeded in showing Prospero's love for his daughter or his affection for Ariel, discounting his one emotional outburst. What eventually pleased me, however, was that the review seemed not to demand a moral ending for the character. Yes, 'years of sitting and brooding, waiting for the opportunity to take revenge on his brother Antonio' should affect one profoundly and emotionally.

Stephen Booth taught me that the truth of an experience is the experience itself, not the intellectualising of it. Most actors find certain roles with which they have a profound connection – an understanding of and with the character that makes every performance a joy, an adventure, and a unique experience. The Prospero I played in that Pennsylvania Shakespeare Festival *Tempest* was one of these for me.

NOTES

Introduction

1. The professor's final sentences are an allusion to *Love's Labour's Lost* (5.1). Behind his hand, Moth abuses Nathaniel, Holofernes, and Armado: 'They have been at a great feast of languages and stolen the scraps' (35–6). Costard responds, 'O, they have lived long on the alms-basket of words!' (37–8).
2. Fish, 110.
3. Adelman, 7.
4. Friedman, 5.
5. Booth, 'Hamlet', 152. Booth is perfectly serious, but the statement is also a joke, since it recasts the notorious voiceover at the beginning of Laurence Olivier's 1948 film of *Hamlet*: 'This is the tragedy of a man who could not make up his mind'.
6. Rabkin, viii.
7. Hartman, 57.
8. Best & Marcus, 5.
9. Jameson, 60.
10. Moretti, 84.
11. Garber, 151.
12. Starr, 50.
13. Starr, 53.
14. Felski, 573.
15. Vendler, *Art*, 40.
16. Hansen, 666.
17. Altieri, 80–81.
18. De Man, 24.
19. For an articulation of 'just reading' see Marcus, 3; for 'strategic formalism' see Levine, 627.
20. Booth makes the same point about a different reading tradition: 'The *Hamlet* that emerges from a critical discussion of it by a critic in a book or a group of critics in a twelfth-grade classroom never survives longer than the discussion that gave it birth. By nightfall, the real *Hamlet* – the monster for which the discussion provided a docile alternative – is out of its coffin and stalking the culture as usual' ('Function', 262).

1: Editorial Emendation and the Opening of *A Midsummer Night's Dream*

1. Andrews.
2. Furness, *Midsummer*, 6.
3. Furness, *Midsummer*, 6.
4. Furness, *Midsummer*, 6.
5. Furness, *Midsummer*, 6–7.
6. E. Johnson.
7. Booth, 'Discourse', 217.
8. Foakes, *Midsummer*, 55.
9. Holland, 132.
10. Brooks, 6.
11. Walsh, 130.

2: The Story of O: Reading Letters in the Prologue to *Henry V*

1. George Wilkins likely composed the prologue to *Pericles*. With varying degrees of certainty, scholars take John Fletcher to be the author of the prologues to *Henry VIII* and *The Two Noble Kinsmen*.
2. Both Bruce Smith (esp. 225, 270, 275) and Joel Fineman pursue important arguments about the potential significance of a single letter, and anticipate some of the observations made here. In particular, Smith notes that 'when the Prologue to *Henry V* attempts to silence the audience gathered within the wooden O, he begins with the most intense phoneme the human voice can make in English speech' (225).
3. Other prologues also approach themes of dramatic inadequacy, but are tepid in comparison to *Henry V*. The prologue to *The Two Noble Kinsmen* worries that the play cannot achieve the greatness of Chaucer, its primary source, but the aid to be provided by the audience is only applause, not the deep, performative thought expected in *Henry V*:

> For, to say truth, it were an endless thing
> And too ambitious to aspire to him,
> Weak as we are, and, almost breathless, swim
> In his deep water. Do you but hold out
> Your helping hands and we shall tack about
> And something do to save us. (1.0.22–7)

In *Henry VIII* the prologue's charge to the audience to 'see' is likewise not performative and does not interrogate the creative failure that *Henry V* owns as its glory:

> Think ye see
> The very persons of our noble story
> As they were living: think you see them great,
> And follow'd with the general throng, and sweat
> Of thousand friends; then, in a moment, see
> How soon this mightiness meets misery (1.0.25–30)

What starts with the possibility of the same subjunctive mood we encounter in *Henry V* – 'Think ye see/The very persons of our noble story/As [if] they were living' – becomes in retrospect a more pedestrian request – 'As they [were when they] were living' – once the passage retreats into a generic statement of the story: greatness come to misery.

4. Though I know of no evidence that the Globe Theatre was ever a venue for animal fights, 'cockpit', as both a venue and as a sexual reference, alludes to the two entertainments that were the dramatic theatres' neighbours both physically and in respectability: cock-fighting rings and bear- and bull-bating pits, and brothels.

5. Booth, *Sonnets*, 520–1 (148.7–9n), 532 (152.9n).

6. *OED* does not provide evidence that 'wood' or associated forms could refer to an erection before 1985. The idea nevertheless seems available to the early modern period. See the conclusion of Robert Herrick's 'The Vine': '… I awoke,/And found (ah me!) this flesh of mine/More like a stock than like a vine' (21–3; Rumrich & Chaplin, 183–4).

7. Obviously, I disagree with T. W. Craik's dismissal (in his Arden 3 edition) of Andrew Gurr's New Cambridge note on the pun of 'casque' with 'cask'. The prologue is absent from the Quarto text (1600) of *Henry V*.

8. *Henry V* is too early for 'spirits' to signify alcoholic beverages; according to *OED*, that sense was not firmly available until the late seventeenth century (*s.v.* 'spirit' n. 21.a–c). However, there is enough evidence to suggest that English was beginning to extend senses (such as 16.a: 'One or other of certain subtle highly-refined substances or fluids … formerly supposed to permeate the blood and chief organs of the body') to mean 'alcohol'. See *2 Henry IV*: '[Sherris-sack] illumineth the face, which, as a beacon, gives warning to all the rest of the little kingdom, man, to arm; and then the vital commoners, and inland petty spirits, muster me all to their captain, the heart' (4.3.106–10); *Othello*: 'O thou invisible spirit of wine, if thou hast no name to be known by, let us call thee devil!' (2.3.277–9); and *Henry V*: 'And shall our quick blood, spirited with wine,/Seem frosty?' (3.5.21–2).

9. See Booth, *Sonnets*, 164–5 (20.12n). Booth also reminds us that '"Nothing" and "naught" were popular cant terms for "vulva" (perhaps because of the shape of a zero)'.

10. See *OED s.v.* 'girdle' n. 3.

3: The Sense of a Beginning

1. All citations from *Paradise Lost* are to Milton, *Works* and will be provided parenthetically in the text.
2. In an autobiographical passage in *The Reason of Church Government* (1642) in Wolfe, 1:810.
3. The cross was commonly referred to as a tree; cf. Donne's 'Good Friday, 1613. Riding Westward': 'and thou look'st towards me/O Saviour, as thou hang'st upon the tree' (35–6). Milton may well have known the tradition that the cross on Calvary stood where the 'forbidden tree' had once stood.
4. The once-conventional names for metric feet are not truly applicable to the accentual-syllabic prosody of English verse. Better to think of stresses placed in a ten-syllable line as the way to read Milton's 'heroic verse'.
5. The alliterated 'f' in 'first', 'fruit', and 'forbidden' ties them in gathering significance, as does the echoing of 'first' and 'taste' in line 2.
6. The root of 'obedience' is in the Latin for 'hear', so that even the grave error of disobeying is to some extent extenuated as a failure to hear (or attend) properly.
7. Parallelisms, doublings, echoes, and mirrorings proliferate throughout *Paradise Lost*; there are also inversions and parodies: one such may be the complex off-rhyming of the 'blissful seat' of God and the 'dismal situation' in which Satan is discovered a few lines later (1.60).
8. An implication is that 'shepherds' are to nurture the 'seed' towards its natural end as 'fruit'.
9. Ariosto, Canto 1, 1.12.
10. Christopher Ricks comments on *instruere* in 'John Milton: Sound and Sense in *Paradise Lost*', originally his Tredegar Memorial Lecture in 1974, reprinted in Ricks, *Force*.
11. Dennis Danielson makes a point of Milton's addressing his theodicy to men (readers), but finds it 'less interesting' than reading the entire phrase, 'the ways of God to men' as the object of 'justify' (10, 236).
12. Milton went completely blind before composing *Paradise Lost*.

4: Spenser Up Close: Temporality in *The Faerie Queene*

1. Augustine, 11.11. Further citations appear parenthetically in the text.
2. Spenser, *Faerie Queene*, 1.9.15. Further citations appear parenthetically in the text.
3. *OED s.v.* 'whilom' A3, citing Henry Bradshaw, *The life of saint werburge of Chester*, 1513.
4. Anchises' prophecy in *The Aeneid*, Book 6, and Merlin's chronicle in *The Faerie Queene*, Book 3 are prime examples.
5. *OED s.v.* 'dare' v^2 5, citing Thomas Cranmer, *Works*, 1556.
6. Attridge, 76, cited in Dolven, 396.
7. 'Sunday Morning', in Stevens, 69.

5: 'at heaven's gate'

1. Booth, *Sonnets.*
2. Edmondson & Wells, 'Plurality' and Edmondson & Wells, *Sonnets.*

6: On Shakespeare's Sonnet 60

1. Original and modernised texts of the *Sonnets* taken from Booth, *Sonnets.*
2. Heaney, *Government*, 15.
3. Heaney, *Seeing Things*, 86.
4. This and other of Vaughan's poems are from Vaughan.
5. Evans & Hecht, 168.
6. Ovid & Golding, 15.240–60.
7. Herbert, *Poems.*
8. This and other of Marvell's poems are from Marvell, *Complete Poems.*

7: Balthasar's Song in *Much Ado About Nothing*

1. Branagh, xiv.
2. Note the possible mondegreen in 'on shore'/*unsure*; such mis-hearings of lyrics are quite common (e.g., hearing the phrase '*Scuse me while I kiss this guy*' for "Scuse me while I kiss the sky' in 'Purple Haze'). Although incorrect, such a hearing would fit smoothly into the context of the lines.
3. Note that 'constant' derives from *sto, stare*, 'to stand', which, in the context of the two feet in the preceding line, creates an unharnessed pun. Obviously, this effect will work only on audience members with some knowledge of Latin.
4. The word 'let' could mean either prevent ('By heaven I'll make a ghost of him that lets me!' [*Hamlet*, 1.4.85]) or permit ('Lo how he mocks me. Wilt thou let him, my lord?' [*The Tempest*, 3.2.29]) depending on context. Shakespeare seems to have been especially fond of such words.
5. Elizabethan audiences might also have understood 'hey nonny-nonny' as a euphemism for 'fucking'. Consider *OED s.v.* 'nonny-nonny' int. A: 'A meaningless refrain, formerly often used to cover indelicate allusions'. *OED* lists 1533 as the first occurrence of this sense.

8: The Persistence of the Flesh in *Deaths Duell*

1. Donne, *Deaths Duell*, 10. Further citations appear parenthetically in the text.
2. New style. Donne preached on 25 February 1630 (old style). He died at the end of March 1631.
3. Targoff, *John Donne*, 173.
4. Donne, *Works*, 32.

9: The Syntax of Understanding: Herbert's 'Prayer (I)'

1. Citations in the text are from Herbert, *Poems*.
2. Gottlieb, 28–9.
3. Vendler, *Herbert*, 38.
4. Erasmus, 38.
5. Greene, 25–6.
6. Burt & Mikics, 88.
7. Greenwood, 28.

10: The Real Presence of Unstated Puns: Herbert's 'Love (III)'

1. All citations of Herbert's English poetry are to Herbert, *Poems*.
2. Booth, *Sonnets*, 489 (Sonnet 141, 13–14n).
3. Strier, 'Ekphrasis', 107n. I owe this reference to Nicholas D. Nace's forth-coming essay, 'On Not Choking in Herbert's "The Collar"'. Strier elsewhere offers an extended reading of 'Love (III)' in which he remarks that 'the "host-Host" pun is literalized in the startling penultimate half-line' (Strier, *Love Known*, 78). Nonetheless, the many astute and sustained readings the poem has attracted for the most part do not discuss this undeveloped pun. Critical notice of the unstated pun has perhaps an appropriately understated history. Michael Schmidt asserts without further attribution that Christopher Ricks 'has pointed out [that] we sense an unstated, underlying pun on the word "host" as the poem unfolds: God is the soul's host at the table; he is also the consecrated host of which the sinner is to partake' (Schmidt, 158). Most critics, however, mention the importance of dining to the poem without noting the conceptual pun on the word 'host'. Less honoured by our silence than by our observance, the unstated pun perhaps epitomises the reticence the poem dramatises.
4. Herbert's single direct translation from the Psalms is 'The Twenty-third Psalm', a related scenario in which God 'dost make me sit and dine, / Ev'n in my enemies' sight' (17–18).
5. In 'Divinity', Herbert engages in a similar inversion of conventional Eucharistic theology, asserting that God 'doth bid us take his blood for wine' (21) rather than the conventional suggestion that wine is by some ritual action turned into blood. 'The Invitation' likewise asks its guest to 'drink this, / Which before ye drink is blood' (11–12).
6. Post, 154.
7. See Charles.
8. Vendler, *Herbert*, 274.
9. See Herbert of Cherbury, *De Veritate*. *De Veritate* was first published in Paris in 1624. In his autobiography, Edward relates that he was moved to publish the controversial work when 'a Loud though yet Gentle noise came from

the heavens' (Herbert of Cherbury, *Life*, 120). This is a kind of veritable yet unverifiable communication that his brother George might likewise have recognised as heavenly in origin.

10. See Schoenfeldt, esp. Chapter 5, 'Standing on Ceremony: The Comedy of Manners in Herbert's "Love (III)"', and Chapter 6, '"That Ancient Heat": Sexuality and Spirituality in *The Temple*'.

11. Booth, *Sonnets*, xi.

12. See Mambrino, 250.

11: 'Hardly they heard'

1. Sidney, *Poems*, 14–20. References in the text are to line numbers in this edition.

2. See, for example, in Gascoigne's 'Certayne Notes of Instruction', where he concedes (somewhat grudgingly) the pre-eminence of the iamb in English verse, and advises that 'in a verse of twelve, [the pause will stand best] in the midst' (456).

3. 'And hath he skill to make so excellent, / Yet hath so little skill to bridle love?' asks Spenser's shepherd Thenot, neatly separating technical skill from emotional self-management (Spenser, *Poems*, 61).

4. Carlo Ginzburg considers these parallel traditions in 'Style as Inclusion, Style as Exclusion'. The dominant sense of 'style' in the sixteenth century is that of its levels, high, middle, and low, which are shareable and teachable. But George Puttenham can still write of a style that is 'many times his peculier by election and arte, and such as either he keepeth by skill, or holdeth on by ignorance, and will not or peraduenture cannot easily alter into any other' (*Art*, 233).

5. And indeed, the technical challenges only mount from there, as Ringler describes (Sidney, *Poems*, 385–6).

6. Puttenham, *Art*, 149.

7. G. Smith, 1:99–100.

8. For example, 'Peace, foolish wit, with wit my wit is mard', in *Astrophil and Stella* 34 (Sidney, *Poems*, 181–2).

12: Having It Both Ways in Juliet's 'Gallop apace' Speech

1. When referring to the 'prevailing' or 'primary' sense of a line, I mean that sense demanded by context and the complete unit of syntax – the paraphrasable content that results when readers take paths of least resistance in comprehending the literal. Of course, the prevailing sense often cannot cancel the momentary ambiguities of syntax and sense that help animate verse lines.

2. The Arden editors emend the plural form 'runawayes' in the First Folio to the singular possessive 'runaway's', which then refers to Phaeton, who, by his absence, seems a good candidate. However, his 'winking' would not matter to Juliet if he is absent for her sexual encounter. More importantly, an audience will always hear 'runaways' as an independent plural subject, a perception that cannot be erased when 'eyes' makes it possessive. Coupled with the comparative prominence of the steeds in Juliet's imagination, readers and audiences are likely to hear 'runaways' as a reference to them, or to them and Phaeton.

3. Note how each word asks the speaker to elide almost entirely its short medial vowel before ending in a long-vowelled, open syllable.

4. See line 1 of Sonnet 130, 'My mistress' eyes are nothing like the sun', as well as 'her sun-bright eye' in *The Two Gentlemen of Verona* (3.1.88).

5. Later in the scene Juliet calls Romeo 'my true knight' (3.2.142), literalising what is implicit in these lines.

6. For an instance of the idiom, see Gardner's speech in Thomas Heywood's *The Fayre Mayde of the Exchange* (1607), 'But such a gallant beautie, or such a forme / I never saw, nor never wore the like'.

13: 'To Celia': Not Too Close

1. Jonson, *Jonson*, 293.

2. Carson, 16. Among others who have discussed the triangulation of desire, see notably Girard, 1–52.

3. On the chief classical source, the *Epistles* of Philostratus, see Fitton Brown. But Ovid's elegy, with its exchange of glances and cup-trick (17–19, 31–2) is clearly also an influence.

4. *OED s.v.* 'pledge' v. 4a.

5. *Ovid's Elegies*, 1.4.31–2, in Ovid & Marlowe, 39.

6. When the poem appears in *The Forest* there may be a husband implied, since both of the earlier lyrics in the same collection addressed to Celia (numbers 5 and 6) concern furtive, adulterous love; but nothing within the poem itself suggests a need for subterfuge.

7. M. H. Abrams discusses this element of poetic pleasure in his lecture 'The Fourth Dimension of Poetry'.

8. See Donaldson's note in Jonson, *Jonson*, 675, and Fitton Brown, 557.

9. Empson, *Seven Types*, 242.

14: Marvell's 'Mourning'

1. All citations from Marvell's poems are from Marvell, *Complete Poems*.

15: On the Value of the *Town-Bayes*

1. Marvell, *Complete Poems*, 193. Subsequent parenthetical citations in the text are to line numbers from this edition.
2. 'A Familiar Epistle to Mr Julian Secretary to the Muses', in Villiers, 2:31.
3. 'The Session of the Poets', in Lord, 1:334.
4. I'm using the title that accompanied the poem on its initial appearance (in the 1674 second edition of *Paradise Lost*), since, as we shall see, Marvell's authorial persona can barely even imagine a world in which such a work might not be the entirety of a poet's legacy. The title furnished in the posthumously published 1681 *Miscellaneous Poems. By Andrew Marvell, Esq*; – 'On Mr Milton's *Paradise Lost*' – suggests, on the other hand, that that epic is but a single component of a broader life and oeuvre. However commonsensical the latter position may seem to us, it's a truth almost wholly beyond the ken of the 'I' of this poem.
5. Milton, *Works*, 355. Subsequent parenthetical citations in the text to *Paradise Lost* are to book and line numbers.
6. Butler, 41.
7. Judges 16:29 (AV).
8. In the Tyndale, Great, and Geneva translations of 2 Corinthians 3:1, the principal verb is 'praise' (e.g. 'do we beginne to praise our selves againe?'). In the Rheims, Bishops', and Authorised translations, it is 'commend' ('Doe we begin againe to commend our selves'). The persona is thus inadvertently using a term with High Church resonance in his commendation of the rather less-than-Laudian Milton. I owe this observation to Nigel Smith (Marvell, *Poems*, 184n52).
9. It's particularly easy to stumble this way when reading the 1674 text, which gives a colon after 'bells', rather than the period with which the 1681 version and the modernised Penguin text end that couplet.
10. Dryden, 'To my Dear Friend Mr. Congreve, On His Comedy, call'd The Double-Dealer', in Congreve, 123. When Dryden visited Milton 'to have leave to putt Paradise Lost into a drama in rhyme' – *The State of Innocence and the Fall of Man* – 'Mr. Milton recieved him civilly, and told him he would give him leave to tagge his verses' (Aubrey, 2:72). To 'tag' a 'point' is to add a metal tip to a lace or cord in order to make it easier to use as a fastener for clothes (much as modern shoelaces have plastic sheaths wrapped around their ends). However, tags were also an easy way of adding something shiny and ornamental to an outfit, hence the persona's confession that 'we for fashion wear' them. Presumably, 'tagge[d] … verses' risk the same kind of gaudy ephemerality.

16: Pointless Milton: A Close Reading in Negative

1. The text of *Paradise Lost* is cited from Milton, *Works*; further line references to *Paradise Lost* will appear in the text.
2. 'Of Education', in Milton, *Works*, 233.
3. Martz, 226.
4. Turner, 245.
5. Leonard, 96.
6. See Samuels; Lewalski.
7. Empson, *Seven Types*, 13.

17: Marlowe's Will, Marlowe's Shall

1. Citations to *Doctor Faustus* are from Marlowe, *Faustus*. Though the textual proliferation of *Doctor Faustus* is complex and places a limit here, both A and B versions of the texts are similarly phrased in this passage.
2. See Kocher, 105–7.
3. Barbour, Book 9, line 147.
4. See Denison, 293.
5. Booth, *Sonnets*, 508.

18: Reading Intensity: Sonnet 12

1. The text is from Booth's legendary edition (Booth, *Sonnets*; further references appear parenthetically in the text), which varies in ten or so commas and semi-colons from Keats's probable text, the 1804 printing of *The Poems of William Shakspeare* (1795), based on Edmond Malone's edition (1:590–91) – both at variance (accidental and substantive) with the 1609 Quarto. Booth's edition presents facing-page Quarto facsimiles (Sonnet 12 [13–15]) and his *Essay* gives the Quarto Sonnet 12 in modern typography (70).
2. Booth, *Essay*, 26–8, on John Crowe Ransom's 'ostentatiously red flag' essay, 'Shakespeare at Sonnets' (1938), and Keats's letter to fellow poet, J. H. Reynolds, 3 February 1818 (Keats, 99). Unless otherwise stated, references to Keats are to this edition's page numbers.
3. Ransom, 533.
4. Ransom, 533.
5. Booth allows that 'sable', heraldic black, could draw 'or' into heraldic punning (Willen & Reed noted this, 14) but he endorses Malone's judgment (1:590n5) that the Quarto's '*Or* was clearly an error of the press'.
6. Booth, *Essay*, 167.
7. Booth, *Essay*, ix.
8. To Helen Vendler, Booth's heroised reader displaces (or effaces) what she regards as the paramount figure: a poet-speaker in the drama of interpretation (*Art*, 17–28, 40n5).

9. For the multiple senses of "gainst' see Booth, *Sonnets* (1978 rpt; 152n13), the last soon echoed in Sonnet 13: 'Against the coming end you should prepare'.

10. Malone, 1:591n8.

11. Text based on Richard Woodhouse's *Letter-Book* (Houghton Library, Harvard University).

12. He hears only objection, dismay or shock (*Essay* 70, 75–6). See also Vendler, who raises the tone to 'anguished protest'; she has, however, misremembered the site as the 'margin of [Keats's] copy of the sonnets now in Harvard's Houghton Library' (*Art*, 100). In a note to me, 26 June 2011, she generously conceded her error. I think the tone of Keats's full letter would have given her a different impression.

13. Woodhouse, *Letter-Book* 51, transcribed with these scriptive elements in Keats, *Letters*, 1:188.

14. Christopher Ricks's term for a sense activated and refused (*Force*, 100).

15. See Booth, *Essay*, 70–85. Garrett Stewart makes the savvy connection to Booth's critical mode in *Reading Voices: Literature as Phonotext* (40). Jakobson's famous (italic) formulation (*The poetic function projects the principle of equivalence from the axis of selection into the axis of combination*), is from 'Closing Statement: Linguistics and Poetics' (358).

16. Booth, *Essay*, 27.

17. Booth, *Essay*, 84, 120.

18. Hazlitt, *Lectures*, 90–91.

19. Hazlitt, *Liber*, 192.

20. Hazlitt, *Liber*, 192.

19: 'Against' Interpretations: Rereading Sonnet 49

1. Booth, *Sonnets*.

2. Evans & Hecht, 158.

3. For an acute analysis of 'against' in Spenser's 'Epithalamion', see Gregerson, 108–9.

4. Certain differences do distinguish the many critics who read 'against' in Sonnet 49 as 'in anticipation of'. Notably, Kevin Curran interprets what others see as humble self-deprecation as adherence to a Levinas-like concept of hospitality that he finds elsewhere in the sequence as well (Curran).

5. Booth, *Sonnets*, 152. Further references appear parenthetically in the text.

6. Vendler, *Art*, 245. Further references appear parenthetically in the text.

7. *OED s.v.* 'against'.

8. *OED s.v.* 'strange'.

9. Recalling that linguists have developed the concept of emotional deixis, in which 'this' suggests positive affective responses in addition to, or instead of, spatial and temporal propinquity, one might perhaps even argue that the distal 'that' in reference to the sun hints at the speaker's desire to distance himself from a strange, potentially harmful celestial body as well as his anticipation of its rejection of him. This reading is, however, more speculative than the

other evidence cited above for coexisting double meanings of 'against'. On emotional deixis, see esp. Lakoff, 347–9.

10. On the putatively normative volta, see Levin's acute essay (xxxviii–xxxix).

11. In contrast to my contention that the primary meaning of 'against' remains 'in defence against', Katherine Duncan-Jones glosses this line as, 'Initially, it may appear that the speaker is consoling himself with the thought of his own merit; but the final couplet indicates that the implication is "my own (lack of) merit"' (208). She also recognises that 'mine own desert' (10) could initially suggest consolation. Thus here, as well as in her comment on the couplet discussed below, she acknowledges evidence for a reading like mine, yet joins other critics in dismissing that possibility and glossing 'against' in terms of expectation of an event in which one willingly participates. Further references to Duncan-Jones appear parenthetically in the text.

20: The Chimney-Sweepers Conceit in the Song for Fidele in *Cymbeline*

1. Thompson & Taylor, *Hamlet*.
2. Warren, 1.
3. Furness, *Cymbeline*, 323–6.
4. S. Johnson, 7:403–4.
5. White, 466.
6. Staunton, 2:749.
7. Rolfe, 244.
8. Lucian, 4:111–31.
9. Warburton, 7:320.
10. Jonson, 'Sonne', 780–81.
11. *Natural History*, 16.3 (Pliny, 4:391).
12. S. Johnson, 7:357.

21: *Mille viae mortis*

1. 'Mille viae mortis' is the title of what is said to be Charles Lamb's earliest poem. Patricia Tatspaugh and her excellent New Cambridge Shakespeare edition (co-edited with Robert Kean Turner), quoted here, were great helps in writing this essay, as was the learning and generosity of my colleague Sander Goldberg, who taught me more than I could put in.
2. Chaucer, *The Knight's Tale*: 'This world nys but a thurghfare ful of wo, / And we been pilgrymes passynge to and fro. / Deeth is an ende of euery worldly soore' (A 2847–9).
3. This is proverb D140 as catalogued by both Tilley and Dent, *Shakespeare's*.
4. See F. P. Wilson, 225a. Here the origin of the proverb is listed as 'Virgil: Mille viae mortis', an error.

5. Quoted from Dent, *Proverbial Language*, under D140.
6. Bradbrook, *Themes*, 88–91.
7. Bradbrook, 'Shakespeare', 30.
8. 'Sudden death, now by sea, now by a thousand ways' as translated by A. S. Kline at wttp://www.poetryintranslation.com/PITBR/Latin/Tibullus.htm#_Toc532635309.
9. R. Abrams, 145; Abrams does later (161) describe the market-place as 'the inevitable rendezvous of high and low'.
10. Thomas Tuke, *Discourse of Death* (1613), sig. C3, as quoted in Dent, W176, lightly modernised. The book's dedication is dated 5 November 1612.
11. *Henry V* (Craik, 1.2.205–11).
12. *The Book of Common Prayer 1559* (Booty, 50).

22: Donne the Time Traveller: Reading 'The Relic'

1. Donne, *Works*, 130.
2. Guibbory, 24.
3. Targoff, 'Facing', 222.
4. See Baker, 159 and Gray, 224.
5. Wootton, 41.
6. Empson, *Essays*, 87.
7. Wootton, 37.
8. Guibbory, 31–2.
9. Wilcox, 131.
10. Gross, 383, 396, 398.

23: Fletcher's *Mad Lover* and the Late Shakespeare

1. Citations in the text are to Fletcher, *Mad Lover*. The play is dated *c.* 1616.

24: 'And Ten Low Words Oft Creep in One Dull Line': Sidney's Perfection of a Sonnet Device

1. All lines from Sidney's *Astrophil and Stella* are taken from Sidney, *Poems*.
2. Wyatt cited from Rollins.
3. Grimald cited from Rollins.
4. All lines from Shakespeare's *Sonnets* are taken from Booth, *Sonnets*.
5. All lines from Donne's poems are taken from Donne, *Works*.
6. All lines from Herbert's poems are taken from Herbert, *Poems*.
7. All lines from Milton's poems are taken from Milton, *Works*.

25: The Fox and His Pause: Punctuating Consciousness in Jonson's *Volpone*

1. Parenthetical citations for *Volpone* are from Jonson & Watson, *Volpone*, but this argument will often (as here) require the use of punctuation from other editions.
2. *English Grammar* in Jonson, *Works*, 690 (1692 edn). The 1640 edition reverses the functions of comma and semi-colon.
3. McDonald, *Shakespeare*, 11.
4. Booth, *Sonnets*, ix.
5. See Ong.
6. *English Grammar* in Jonson, *Works*, 690.
7. *English Grammar* in Jonson, *Works*, 690.
8. Booth, *Precious*.
9. McDonald, 'Jonson', 114.
10. Watson.

26: Some Similes in Paradise Lost, Book 9

1. Citations in the text are to Milton, *Works*. Further references to *Paradise Lost* will appear by book and line number in the text.
2. Todd, *ad loc.*
3. Fowler, *ad loc.*
4. Forsyth, 282.
5. Empson, *Seven Types*, 9.
6. Kermode, 275.
7. Teskey, *ad loc.*
8. Ovid, 4.572–603.
9. Fowler, *ad loc.*
10. Empson, *Pastoral*, 176.
11. Hale, 145.

27: Telling Stories

1. Mahood, 144.
2. Dekker, sig. F.
3. Tusser, sig. Biiii.
4. Bawcutt, 2.1.118n.
5. Gibbons, 104.
6. Quintilian, 8.3.61.
7. Quintilian, 8.3.61.

28: Richard's Soliloquy: *Richard II*, 5.5.1–49

1. Righter, 60. After almost half a century, Righter's book remains in my opinion the best of its kind on this topic.
2. Righter, 57.
3. Personal communication. My understanding of *Richard II* has benefited enormously from Professor Potter's writings and suggestions about the play, and it gives me pleasure to record my gratitude here.
4. Iser, 94.
5. Kierkegaard, 18, 20.

29: Virtual Presence and Vicarious Identity in the First Tetralogy

1. More precisely, it is a simile-turned-metaphor, as the comparison from nature fuses with the speaker's experience.
2. For discussion of authorship and dating, see Taylor.
3. See 1.1.221; 2.2.63–5; 3.1.89–90, 337–8.
4. The Catholic doctrine of real presence held that during Communion the Eucharist actually becomes the body and blood of Christ, empowering the participant with the gift of life everlasting. The Church of England taught that Christ's presence was virtual and that the efficacy of the sacrament lay in its faithful reception by the participant.

30: Unmuffling Isabella

1. G. Wright, 'Supposing'.

31: Hamlet's 'Serious Hearing': 'Sound' vs. 'Use' of 'Voice'

1. Booth, 'Value', 141.
2. Stewart, 55.
3. Empson, *Seven Types*, 90–101; G. Wright, 'Hendiadys'.
4. Moretti, 92–3.
5. Cavell, 179–91.

32: Hamlet's Couplets

1. Pope, *Poems*, 155 (lines 352–3).
2. Thompson & Taylor, Q1 *Hamlet*, 2.38–9; retention of the couplet or its rhyme occurs throughout Q1, which in one instance *adds* a couplet (10.12–13, the King's attempt to pray).

3. Q2's 'most' in 3.4.213 breaks the metre.
4. This is the *sole* evidence for *OED* s.v. 'couplet' n.2 ('a pair or couple'), since the *Twelfth Night* citation includes the metrical sense and in the third citation Mary Mitford quotes Gertrude directly.

33: The Dumb Show in *Hamlet*

1. Stern, 63–80.
2. Quarles, 4.
3. Mehl, 113.
4. Greg, 'Hallucination'; J. D. Wilson, 151.
5. For more on F *Hamlet* as a revision, see Ann Thompson and Neil Taylor's introduction to their Arden 3 *Hamlet*, which chooses Q2 as copy text.
6. Cropped note on copy of *Locrine* (London, 1595), reconstructed in Greg, *Papers*, 226–35. Contractions have been expanded.

34: Claudius on His Knees

1. *OED* s.v. 'rank' adj. 11, 12, 13, 14.
2. Cf. Genesis 4:1–14, especially 13, 'And Cain said unto the Lord, My punishment is greater than I can bear' (Geneva).
3. Jenkins, *ad loc.*
4. In his edition of Shakespeare's Sonnets, Stephen Booth's head note to Sonnet 135 lists some of the meanings of 'will' that operate in that sonnet, these among them (Booth, *Sonnets*, 466).
5. Jenkins, *ad loc.*
6. Jenkins, 2.448–514 long note.
7. Targoff, *Common*, 3.
8. Foakes, 'Neglect', 93.
9. T. Wright, 27.
10. De Grazia, chapter 6, 'Hamlet's Delay', 158–203, esp. 168–71.

35: Gertrude's Gallery

1. Dessen, 151–4. The author is grateful to Alan Dessen for reading and commenting on an early version of this essay, as also to the late Bernice Kliman.
2. Harrison, 200.
3. Summerson, 124.
4. Girouard, 101–2.
5. Orlin, *Locating*, 240.
6. *Warning*, 134.
7. Webster, 2.2.23sd.
8. Shirley, 5.2.22sd.

9. Orlin, *Locating*, 260.

10. Bullough, 144–5; Clary, 183.

11. Donne, *Variorum*, 246–7; Jonson & Parker, *Volpone*, 1.2.86–7, 3.7.12–13; Beaumont & Fletcher, 4.1.8.

12. Jonson, *Epicene*, 4.5.27–33.

13. Orlin, 'Closet', 56–7.

14. Jonson, *Epicene*, 4.5.28–9.

15. Thurley, *Royal Palaces*, 125.

16. Thurley, *Royal Palaces*, 31, 125.

17. Thurley, 'Henry VIII', 21.

18. Emmison, 32–3, 83.

19. Coope, 61.

20. *Wills*, 132.

21. Machyn, 129.

22. Beckerman, 64.

23. Jardine, 150–51.

36: The Fool's Promised Exit

1. According to Hinman's through-line numbering of the 1623 Folio, the Fool's millenarian prophecy begins at line 1,734 of the play's 3,302 lines (804–5).

2. See *The History of King Lear* (9.78) in Greenblatt (2nd edn).

3. *The Life and Death of King Lear*, in Warburton, 6:76–7.

4. According to the 1880 Variorum editor, Warburton's emendation was followed by all the major subsequent editors until Malone in 1790 (Furness, *King Lear*, 179). In 1960, the editors of the Cambridge edition reverted to Warburton's emendation (only reversing the order of his two inferences), trusting that the resulting 'rearrangement will be accepted as … genuine Shakespeare' (Duthie & Wilson, 204, 263). All major editions of Shakespeare's complete works since then have followed the 1747/1960 emendation: Bevington; Evans & Tobin; Wells & Taylor; Greenblatt (2nd edn), in the Folio *Lear*, but not the Conflated Text. John Kerrigan in 'Revision, Adaptation, and the Fool in *King Lear*' and Gary Taylor in 'The Date and Authorship of the Folio Version' both assume two prophecies, in Taylor & Warren, 238n93, 382.

5. For much of the twentieth century, the prophecy was considered spurious; see Zitner.

6. See Hawkes. R. A. Foakes (editor of the Arden 3 edition cited throughout) endorses Hawkes in his note on these lines (3.2.79–96); see also *King Lear* (Conflated Text) in Greenblatt (2nd edn), 2516.

7. In Britain, this tradition extended back to Shakespeare's source for the story of Lear and his three daughters: Geoffrey of Monmouth's *Historia Regum Britanniæ* (c. 1136). This work includes a chapter, *Prophetiae Merlini*, of over a hundred prophecies; see Geoffrey of Monmouth. For a genealogical sketch of the Fool's Merlinic prophecy, see Fawtier & Fawtier.

8. Puttenham, *Arte* facsimile, 232.
9. *Macbeth*, 5.10.20.
10. On the clown's conventional stalling technics, see De Grazia, 175–80.
11. *The Summoning of Everyman*, in *Everyman*, 131, 122, 130.
12. Puttenham, *Arte* facsimile, 230.
13. On *King Lear* as 'a play that has been ready to end since it began', see 'On the Greatness of *King Lear*', in Booth, *Indefinition*, 3–56, at 17.

37: How Can Act 5 Forget Lear and Cordelia?

1. Muir, 5.3.235, note.
2. Not surprisingly Stephen Booth notices this anomaly. He offers a persuasive and moving account of how the play by this point constantly refuses to provide the ending that characters like Gloucester desire. Booth figures the audience as stretched on a rack in frustrated fascination with the possibility that the play will never end but keep discovering these momentarily forgotten locales of suffering (Booth, *Indefinition*, 9–17). I don't quite disagree, but I want to stress the specific states that the play invites the audience to try on as a reward for their endurance, or, better, as a contrast to the torture that only such torture prepares us to see.
3. Wittgenstein, *Tractatus*, 145 (§6.41).
4. Wittgenstein, *Tractatus*, 151 (§6.52). Wittgenstein concludes this statement with one more sentence: 'They are what is mystical'. I drop it from my argument because it is easy to mistake what Wittgenstein means by the mystical. He does not mean anything transcendental. His view is summarised by a statement a page back, 'Feeling the world as a limited whole – it is this that is mystical' (Wittgenstein, *Tractatus*, 147 [§6.45]). Ultimately what is mystical is the fact that the world can fit logical form that gives shape to propositions. And because we would have to use logic to describe logic, there is no way to get outside of logic. The force of logic can only be displayed. Perhaps that is also true of theatre at its most intense and demanding.
5. Wittgenstein, *Investigations*, 222 (§2.11). The passion behind this formulation emerges in Wittgenstein's private writing: 'The Christian Faith – as I see it is a man's refuge in this ultimate torment. Anyone in such torment who has the gift of opening his heart, rather than contracting it, accepts the means of salvation in his heart. Someone who in this way penitently opens his heart to God in confession lays it open for other men too. In doing this he loses the dignity that goes with his personal prestige and becomes like a child. ... A man can bare himself before others only out of a particular kind of love. A love which acknowledges, as it were, that we are all wicked children. We could also say: Hate between men comes from our cutting ourselves off from each other' (*Culture*, 46).

38: Exits without Exiting

1. Citations from *Macbeth* are from Greenblatt.
2. Booth, 'Close', 56.
3. I directed this production. J. P. Scheidler was the Associate Director and was responsible for the fight and dance choreography. Jeremy Fiebig was my Assistant Director. Erin M. West designed the costumes. Alvaro Mendoza played Macbeth and Celia Madeoy played Lady Macbeth. George Walton Williams worked as the production's dramaturge, and this essay owes much to the delight of doing table work with him and the cast.
4. McDonald, *Bedford*, 50.
5. In our 2006 production Celia Madeoy's Lady Macbeth went back to get Macbeth (Alvaro Mendoza) and pulled him by the hand through the door.
6. See Palfrey & Stern for a consideration of the embedded stage directions in 3.2.
7. These lines follow two previous couplets, and originally I had planned to argue here that this series of couplets and the other such instances in the play would allow the actor a false exit on every couplet, giving him as many as five. We used the couplets in this way in our ASC production and the false exits 'worked' (by which I mean the actor made them make sense and the audience didn't laugh at them). So I still want to argue for it, but I have run out of room.
8. I have looked here only at the scene endings involving Macbeth and Lady Macbeth (1.5, 2.1, 3.2, 3.4), but all of the following scenes have a similar pattern of *exit interruptus* at the end: 1.2.63–7 (Duncan and Ross), 1.3.145–56 (Macbeth and Banquo), 1.4.52–8 (Macbeth and Duncan), 2.4.38–42 (Macduff, Ross, and Old Man), 4.1.169–72 (Macbeth), 5.1.67–9 (Doctor and Gentlewoman), 5.2.29–31 (Caithness and Lennox), 5.3.61–4 (Macbeth and Doctor), 5.4.17–21 (Siward and Macduff), 5.5.45–50 (Macbeth and Messenger).
9. 'Start' here is an antagonym, a word that has opposite meanings – both to swerve from and to hasten to (*OED s.v.* 'start' v.). Those two meanings seem apposite to the re-appearing attempted exits in *Macbeth*.

39: Playing Prospero Against the Grain

1. Montaigne, 2:108.
2. Mazer.

r

BIBLIOGRAPHY

Abrams, M. H.

M. H. Abrams, 'The Fourth Dimension of Poetry', http://www.cornell. edu/
video/?videoID=1088

Abrams, R.

Richard Abrams, '*The Two Noble Kinsmen* as Bourgeois Drama', in *Shakespeare,
Fletcher, and* The Two Noble Kinsmen, ed. Charles H. Frey (Columbia, MO,
1989) 145–62

Adelman

Janet Adelman, *The Common Liar: An Essay on* Antony and Cleopatra (New
Haven, 1973)

Altieri

Charles Altieri, 'The Sensuous Dimension of Literary Experience: An
Alternative to Materialist Theory', *New Literary History* 38 (2007): 71–98

Andrews

William Shakespeare, *A Midsummer Night's Dream*, ed. John F. Andrews,
Everyman Shakespeare (London, 1993)

Ariosto

Ludovico Ariosto, *Orlando Furioso*, ed. L. Caretti (Torino, 1982)

Attridge

Derek Attridge, *Well-Weighed Syllables: Elizabethan Verse in Classical Metres*
(London, 1974)

Aubrey

John Aubrey, *'Brief lives', chiefly of contemporaries, set down by John Aubrey,
between the years 1669 & 1696*, ed. Andrew Clark, 2 vols (Oxford, 1898)

Augustine

Saint Augustine, *Confessions*, trans. R. S. Pine-Coffin (Harmondsworth, 1986)

AV (Authorised Version)

*The Holy Bible, conteyning the Old Testament, and the New, newly translated out
of the originall tongues, and with the former translations diligently compared and
reuised, by His Maiesties speciall comandement* (London, 1611)

Baker

Christopher Baker, 'Bone Lace and Donne's "bracelet of bright haire about
the bone"', *John Donne Journal* 28 (2009): 159–61

Barbour

John Barbour, *The Bruce*, ed. A. A. M. Duncan (London, 1997)

Bawcutt

William Shakespeare, *Measure for Measure*, ed. N. W. Bawcutt (Oxford, 1991)

Beaumont & Fletcher
Francis Beaumont and John Fletcher, *The Maid's Tragedy*, ed. T. W. Craik, The Revels Plays (Manchester, 1988)

Beckerman
Bernard Beckerman, *Shakespeare at the Globe, 1599–1609* (New York, 1962)

Best & Marcus
Stephen Best and Sharon Marcus, 'Surface Reading: An Introduction', *Representations* 108 (2009): 1–21

Bevington
William Shakespeare, *The Complete Works of Shakespeare*, ed. David Bevington, 6th edn (New York, 2008)

Booth, 'Close'
Stephen Booth, 'Close Reading without Readings', in *Shakespeare Reread: The Texts in New Contexts*, ed. Russ McDonald (Ithaca, 1994) 42–56

Booth, 'Discourse'
Stephen Booth, 'A Discourse on the Witty Partition of *A Midsummer Night's Dream*', in *Inside Shakespeare: Essays on the Blackfriars Stage*, ed. Paul Menzer (Selinsgrove, 2006), 216–22

Booth, *Essay*
Stephen Booth, *An Essay on Shakespeare's Sonnets* (New Haven, 1969)

Booth, 'Function'
Stephen Booth, 'The Function of Criticism at the Present Time and All Others', *Shakespeare Quarterly* 41 (1990): 262–8

Booth, *Indefinition*
Stephen Booth, King Lear, Macbeth, *Indefinition, and Tragedy* (New Haven, 1983)

Booth, *Precious*
Stephen Booth, *Precious Nonsense: The Gettysburg Address, Ben Jonson's Epitaphs on His Children, and* Twelfth Night (Berkeley, 1998)

Booth, *Sonnets*
William Shakespeare, *Shakespeare's Sonnets*, edited with analytic commentary by Stephen Booth (New Haven, 1977; rpt 1978, corrected with additional notes)

Booth, 'Value'
Stephen Booth, 'On the Value of *Hamlet*', in *Reinterpretations of Elizabethan Drama: Selected Papers from the English Institute*, ed. Norman Rabkin (New York, 1969), 137–76

Booty
The Book of Common Prayer 1559, ed. John E. Booty (Washington, 1976)

Bradbrook, 'Shakespeare'
M. C. Bradbrook, 'Shakespeare and His Collaborators', in *Shakespeare 1971*, ed. Clifford Leech and J. M. R. Margeson (Toronto, 1972)

Bradbrook, *Themes*
M. C. Bradbrook, *Themes and Conventions of Elizabethan Tragedy* (Cambridge, 1935, rpt 1960)

Branagh

Branagh, Kenneth, Much Ado About Nothing: *Screenplay, Introduction, and Notes on the Making of the Movie* (New York, 1993)

Brooks

William Shakespeare, *A Midsummer Night's Dream*, ed. Harold F. Brooks, Arden 2 (London, 1979)

Bullough

Fratricide Punished (Der bestrafte Brudermord), in Geoffrey Bullough, *Narrative and Dramatic Sources of Shakespeare*, vol. 7 (London, 1978), 128–58

Burt & Mikics

Stephen Burt and David Mikics, *The Art of the Sonnet* (Cambridge, MA, 2010)

Butler

[Samuel Butler], *The Transproser Rehears'd: or the Fifth Act of Mr. Bayes's Play* (Oxford, 1673)

Carson

Anne Carson, *Eros the Bittersweet: An Essay* (Princeton, 1986)

Cavell

Stanley Cavell, *Disowning Knowledge in Six Plays of Shakespeare* (Cambridge, 1987)

Charles

Amy Charles, ed., *The Williams Manuscript of George Herbert's Poems* (Delmar, NY, 1977).

Chaucer

Geoffrey Chaucer, *The Works of Geoffrey Chaucer*, ed. F. N. Robinson, 2nd edn (Boston, 1961)

Clary

Frank Nicholas Clary, 'Pictures in the Closet: Properties and Stage Business in *Hamlet* 3.4', in *Stage Directions in* Hamlet*: New Essays and New Directions*, ed. Hardin L. Aasand (Madison, 2003), 170–88

Congreve

William Congreve, *The Complete Plays of William Congreve*, ed. Herbert Davis (Chicago, 1967)

Coope

Rosalys Coope, 'The "Long Gallery": Its Origins, Development, Use and Decoration', *Architectural History* 29 (1986): 43–84

Craik

William Shakespeare, *Henry V*, ed. T. W. Craik, Arden 3 (London, 1995)

Curran

Kevin Curran, 'Hospitable Justice: Law and Selfhood in Shakespeare's Sonnets', *Law, Culture and the Humanities* (30 June 2011): n.p., doi: 10.1177/1743872111407450.

Danielson

Dennis Danielson, *Milton's Good God* (Cambridge, 1982)

De Grazia
    Margreta de Grazia, Hamlet *without Hamlet* (Cambridge, 2007)
De Man
    Paul de Man, *The Resistance to Theory* (Minneapolis, 1986)
Dekker
    Thomas Dekker, *The pleasant comœdie of patient Grissill* (London, 1603)
Denison
    David Denison, 'Modals and related auxiliaries', *English Historical Syntax: Verbal Constructions* (London, 1993)
Dent, *Proverbial Language*
    R. W. Dent, *Proverbial Language in English Drama exclusive of Shakespeare, 1495–1616, an index* (Berkeley, 1984)
Dent, *Shakespeare's*
    R. W. Dent, *Shakespeare's Proverbial Language* (Berkeley, 1981)
Dessen
    Alan C. Dessen, *Recovering Shakespeare's Theatrical Vocabulary* (Cambridge, 1995)
Dolven
    Jeff Dolven, 'Spenser's Metrics', in *The Oxford Handbook of Edmund Spenser*, ed. Richard A. McCabe (Oxford, 2010), 385–402
Donne, *Deaths Duell*
    John Donne, *Deaths Duell, or, A Consolation to the Soule, against the dying Life, and living Death of the Body*, HBLL Digital Collections, http://lib.byu.edu/digital/donne/, ed. Kimberly Johnson (2005); text based on *The Sermons of John Donne*, ed. George Potter and Evelyn Simpson, 10 vols (Berkeley, 1953–62)
Donne, *Variorum*
    John Donne, *The Variorum Edition of the Poetry of John Donne, vol. 2: The Elegies*, Gary A. Stringer, gen. ed. (Bloomington, 2000)
Donne, *Works*
    John Donne, *The Major Works*, ed. John Carey (Oxford, 1990)
Duncan-Jones
    William Shakespeare, *Shakespeare's Sonnets*, ed. Katherine Duncan-Jones, Arden 3 (n.p., 1997)
Duthie & Wilson
    William Shakespeare, *King Lear*, ed. George Ian Duthie and John Dover Wilson (Cambridge, 1960)
Edmondson & Wells, 'Plurality'
    Paul Edmondson and Stanley Wells, 'The Plurality of the Sonnets', *Shakespeare Survey 65* (Cambridge, 2012)
Edmondson & Wells, *Sonnets*
    Paul Edmondson and Stanley Wells, *Shakespeare's Sonnets* (Oxford, 2004)
Emmison
    F. G. Emmison, *Tudor Secretary: Sir William Petre at Court and Home* (London, 1961)

Empson, *Essays*
William Empson, *Essays on Renaissance Literature, Volume I: Donne and the New Philosophy*, ed. John Haffenden (Cambridge, 1993)

Empson, *Pastoral*
William Empson, *Some Versions of Pastoral* (London, 1935)

Empson, *Seven Types*
William Empson, *Seven Types of Ambiguity* (n.p., 1930, 3rd edn 1963)

Erasmus
Desiderius Erasmus, [*De Copia*] *On Copia of Words and Ideas*, trans. Donald B. King and H. David Rix (Milwaukee, 2005)

Evans & Hecht
William Shakespeare, *The Sonnets*, ed. G. Blakemore Evans and Anthony Hecht, New Cambridge Shakespeare (Cambridge, 1996)

Evans & Tobin
William Shakespeare, *The Riverside Shakespeare*, ed. G. Blakemore Evans and J. J. M. Tobin, 2nd edn (Boston, 1997)

Everyman
Everyman *and* Mankind, ed. Douglas Bruster and Eric Rasmussen (London, 2009)

Fawtier & Fawtier
E. C. Fawtier and R. Fawtier, 'From Merlin to Shakespeare: Adventures of an English Prophecy', *Bulletin of the John Rylands Library* 5 (1919): 388–92

Felski
Rita Felski, '"Context Stinks!"', *New Literary History* 42 (2011): 573–91

Fineman
Joel Fineman, 'The Sound of *O* in *Othello*: The Real of the Tragedy of Desire', *October* 45 (1988): 76–96

Fish
Stanley Fish, *Professional Correctness: Literary Studies and Political Change* (Oxford, 1995)

Fitton Brown
A. D. Fitton Brown, 'Drink to me, Celia', *Modern Language Review* 54 (1959): 554–7

Fletcher, *Mad Lover*
John Fletcher, *The Mad Lover*, in *The Dramatic Works in the Beaumont and Fletcher Canon*, vol. 5, ed. Robert Kean Turner, gen. ed. Fredson Bowers (Cambridge, 1983)

Foakes, *Midsummer*
William Shakespeare, *A Midsummer Night's Dream*, ed. R. A. Foakes, updated ed., New Cambridge Shakespeare (Cambridge, 2003)

Foakes, 'Neglect'
R. A. Foakes, 'Hamlet's Neglect of Revenge', in Hamlet: *New Critical Essays*, ed. Arthur F. Kinney (New York, 2002)

Forsyth
Neil Forsyth, *The Satanic Epic* (Princeton, 2003)

Fowler
 John Milton, *Paradise Lost*, ed. Alastair Fowler, rev. 2nd edn (New York, 2007)
Friedman
 Donald M. Friedman, 'The Mind in the Poem: Wyatt's "They Fle From Me"', *Studies in English Literature, 1500–1900* 7 (1967): 1–13
Furness, *Cymbeline*
 William Shakespeare, *Cymbeline*, ed. Horace Howard Furness, Variorum Shakespeare (Philadelphia, 1913)
Furness, *King Lear*
 William Shakespeare, *King Lear*, ed. Horace Howard Furness, Variorum Shakespeare (Philadelphia, 1880)
Furness, *Midsummer*
 William Shakespeare, *A Midsummer Night's Dream*, ed. Horace Howard Furness, Variorum Shakespeare (Boston, 1895)
Garber
 Marjorie Garber, 'Shakespeare in Slow Motion', *Profession* (2010): 151–64
Gascoigne
 George Gascoigne, 'Certayne Notes of Instruction', in *A Hundreth Sundrie Flowres*, ed. G. W. Pigman (Oxford, 2000)
Geneva
 The Geneva Bible: A Facsimile of the 1560 Edition, introd. Lloyd E. Berry (Madison, 1969)
Geoffrey of Monmouth
 Geoffrey of Monmouth, *History of the Kings of Britain*, ed. Michael D. Reeve, trans. Neil Wright (Woodbridge, 2007)
Gibbons
 William Shakespeare, *Measure for Measure*, ed. Brian Gibbons updated edn, New Cambridge Shakespeare (Cambridge, 2006)
Ginzburg
 Carlo Ginzburg, 'Style as Inclusion, Style as Exclusion', in *Picturing Science, Producing Art*, ed. Peter Gallison and Caroline Jones (New York, 1989), 27–54
Girard
 René Girard, *Deceit, Desire, and the Novel: Self and Other in Literary Structure*, trans. Yvonne Freccero (Baltimore, 1966)
Girouard
 Mark Girouard, *Life in the English Country House: A Social and Architectural History* (New Haven, 1978)
Gotch
 J. Alfred Gotch, *Architecture of the Renaissance in England* (London, 1894)
Gottlieb
 Sidney Gottlieb, 'How Shall We Read Herbert? A Look at "Prayer" (I)', *George Herbert Journal* 1 (1977): 26–38
Gray
 Erik Gray, 'Severed Hair from Donne to Pope', *Essays in Criticism* 47 (1997): 220–39

Greenblatt
    William Shakespeare, *The Norton Shakespeare*, ed. Stephen Greenblatt,
    Walter Cohen, Jean E. Howard, and Katharine Eisaman Maus (New York,
    1997, 2nd edn 2008)
Greene
    Thomas M. Greene, *The Light in Troy: Imitation and Discovery in Renaissance
    Poetry* (New Haven, 1982)
Greenwood
    E. B. Greenwood, 'George Herbert's Sonnet "Prayer": A Stylistic Study',
    Essays in Criticism 15 (1965): 27–45
Greg 'Hallucination'
    W. W. Greg, 'Hamlet's Hallucination', *MLR* 12 (1917): 393–421
Greg, *Papers*
    W. W. Greg, *Collected Papers*, ed. J. C. Maxwell (Oxford, 1966)
Gregerson
    Linda Gregerson, 'Anatomizing Death', in *Imagining Death in Spenser and
    Milton*, ed. Elizabeth Jane Bellamy, Patrick Cheney, and Michael Schoenfeldt
    (New York, 2003)
Gross
    Kenneth Gross, 'John Donne's Lyric Skepticism', *Modern Philology* 101
    (2004): 371–99
Guibbory
    Achsah Guibbory, '"The Relique," the *Song of Songs* and Donne's *Songs and
    Sonets*', *John Donne Journal* 15 (1996): 23–44
Gurr
    William Shakespeare, *Henry V*, ed. Andrew Gurr, New Cambridge
    Shakespeare (Cambridge, 1992)
Hale
    John K. Hale, *Milton's Languages* (Cambridge, 1997)
Hansen
    Jim Hansen, 'Formalism and Its Malcontents: Benjamin and de Man on the
    Function of Allegory', *New Literary History* 35 (2004): 663–83
Harrison
    William Harrison, *The Description of England* (1577), ed. Georges Edelen
    (Ithaca, 1968)
Hartman
    Geoffrey H. Hartman, *Beyond Formalism: Literary Essays, 1958–1970* (New
    Haven, 1970)
Hawkes
    Terence Hawkes, 'The Fool's "Prophecy" in *King Lear*', *Notes and Queries*,
    n.s. 7 (1960): 332–3
Hazlitt, *Lectures*
    William Hazlitt, *Lectures on the English Poets* (London, 1818)
Hazlitt, *Liber*
    [William Hazlitt], *Liber Amoris; or The New Pygmalion* (London, 1823)

Heaney, *Government*
  Seamus Heaney, *The Government of the Tongue* (London, 1988)
Heaney, *Seeing*
  Seamus Heaney, *Seeing Things* (London, 1991)
Herbert, *Poems*
  George Herbert, *The Complete English Poems*, ed. John Tobin (London, 2004)
Herbert of Cherbury, *De Veritate*
  Edward, Lord Herbert of Cherbury, *De Veritate*, trans. Meyrick Carre (Bristol, 1937)
Herbert of Cherbury, *Life*
  Edward, Lord Herbert of Cherbury, *The Life of Lord Herbert of Cherbury*, ed. J. M. Shuttleworth (London, 1976)
Heywood
  Thomas Heywood, *The Fayre Mayde of the Exchange* (London, 1607)
Hinman
  Charlton Hinman, *The First Folio of Shakespeare*, facsimile (New York, 1968)
Holland
  William Shakespeare, *A Midsummer Night's Dream*, ed. Peter Holland, Oxford Shakespeare (Oxford, 1994)
Iser
  Wolfgang Iser, *Staging Politics: The Lasting Impact of Shakespeare's Histories*, trans. David Henry Wilson (New York, 1993)
Jakobson
  Roman Jakobson, 'Closing Statement: Linguistics and Poetics', in *Style in Language*, ed. Thomas A. Sebeok (Cambridge, 1960)
Jameson
  Fredric Jameson, *The Political Unconscious: Narrative as a Socially Symbolic Act* (Ithaca, 1981)
Jardine
  Lisa Jardine, *Reading Shakespeare Historically* (London, 1996)
Jenkins
  William Shakespeare, *Hamlet*, ed. Harold Jenkins, Arden 2 (London, 1982)
Johnson, E.
  Eric M. Johnson, *Open Source Shakespeare: Concordance of Shakespeare's Complete Works*, http://www.opensourceshakespeare.org/concordance/
Johnson, S.
  William Shakespeare, *The Plays of William Shakespeare*, ed. Samuel Johnson, 7 vols (London, 1765; rpt New York, 1968)
Johnson & Steevens
  William Shakespeare, *The Plays of William Shakespeare*, ed. Samuel Johnson and George Steevens, 10 vols (London, 1778)
Jonson, *Epicene*
  Ben Jonson, *Epicene, or The Silent Woman*, ed. Richard Dutton, The Revels Plays (Manchester, 2003)

Jonson, *Jonson*

  Ben Jonson, ed. Ian Donaldson (Oxford, 1985)

Jonson, 'Sonne'

  Ben Jonson, 'On My First Sonne', in *The Workes of Beniamin Jonson* (London, 1616)

Jonson, *Works*

  Ben Jonson, *The Works of Ben Jonson* (London, 1692)

Jonson & Parker, *Volpone*

  Ben Jonson, *Volpone, or The Fox*, ed. Brian Parker, The Revels Plays, rev. edn (Manchester, 1999)

Jonson & Watson, *Volpone*

  Ben Jonson, *Volpone*, ed. Robert N. Watson, New Mermaids, 2nd edn (London, 2003)

Jourdain

  M. Jourdain, *English Decoration and Furniture of the Early Renaissance* (London, 1924)

Keats

  John Keats, *John Keats: A Longman Cultural Edition*, ed. Susan J. Wolfson (New York, 2007)

Keats, *Letters*

  The Letters of John Keats, ed. Hyder E. Rollins, 2 vols (Cambridge, MA, 1958)

Kermode

  Frank Kermode, *Shakespeare, Spenser, Donne; Renaissance Essays* (London, 1971)

Kierkegaard

  Soren Kierkegaard, *The Sickness Unto Death: A Christian Psychological Exposition for Upbuilding and Awakening*, ed. and trans. Howard V. Hong and Edna H. Hong (Princeton, 1980)

Kocher

  Paul Kocher, *Christopher Marlowe: A Study of His Thought, Learning, and Character* (Chapel Hill, 1946)

Lakoff

  Robin Lakoff, 'Remarks on *This* and *That*', in *Papers from the Tenth Regional Meeting, Chicago Linguistic Society*, ed. Michael W. La Galy, Robert A. Fox, and Anthony Bruck (Chicago, 1974) 345–56

Leonard

  John Leonard, 'Milton's Jarring Allusions', in *Of Paradise and Light: Essays on Henry Vaughan and John Milton in Honor of Alan Rudrum*, ed. Donald R. Dickson and Holly Nelson (Newark, DE, 2004) 71–100

Levin

  Phillis Levin, 'Introduction', in *The Penguin Book of the Sonnet: 500 Years of a Classic Tradition in English* (London, 2001) xxxvii–lxxiv

Levine

  Caroline Levine, 'Strategic Formalism: Towards a New Method in Cultural Studies', *Victorian Studies* 48 (2006): 625–57

Lewalski

Barbara Kiefer Lewalski, 'The Genres of *Paradise Lost*', in *The Cambridge Companion to Milton*, ed. Dennis Danielson, 2nd edn (Cambridge, 1999) 113–29.

Lord

George deF. Lord *et al.*, eds., *Poems on Affairs of State: Augustan Satirical Verse, 1660–1714*, 7 vols (New Haven, 1963)

Lucian

'On Funerals', trans. A. M. Harmon, Loeb Classical Library (Cambridge, MA, 1969)

Machyn

Henry Machyn, *The Diary of Henry Machyn, Citizen and Merchant-Taylor of London*, ed. John Gough Nichols, Camden Society 42 (London, 1848)

Mahood

M. M. Mahood, *Playing Bit Parts in Shakespeare* (London, 1988)

Malone

Edmond Malone, *Supplement to the Edition of Shakespeare's Plays Published in 1778 by Samuel Johnson and George Steevens*, 2 vols (London, 1780)

Mambrino

Jean Mambrino, 'Simone Weil et George Herbert', *Etudes* 340 (1974): 247–56

Marcus

Sharon Marcus, *Between Women: Friendship, Desire, and Marriage in Victorian England* (Princeton, 2007)

Marlowe, *Faustus*

Christopher Marlowe, *Dr Faustus*, ed. Roma Gill and Ros King, New Mermaids (London, 2008)

Martz

Louis L. Martz, *Milton: Poet of Exile*, 2nd edn (New Haven, 1986)

Marvell, *Complete Poems*

Andrew Marvell, *Andrew Marvell: The Complete Poems*, edn Elizabeth Story Donno (London, 2005)

Marvell, *Poems*

Andrew Marvell, *The Poems of Andrew Marvell*, ed. Nigel Smith, rev. ed. (Harlow, 2007)

Massai

Sonia Massai, *Shakespeare and the Rise of the Editor* (Cambridge, 2007)

Mazer

Cary M. Mazer, 'Storm King', *Philadelphia City Paper*, 8–15 July 1999, http://archives.citypaper.net/articles/070899/ae.theater.tempest.shtml

McDonald, *Bedford*

Russ McDonald, *The Bedford Companion to Shakespeare: An Introduction with Documents*, 2nd edn (Boston, 2001)

McDonald, 'Jonson'

Russ McDonald, 'Jonson and Shakespeare and the Rhythm of Verse', in *The Cambridge Companion to Ben Jonson*, ed. Richard Harp and Stanley Stewart (Cambridge, 2000) 103–18

McDonald, *Shakespeare*
   Russ McDonald, *Shakespeare and Jonson, Jonson and Shakespeare* (Brighton, 1988)
Mehl
   Dieter Mehl, *The Elizabethan Dumb Show* (London, 1965)
Milton, *Works*
   John Milton, *The Major Works*, ed. Stephen Orgel and Jonathan Goldberg (Oxford, 2008)
Montaigne
   Michel de Montaigne, *Montaigne's Essays*, trans. John Florio (London, 1603; 3 vols, London, 1910)
Moretti
   Franco Moretti, 'Network Theory, Plot Analysis', *New Left Review* 68 (2011): 80–102
Muir
   William Shakespeare, *King Lear*, ed. Kenneth Muir, Arden 2 (London, 1972)
Ong
   Walter Ong, 'Backgrounds of Elizabethan and Jacobean Punctuation Theory', *PMLA* 59 (1944): 349–60
Orlin, 'Closet'
   Lena Cowen Orlin, 'Gertrude's Closet', *Shakespeare Jahrbuch* 134 (1998): 44–67
Orlin, *Locating*
   Lena Cowen Orlin, *Locating Privacy in Tudor London* (Oxford, 2007)
Ovid
   Ovid, *Metamorphoses*, trans. F. J. Miller, rev. G. P. Goold, Loeb Classical Library (Cambridge, MA, 1977)
Ovid & Golding
   Ovid, *Metamorphoses*, trans. Arthur Golding (1567), ed. John Frederick Nims (New York, 1965)
Ovid & Marlowe
   Christopher Marlowe, *The Collected Poems*, ed. Patrick Cheney and Brian J. Striar (Oxford, 2006)
Palfrey & Stern
   Simon Palfrey and Tiffany Stern, *Shakespeare in Parts* (Oxford, 2007)
Pliny
   Pliny, *Natural History*, trans. H. Rackham, 10 vols, Loeb Classical Library (Cambridge, MA, 1968)
Pope, *Poems*
   Alexander Pope, *The Poems of Alexander Pope: A Reduced Version of the Twickenham Text*, ed. John Butt (New Haven, 1966)
Post
   Jonathan F. S. Post, *English Lyric Poetry: The Early Seventeenth Century* (New York, 1999)

Puttenham, *Art*
  George Puttenham, *The Art of English Poesy*, ed. Frank Whigham and Wayne
  A. Rebhorn (Ithaca, 2007)
Puttenham, *Arte* facsimile
  George Puttenham, *The Arte of English Poesie* (London, 1589), facsimile rpt,
  ed. Gladys Doidge Willcock and Alice Walker (Cambridge, 1970)
Quarles
  Francis Quarles, *Divine Fancies* (London, 1632)
Quintilian
  Quintilian, [*Institutio Oratoria*] *The Orator's Education*, ed. and trans. Donald
  Russell, Loeb Classical Library, Books 6–8 (Cambridge, MA, 2001)
Rabkin
  Norman Rabkin, 'Foreword', *Reinterpretations of Elizabethan Drama: Selected
  Papers from the English Institute* (New York, 1969) v–x
Ransom
  John Crowe Ransom, 'Shakespeare at Sonnets', *Southern Review* 3 (1938):
  531–3
Ricks, *Force*
  Christopher Ricks, *The Force of Poetry* (Oxford, 1984)
Righter
  Anne Righter, *Shakespeare and the Idea of the Play* (London, 1962)
Rolfe
  William Shakespeare, *Shakespeare's Tragedy of Cymbeline*, ed. William James
  Rolfe (New York, 1905)
Rollins
  Hyder Edward Rollins, ed., *Tottel's Miscellany (1557–1587)*, 2 vols (Cam-
  bridge, MA, 1965)
Rowe
  William Shakespeare, *The Works of Mr. William Shakespear*, ed. Nicholas
  Rowe, 8 vols (London, 1709)
Rumrich & Chaplin
  John P. Rumrich and Gregory Chaplin, eds., *Seventeenth-Century British
  Poetry: 1603–1660*, Norton Critical Edition (New York, 2006)
Samuels
  Peggy Samuels, 'Milton's Use of Sonnet Form in *Paradise Lost*', *Milton
  Studies* 24 (1988): 141–54
Schmidt
  Michael Schmidt, *A Reader's Guide to Fifty British Poets 1300–1900* (London,
  1980)
Schoenfeldt
  Michael Schoenfeldt, *Prayer and Power: George Herbert and Renaissance
  Courtship* (Chicago, 1991)
Shirley
  James Shirley, *The Traitor*, ed. John Stewart Carter, Regents Renaissance
  Drama (London, 1965)

Sidney, *Poems*
> Philip Sidney, *The Poems of Sir Philip Sidney*, ed. William A. Ringler, Jr (Oxford, 1962)

Smith, B.
> Bruce R. Smith, *The Acoustic World of Early Modern England: Attending to the O-Factor* (Chicago, 1999)

Smith, G.
> G. Gregory Smith, ed., *Elizabethan Critical Essays*, vol. 1 (Oxford, 1904)

Spenser, *Faerie Queene*
> Edmund Spenser, *The Faerie Queene*, ed. A. C. Hamilton *et al.*, 2nd edn (Harlow, 2007)

Spenser, *Poems*
> Edmund Spenser, *The Shorter Poems*, ed. Richard McCabe (Harmondsworth, 1999)

Starr
> G. Gabrielle Starr, 'Poetic Subjects and Grecian Urns: Close Reading and the Tools of Cognitive Science', *Modern Philology* 105 (2007): 48–61

Staunton
> Howard Staunton, ed., *The Plays of Shakespeare*, 3 vols, (London, 1858–60)

Stern
> Tiffany Stern, *Documents of Performance in Early Modern England* (Cambridge, 2009)

Stevens
> Wallace Stevens, *Collected Poems* (New York, 1968)

Stewart
> Garrett Stewart, *Reading Voices: Literature as Phonotext* (Berkeley, 1990)

Strier, 'Ekphrasis'
> Richard Strier, 'George Herbert and Ironic Ekphrasis', *Classical Philology* 102 (2007): 96–109

Strier, *Love Known*
> Richard Strier, *Love Known: Theology and Experience in George Herbert's Poetry* (Chicago, 1983)

Summerson
> John Summerson, 'The Building of Theobalds, 1564–1585', *Archaeologia*, 2nd series 97 (1959): 107–26

Taylor
> Gary Taylor, 'Shakespeare and Others: The Authorship of *Henry the Sixth, Part One*', *Medieval and Renaissance Drama in England* 7 (1995): 145–205

Taylor & Warren
> Gary Taylor and Michael Warren, eds., *The Division of the Kingdoms: Shakespeare's Two Versions Of* King Lear (Oxford, 1983)

Targoff, *Common*
> Ramie Targoff, *Common Prayer: The Language of Public Devotion in Early Modern England* (Chicago, 2001)

Targoff, 'Facing'
>   Ramie Targoff, 'Facing death', in *The Cambridge Companion to John Donne*, ed.
>   Achsah Guibbory (Cambridge, 2006) 217–32

Targoff, *John Donne*
>   Ramie Targoff, *John Donne, Body and Soul* (Chicago, 2008)

Teskey
>   John Milton. *Paradise Lost*, ed. Gordon Teskey (New York, 2005)

Thompson & Taylor, *Hamlet*
>   William Shakespeare, *Hamlet*, ed. Ann Thompson and Neil Taylor, Arden 3
>   (London, 2006)

Thompson & Taylor, Q1 *Hamlet*
>   William Shakespeare, *Hamlet: The Texts of 1603 and 1623*, ed. Ann Thompson
>   and Neil Taylor, Arden 3 (London, 2007)

Thurley, 'Henry VIII'
>   Simon Thurley, 'Henry VIII and the Building of Hampton Court: A Recon-
>   struction of the Tudor Palace', *Architectural History* 31 (1998): 1–57

Thurley, *Royal Palaces*
>   Simon Thurley, *The Royal Palaces of Tudor England* (New Haven, 1993)

Tilley
>   Morris Palmer Tilley, *A Dictionary of the Proverbs in England in the Sixteenth
>   and Seventeenth Centuries* (Ann Arbor, 1950)

Todd
>   Henry J. Todd, ed., *The Poetical Works of John Milton, with Notes of Various
>   Authors*, 7 vols (London, 1809)

Turner
>   James Grantham Turner, *One Flesh: Paradisal Marriage and Sexual Relations
>   in the Age of Milton* (Oxford, 1987)

Turner & Tatspaugh
>   William Shakespeare, *The Two Noble Kinsmen*, ed. Robert Kean Turner and
>   Patricia Tatspaugh, New Cambridge Shakespeare (Cambridge, 2012)

Tusser
>   Thomas Tusser, *A hundreth good pointes of husbandrie* (London, 1557)

Vaughan
>   Henry Vaughan, *Poetry and Selected Prose*, ed. L. C. Martin (Oxford, 1963)

Vendler, *Art*
>   Helen Vendler, *The Art of Shakespeare's Sonnets* (Cambridge, MA, 1997)

Vendler, *Herbert*
>   Helen Vendler, *The Poetry of George Herbert* (Cambridge, MA, 1975)

Villiers
>   George Villiers, *Plays, Poems, and Miscellaneous Writings Associated with
>   George Villiers, Second Duke of Buckingham*, ed. Robert D. Hume and Harold
>   Love, 2 vols (Oxford, 2007)

Walsh
>   Marcus Walsh, *Shakespeare, Milton and Eighteenth-Century Literary Editing:
>   The Beginnings of Interpretative Scholarship* (Cambridge, 1997)

Warburton

William Shakespeare, *The Works of Shakespear*, 8 vols, ed. William Warburton, 8 vols (London, 1747; facsimile rpt, New York, 1968)

Warning

A Warning for Fair Women: A Critical Edition, ed. Charles Dale Cannon (The Hague, 1975)

Warren

William Shakespeare, *Cymbeline*, ed. Roger Warren, The Oxford Shakespeare (Oxford, 1998)

Watson

Robert N. Watson, *Ben Jonson's Parodic Strategy: Literary Imperialism in the Comedies* (Cambridge, MA, 1987)

Webster

John Webster, *The White Devil*, ed. John Russell Brown, The Revels Plays (Cambridge, MA, 1960)

Wells & Taylor

Williams Shakespeare, *The Oxford Shakespeare*, ed. Stanley Wells and Gary Taylor (Oxford, 1986)

White

Richard Grant White, *Shakespeare's Scholar* (New York, 1854)

Wilcox

Helen Wilcox, 'Miracles of Love and Wit: John Donne's "The Relic"', *GRAAT* 25 (2002): 119–37

Willen & Reed

Gerald Willen and Victor B. Reed, eds., *A Casebook on Shakespeare's Sonnets* (New York, 1964)

Wills

Wills and Inventories Illustrative of the History … of the Northern Counties of England, ed. James Raine, Publications of the Surtees Society 2 (1835)

Wilson, F. P.

F. P. Wilson, *Oxford Dictionary of English Proverbs* (Oxford, 1970)

Wilson, J. D.

John Dover Wilson, *What Happens in Hamlet* (Cambridge, 2003)

Wittgenstein, *Culture*

Ludwig Wittgenstein, *Culture and Value*, ed. G. H. von Wright, trans. Peter Winch (Chicago, 1980)

Wittgenstein, *Investigations*

Ludwig Wittgenstein, *Philosophical Investigations*, trans. G. E. M. Anscombe (New York, 1958).

Wittgenstein, *Tractatus*

Ludwig Wittgenstein, *Tractatus Logico-Philosophicus*, trans. D. F. Pears and B. F. McGuiness (London, 1961)

Wolfe

John Milton, *Complete Prose Works of John Milton*, ed. Don M. Wolfe, 8 vols (New Haven, 1953–82)

Wootton

David Wootton, 'John Donne's Religion of Love', in *Heterodoxy in Early Modern Science and Religion*, ed. John Brooke and Ian MacLean (New York, 2005) 31–58

Wright, G., 'Hendiadys'

George T. Wright, 'Hendiadys and *Hamlet*', *PMLA* 96 (1981) 168–93

Wright, G., 'Supposing'

George T. Wright, 'Supposing a Measure for *Measure for Measure*', in *Hearing the Measures: Shakespearean and Other Inflections* (Madison, 2001) 73–95

Wright, T.

Thomas Wright, *The Passions of the Minde in generall* (London, 1630), rpt with introduction by Thomas O. Sloan (Urbana, 1971)

Zitner

Sheldon P. Zitner, 'The Fool's Prophecy', *Shakespeare Quarterly* 18 (1967): 76–80

INDEX